The Lake District

timeout.com

Time Out Guides Ltd
Universal House
251 Tottenham Court Road
London W1T 7AB
United Kingdom
Tel: +44 (0)20 7813 3000
Fax: +44 (0)20 7813 6001
Email: guides@timeout.com
www.timeout.com

Published by Time Out Guides Ltd, a wholly owned subsidiary of Time Out Group Ltd.
Time Out and the Time Out logo are trademarks of Time Out Group Ltd.

10 9 8 7 6 5 4 3 2 1

This edition first published in Great Britain in 2010 by Ebury Publishing.
A Random House Group Company
20 Vauxhall Bridge Road, London SW1V 2SA

Random House Australia Pty Ltd 20 Alfred Street, Milsons Point, Sydney, New South Wales 2061, Australia
Random House New Zealand Ltd 18 Poland Road, Glenfield, Auckland 10, New Zealand
Random House South Africa (Pty) Ltd Isle of Houghton, Corner Boundary Road & Carse O'Gowrie,
Houghton 2198, South Africa
Random House UK Limited Reg. No. 954009
Distributed in USA by Publishers Group West
1700 Fourth Street, Berkeley, California 94710
Distributed in Canada by Publishers Group Canada
250A Carlton Street, Toronto, Ontario M5A 2L1
For further distribution details, see www.timeout.com.

ISBN: 978-1-84670-203-7

A CIP catalogue record for this book is available from the British Library.

Printed and bound by Firmengruppe APPL, aprinta druck, Wemding, Germany.

The Random House Group Limited supports The Forest Stewardship Council (FSC), the leading international
forest certification organisation. All our titles that are printed on Greenpeace approved FSC certified paper
carry the FSC logo. Our paper procurement policy can be found at http://www.rbooks.co.uk/environment.

Time Out carbon-offsets its flights with Trees for Cities (www.treesforcities.org).

While every effort has been made by the author(s) and the publisher to ensure that the information contained
in this guide is accurate and up to date as at the date of publication, they accept no responsibility or liability
in contract, tort, negligence, breach of statutory duty or otherwise for any inconvenience, loss, damage, costs
or expenses of any nature whatsoever incurred or suffered by anyone as a result of any advice or information
contained in this guide (except to the extent that such liability may not be excluded or limited as a matter of
law). Before travelling, it is advisable to check all information locally, including without limitation, information
on transport, accommodation, shopping and eating out. Anyone using this guide is entirely responsible for
their own health, well-being and belongings and care should always be exercised whilst travelling.

Published by

Time Out Guides Limited
Universal House
251 Tottenham Court Road
London W1T 7AB
Tel +44 (0)20 7813 3000
Fax +44 (0)20 7813 6001
email guides@timeout.com
www.timeout.com

Thanks to Alex Brodie, CAMRA, Julie Darroch, Lake District National Park Authority, Lakeland Arts Trust, Grant McKee, Daniela Morosini, Patterdale & Wasale Mountain Rescue Teams, Libby Raper, Ros Sales, Jane Watson, Wordsworth Trust, Mandy Wragg.

Maps pages 18-19 Kei Ishimaru.

This product contains mapping from Ordnance Survey with permission of HMSO. © Crown Copyright, all rights reserved. Licence number: 100049681.

Cover photography David Noton Photography.

Back cover photography Church House Inn, see page 65; Stephen Meese; Good Taste Café, see page 168.

Photography pages 2, 153 (top and middle left) Ian O'Hanlon; page 11 Royal Air Force; page 13 Holker Estate 2008; pages 16/17, 77, 98/99, 132, 181, 186/187, 271 Stewyphoto; pages 22/23 Sacha Khamnei-Brooks; page 27 Tony West; page 34 Lakeland Arts Trust; page 35 Nick Wood; page 45 (bottom) Robert Ford; pages 46, 47 Hawkshead Grammar School Foundation; page 50 NTPL/Ian West; pages 58 (top), 74, 82/83, 85, 90, 103, 108, 152, 153 (middle right), 174/175, 204/205, 233, 234, 237, 245, 252, 256, 259, 272, 275, 267 Kevin Eaves; page 59 (bottom) David Woolfenden; page 68 NTPL; page 72 NKT-IKBU; pages 88, 89 copyright The Wordsworth Trust; page 94 Steve Barber; pages 100/101 Bill Birkett; pages 102, 153 (bottom) Len Green; pages 106 (top and middle), 109, 112, 131 (bottom), 136/137, 224, 228 (top right and bottom), 229 (bottom) John Oakey; page 110 Brian Sherwen; pages 124/125 David Hughes; pages 131 (top), 196, 201, 238, 239, 242 Alamy; pages 133, 246/247 Photolibrary.com; pages 134, 135 Bob Shaw; pages 142/143 YHA (England & Wales) Ltd; pages 141, 145, 151, 154, 190/191 Peter Guess; page 167 www.stevebarberphoto.co.uk; pages 170/171 Darren Turner; page 176 Mandy Willett; pages 194, 195 Chris Crowder; pages 156, 157, 161 www.briansherwen.co.uk; page 197 James A Gordon; pages 206, 207 Adrian Wanless www.mawbray.com; page 210 Nick Jones; pages 213, 214 Annie Swarbrick; page 221 NTPL/Andy Williams; pages 222/223, 228 (top left and middle), 229 (top) Michael Sayles; page 231 (bottom right) Matthew Harrison; page 254 Tony West.

The following images were provided by the featured establishments: pages 30, 31, 33, 36, 38, 39, 45 (top), 48, 49, 51, 52, 54, 55, 60, 61, 63, 65, 67, 70, 71, 75, 76, 78, 79, 80, 81, 84, 87, 91, 92, 93, 95, 97, 114, 115, 116, 120, 122, 123, 126, 127, 145, 146, 148, 156, 157, 158, 159, 165, 169, 172, 179, 184, 185, 192, 198, 199, 200, 209, 218, 219, 225, 226, 231, 232, 240, 241, 249, 250, 253, 255, 257, 259, 260, 261, 262, 263.

About the guide

The Lake District is one in a new series of Time Out guides covering Britain. We've used our local knowledge to reveal the best of the region, and while we've included all the big attractions, we've gone beneath the surface to uncover plenty of small or hidden treasures too.

This is a landscape of breathtaking beauty: of still lakes, surrounded by forest and fells; of tranquil valleys and jagged summits; of plunging cascades and remote, reed-fringed tarns. Its pleasures are timeless, whether you're tramping up the Langdale Pikes, lingering over a cream tea on the lawns of one of Ullswater's grand hotels, idling on a rowing boat on Windermere or following in the footsteps of Wordsworth.

If, sometimes, the paths seem a little too well trodden, and the chocolate-box hamlets, daffodils and Beatrix Potter theming a little cloying, then the other, wilder side of the Lakes is never far away. The names of the great peaks – Scafell Pike, Skiddaw, Helvellyn – possess an older, harsher poetry of their own, and the untamed fells, lonely churches and windswept high passes exude an irresistible siren song.

TELEPHONE NUMBERS

All phone numbers listed in this guide assume that you are calling from within Britain. If you're calling from elsewhere, dial your international access code, then 44 for the UK; follow that with the phone number, dropping the first zero of the area code.

OPENING TIMES

Part of the charm of the countryside is that it's not like the city. But this means beware opening times: places shut up shop for the winter months, or only open at weekends, and some shops still close for lunch. If you're eating out, many places still stop serving at 2pm sharp for lunch and at 9pm for dinner. If you're making a journey, always phone to check. This goes for attractions too, especially outside the summer holiday season. While every effort has been made to ensure the accuracy of the information contained in this guide, the publisher cannot accept any responsibility for errors it may contain.

ADVERTISERS

The recommendations in The Lake District are based on the experiences of Time Out's reviewers. No payment or PR invitation has secured inclusion or influenced content. The editors choose which places to include. Advertisers have no influence over content; an advertiser may receive a bad review or no review at all.

FEEDBACK

We hope you enjoy the guide. We always welcome suggestions for places to include in future editions and take note of your criticism of our choices. You can email us at guides@timeout.com.

Contents

Festivals & Events

APRIL

Damson Day
www.lythdamsons.org.uk. Date mid Apr.
Held at Low Farm near Kendal, this celebration of the small, plum-like fruit involves morris dancing, dog agility contests, damson gin and walks through the blossom-clad orchards. For children, there's a funfair, crafts and various animals to meet, including wobbly-legged lambs.

Ulverston Walking Festival
www.goulverston.co.uk. Date late Apr-early May.
Events at Ulveston's ten-day Walking Festival run from map-reading skills sessions to wildflower rambles.

MAY

Morecambe Bay Walks
Date May-Sept.
Guided group walks across the treacherous sands of Morecambe Bay; book well ahead. *See p251.*

Cockermouth Georgian Fair
www.cockermouth.org.uk/georgianfair. Date early May.
Gentlemen in tailcoats and ladies in empire-line frocks stroll Cockermouth's streets during the biennial Georgian Fair, along with companies of musket-wielding soldiers. The sedan chair race is a highlight.

Windermere Air Show. See p13.

Printfest
07812 172193, www.printfest.org.uk. Date early May.
Around 40 contemporary printmakers are selected to show their work at this two-day fair, held in Ulverston's Coronation Hall; there are open workshops too.

Keswick Jazz Festival
017687 74411, www.keswickjazzfestival.co.uk. Date early-mid May.
Four days of jazz and over 100 events make for a packed programme, with an international line-up of musicians.

Fred Whitton Challenge
www.fredwhittonchallenge.org.uk. Date Sun after May Day Bank Holiday.
This 112-mile one-day cycling race is held in memory of local bike enthusiast Fred Whitton, who died in 1998. The route starts and ends at Coniston, and includes all the hardest, highest road passes: Kirkstone, Honister, Newlands, Whinlatter, Hardknott and Wrynose.

Brathay Windermere Marathon
0844 225 3100, www.brathaywindermeremarathon. org.uk. Date mid May.
Skirting Lake Windermere and Esthwaite Water, the marathon's course adds up to just over 26 miles.

Country Fest
015395 67804, www.westmorlandshow.co.uk. Date late May.
Sheep-shearing contests and the chance to milk a cow are among the rural diversions at this two-day event at Crooklands, near Kendal. Other attractions range from terrier racing to foodie tastings and talks.

Keswick Mountain Festival
01539 729048, www.keswickmountainfestival.co.uk. Date late May.
Outdoor activities loom large on this five-day festival's agenda – triathlons, wild swims, biking, climbs and hikes among them. Film screenings, photography workshops, and top-notch speakers also feature.

Troutbeck Garden Trail
www.troutbeck.org. Date Spring Bank Holiday.
This biennial trail offers the chance to have a nosey through a dozen of Troutbeck's loveliest private gardens; don't miss the superb teas in the Village Institute.

Duddon Valley Fell Race
01229 716869, www.duddonvalleyfellrace.org.uk. Date late May-early June.
This is one of the toughest of the fell races: the short course is 11 miles with a climb of 3,000 feet; the full course covers 18 miles with 6,000 feet of climb.

JUNE

Holker Hall Garden Festival
015395 58328, www.holker-hall.co.uk. Date early June.

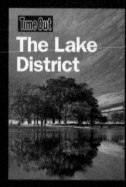

Holker's three-day festival is a lively affair, with plant sales, show gardens, horticultural talks, musicians, Cumbrian produce stalls and children's activities.

Boot Beer Festival
www.bootbeer.co.uk. Date mid June.
Boot's three pubs all participate in the village's beer fair, when you can sample myriad brews from small producers.

Ennerdale Horseshoe Fell Race
01539 735134, www.cfra.co.uk/calendar.php. Date mid June.
Organised by the Cumbrian Fellrunner's Association, this 23-mile race over the fells is seriously challenging, taking in the likes of Kirk Fell, Pillar and Haystacks.

Coniston Walking Festival
015394 41533, www.conistonwalkingfestival.org. Date late June.
Coniston's three-day walking festival includes walks for all abilities, from gentle ambles to serious summit hikes.

Whitehaven Festival
www.thefestival.org.uk. Date late June.
Whitehaven's three-day shindig brings all manner of events, with celebrity chefs on the quay, market stalls lining the streets and stately tall ships in the harbour. It's held every two years.

JULY

Coniston Water Festival
www.conistonwaterfestival.org.uk. Date early July.
Events on and around the water run from canoe races, duck races and stone skimming championships to lake cruises on the National Trust's steam yacht, *Gondola*, and the chance to try your hand at sailing.

Furness Tradition Festival
www.furnesstradition.org.uk. Date early July.
Run by a folk arts group and held in the market town of Ulverston, this three-day event brings ceilidhs, dancing and craft displays, workshops and storytelling.

Rushbearing Ceremony
Date 1st Sat in July.
On the first Saturday in July, children parade through Ambleside to St Mary's church, carrying flowers and rushes from the lakeside. After a short church service, there's a children's sports day.

Staveley Carnival
www.staveleycarnival.com. Date mid July.
This riotously colourful carnival is held in Staveley over a weekend in mid July, biennially. Expect vibrant costumes, dancers, samba bands and street theatre.

Le Tour de Staveley
015398 21443, www.wheelbase.co.uk. Date mid July.
Wheelbase, the cycle mega-store in Staveley, holds an annual non-competitive road race to coincide with the Tour de France. Some 300 cycle nuts embark on Le Tour de Staveley, which takes in the Lyth and Winster valleys. Those with thighs of steel can tackle the 45-mile 'tough' course; there's also a softer 22-mile option.

Windermere Air Show
www.windermereairshow.co.uk. Date late July.
No one is long in Lakeland without being startled by a low-flying fighter jet snarling through the valleys. The RAF makes its annual apology/thank-you at this Bowness-based show, which features Red Arrows, helicopter displays, Hawks, wingwalkers, parachutists and more.

Ambleside Sports
015394 35351, www.amblesidesports.co.uk. Date last Thur in July.
The sports include fell, cycle and track races, along with traditional Cumberland and Westmorland wrestling; even if you can't appreciate the technicalities, it's entertaining to watch grown men in white long johns and big embroidered knickers, locking arms to bring each other to the ground. Bookies are on hand to take bets on the hound trails, a traditional Cumbrian pastime that resembles fox hunting without the fox. An aniseed soaked rag is dragged around a ten-mile route, then the hounds are released to follow the trail back to the arena. The finish is exciting, especially if you have a tenner on it.

Kendal Calling
www.kendalcalling.com. Date late July-early Aug.
This two-day music festival draws a friendly crowd and an enjoyably varied line-up: Beardy Man, DJ Yoda, Dizzee Rascal, Ash and Mystery Jets have all graced the stage.

Holker Hall Garden Festival. See p11.

A world of experience on your doorstep

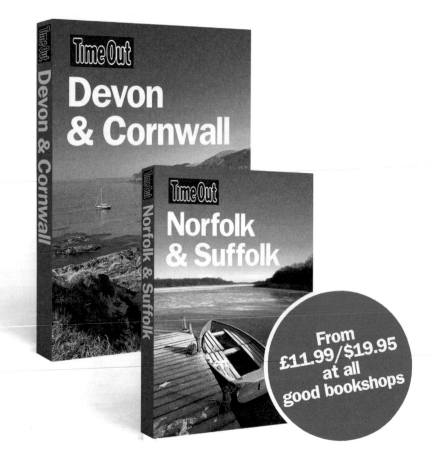

The Lake Artists' Society Summer Exhibition

www.lakeartists.org.uk. Date late July-early Sept.
Founded in 1904, the Lake Artists' Society held its first exhibition in 1905. Nowadays, the exhibition is held in Grasmere's New Hall, and attracts over 10,000 visitors.

AUGUST

Windermere Two Way

Date early Aug.
An epic swim across Windermere's waters, taking place biennially. See p41.

Lake District Summer Music Festival

www.ldsm.org.uk. Date early-mid Aug.
This two-week event has become one of the top classical music festivals in the country, attracting world-class performers as well as providing a showcase for young musicians and rising stars. Chamber musicians rub shoulders with sitar players, brass ensembles with virtuoso pianists in village halls, churches and theatres.

Borrowdale Fell Race

www.borrowdale-fell-runners.org.uk. Date mid Aug.
Only the experienced need apply to take part in this 17-mile race. The route takes in 6,500 feet of ascent, and starts and finishes at Rosthwaite's Scafell Hotel.

Lakes Chilli Fest

www.chillifest.co.uk. Date mid Aug.
Chilli-related edibles take pride of place at this annual celebration, held at the lovely Levens Hall: jams, jellies, chocolate, ice-cream and chutneys are all infused with a fiery kick. Steel bands, salsa dancers, fire-eaters and cookery demonstrations might also feature.

Eskdale Fête

www.eskdale.info. Date Sun Aug Bank Holiday.
The Outward Bound Centre's grounds come alive on August Bank Holiday Sunday, when Eskdale's fête swings into action. It's a delightfully traditional day out, with face-painting, a fancy dress contest, a bouncy castle, competitions and stalls plying books, crafts and produce.

SEPTEMBER

Great North Swim

www.greatswim.org. Date early Sept.
Thousands of swimmers take the plunge for this one-mile swim around Windermere. See p41.

Loweswater Show

www.loweswatershow.co.uk. Date early Sept.
Along with livestock displays, hound trails and sheepdog trials, this agricultural show features Cumberland wrestling, fell racing and family-friendly entertainment.

Windermere Swim

www.bldsa.org.uk. Date early Sept.
Tough nuts only need apply for this cold, ten-and-a-half mile swim. See p41.

Westmorland County Show

015395 67804, www.westmorlandshow.co.uk.
Date 2nd Thur in Sept.

Held at Crooklands, near Kendal, the Westmorland County Show is one of the biggest and oldest agricultural shows in the country. Heavy horses, sheep, pigs, dogs and goats are among the animals competing for prize rosettes; there's also show jumping, traditional Cumbrian sports and crafts, and a splendid food hall.

Borrowdale Show

www.borrowdaleshow.org.uk. Date mid Sept.
Visitors flock to Rosthwaite for this one-day show. All the usual Lakeland pursuits are embraced, from fell races, sheepdog trials and hound trails to wrestling and tug-of-war. In the main ring there are Herdwick hand-clipping contests, duck-herding displays and fell pony judging.

Egremont Crab Fair & Sports

01946 821220, www.egremontcrabfair.com.
Date mid Sept.
Established in 1267, this is one of the oldest fairs in the world. Its best-known draw is the World Gurning Championship, in which competitors strive to pull the most outlandish faces; look out for Tommy Mattinson, who won first prize eight years in a row. Other time-honoured attractions include greasy pole climbing, morris dancing, a children's fancy dress contest and assorted field events (ferret racing, wheelbarrow races and more).

Kendal Torchlight Carnival

01539 721360, www.kendaltorchlightcarnival.co.uk.
Date mid Sept.
The inaugural Kendal Torchlight Carnival took place in 1970, and since then the event has gone from strength to strength. A carnival, fun fair and fancy dress parade all rolled into one, it culminates with a torchlight procession through town: pennyfarthing riders, folk dancers, heavy horses and pipe bands all join the good-natured throng.

Eskdale Show

www.eskdale.info. Date last Sat in Sept.
This country show is set against the backdrop of the stunning Eskdale Fells, in the field by the George IV pub. There are classes for Herdwick sheep, foxhounds and terriers, along with hound trails where dogs race across the fells, following an aniseed trail. Handicrafts, fell races and children's sports events round off the day, and the beer and tea tents do a roaring trade.

Lakeland Festival of Storytelling

015394 35641, www.taffythomas.co.uk.
Date last weekend in Sept.
On the last weekend in September, the schools, church halls and pubs of Ings and Staveley stage the Lakeland Festival of Storytelling. Its host, Laureate for Storytelling Taffy Thomas, is joined by storytellers from all over the country; plays, parades and musicians also feature. The event is biennial.

NOVEMBER

Coniston Power Boat Records Week

www.conistonpowerboatrecords.co.uk. Date early Nov.
Coniston Water's 10mph speed limit is set aside for one week in November, when all kinds of powerboats from around the world take to the lake to break records.

Grasmere. See p85.

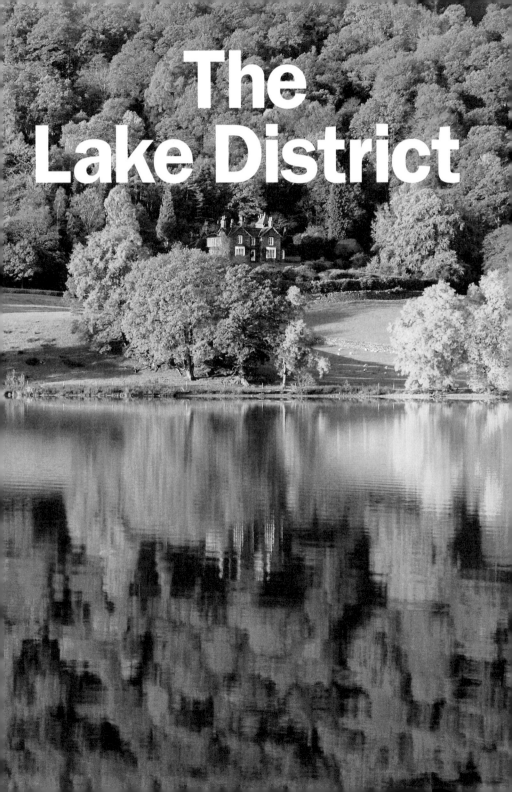

The
Lake District

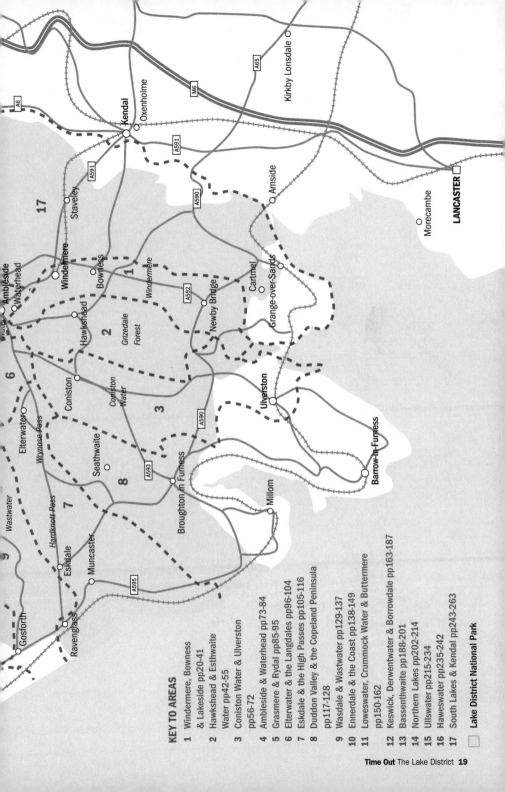

KEY TO AREAS

1 Windermere, Bowness & Lakeside pp20-41
2 Hawkshead & Esthwaite Water pp42-55
3 Coniston Water & Ulverston pp56-72
4 Ambleside & Waterhead pp73-84
5 Grasmere & Rydal pp85-95
6 Elterwater & the Langdales pp96-104
7 Eskdale & the High Passes pp105-116
8 Duddon Valley & the Copeland Peninsula pp117-128
9 Wasdale & Wastwater pp129-137
10 Ennerdale & the Coast pp138-149
11 Loweswater, Crummock Water & Buttermere pp150-162
12 Keswick, Derwentwater & Borrowdale pp163-187
13 Bassenthwaite pp188-201
14 Northern Lakes pp202-214
15 Ullswater pp215-234
16 Haweswater pp235-242
17 South Lakes & Kendal pp243-263

▢ Lake District National Park

Windermere, Bowness & Lakeside

It is the best of the Lakes and the worst of the Lakes, the most popular and the most deplored, the cheapest and the dearest. In some parts it is horribly crowded, in others highly exclusive. There's not much middle ground with England's biggest lake: most people love it or hate it.

Windermere anchors the southern end of the Lake District – and as most visitors arrive from the south, funnelling in from the M6 to the conjoined twin towns of Windermere and Bowness, these tourist honeypots are where almost everyone experiences their first, rather untypical taste of the Lakes.

While it may be tempting to push straight on to more isolated spots, there is plenty to enjoy around Windermere, from a treasury of Arts and Crafts architecture and a clutch of museums and attractions to extravagant hotels and restaurants – not forgetting the great lake itself.

The distant Langdale Pikes brood magnificently over the northern end of Windermere, but the lake's flanks have all but subsided by the time it turns into the River Leven at its southernmost end. It doesn't have a defining mountain or high waterfall, nor the trademark Lakes feel of being hemmed in by sheer-sided fells. Catch Windermere from the right angle, though, and it is a spectacle in itself, best appreciated from out on the water, or from a high point such as Wansfell Pike. Towards the end of the day, as the ten-and-a-half mile expanse of water stretches gracefully and mistily into the distance, it's a sight to behold – it's no surprise that generations of poets and artists have fallen for its charms.

Nowhere in the Lakes is as built up as Bowness and Windermere town, with their countless guesthouses and touristy shops, and no stretch of water is criss-crossed by quite so many crafts, from colourful windsurfing boards to floating gin palaces. Yet on the other side of the lake, the western shore is another world. Vast swathes of land are held by the National Trust or covered by the forest plantation of the Graythwaite estate, which means it is barely inhabited; with only a single ferry to link the two shores, the west looks more naturally to Hawkshead and is covered in that chapter (*see p42*).

The contrast between populist Windermere and walled-off Windermere is never far away. It was only in 1939 that the local council, funded by a brewery family philanthropist, was able to buy the lake bed, which formerly belonged to the Earl of Lonsdale. Great tracts of its shoreline are still privately owned, and out of bounds to the public. Many of the plum sections were corralled by a long line of wealthy Victorian barons, who came to Windermere to find – and buy up – its green and pleasant land, away from the satanic mills that enriched them. Their legacy is a mind-boggling collection of 'brass castles': some

fabulous, some gaudy, all large. Usually half-hidden at the end of long drives, among mature trees and rhododendron bushes, their lawns sweep down to private landing stages, cocooned from what William Wordsworth called the 'contaminating' tourists.

Nowadays, many of the mansions are hotels. Even the snootiest establishments welcome non-residents for that very Lake District institution, afternoon tea with dainty sandwiches, Borrowdale tea bread and scones on bone china, and tea from a silver teapot. Stand by with a £20 note. Others have become adventure centres, youth hostels, schools and nursing homes, while some remain discreetly in private hands.

It is easy to be sniffy about Windermere and its summer hordes. Wordsworth predicted the worst excesses of mass tourism when he campaigned against the arrival of the railway in 1845. But it is worth recalling too the Board of Trade's reply: 'an argument which goes to deprive the artisan of the offered means of occasionally changing his narrow abode, his crowded streets, his wearisome task and unwholesome toil, for the fresh air and the healthful holiday, which sends him back to work refreshed and invigorated – simply that individuals may retain to themselves the exclusive enjoyment of scenes which should be open alike to all, seems to us to be an argument wholly untenable.'

Wordsworth did, at least, prevent the railway from being driven on to its intended destination of Grasmere; and that, perhaps, was a significant victory. After all, if so many visitors didn't gravitate to Windermere, the rest of the Lakes would be vastly more crowded than they are as things stand. And as with other Lakeland locales, if you want to escape the crowds, then simply climb. It remains quite the best way to appreciate Windermere's indestructible beauty.

Windermere. See p25.

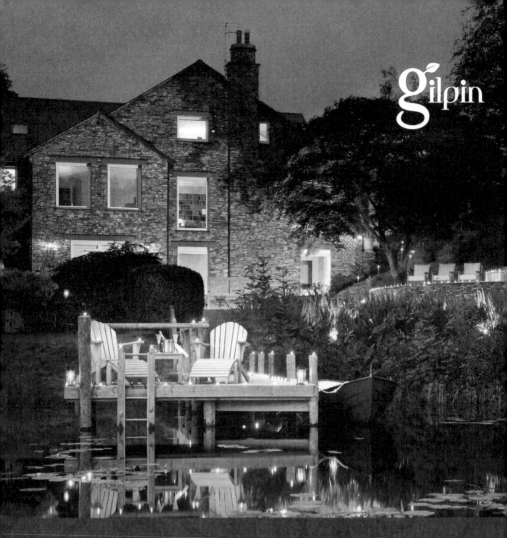

WINDERMERE & BOWNESS

Windermere town

The town of Windermere, set on a hill and with a dominant vernacular of Victorian slate and stone, is not actually on the shores of Windermere; in fact, the lake is largely invisible from ground level in the town. Bowness (properly Bowness-on-Windermere) is the town on the lake. The fact that the two towns are really one conurbation hardly makes things clearer, but it soon sorts itself out once you're there.

In any case, with the whole of the Lake District beyond, there's not much to detain new arrivals at the top of the town, save stocking up on essentials and information. Here is the Victorian railway terminus that Wordsworth fulminated against, which has now been disgorging tourists for some 160 years. You can hop straight on a rental bike at Country Lanes (015394 44544, www.countrylanes lakedistrict.co.uk), which is based at the station; staff can suggest routes around the Lakes that minimise car traffic. Alongside it are two of the north's best stores: a branch of Booths, the quality mini-chain of Lancashire supermarkets, and the headquarters of Lakeland, with an atrium full of household goods and kitchenware, and the fine First Floor Café (see p33) upstairs.

Scoop up free street maps and current what's-on advice at the Tourist Information Centre (Victoria Street, 015394 46499, www.southlakeland.gov. uk/tourism). It's a good habit to develop: the Lake District is blessed with a network of superb tourist offices, both council-run and independent, with helpful, well-informed staff and an endless supply of leaflets.

Shopping roads fan out before regathering at the main road down to Bowness and the lake. Further down Victoria Street, Fireside (015394 45855, www.firesidebookshop.co.uk) is a cherishable example of the dying breed of second-hand bookshops. Amid a plethora of routine eateries, two stand out: Jerichos (see p35) is a smart, dinner-only affair, while Francine's (see p33) is a homely bistro that works its socks off to offer brilliant quality and value.

Bowness

There's nothing so brash here as amusement arcades; nonetheless, Bowness has something of the air of a seaside town, with its coachloads of day-trippers and throng of sweet shops, ice-cream parlours, dinky gift shops and tearooms, pubs and pizza takeways. The little lanes around St Martin's Church and Ash Street struggle to retain their charm under the weight of crowds and commerce. Finally – and blessedly – at the bottom of the hill is the Promenade, the pier and the lake, in a setting that reveals what all the fuss is about. Across the water is Belle Isle and the undeveloped woodland of Claife Heights. Feed the swans and watch the cormorants dive, find a patch of grass on the Glebe or play a round of crazy golf; above all, though, get out on the water.

Anyone landing at Bowness pier can't miss the Belsfield Hotel, a white wedding cake of a mansion, set in a commanding position above the Promenade. It belonged to Victorian industrialist Henry Schneider, chairman of Barrow Steelworks, who enjoyed what must have been the most scenic commute in England. After breakfasting aboard his private steam yacht, en route to the southern end of the lake, he would board a private train carriage for the final leg of the journey to his office in Barrow.

Here too is the World of Beatrix Potter Attraction (see p34); while there are more subtle ways in which to explore the author's Lakeland legacy, children still susceptible to the lure of Peter Rabbit, Mrs Tittlemouse and friends will enjoy the tableaux of Potter's timeless characters.

Sadly, the splendid Windermere Steamboat Museum (www.steamboats.org.uk) on Rayrigg Road is currently closed for a large-scale refurbishment. Among the vessels in its collection are Henry Schneider's *Esperance*, and *Mavis*, one of the children's dinghies that inspired Arthur Ransome's *Swallows and Amazons*. Check the website to find out if any site tours or open days are running, and for information on the restoration.

To rise above it all, take a picnic up to Biskey Howe, a little rock and grass outcrop at the back of the town, or keep climbing to the town's highest point, the 626-foot summit of Brant Fell.

The lake

Above all, Windermere is about taking to the water. The lake is a playground for some 10,000 registered craft, and on a busy weekend 100,000 people can be found on or around the water. The volume of waterborne traffic has long been a headache for the National Park, in terms of safety as well as noise and pollution: in 1991, a survey revealed that on an average day, 368 of the 812 craft on Windermere's six square miles were fast powerboats, creating potentially dangerous levels of congestion.

It took a public enquiry and a five-year period of grace – in the teeth of opposition from the speedboat lobby and from local traders, who feared damage to Windermere's economy – before a ten-knot speed limit was imposed on the lake in 2005. Some powerboat owners continue to oppose the ban with a Keep Windermere Alive campaign, while others rev up their engines in hidden bays, playing cat and mouse with the Lake Patrol and their speed guns. Nonetheless, Windermere has reclaimed a measure of peace, while the sailing dinghies, rowing boats and canoeists are all a little safer.

Bowness – and Low Wood, near the north-eastern corner of the lake – are the two main boat hire centres, but the quintessential Windermere experience is to take a steamer trip with Windermere Lake Cruises (see p26).

Dotted around the lake are 18 little wooded islands, mostly grouped off Bowness. There is a cormorant colony on Lady Holme, while monks used to keep poultry on Hen Holme. The smallest, Maiden Holme, appears to consist of a single tree; it is still officially an island, according to the Ordnance Survey maps, even though it keeps moving. Most of the islands can be visited, in

Things to do

WINDERMERE & BOWNESS

Bowness Theatre & Film
Old Laundry Theatre, Crag Brow, Bowness, LA23 3BX (015394 88444, www.oldlaundrytheatre.co.uk). Open Box office 9am-5pm Mon-Sat; noon-7.45pm on performance days.

The Old Laundry hibernates in winter, overshadowed by the World of Beatrix Potter Attraction (*see p34*), which shares its premises. Its theatre-in-the-round comes alive in the summer, culminating in a three-month autumn festival of drama, dance, music, film and comedy.

Classic Cruises on Windermere
07879 665237, www.classic-cruises.co.uk. Prices from £100 per hr.

To push the boat out in style, take a cruise on *Ginny* – a glamorous, ten-seater, 1930s motorboat. The company can organise picnic cruises for up to four passengers, sightseeing trips and wedding cruises, along with pick-ups from four hotels (Beech Hill, Langdale Chase, Storrs Hall and Crag Wood).

Royalty Cinema
Lake Road, Bowness (015394 43364, www.nm-cinemas.co.uk). Tickets £4-£5; £3-£4.50 reductions.

Built in 1926, the Royalty is appealingly old-fashioned in looks, with a choice of circle or stall seats in the main auditorium. A second screen shows big-budget movies, with more adventurous fare in the 65-seater studio.

Windermere Lake Cruises ★
Bowness Pier, Bowness, LA23 3HQ (015394 43360, www.windermere-lakecruises.co.uk). Cruises and rates vary; check website for details.

For more than a century, sightseers have queued on Bowness pier to board the 1891 MV *Tern*, or its equally handsome 1930s sister ships, MV *Teal* and MV *Swan*. Despite their vintage good looks, they are diesel-powered and sail the length of the lake all year, carrying up to 530 passengers in total. Various cruises are on offer, calling at Lakeside, at the southern end of the lake; Waterhead at the northern end for Ambleside; and sometimes at the landing stages of Wray Castle and the Lake District National Park Visitor Centre. You can also hire motor boats and rowing boats.

LAKESIDE & NEWBY BRIDGE

Lakeside & Haverthwaite Railway
015395 31594, www.lakesiderailway.co.uk. Open Apr-Oct 10.45am-4.15pm daily. Tickets Return £5.90; free-£2.95 reductions; £16.95 family.

Polished, dapper steam trains chug along a three-and-a-half-mile stretch of the Leven Valley, before linking up with the launches at Lakeside. The track forms part of the old Furness line that used to link Windermere with Ulverston and Barrow – essential to an area that was once a hotbed of charcoal, gunpowder, iron and bobbin production. Closed in the 1960s, the railway's revival (like that of most revived steam lines) involves a heroic tale of enthusiasts battling institutional indifference. The vintage engines and rolling stock, saved from the scrapyard and lovingly restored, exert a headily nostalgic appeal. A café at Haverthwaite station serves coffee, ice-cream and sturdy grub (own-made pies, toasties and so on), while the gift shop is stocked with books, model trains, crafts and toys.

the spirit of *Swallows and Amazons* – indeed, Arthur Ransome used islands on Windermere and Coniston Water as the inspiration for his fictional Wild Cat Island.

The largest island, the mile-long, 38-acre Belle Isle, is the only one that is inhabited and closed to visitors. Its colourful history dates from Roman times, when the commander at Ambleside built a villa here. During the Civil War it was a Royalist stronghold, and came under musket fire. In 1774 its then-owner, Thomas English, commissioned the construction of an unusual round house, at a cost of £6,000. Wordsworth and his friends were appalled at the building, and derided it as a tea caddy or a pepperpot. Humiliated, English sold it for the knockdown price of £1,700; the new owner gave it to his bride, Isabella Curwen, renaming the island Belle Isle in her honour. It is currently owned by the Lefton family, *Sunday Times* Rich List multi-millionaires. Landing on the island is strictly forbidden, so you'll have to pass judgment on Wordsworth's Grade I-listed pepperpot from the ferry crossing.

North towards Waterhead
Those in possession of a banker's bonus or a lottery win could put a sizeable dent in it by hitting the palatial hotels and Michelin-starred restaurants

dotted around these parts. All come with obligatory knock-out lake views. There's Miller Howe (*see p38*), made nationally famous in the 1970s by its early superstar chef, John Tovey. Langdale Chase, built for yet another Manchester industrialist, features so much carved oak that you half expect to find Henry VIII feasting there. Its landscaped grounds, sloping gently down to the lake, were the work of Thomas Mawson, the Lake District's greatest garden designer. A little further north, off the Ambleside road, are Holbeck Ghyll (*see p33*), once Lord Lonsdale's hunting lodge, and the Samling (*see p35*); both establishments discreetly polish their Michelin stars in gracious country houses, set high above the lake at the end of long private driveways.

Alternatively, park in one of the two public car parks on either side of Miller Howe and enjoy the same glorious lake panorama as the hotel guests. These are some of the best views of Windermere, because you can't see all the development around Bowness and Windermere town. Walk down to the lakeside at Millerground, passing some delightful little waterfalls en route, and bathe at one of the three formally designated swimming areas on the lake; the others are at Fell Foot Park (*see p29*) and Lakeside (*see p41*). Expect summer temperatures of about 15°C.

Blackwell Tea Rooms. See p33.

Cumbria

Luxury in the Lakes – The Queen's Head Hotel

The UK has some of the most stunning landscape in the world, boasting superb scenery, and views to remember. No more so is this true than in the Lake District, so we've found the ideal base from which you can experience this – The Queen's Head Hotel.

Tucked away in the Troutbeck Valley near Windermere, at The Queen's Head you'll experience luxurious rooms and an array of tantalising dishes. Plus, you'll have no trouble discovering the area, with a maze of footpaths linking ancient hamlets and luring you into some beautiful gardens. You can expect a choice of

double and four-poster bedrooms, not to mention the original coaching inn and beautifully transformed ancient barn. There's an extensive menu, with locally sourced produce, including poached local duck eggs, their own Cumberland sausage and the old favourite of real ale battered fish and chips! With so much choice, the most stressful part of your break will be what to choose from the menu, and there's even a selection of local ales to wash everything down!

So, take advantage of The Queen's Head Hotel NOW and book your next Lakeland adventure.

The Queen's Head Hotel
Townhead, Troutbeck
Near Windermere,
Cumbria, LA23 1PW
Tel: 015394 32174
www.queensheadtroutbeck.co.uk

The Lake District Visitor Centre (see p34) at Brockhole is much more than just another place to pick up pamphlets. A tourist attraction in its own right, it has a 30-acre ornamental terraced garden (Thomas Mawson, again), an adventure playground, a café, a calendar of Lakes-linked events and festivals, and displays on local traditions and wildlife, and is a stop-off for Windermere Lake Cruises. It's also the starting point for an enjoyable walk up Wain Lane to Middlerigg Tarn.

After Brockhole, there are only a few sporadic chances to access the lake before it ends at Waterhead; nearby beauty spots include Jenkyn's Crag and Stagshaw Gardens, and you can hire boats and enjoy assorted water-based activities at Low Wood Watersports Centre (see p75).

South to Ferry Nab & Fell Foot Park

On the southern outskirts of Bowness, amid a forest of marina masts, the lake narrows – which explains why Ferry Nab has been a ferry crossing point for more than 500 years. Today, the Lake District's only car ferry runs to the western shore year round. The chain-driven ferry provides a neat shortcut for the Sawreys, Hawkshead, Grizedale Forest and Coniston, and is an easy way to reach some of Windermere's best shoreline walking.

Heading south from the landing takes you to Jemmy Crag; to the north, you can follow the lakeside for four miles to Bass Rock, the longest stretch of public shoreline on Windermere. Returning via the woodlands of Claife Heights completes a satisfying low- and high-level circuit. With just one ferry, carrying 18 cars (and horses, if required), there are inevitable summer and peak-time queues. Signs on the approach road indicate how long a wait to expect before you can embark on the simple five-minute crossing. Alternatively, use the car park and beat the queue as a pedestrian. Another way to escape the crowds is by hiring your own craft at Windermere Canoe & Kayak (015394 44451, www.windermerecanoekayak.com, closed Wed winter), based close to the slipway at Ferry Nab.

Back on the eastern side of the lake, looking loftily down on it all, is Blackwell (see p34). The jewel in the crown of Windermere's cluster of Arts and Crafts houses, it was designed by Mackay Hugh Baillie Scott, a contemporary of William Morris and John Ruskin. Behind its angular white exterior the house is remarkably well preserved, down to the last decorative detail.

To the south lies a private millionaires' mile between the road and the lake, which peaks at the Storrs Hall Hotel. Set on its own 17-acre lakeside promontory, with a fearless marriage of Greek temple and Georgian architecture, its former owners include John Bolton, a Liverpool slave trader who entertained Wordsworth and Sir Walter Scott at his Windermere regattas.

More immediately lovable is Broad Leys, a little further south at Ghyll Head. Fronted by three enormous bay windows, it was designed by Arts and Crafts architect CFA Voysey, at the behest of a Yorkshire pit owner. Long the clubhouse of the Windermere Motor Boat Racing Club, it is generally closed to the public, although six beautifully restored rooms are available for B&B (see p37).

There is a small lakeside public car park and picnic area beyond the nearby Beech Hill Hotel, but for the best of the south-east section of Windermere, head on to National Trust-owned Fell Foot Park (015395 31273, www.nationaltrust.org.uk/main/w-fellfootpark). Paths meander through the gardens and expansive lawns; down by the lakeside you'll find a seasonal café, trestle tables, little pebbly beaches and another of Windermere's designated swimming spots.

The conical summit of Gummer's How (see p37) is another popular spot at which to rest and survey the surroundings. Walk up from Fell Foot (mostly by road), or cheat by using the car park two-thirds of the way up.

Where to eat & drink

Hotel dining rooms in England are seldom known for their exceptional food, but the opposite applies in the Lake District. Here, some of the finest food in the north of England is served in hotel restaurants – of which Windermere has an abundance of luxurious (and expensive) examples. Some, however, are classic examples of emperor's new clothes, or are living off past glories, so choose carefully. Storrs Hall Hotel (015394 33773, www.elh.co.uk/hotels/storrshall) adheres to a rather old-fashioned concept of luxury, with its chandeliers, statues and dress code for dinner. Stroll down the lawns to the water's edge with a drink on a summer evening, though, and all will seem right with the world. If you manage to reserve a table, and your finances are in good shape, Holbeck Ghyll (see p33) is the starriest turn.

For gastropub and Modern British cooking, it's best to pop over to the Lyth Valley: with the honourable exception of Francine's (see p33), Windermere and Bowness abound in places that process tourists and process food. At the top end of the lake, go the extra mile to reach Ambleside (see p73); at the bottom, sample creative home-cooking at the Knoll (see p41).

Angel Inn

Helm Road, Bowness, LA23 3BU (015394 44080, www.the-angelinn.com). Open 9am-11pm daily. Breakfast served 9-11.30am, lunch served 11.30am-4pm, dinner served 5-9pm daily.
'Beer garden' sounds too uncouth a description for the Angel's terraced garden with its smart canvas parasols, where you can sup Lake District beers, proper West Country cider or a globe-trotting array of wines. The menu runs from hearty breakfasts to superior sandwiches and salads, along with polished pub favourites: fell-bred lamb burger with apple chutney, say, or beer-battered cod with marrowfat peas, chips and own-made tartare sauce. Inside, it has the trappings of a modern gastropub, with stripped wooden floorboards and chunky leather sofas. There are also 13 B&B rooms (£90-£175 double incl breakfast) in the main building and nearby Gatehouse. Aimed more at the boutique hotel market (unusual in these parts), they nod to the genre with muted colour schemes and flatscreen TVs.

World of Beatrix Potter Attraction. See p34.

Blackwell Tea Rooms

Bowness, LA23 3JT (015394 46139, www.blackwell.org.uk). Open Summer 10am-5pm daily. Winter 10am-4pm daily.

The pleasant café at this Arts and Crafts gem (*see p34*) is an excellent spot for a coffee or a light lunch. The interior has a Shaker-like simplicity, while the garden terrace offers lofty lake views. Options include toasted open sandwiches – stilton with red onion marmalade, gravadlax with crème fraîche – own-baked chocolate hazelnut brownies, or slices of Blackwell tea bread. Wine, cider and beer can be served with meals: raise a glass of hoppy, award-winning Holt ale to the memory of Edward Holt, the Manchester brewer who built Blackwell.

First Floor Café

Lakeland, Alexandra Buildings, Windermere, LA2 1BQ (015394 88100, www.lakeland.co.uk). Open 9am-6pm Mon-Fri; 9am-5pm Sat; 10.30am-4pm Sun.

The modern, semi-circular glass building beside Windermere railway station is the flagship store of the Lakeland kitchenware company. After browsing the pastry cutters and banana holders, head upstairs to the First Floor Café, presided over by Roux-trained Steven Doherty. After a stint as head chef at Le Gavroche, Doherty moved on to the Punch Bowl at Crosthwaite (*see p249*), before creating this café. Expect simple dishes, quality ingredients and accomplished cooking, along with a wait of up to two hours at peak times. Once you've bagged a seat, though, satisfaction is guaranteed, whether you order chargrilled chicken breast with black pudding, mash and veg, a generous plate of grilled mushrooms on toast or the fluffiest of fresh-baked scones.

Francine's Coffee House & Restaurant ★

27 Main Road, Windermere, LA23 1DX (015394 44088, www.francinesrestaurantwindermere.co.uk). Lunch served 10am-3pm Tue-Sun. Dinner served 6.15-9.30pm Wed-Sat.

Amid the chaff of Windermere's commercial heart, Francine's is a delightful little find. It has an agreeably haphazard layout and an all-day, all-purpose repertoire, often with a Mediterranean slant. The specials board includes plenty of game in season, while the herby spaghetti marinara, loaded with clams, mussels, plump prawns and sea bream, epitomises the kitchen's generous approach. Earlier in the day, drop by for cooked breakfasts or simple lunches (think melted brie and bacon ciabatta, a bowl of mussels, or a plate of papperdelle with parmesan and own-made pesto).

Holbeck Ghyll Country House Hotel

Holbeck Lane, Windermere, LA23 1LU (015394 32375, www.holbeck-ghyll.co.uk). Breakfast served 8-10am, lunch served noon-1.30pm, dinner served 6.30-9.30pm daily.

Perched above the lake, amid acres of woodland, Holbeck Ghyll was once Lord Lonsdale's hunting lodge. It's now a country house hotel furnished to palatial standards. The restaurant is suitably sophisticated, with stately oak panelling and a French-influenced, Michelin-starred chef, David McLaughlin, at the helm. There's a three-course dinner menu and a pricier six-course gourmet tasting menu, which might feature hand-dived scallops with spiced cauliflower, apple and raisin purée, or loin of Lakeland

venison with herb spätzle. Those with sufficient funds can choose from 23 richly appointed rooms (£190-£330 double incl breakfast) and suites, where appealing little extras include fresh flowers and a decanter of sherry.

Hole in t' Wall

Lowside, Robinson Place, Bowness, LA23 3DH (015394 43488). Open 11am-11pm Mon-Sat; noon-10.30pm Sun. Lunch served noon-2.30pm Mon-Thur, Sun; noon-3pm Fri, Sat. Dinner served 6-8pm Mon-Thur; 4-7pm Fri, Sat.

Formerly known as the New Hall Inn, the best-known boozer in Bowness is now the Hole in t' Wall – a nickname it received thanks to a serving window that allowed the

First Floor Café

Places to visit

WINDERMERE & BOWNESS

Blackwell ★
*The Arts and Crafts House, Bowness, LA23 3JT
(015394 46139, www.blackwell.org.uk). Open Apr-Oct
10.30am-5pm daily. Nov-Mar 10.30am-4pm daily.
Admission £6.50; £3.80 reductions; £17.25 family.*
Blackwell was built at the turn of the 20th century as
a holiday home for Edward Holt, a brewing magnate
from Manchester. Holt gave carte blanche to his
architect, Mackay Hugh Baillie Scott, and the result
was an Arts and Crafts classic – even if, ironically,
the Arts and Crafts aesthetic was a reaction against
the mass production values of the industrial revolution
from which Holt derived his wealth. The interior is
a delight, blending bold simplicity with intricate
plasterwork, carved panelling and stained glass, setting
Delft tiles in modernist fireplaces, and juxtaposing
mock Tudor beams and Art Nouveau-ish rugs. The most
compelling room is the White Drawing Room. Offering
a stark contrast to the baronial feel of the Main Hall
and Dining Room, it is flooded with light and elegantly
minimalist; walking in, you are irresistibly drawn to the
cushioned window seats, with their bird's-eye views of
Windermere. Elsewhere, the house has some superb
examples of Arts and Crafts furniture, ceramics and
glass, along with varied temporary exhibitions. After a
visit to the excellent tea room (*see p33*), stroll through
the terraced gardens and fragrant herbaceous borders.

Blackwell

Lake District Visitor Centre & Gardens
*Brockhole House, Rayrigg Road, Windermere, LA23
1LJ (015394 466601, www.lakedistrict.gov.uk). Open
Visitor Centre Apr-Nov 10am-5pm daily. Feb, Mar 10am-
4.30pm daily. Gardens 24hrs daily. Admission free.*
Rather grandly, the National Park's visitor centre
occupies the late Victorian Brockhole House – once
»the home of a Lancashire cotton king. Now it explains
everything there is to know about the Lake District and
the National Park, with various interactive exhibits and
low-tech children's entertainment, such as a 'magic
carpet' ride over Lakeland. There's also a shop, a
café, and 30 acres of grounds to explore, running right
down to the lake shore, where it is possible to catch
the launch to Bowness or Lakeside. Picnic areas, an
adventure playground, treasure trails and a wildflower
meadow add to the appeal. Ambitious expansion
plans are afoot, with talk of a watersports centre,
a high ropes course, improved exhibition spaces and
a new ferry hub; check the website for updates.

World of Beatrix Potter Attraction
*The Old Laundry, Crag Brow, Bowness, LA23 3BX
(015394 884444, www.hop-skip-jump.com). Open
Apr-Sept 10am-5.30pm daily. Oct-Mar 10am-4pm
daily. Admission £6.75; £5.75 reductions.*
Peter Rabbit, Squirrel Nutkin, Jemima Puddleduck,
the Flopsy bunnies – all are here, in a series of artfully
constructed vignettes. After watching a short video
about Potter's work, visitors follow a winding path
past various tableaux from the stories: Mrs Tiggy-
Winkle doing her ironing, say, or Squirrel Nutkin on
his raft, using his tail as a sail. The attention to detail
is impressive, and the scenes thoughtfully set at small
person height. A recent addition is the little Peter

Rabbit garden, planted with gooseberry bushes, fruit
trees, lettuces and carrots; here too is the potting
shed, and poor Peter's little blue coat and shoes,
used to dress the scarecrow in Mr McGregor's garden.

LAKESIDE & NEWBY BRIDGE

Aquarium of the Lakes
*Lakeside, LA12 8AS (015395 30153, www.lakes
aquarium.co.uk). Open Summer 9am-5pm daily.
Winter 9am-4pm daily. Admission £8.95; free-£7.50
reductions; £26.95-£32.25 family.*
Get close to the underwater life of England's biggest
lake and follow the recreated journey of a waterway,
from mountains to sea. Along the way you can see
salmon, trout, otter, pike, perch, diving ducks and the
Lake District's very own Arctic charr. There are tropical
sections, coastal sharks and a virtual dive bell, too, but
it's the freshwater displays that set this aquarium apart.

Holehird Gardens
*Patterdale Road, LA23 1NP (015394 46008,
www.holehirdgardens.org.uk). Open Gardens dawn-
dusk daily. Reception Apr-Oct 10am-5pm daily.
Admission free; £3 donation.*
Given to the people of Windermere by a Manchester
brewing dynasty in 1945, the ten-acre hillside gardens
at Holehird are run by the Lakeland Horticultural
Society, and expertly maintained by its volunteers.
This is a lovely spot for a walk, with a colourful walled
garden, a lake and national collections of polystichum
ferns, astilbe and hydrangeas. The views, meanwhile,
are exceptional enough to have earned the gardens
an Ordnance Survey 'beautiful viewpoint' symbol.

Lakeland Motor Museum
*Old Blue Mill, Backbarrow, LA12 8TA (015395 58509,
www.lakelandmotormuseum.co.uk). Open Mid May-
mid Dec 10am-5.30pm daily. Admission varies; phone
or check website for details.*

blacksmith next door to slake his thirst. Built in 1612, this place is almost a parody of a traditional English hostelry, with its tales of a Victorian landlord who was the champion wrestler of all England, a Charles Dickens connection, hanging baskets outside, hanging hops inside, stuffed animals and china chamber pots galore, and a summer scrum for its standard beers and pub food.

Jerichos
College Road, Windermere, LA23 1BX (015394 42522, www.jerichos.co.uk). Dinner served 7-9pm Mon-Wed, Fri-Sun.
This well-established evenings-only restaurant occupies a appealing Victorian property in the heart of town. Chef and co-proprietor Chris Blaydes' CV includes a stint with John Tovey at Miller Howe (*see p38*), while his compact, ever-changing menu reflects a passion for seasonal game, meat and seafood. The cooking is quietly accomplished: typical offerings might include cream of cauliflower and blengdale blue cheese soup, laced with truffle oil, to start, followed by slow-roasted knuckle of Lune Valley lamb with all the trimmings, then orange, honey and prune parfait with own-made sorbet. The lengthy wine list includes plenty of modestly priced bottles. There are ten smart double rooms (£85-£120 incl breakfast), equipped with wonderfully comfortable beds, iPod docks, Wi-Fi and flatscreen TVs.

Lucy Restaurant & Bar
3 Ash Street, Bowness, LA23 3EB (015394 42793, www.lucysofambleside.co.uk/lucy4). Lunch served noon-4pm Sun. Dinner served 5-9.30pm daily.
Set in quaint, pedestrianised Ash Street, the first franchise of the Ambleside-based chain of Lucy eateries (*see p78*) takes a different approach to the more traditional restaurants that surround it. An expansive menu of Italian-influenced tapas encourages sharing and relaxed, leisurely suppers, while numerous wines are offered by the glass. The setting is appealing, whether you dine by candlelight inside, at the streetside tables at the front or on the rear patio. Its critics focus on sometimes slipshod cooking and service; its supporters welcome it as a breath of fresh air.

The Samling
Ambleside Road, Windermere, LA23 1LR (015394 31922, www.thesamlinghotel.co.uk). Lunch served noon-1.30pm, dinner served 7-9.30pm daily.
The Samling's restaurant is on splendid form, having won its first Michelin star in 2010. It offers a suave fine dining experience, from the moment the maître d' ushers you to a sofa in front of the fireplace for an aperitif, to the last sumptuous spoonful of dessert. No one could deny the polish and precision that goes into both the à la carte and the gourmand menu, which combine contemporary culinary flourishes with time-honoured local ingredients such as Herdwick mutton and Hawkshead venison. With just 11 individually decorated rooms (£190-£490 double), the hotel has an intimate feel – though there's nothing small-scale about its setting, amid 67 acres of grounds overlooking the lake.

Set to open in May 2010, this massive new venture will bring a new modern building on the River Leven, on the site of one of Backbarrow's old 'Dolly Blue' dyeworks, and a new railway halt on the Lakeside & Haverthwaite line. It will certainly provide a welcome boost for the former ironworks village, which was hard hit when the river burst its banks in the floods of November 2009. Many of the museum's exhibits will be familiar to those who visited its previous incarnation at Holker Hall, where motoring enthusiast Don Sidebottom built up an ever-growing collection of memorabilia and some 150 classic and American cars, motorbikes and tractors. Star exhibits include full-size replicas of Malcolm Campbell's *Bluebird* racing car, in which he broke the land speed record in 1935, the *Bluebird K4* hydroplane, in which he broke the water speed record on Coniston Water in 1939, and the *Bluebird K7*, in which his son Donald died on Coniston Water in 1967.

Stott Park Bobbin Mill
Finsthwaite, LA12 8AX (015395 31087, www. english-heritage.org.uk/stottpark). Open Apr-Oct 11am-5pm Mon-Fri. Admission £4.80; £2.40-£4.10 reductions; £12 family.
Built in 1835, the bobbin mill at Stott Park didn't close until 1971; nonetheless, it feels positively Dickensian. Workhouse boys were part of a labour force that endured grim conditions to turn out some ten million wooden bobbins a year for the Lancashire cotton mills. With abundant water to power the waterwheel, and plenty of ash, sycamore and birch in the local woods, bobbin-manufacturing became a prime Lakeland industry. The mill's belts and lathes are still in working order, and visitors can make and take away their own bobbin. Outside, a hefty ash tree illustrates the way in which Lakeland's woods were coppiced to provide a regular supply of wood, rather than being felled outright.

Where to stay
The area around Windermere has an embarrassment of riches when it comes to top-end hotels; indeed, there are simply too many to list. As a broad rule,

Holbeck Ghyll Country House Hotel. See p33.

the hotels with the best restaurants are the ones that take most trouble elsewhere too. Holbeck Ghyll (*see p33*) and the Samling (*see p35*) are two enticing options, finances permitting.

At the other end of the spectrum, the dependable Low Wray Campsite and pioneering Windermere YHA (for both, *see p38*) are excellent budget choices, while the Angel Inn (*see p29*) and Jerichos (*see p35*) may appeal to those in search of a few more home comforts.

Broad Leys
Ghyll Head, Newby Bridge Road, Windermere, LA23 3LJ (015394 43284, www.wmbrc.co.uk). Rates £130 double incl breakfast.
This place is one of a kind, and a Windermere classic: think Grade I-listed Arts and Crafts mansion meets timeless gentlemen's club, with an unlikely sideline as a B&B. Reckoned to be architect CFA Voysey's masterpiece, the house has been impeccably preserved. The Windermere Motor Boat Racing Club has been headquartered here since 1950, and silver trophies and club pennants abound; whatever side you take in the current controversy over speedboats on Windermere, it's hard to resist the photographs and mementoes of a seemingly innocent golden age, when dashing chaps with goggles and moustaches pushed their boats to the limits and beyond for sport and the glory of the Empire. Six spacious rooms (three en suite) are available on a B&B basis, generally midweek only; the Arts and Crafts-style decor and original fireplaces are utterly charming. The lounge, dining room and hall – check out the fireplace – are glorious; outside, well-tended grounds roll down to the club's jetties and private foreshore.

Gillthwaite Rigg
Lickbarrow Road, Windermere, LA23 2NQ (015394 46212). Rates £80 double incl breakfast. No credit cards.
It's easy to forget the bright lights of Windermere once you're tucked up in this beautiful B&B, located on a quiet road above the town. Built in 1906, it is relatively unsung among the district's remarkable array of Arts and Crafts houses. Nonetheless, it is packed with period features, including a panelled sitting room, a herringbone fireplace, ornate window catches and decorative plasterwork. Gillthwaite Rigg has two simple but elegant en suite double rooms and a small kitchen for making snacks, plus 14 acres of gardens and lovely views of the fells. The breakfasts are excellent.

Gilpin Lodge Country House Hotel
Crook Road, Windermere, LA23 3NE (015394 88818, www.gilpinlodge.co.uk). Rates £290 double incl breakfast.
This long-standing, family-run favourite is more intimate than some of Windermere's other luxury hotels, with 20 rooms and junior suites, and six bright, boldly decorated garden suites. You get plenty of pamper for your pound, with a three-page breakfast menu, supremely attentive service and a dinner menu that's dotted with foie gras and truffles; vegetarians are well catered for too. On-call therapists can provide in-room massages, reflexology, facials and manicures, while each of the garden suites has a cedarwood hot tub.

FIVE WINDERMERE WALKS

Claife Heights
Follow a time-honoured route, trodden by generations of tourists, by taking the ferry across the lake and scaling Claife Heights via the ruined viewpoint at Claife Station. Turn it into a circular walk via Moss Eccles Tarn and Far Sawrey, or drop down to Bass Rock and return along the waterside.

Ferry House to Lakeside
Probably the most peaceful stretch of Windermere. Catch the ferry at Ferry Nab across to the western side of the lake and head south, following shoreline footpaths and quiet roads to Lakeside, where you can catch the launch back to Bowness.

Gummer's How ★
Parking at the Astley's Plantation car park on the back road above Fell Foot Park will take some of the sting out of a short, stiff climb (1,391 feet) to the elaborate trig point at the top of Gummer's How. On a clear day, the reward is superb views over Lakeside, to Coniston Old Man and beyond to Morecambe Bay, or to the Pennines in the east.

Orrest Head
From outside Windermere's Tourist Information Centre, cross the A591 and follow the footpath sign to Orrest Head. It's an easy one-mile walk, climbing 784 feet; for many it is a pilgrimage, as this was the first summit tackled by a 23-year-old Alfred Wainwright in 1930 – and the inspiration for his life's work. 'It was a moment of magic, a revelation so unexpected that I stood transfixed, unable to believe my eyes. Those few hours on Orrest Head cast a spell that changed my life,' he later explained. A plaque on the summit is dedicated to his memory.

Windermere Way
A spectacular 45-mile circuit of Windermere, covering both low and high ground. The walk is designed to take four days, and can be followed in either direction; alternatively, you can tackle a single section. A map and guide are available from www.windermere-way.co.uk.

Gossel Ridding ★

Nr Bowness (07810 091008, www.gosselridding.com).
Rates £6,500-£7,950 per week.
Available to rent out in its entirety, this seven-bedroom Arts and Crafts house offers a heady blend of classic craftsmanship and modern gloss. Along with beautifully carved fireplaces, mouldings and an oak-panelled hallway, there are white leather sofas and fluffy white rugs, a private cinema, swish bathrooms and an immense, glossy kitchen, straight from the pages of an interiors magazine. Outside, beyond the elegant terrace, stretch eight acres of lawns, woodland and meadows. Prices, as you might expect, are eye-watering – though considerably less painful if you're dividing the cost between a big group. The concierge service can arrange various little extras, from a private chef to yoga sessions and yacht hire.

Linthwaite House

Crook Road, Windermere, LA23 3JA (015394 88600, www.linthwaite.com). Rates £198-£495 double incl breakfast.
Set in 14 acres of gardens, with its own tarn, Linthwaite is another rich man's mansion reborn as a luxury hotel. The 30 bedrooms, from standard doubles to the new loft suite with freestanding bath and telescope, are the epitome of restrained elegance, with plenty of posh toiletries to test your inner magpie. The public rooms are equally sumptuous, with deep sofas, thick drapes and log fires. Guests can sit back with newspapers, games and glossy magazines, then stroll through the grounds or play a round of croquet before dinner – an indulgent three-course affair with canapés and coffee. Although the country house theme wears a little thin in places (witness the scuffed cabin trunks, old books that look as though they were bought in job lots, and coal-effect fires) this is a top-drawer establishment, with prices to match.

Low Wray Campsite

Low Wray, LA22 0JA (015394 63862, www.national trust.org.uk/campsites/lakedistrict). Rates Camping £7.50-£10.50 per person. Pods £40.
One of four National Trust campsites in the Lake District, Low Wray is enviably positioned on Windermere's wooded north-western shore. The main camping field is the pleasant Vic's Meadow, but it's worth paying a little extra for a woodland pitch and a breathtaking lake view in the other field, Ransoms. Camping softies can opt for a wooden camping pod, a pre-erected Eurocamp tent, a canvas tipi, or a bell tent with its own wood-burning stove and solar-powered fairy lights; check the website for details. The National Trust's site rules require that visitors maintain a 20-foot gap between tents, refrain from parking on the grass and keep noise to a minimum between 10pm and 7am. For all of which you'll be grateful when you wake to the sound of moorhens paddling past, and a glorious view of the lake.

Miller Howe

Rayrigg Road, Windermere, LA23 1EY (015394 42536, www.millerhowe.com). Rates £230-£290 incl breakfast & dinner.
Internationally famous in the 1970s and '80s thanks to its flamboyant owner John Tovey, one of the UK's first celebrity chefs, Miller Howe is now under the direction of Martin and Helen Ainscough. It has been given a smart new refurb, with 15 bright, fresh bedrooms that mix rich fabrics and wallpapers, antique furniture and modern comforts with considerable aplomb. If you don't score one of the six rooms with lake views and balconies, the same lovely vista can be enjoyed over tea on the terrace, or from the restaurant. Head chef Andy Beaton, who trained with Raymond Blanc, is stamping his mark on the kitchen with sophisticated, modern evening menus and some pleasingly simple lunches (mushrooms on toasted muffin with poached egg, say, or Cumbrian ham, egg and chips). For extra privacy and space, book the Gardener's Cottage in the grounds, which has three bedrooms, a kitchen and a peaceful private garden.

Windermere YHA

Bridge Lane, Troutbeck, LA23 1LA (0845 371 9352, www.yha.org.uk). Rates from £13.95 per person.
Acres of grounds; a panorama of lakes, meadows and mountains; a location high up at the end of a private drive, two miles north of Windermere town. Another sumptuously expensive hotel? No, it's the £13.95-a-night Windermere Youth Hostel. Buffet breakfasts, packed lunches and hot dinners are available, and facilities include a cycle store, shop, barbecue areas, a drying room and a laundry. The

Aquarium of the Lakes. See p34.

Lakeside

boxy, white-painted building was one of the first houses in England to be built of concrete; when the stately wooden mansion that once stood on the site burned down, the owner vowed it would never happen again.

LAKESIDE & NEWBY BRIDGE

The southern end of Windermere was hard hit by the floods of November 2009, with Newby Bridge, Lakeside, Backbarrow and the River Leven bearing the brunt. Happily, all the major attractions and hotels were scheduled to be back in full swing by summer 2010.

On Windermere's western shore, the little community of Lakeside packs in a disproportionate number of features for its size. It acts as a terminal for both the year-round launches of Windermere Lake Cruises (*see p26*) and the seasonal Lakeside & Haverthwaite Railway (*see p26*). The Aquarium of the Lakes (*see p34*) is in the same complex as the train terminus, and it's a ten-minute walk to the historic Stott Park Bobbin Mill (*see p35*).

A mile south of Lakeside, on the River Leven, is Newby Bridge – which, when the A592 hits the A590 at the bottom of Windermere, appears to consist of little more than a roundabout and a petrol station. The fine five-arched bridge takes you across the Leven to the Swan Hotel (*see below*) and the Newby Bridge halt on the Lakeside & Haverthwaite railway.

Where to eat & drink

Without being quite state-of-the-art, both the Swan Hotel (015395 31681, www.swanhotel.com) at Newby Bridge, on the riverbank, and the Lakeside (015395 30001, www.lakesidehotel.co.uk) at Lakeside are fine locations for afternoon tea or a sundowner. Non-residents are also very welcome to dine at the Knoll (*see below*), although advance booking is essential.

For a wider range of options head on to Cartmel, where there's seriously sophisticated new wave dining at Simon Rogan's restaurant L'Enclume (*see p256*), or cut back over to the Lyth Valley for its mini-constellation of gastropubs (*see p249*).

Where to stay

The Knoll
Lakeside, LA12 8AU (015395 31347, www.theknoll-lakeside.co.uk). Rates £90-£150 double incl breakfast.
A short stroll north of Lakeside, this upmarket B&B is a wonderfully relaxed, tranquil retreat. Another asset (especially valuable given the limited dining options nearby) is the kitchen's prowess. Jenny Meads and her all-woman team break the mould, offering vegan beancakes and home-made, madras curry-laced kedgeree for breakfast, along with more conventional cooked breakfasts; cereals, fruit salads and porridge; come the evening, inventive two- or three-course dinners showcase the best local produce. The eight double rooms transcend their Edwardian origins with bold chocolate and hot pink colour schemes and sleek bathrooms.

In the swim

A fine drizzle over Windermere; a water temperature of 15°C; south-west winds gusting up to force three, with the current pulling in the opposite direction and more rain forecast. Such were the conditions on 5 September 2009 for the 59th Windermere Long Distance Swim, when competitors set out to swim the ten-and-a-half-mile length of Windermere, from its southern tip at Fell Foot to Waterhead at the north. It's a demanding event: only approved swimmers are allowed to compete, wetsuits are banned, and the water temperature drops again a foot below the surface. Of the 31 competitors in the 2009 swim, ten had to retire, too cold to continue. The race was won in four hours, three minutes and 19 seconds by William Bott, from Sandwell in the West Midlands.

Then there's the Windermere Two Way, staged every other year on a moonlit night in August. Caked in Vaseline, the swimmers set off at 5pm to reach Fell Foot by midnight, then turn around for the long crawl back to Waterhead. A rowing boat accompanies each swimmer, providing high-calorie snacks, encouragement and a get-out clause. All this makes the Great North Swim (www.greatswim.org), a one-mile circuit around Windermere in a wetsuit, look like a doddle. Some 6,000 swimmers took part in 2009.

All these events are prime dates in the calendar of the British Long Distance Swimming Association (www.bldsa.org.uk); check the website for details of other races organised on Coniston Water, Derwentwater and Ullswater.

For more leisurely forays into the Lakes, the Outdoor Swimming Society (www.outdoorswimming society.com) organises various open water swims. For a simple dip, it recommends Millerground Landing or Red Nab at Windermere, and Machell's Coppice at Coniston Water. Those in search of serious thrills should head for Wastwater or Stickle Tarn, high in the Langdale Pikes.

Wild Swimming (www.wildswimming.co.uk) suggests the pools along the Eskdale route up Scafell Pike, the waterfall pools of Rydal Beck, or Ulpha Bridge in the Duddon Valley. Black Moss Pot in the Langstrath valley is another popular spot, and zingingly refreshing on a sweltering summer walk.

Even on the warmest summer day, though, never underestimate how cold these glacial waters can be; there have been enough tragedies down the years. Indeed, Thirlmere's water is so cold that swimming is banned. Don't stay in too long without a wetsuit, and bring a thermos of hot chocolate for afterwards.

Hawkshead & Esthwaite Water

At first sight the countryside between Windermere and Coniston Water appears dominated by forestry, with the two great estates of Grizedale and Graythwaite clogging the map with seemingly impenetrable green, but when it opens up the National Trust are stewards of much lovely countryside that has a timeless calm. There's nothing wild or mountainous about the landscape, but it's exceedingly easy on the eye. Visitors flock in from Ambleside or the Windermere Ferry in formidable numbers. Few destinations in the Lake District are as deservedly popular as the tourist magnet of Tarn Hows, the epicentre of Beatrix Potter's world at Hill Top, the Grizedale sculpture trail and the picturesque old market centre of Hawkshead. But it's also easy to wander a little more lonely up to Latterbarrow and Claife Heights, to row a boat among the water lilies on Esthwaite Water, or to saunter through the lordly grounds of Graythwaite Hall or Wray Castle.

Come the end of the day there are some brilliant places to relax: a pint at the Sawrey Arms, a meal at the Drunken Duck, and a pillow in a historic farmhouse B&B such as High Wray Farm would add up to an evening of pleasures to match anywhere in the Lakes.

HAWKSHEAD & AROUND

Hawkshead

The popularity of Hawkshead village is easy to understand. Never shy to describe itself as the prettiest village in the Lake District, it's almost an Olde England theme park, with its greystone archways, narrow cobbled alleys with such names as Rag Street and Leather Street, and jumble of whitewashed cottages with window boxes and overhanging eaves. What's more, it has powerful connections to William Wordsworth and Beatrix Potter, and is a natural base for exploring the surrounding attractions of Esthwaite Water, the villages of Near and Far Sawrey and Grizedale Forest. The downside is that it can feel like a tourist trap: the car park is almost as big as the village; the shops are top-heavy with trinkets and tweeness; the throng of visitors in the pedestrianised centre is oppressive throughout the summer. Decide for yourself – but be prepared to brave the crush.

The Tourist Information Centre (015394 36946) is in the main car park in the centre of town. Hawkshead Grammar School Museum (see p46) opposite, with its exuberant sundial over the front door, is well worth the £2 entrance fee for the talk and tour through the room where Wordsworth was educated and carved his name on a desk. The future poet laureate also liked to sit peacefully in the graveyard of the church of St Michael & All Angels. In The Prelude he compared the church to 'a throned lady sending out a gracious look over all her domain'. The same domain still takes in a fine

sweep from the Langdale Pikes past Claife Heights to Esthwaite Water. To complete the Wordsworth trail, there's the suitably sweet Ann Tyson's House (see p51), where Wordsworth first lodged as a schoolboy. It's now a B&B, although it seems unnecessary to have changed the street name from Putty Street to Wordsworth Street.

Close by is the National Trust's Beatrix Potter Gallery (see p46) a quaint 17th-century building that housed the office of her solicitor husband William Heelis, and was supposedly the model for Tabitha Twitchit's shop. It shows a changing – and exquisite – selection of Potter's watercolours and sketches.

Of all the village's gift shops, it's worth popping into the Hawkshead Relish Company (The Square, 015394 36614, www.hawksheadrelish.com) for a jar of their award-winning chutneys, jams or pickles; the vast range runs from Indian capsicum pickle to fig and orange jam. Also on the Square is a branch of Henry Roberts bookshops (Laburnum House, 015394 36650) with a strong Lakeland section and two floors of bargain books upstairs.

A quarter of a mile out of town on the Coniston road is Hawkshead Courthouse, all that is left of a medieval manor house built by the monks of Furness Abbey – everything else was destroyed during the dissolution. Walk through the archway and see how a downstairs farm store was combined with an upstairs courtroom. It's owned by the National Trust, and you'll need to borrow the key from the NT shop on the Square in Hawkshead.

A couple of miles north of Hawkshead, at the Barnsgate crossroads, the Drunken Duck inn and

restaurant (see p49) is almost as famous a Lake District location as Tarn Hows or Beatrix Potter's Hill Top. Whether you want a gastropub lunch, a slap-up dinner or an overnight stay, nowhere else compares for miles around.

Tarn Hows

It would be churlish to resist Tarn Hows (and not many do): a perfect lake in miniature, set in an equally perfect amphitheatre of surrounding hills and distant fells. More than a century ago, charabancs bought sightseers daily from Ambleside to admire its legendary beauty. These days, more than half a million visitors a year traipse the mile-and-a-half circuit around the tarn; the paved pathways are easily scorned by righteous fell walkers, but are ideal for wheelchair and pushchair users.

If the place looks too good to be true, that's because there's more than a little artifice to the scene. In typical Lake District tradition, the land belonged not to a local farmer but to a Yorkshire mill owner, James Marshall. In 1862 he decided to improve on nature by turning his three small tarns

into one, planting the new shoreline with a blend of exotic conifers and native broadleaf trees. The result is hardly characteristic of the Lake District, but no one can gainsay the success of his vision – as evident from the countless calendar covers and guesthouse watercolours that reproduce the beauty spot. Beatrix Potter bought Tarn Hows in 1929 and bequeathed it to the National Trust, who manage the daily invasion with two car parks, an information centre, picnic areas and a clean-up regime that keeps the place remarkably tidy.

The tarn is also a designated Site of Special Scientific Interest for its waterlife, its mires and its woodland, frequented by deer, red squirrels and woodpeckers. When the main lake orbital becomes too much like the M25, branch off on to trails less travelled – into the woods, to Tom Heights or to the often bypassed waterfalls on Tom Ghyll (also called Glen Mary, a name bestowed by John Ruskin). Another path leads through the grounds of Monk Coniston Hall (see p53), the Victorian home of James Marshall that now provides accommodation for a walking holidays company.

Tarn Hows. See p43.

It's less than two miles from Hawkshead to Tarn Hows. Take the Coniston road (B5285), turn north to Hawkshead Hill and at the crossroads go straight over. There's only one access road, no roadside parking and the car parks are often full. Better to walk or catch the X31 bus, which links Tarn Hows with Hawkshead, Coniston, Ulverston and Newby Bridge.

Wray Castle

From Hawkshead the road north-east to Wray Castle follows a pleasant curling route past the hamlet of Colthouse, the isolated fell of Latterbarrow and Blelham Tarn. Colthouse is the second place that Wordsworth lodged with Ann Tyson when he was a Hawkshead schoolboy. The National Trust's Greenend Cottage (closed to the public) is presumed to be the place, though no one is sure.

Latterbarrow is quite simply one of the best climbs around. It's not that high – only 803 feet – but because it's bigger than anything else in the

vicinity there are exceptional 360-degree views from the summit that take in Windermere and most of the peaks in the southern lakes, showing clearly how the Fairfield Horseshoe got its name. And among the good, the bad and the ugly of Lakeland cairns, the elaborate obelisk at the top of Latterbarrow might qualify for listed building status.

For those most familiar with the Windermere shoreline from the buzz points of Bowness and Waterhead, take a right turn at High Wray and follow the unclassified – but perfectly driveable – track down to the (free) National Trust car park at Red Nab. Here you can see England's biggest lake in unsuspected peace and calm, with Wansfell Pike opposite and a surprisingly underused footpath hugging the water to High Wray Bay. Carry on by foot to circumnavigate reedy Blelham Tarn, or march down the sweeping drive of Wray Castle, a rather pompous grey Gothic fortress, castellated as if civil war were about to break out. It was built in 1840 for a gin heiress who apparently took one look at it and refused to live there, after which the architect supposedly drank himself to death.

Beatrix Potter holidayed here as a teenager, which is when she first met the Canon Hardwicke Rawnsley, poet, Lakes champion and friend of Ruskin, who was a great mover in the foundation of the National Trust. The castle (now owned by the NT) has had a wayward modern history with its rooms given over to business occupancy, NT office space and occasional public openings in summer. For the last five years it has lain empty; the latest plan is to lease it as a hotel. Meanwhile, its rolling parkland gardens, which run down to Windermere and a public access jetty, are free and open all year. Windermere Lake Cruises (*see p26*) and the NT are planning a waterbus service from the jetty, though this hadn't come to fruition at time of writing.

Esthwaite Water

Directly south of Hawkshead, Esthwaite Water is pleasingly set among pastoral countryside and low fells. Wordsworth liked it here – although admitted he 'knew not why' – and it has an enigmatic quality. Inevitably overshadowed by its larger neighbours, Windermere and Coniston Water, most people only see the lake from a car window en route to the Sawreys or the southern tip of Windermere. Accordingly, it is often praised for its peace and freedom from crowds. One reason for its solitude is that there's precious little public access to the lakeside; frustratingly, not one stretch of the four-mile perimeter has a shoreline footpath.

Approaching from Hawkshead, take the Grizedale turn-off and follow the footpath; you can walk to the water's edge but no further. At the southern end, at Ridding Wood car park, lay out a picnic and go for a paddle. Anglers gather here too, for above all Esthwaite Water is a prime fishing lake. Something about its combination of deep troughs, shallow bays and nutrient-rich water has allowed a wide range of fish to flourish, including pike, perch, roach and rudd. The boatyard of Esthwaite Water Trout Fishery (015394 36541, www.hawksheadtrout.com), about halfway down the lake's western side, is the place to buy bait or get fly fishing tuition. Any doubts about the quality of Esthwaite pike are immediately dispelled by the stuffed 40lb monster in the tackle shop – it's only a few pounds shy of the all-time British record. The lake is teeming with trout too. There have been trout cages here for 30 years, although these are being phased out to encourage a more natural population and to free a passage for salmon migrating to the mountain becks.

Alternatively, hire a rowing boat from the fishery for some gentle messing about. The romantically inclined may be disappointed to discover that (as at most boat hire establishments in the Lakes) the vessels are not vintage craft made of varnished wood but fibreglass moulded to resemble old-fashioned clinker-built boats. Still, romance returns as you watch the wildfowl scuttling through the reeds, drift towards the water lilies that smother the lake every summer, and remember that this is where Beatrix Potter's hapless Jeremy Fisher embarked on his calamitous fishing trip.

Hawkshead Relish Company. See p42.

St Michael & All Angels. See p42.

Places to visit

HAWKSHEAD & AROUND

Beatrix Potter Gallery ★
*Main Street, Hawkshead, LS22 0NS (015394 36355,
www.nationaltrust.org.uk/main/w-beatrixpottergallery).
Open June-Aug 10.30am-5pm Mon-Thur, Sat, Sun.
Apr, May, Sept, Oct 11am-5pm Mon-Thur, Sat, Sun.
Mar 11am-3.30pm Mon-Thur, Sat, Sun. Admission
£4.40; £2.10 reductions; £10.50 family.*
Formerly the law office of Beatrix Potter's husband,
William Heelis, this modest townhouse is the best
place in the Lake District (along with the Armitt
Collection in Ambleside; *see p84*) to appreciate what
a talented illustrator and artist Potter was. The display
of watercolours and original sketches for her stories
changes regularly (the centenary of *The Tale of Mrs
Tittlemouse* was celebrated recently), as well as
showcasing Potter's exceptional legacy as a
conservationist farmer, philanthropist and leading
light of the nascent National Trust. The most notable
gap in the collection is the original work for *The Tale
of Peter Rabbit*, which is kept in the archive of Potter's
publisher, Frederick Warne. Not that Peter Rabbit
imagery is hard to find in Hawkshead.

Graythwaite Hall Gardens
*Graythwaite Hall, Graythwaite, LA12 8BA (015395
31333, www.graythwaitehall.co.uk). Open Apr-Aug
10am-6pm daily. Admission £3; free reductions.
No credit cards.*
Graythwaite Hall's lovely gardens are notable for being
the first commission of Thomas Mawson, the Lake
District's most celebrated landscape architect (*see*
p53). His Arts and Crafts influences are apparent in
the Dutch garden and the terraces. The rhododendrons
and azaleas are a delight to behold in spring, and there
is also a mature arboretum to admire. Inevitably,
Wordsworth beat Mawson to it as he gathered

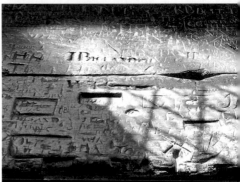

hazelnuts from the woods. Inevitably again, Beatrix
Potter adopted the location for one of her books, the
little-read *The Gypsy Caravan*.

Hawkshead Grammar School Museum
*Main Street, Hawkshead, LA22 0NT (015394 36735,
www.hawksheadgrammar.org.uk). Open Apr-Sept
10am-12.30pm, 1.30-5pm Mon-Sat; 1-5pm Sun. Oct
10am-12.30pm, 1.30-4.30pm Mon-Sat; 1-4.30pm
Sun. Admission £2; free-£1 reductions. No credit cards.*
An evocative short talk on and tour of Wordsworth's
former school reveals not some cruel Dickensian hell-
hole, but a rather noble institution where it was not
exceptional for boys to pass on to Oxford or Cambridge.
Beer and tobacco featured as part of the curriculum,
and the school also ran a pub in the village.
  The main room is a wonderfully atmospheric spot,
with its ancient oak doors, tables and benches, the
school's charter signed by Elizabeth I, and the desk

Hawkshead Grammar School Museum

where Wordsworth, a pupil from 1778 to 1787, unmistakeably carved his name – with the teacher's blessing. The headmasters, in their upstairs study, wielded the birch, but were not above reproach themselves – one, history records, got his housemaid pregnant. Although the school closed in 1909, its governing body, unchanged in its set-up since 1585, still exists and uses profits from the museum for the further education of local children.

Hill Top

Near Sawrey, LA22 0LF (015394 36269, www.nationaltrust.org.uk/hilltop). Open House June-Aug 10am-4.30pm Mon-Thur, Sat, Sun. Apr, May, Sept, Oct 10.30am-4.30pm Mon-Thur, Sat, Sun. Feb, Mar 11am-3.30pm Mon-Thur, Sat, Sun. Gardens Mid Feb-Dec daily; times vary, check website for details. Admission House £6.50; £3.10 reductions; £16 family. Gardens free.

From the outside, this 17th-century farmhouse is handsome rather than beautiful, but looks aren't the point: Beatrix Potter's former home is a place of devout pilgrimage. In fact, she rarely spent more than a few days at a time here, using it first as a bolthole from her parents in London and then, after she married and moved to Castle Farm, as a studio for her writing and painting. Still, some of her best-loved characters, including Tom Kitten, Samuel Whiskers and Jemima Puddle-Duck, were created here.

The small rooms are immaculate, each like a set for one of her stories, styled and furnished by the author with good-quality country oak furniture. In her will Potter stipulated that Hill Top should never be lived in and the rooms should be 'kept in their present condition'. Despite the press of visitors, the instruction has been fulfilled: the door with the mouse hole in it, the pretty card table, her tester bed, a jug filled with garden flowers; even her spectacles are there, as if she'd just popped out to feed the ducks. The house is closed on Fridays and all winter, so that its 'fragile interior' can recover from the onslaught, but the gardens are open almost all year round. The pretty cottage garden next to the house will seem familiar to fans, with its upturned plant pots, a wooden spade stuck in a flower bed as a tempting perch for passing robins, and a little gate just like the one Peter Rabbit squeezed under.

So popular is Hill Top, with 90,000 visitors a year, that the National Trust sets a quota of visitors each day, with timed entry. When the quota is reached, the doors are closed. Some 20,000 of those visitors are from Japan, so it's not surprising that the car park signs are in Japanese as well as English. Beatrix Potter has a special place in Japanese hearts, as generations of schoolchildren have learnt English through her books, and an exact replica of Hill Top stands in a zoo near Tokyo.

The Sawreys

The name of Beatrix Potter crops up all over the Lake District, but this is her heartland. It can seem as if every other building and B&B in Near Sawrey claims a connection to one of her books, but there's no dispute over Hill Top (*see p47*) where she did the bulk of her writing. Preserved to her own exacting specifications, it is rightly one of Britain's most cherished literary shines. If you visit on a Friday or in winter, when it's closed, don't discount a walk in the small garden, which is open almost all year. Despite appearances, it wasn't actually Mr McGregor's garden in *Peter Rabbit*. Half a mile away in Far Sawrey, Castle Cottage (closed to the public) was Potter's final home and where she died. She regularly walked between the two attractive hamlets and through the surrounding countryside.

Near Sawrey has one of the Lake District's best pubs in the shape of the Tower Bank Arms (*see p51*), or you could pop into the Claife Crier Bar (*see p49*) in Far Sawrey. From here it's a couple of downhill turns on the B5285 to reach the landing stage for the Windermere Ferry, which carries cars and passengers across to Ferry Nab on the eastern side of the lake.

A fine short walk, from either of the Sawreys, leads up to Claife Heights, taking in a succession of tarns along the way. First comes Moss Eccles Tarn ★, where you can walk right around the water's

Esthwaite Water Trout Fishery. See p45.

edge. It rivals Esthwaite Water and the River Tay as the spot that inspired *The Tale of Jeremy Fisher*. Beatrix Potter fished here from a little boat that is now in the Windermere Steamboat Museum; with a permit (from the Tower Bank Arms or the tourist offices in Bowness and Ambleside) you can fly fish for the tarn's brown trout. Within a mile come Wise Een Tarn, Scale Head Tarn and High Moss Tarn, each with varying degrees of accessibility to the water. At the summit of Claife Heights, Windermere appears between the trees.

The most famous view of Windermere and Bowness, however, is from Claife Station, on the route down to the Windermere Ferry. A belvedere built for tourists in the 1790s, it was mentioned in Thomas West's very first guide to the Lakes. Not satisfied with what nature had provided, its designer tinted the windows to suggest different times of day, season and weather conditions. Not a pane of glass remains, but the ruined edifice – and the view – are still impressive.

Three minor roads run south of Esthwaite and the Sawreys, eventually linking up with the A590, which runs along the bottom end of the Lake District. There is much dense forest, especially on the westernmost road through Dale Park. The easternmost road follows the Windermere shore before plunging into the second of the area's major forestry plantations, part of the Graythwaite estate, and converging with the middle road at Graythwaite Hall. This is the residence of one of the Lake District's oldest families, the Sandys. Edwin Sandys founded Hawkshead Grammar School in 1585 (there is still a Sandys on the school's governing body) and went on to become Archbishop of York. In the 20th century Duncan Sandys was a Tory cabinet minister; he was posthumously outed as the 'Headless Man' being pleasured by the Duchess of Argyll in a photograph that appeared in a scandalous 1960s high society divorce case. The Hall is closed to the public, but the gardens (*see p46*) are open in spring and summer.

Where to eat & drink
In the centre of Hawkshead, two historic pubs stand out from the pack: the Queen's Head Hotel (Main Street, 015394 36271, www.queensheadhotel. co.uk) and the King's Arms (The Square, 015394 36372, www.kingsarmshawkshead.co.uk). The Queen offers wood panelling, sepia photos and sit-down dinners, while the King is better for bar meals, a game of darts and a local vibe. Both have done well to retain their identity.

Claife Crier Bar
Sawrey Hotel, Far Sawrey, LA22 0LQ (015394 43425, www.sawrey-hotel.co.uk). Open Summer 11am-11pm Mon-Sat; noon-10.30pm Sun. Winter 11am-2.30pm, 5.30-11pm Mon-Sat; noon-2.30pm, 5-10.30pm Sun. Lunch served noon-2pm daily.
The Sawrey Hotel's Claife Crier Bar, once the stables, is where locals repair to sup Hawkshead Bitter, the creation of the village's Alex Brodie, formerly the BBC's man in the Middle East. While savouring your pint, consider two

legends: that the pub's beams came from a Spanish Armada galleon wrecked on the Cumbrian coast; and that people are afraid to go up Claife Heights at night because of the hooded ghost of the Claife Crier, a medieval monk who went mad from unrequited love and terrified the Windermere ferrymen. The menu in the restaurant (lunch only) is an old-fashioned affair, with tomato juice as a starter and roast beef and yorkshire pudding the highlight of the mains. A similar vibe applies to the 19 bedrooms (£80 double with breakfast).

Drunken Duck ★
Barngates, LA22 0NG (015394 36347, www.drunken duckinn.co.uk). Open 11am-11pm daily. Lunch served noon-3pm, dinner served 6.30-9pm daily.
Since Stephanie and Peter Barton took over the Duck in the mid 1970s, it has grown from an ordinary inn at a minor crossroads between Hawkshead and Ambleside into the Lake District's most famous gastropub. It's probably its most sought-after weekend stay too, with a six-month waiting list. You'll need to plan well in advance for dinner; lunch might be a better option (there's no booking), especially if you visit midweek out of high season. Then you can sample the Duck in less rarified mood, when the hop-strewn bar is the focus, thanks to its excellent selection of Barngates ales (the brewery is at the back of the inn).

If the pewter tankards and corny 'Wanted' posters are a bit passé, modern sophistication is evident in the chalky green colour scheme, Brathay slate bar and funky leather bar stools. The pin-sharp cooking features such dishes as

Tower Bank Arms. See p51.

Local heroes: Beatrix Potter

Hill Top. See p47.

Helen Beatrix Potter was born in 1866 into a genteel London family. It was a lonely childhood, despite the presence of her younger brother, Bertram; as she would wistfully confess to her journal, years later, 'I used to half believe and wholly play with fairies when I was a child.' Looked after by a governess, Miss Hammond, and educated at home, Beatrix seldom mixed with other children. Instead, her companions were a succession of beloved pets, secretly carried up to the nursery: rabbits, newts and even a hedgehog. Beatrix spent hours drawing them – and took them, along with her sketchbooks, on the family's summer holidays to the Lake District.

The holidays afforded endless opportunities for studying and drawing the natural world, and Beatrix developed into a talented artist and naturalist. Mushrooms and toadstools, in particular, fascinated her: today, her fungi illustrations are displayed in the Armitt Collection (see p84) in Ambleside.

It was an illustrated letter to the son of her former governess, describing a rabbit she encountered at Lingholm, that inspired her first and most famous book, The Tale of Peter Rabbit. Unable to find a publisher to accept it, she had it printed privately, in a 250-edition run, in 1901. A year later, publisher Frederick Warne finally agreed to print the story that would become one of the best-loved children's books in the English language, and sell over 40 million copies worldwide.

Beatrix's contact at the company was the youngest Warne brother, Norman – who, in 1905, asked her to marry him. Much against her parents' wishes, the pair

became engaged, although they refused to let their 39-year-old daughter announce the engagement. A few months later, Norman fell ill and died.

Envisaging a stultifying future in London, living with her parents, Beatrix fled to Lakeland, buying Hill Top (see p47) in Near Sawrey with the royalties from her work – according to her journal, 'as nearly perfect a little place as I ever lived in, and such nice old-fashioned people in the village.' Here, she wrote and illustrated seven of her classic miniature books, inspired by the local villages and countryside.

In 1909 she purchased a second property in Near Sawrey, Castle Farm. Her advisor was a local solicitor, William Heelis, who asked her to marry him three years later. Despite more objections from her parents, they were wed in 1913. At Castle Farm, Beatrix pursued her interests in breeding pigs and sheep; a regular winner at agricultural shows, she was instrumental in ensuring the survival of Lakeland's distinctive Herdwick sheep.

As failing eyesight stopped her from producing more books, Beatrix devoted her energies to farming and conservation, buying more houses, farms and estates (such as Monk Coniston) as the income flowed in from her 23 books. When she died in 1943, her ashes were scattered between Near Sawrey and Esthwaite Water on land that she left to the National Trust – along with 14 farms, 20 houses, Tarn Hows, her flocks of Herdwick sheep and over 4,000 acres of land. The swathes of land that she gave to the Trust are an extraordinary legacy – and a greater gift to the nation, perhaps, than even her much-loved books.

rose veal with skin-on fries, and grilled mushrooms on toast with two perfect poached eggs. Prices are fair too. At dinner, white linen tablecloths appear and you can enjoy the likes of crab and shrimp tortellini, turbot and caviar butter sauce, dark chocolate panna cotta and some tip-top wines. It's a class act, and significantly better value than some of Windermere's fancier dining rooms. Needless to say, the 17 bedrooms (£95-£275 per room incl breakfast and afternoon tea) are uniformly gorgeous and lavishly equipped. Superior rooms have the best fell views to the Fairfield Horseshoe.

Tower Bank Arms ★
Near Sawrey, LA22 0LF (015394 36334, www.tower bankarms.com). Open 11.30am-11pm Mon-Sat; noon-10.30pm Sun. Lunch served Summer noon-2pm daily. Dinner served Summer 6-9pm Mon-Sat; 6-8pm Sun. Winter 6-8pm Mon-Thur, Sun; 6-9pm Fri, Sat.
The Lake District has inns the rest of the country would drool over, and this is one of the best, even when it's packed on a summer weekend. Pay heed to the wood-framed porch and clock – it appeared as an illustration in *The Tale of Jemima Puddle-Duck* – but then put away the Beatrick Potter checklist, and focus on the pub itself. The interior oozes atmosphere; witness the undulating flagstone floor, Windsor chairs and slate-topped tables, and the fire glowing in a cast-iron range. A grandfather clock strikes the hour, and Donald Campbell's pennant from *Bluebird* takes pride of place among an evocative collection of old photos. A tiny garden has picnic tables for sunny days. The food is simple but good: Woodall's Cumberland sausage and mash, mussels in wine and cream, and the juiciest of fat chips. In the evening, dishes might include chicken liver pâté, smoked duck and orange salad, and comfort puddings (sticky toffee, bread and butter). The beer is Lakeland's best, from the Hawkshead and Barnsgate breweries. The four bedrooms (£88-£105 double incl breakfast) have been smartly updated; all have en suite bathrooms, iron bedsteads and lovely outlooks.

Where to stay
The Hawkshead area offers some of the finest B&Bs and guesthouses in Lakeland, which tend to get booked up well in advance by guests who return year after year – so plan accordingly. Of the options, the superb Low Graythwaite Hall (*see p53*) is perhaps the most undersung. The area is blessedly free of Victorian piles – which are too big for the scenery – but if you want to trade up, Randy Pike (*see p53*) is the exotic choice, while for all-round creature comfort it has to be the Drunken Duck (*see p49*).

Ann Tyson's House
Wordsworth Street, Hawkshead, LA22 0PA (015394 36405, www.anntysons.co.uk). Rates B&B £62-£70 double incl breakfast. Self-catering £235-£425 per week.
Wordsworth supposedly lodged in this cottage for a few years as a boy with 'my aged dame' Ann Tyson (let the scholars argue over exactly where and when). The cutesy exterior will certainly appeal to foreign tourists; they might also enjoy the copper kettles hanging from the beams in the breakfast room, the china dogs on the mantlepiece, and the floral fabrics in the five bedrooms and adjoining self-catering cottage, which sleeps five. Double up on the literary heritage stakes by asking for the room with 'John Ruskin's bed', purchased from a Brantwood estate auction in 1933. Wordsworth was well looked after by the Tysons, and current owners the Waltons enjoy the same reputation with their guests.

High Wray Farm
High Wray, LA22 0JE (015394 32280, www.high wrayfarm.co.uk). Rates B&B £70 double incl breakfast. Self-catering £300-£600 per week.
A couple of miles outside Hawkshead, on the road to Hawkshead and Wray Castle, this charming B&B occupies

Ann Tyson's House

Randy Pike

another of the farms given to the National Trust by the Beatrix Potter estate. The building dates from 1628, but looks even older thanks to the magnificent oak features and a residents' lounge that resembles an Elizabethan stately home in miniature. Highlights include the three pretty bedrooms (all en suite), breakfast sausages and eggs from the family farm, and walks from the front door up to Latterbarrow or down to Blelham Tarn. The more modern two-bedroom apartment across the farmyard is very popular with self-catering visitors.

Low Graythwaite Hall ★

Graythwaite, LA12 8AZ (015395 31676, www.low graythwaitehall.co.uk). Rates B&B £90-£100 double incl breakfast. Self-catering £325-£650 per week.

You can't miss this handsome house from the road, thanks to its extravagant topiary. Imposing outside, friendly inside, it feels more like a boutique hotel than a B&B. The five spacious bedrooms have an assured contemporary style, with sumptuous velvet and satin fabrics, chunky wood and leather furniture, and cool slate surfaces. Vibrantly coloured modern art plays against old timber. There's a lord-of-the-manor-style residents' lounge with a mighty fireplace, and an even bigger breakfast room. A river passes through the gardens, with a fine collection of ducks relaxing by the weir. The hotel is independently run, but part of the Graythwaite estate, which means there's free fishing in the estate's tarn and use of its boathouse on Windermere. There's also the separate self-catering Dairy Cottage, which sleeps six.

Monk Coniston Hall

Coniston, LA21 8AQ (0845 470 7558, www.hf holidays.co.uk). Rates vary, check website for details.

This 33-bedroom country house has been leased from the National Trust by a company that runs house party-style guided walking holidays. Walks are graded from easy strolls around Rydal Water or Tarn Hows to full-day treks up Coniston Old Man and Wetherlam. It's a sociable set-up, with communal dinners of homely British food, a programme of evening events and a bar. Rooms tend to be plain and functional; it's worth paying the extra £5 per person per night to upgrade to a premium room with more space or superior views. Non-walking guests are welcome too.

Randy Pike ★

Outgate, LA22 0JP (015394 36088, www.randypike. co.uk). Rates £180-£200 double incl breakfast.

'Wow' is the usual response to the utterly indulgent two-bedroom B&B that Chrissy and Andy Hill have created at their home, a former hunting lodge on the Wray Castle estate. Each suite has its own entrance from a garden that delivers a long-distance view to the Kirkstone Pass. The rooms, all rugs and polished floorboards, are hyper-glamorous: think rococo headboards, top-of-the-range kingsize beds, flatscreen TVs and iPod docking stations. If the feather-trimmed scarlet bedside lamps and the impossibly high-backed easy chairs are Laurence Llewelyn-Bowen in overdrive, then let the bathrooms seduce you with their acres of glass, subtle lighting and rather fabulous walk-in showers. Breakfast is delivered to your room – there are no public rooms – and a chauffeur-driven 4WD can drop you in Grasmere for dinner at the Randy Pike's sister establishment, the well-regarded Jumble Room restaurant (*see p91*).

Local heroes: Thomas Mawson

Born in 1861, Thomas Mawson was the builder's lad from Lancashire who went on to design some of the most important gardens and parks in Britain and around the world, from Blackpool's Stanley Park to the Peace Palace gardens at the Hague. Much of his finest work, though, can be found in the Lake District; he owned a plant nursery in Windermere, and was commissioned to lay out some 20 major gardens during the area's Victorian and Edwardian building boom. After his death in 1933, Mawson's work went out of fashion: TV and tourism have spurred a revival of interest, however, and several of his finest gardens are now open to the public.

Blackwell
A stunning Arts and Crafts mansion with superb vistas over Windermere, Blackwell was designed by architect Mackay Hugh Baillie Scott in 1900, as the holiday home for brewing millionaire Sir Edward Holt. Mawson laid out simple, low-maintenance terraces – something of a signature touch – to make best use of the views to the lake. Today, it's a lovely place to go for a stroll, followed by afternoon tea on the terrace. See p34.

Brockhole
The Lake District Visitor Centre in Windermere occupies the stately Victorian Brockhole House, which is set amid five acres of highly formal gardens, beds and borders. A further 25 acres, also lovely but more loosely landscaped, lead spectacularly down to Windermere's shoreline. The head gardener provides regular free walks. See p34.

Graythwaite Hall Gardens
Halfway down the western shore of Windermere, Graythwaite was one of Mawson's first designs. Commissioned in 1896, it is a mix of formal and informal areas in Arts and Crafts style, with yew hedges, topiary, a Dutch garden, a rose garden and an extensive rhododendron and azalea collection. Look out for the sundial, which appeared on the cover of Mawson's pioneering book *The Art and Craft of Garden Making*. See p46.

Holehird
Commissioned to extend and improve the walled garden at Holehird, Mawson added a rock garden and a 160ft glasshouse. The garden fell into tangled neglect after World War II, but has been given a new lease of life by the Lakeland Horticultural Society and its volunteers, who have restored the ten-acre site to its former glory. Although the glasshouse had to be demolished, the walled garden and its herbaceous borders remain. See p34.

Rydal Hall
Mawson designed the gardens at Ambleside's Rydal Hall in 1909, installing grand Italianate terraces with fountains and statues. Beyond the orderly columns, arbours and formal flowerbeds, the mossy woodland provides a dramatic backdrop. The house itself is now a conference centre and religious retreat; the gardens, restored in 2005, are open to the public. See p91.

Things to do

HAWKSHEAD & ESTHWAITE WATER

Woodsmoke
01900 821733, www.woodsmoke.uk.com.
Rates vary, check website for details.
For bushcraft, wilderness skills and backwoods wisdom, contact Esthwaite-based Woodsmoke. Foraging for food, lighting fires, building shelters, skinning game and trout fishing: all feature in an array of courses for all ages and abilities. You can learn to live like a 'British aboriginal' or take a seven-day 'travelling light' nomad's journey on foot and canoe through some of the wildest parts of the Lakes. A two-day introductory course starts at £225.

GRIZEDALE FOREST

Go Ape!
Grizedale Forest, LA22 0QJ (0845 643 90860, www.goape.co.uk). Open Feb, Mar, Nov 8am-dusk Sat, Sun. Apr-Oct 8am-6pm Mon, Wed-Sun. Admission £30; £20 reductions.
Surveying the forest from ground level is all well and good, but the Grizedale Go Ape! outpost offers a loftier – and far more thrilling – perspective. Ladders, ropes, walkways and zipwires weave through the trees at positively dizzying heights: you're given a half-hour briefing and training session before being let loose amid the treetops, and are securely strapped into a safety harness. Check online for the minimum age and height restrictions. Nervous parents should bear in mind that under-18s must be supervised (and not from the ground, either).

Walker Ground Manor
Vicarage Lane, Hawkshead, LA22 0PD (015394 36219, www.walkerground.co.uk). Rates B&B £72-£98 double incl breakfast. Self-catering £338-£642 per week. No credit cards.
If you're in anything wider than a small car, you'll be worried for your paintwork as you edge through Hawkshead's narrow streets and up Vicarage Lane. It's worth the wriggle: this is the best place to stay in the village. The handsome stone and slate house, dating from the 16th century, should win awards for its antique oak panelling – and that's before you start climbing the barley-twist oak staircase to the three ample guest rooms (all en suite) that don't stint on the oak either. There's a conservatory for summer breakfasts. The woodland garden with its own stream is a charmer, and a footpath leads through the fields to Hawkshead church.

GRIZEDALE FOREST

South-west of Hawkshead, across the crown of Hawkshead Moor, lies the 6,000-acre expanse of Grizedale Forest. If the Forestry Commission sometimes gets a bad press for covering the countryside with boring conifers, then its efforts at Grizedale to give something back to the public are undeniable.

The forest's information complex is about three miles south of Hawkshead, on the road to Sattherwaite. A handsome visitor centre (01229 860010, www.forestry.gov.uk/grizedalehome), a bike hire shop (01229 860369, www.grizedale mountainbikes.co.uk), a food and craft shop and the Café in the Forest (*see right*) occupy a set of elegantly restored buildings that were once part of the private Grizedale estate owned in the early 20th century by Harold Brocklebank, a Liverpool shipping magnate. During World War II, they housed high-ranking German POWs. The forest's isolated location made all escape attempts futile – even the one in which an officer had himself sewn into an armchair. The latest addition, a new community, education and wedding venue called the Yan (the Cumbrian term for number one), opened in 2008. An impressive slate, glass and cedarwood structure, it is one of the few contemporary buildings to be found in the National Park.

The information complex is the starting point for exploring the forest; there are eight waymarked footpaths and five cycle trails. There's also a branch of high-wires adventure course Go Ape! (*see above*). But Grizedale's most famous attractions are the 60 or so sculptures dotted throughout the forest; when the head forester came up with the idea of placing artworks among the trees in the mid 1970s, it changed the direction of outdoor art in Britain. The Ridding Wood Trail provides access to a fair selection, and a map will show you the rest.

The sculptures by Andy Goldsworthy are the most famous, and the most controversial. His work has

Go Ape!

been dogged with arguments over preservation and selling policy, and disparaged by sections of the art world. He first visited as a student and then on a prolonged residency with Grizedale Arts, which is when he made his best-known piece *Take a Wall for a Walk* – a full-size drystone wall that twists tightly between the forest firs. Damaged by felling and then repaired, it now stands within a mix of fallen and newly planted trees. The Forestry Commission is now in charge of the administration of the sculptures, and says it's allowing the wall to collapse naturally, as Goldsworthy preferred. Nonetheless, the *Wall* remains one of the public's favourites. New pieces are being added all the time; the latest, Keith Wilson's *Boat Race*, is a steel walkway that winds through the trees in the shape of the River Thames.

South of Grizedale is the sleepy backwater of Satterthwaite, once a thriving centre with charcoal makers, an iron forge and a sawmill. Nearby, there are picnic areas around Force Mills and waterfalls within easy walking distance at Force Falls.

Where to eat & drink

Café in the Forest
Grizedale Forest, LA22 0QJ (01229 860455, www.forestry.gov.uk/grizedalehome). Open Summer 9.30am-5.30pm daily. Winter 10am-4pm daily.

A contemporary remodelling of existing buildings has breathed new life into what is now the Café in the Forest. Easy chairs in the coffeeshop mix comfortably with the hefty wooden tables in the dining room. Picture windows provide views of the forest, and there's a shaded terrace for outdoor eating. Simple meals of soups, sandwiches, cakes and ice-creams generally hit the spot.

Where to stay
Accommodation options in the forest are very limited, but it's only a few miles to the multifarious options in and around Hawkshead.

Grizedale Camping
Bowkerstead Farm, Satterthwaite, LA12 8LL (01229 860208, www.grizedale-camping.co.uk). Rates vary, phone for details.

A mile and a half south of the Grizedale Forest visitor centre (*see left*), this farm campsite will appeal to back-to-basics campers, who don't expect any bells and whistles (or electric hook-ups, for that matter). Instead, pitch your tent in one of the grassy fields or wooded areas below the farm, and be prepared for clean but spartan toilet and shower facilities. Dotted among the trees are three charming camping pods: insulated, arch-roofed wooden huts with a window and double-glazed french door, which look rather like hobbit dwellings. The farm also incorporates a small riding centre with ten resident ponies and horses, should you fancy a trot through the trees; prices start at £25 for a one-hour ride.

Coniston Water & Ulverston

That Coniston Water enjoys such a distinct identity is largely down to three dead men: John Ruskin, Arthur Ransome and Donald Campbell. The third largest lake in the Lake District is indelibly associated with Ruskin, the great prophet of social reform and his lakeside home Brantwood; with the children's escapism of Ransome's *Swallows and Amazons* novels; and with Campbell's dramatic 300mph death in his somersaulting, jet-propelled *Bluebird* hydroplane.

There's much more of interest, of course. Boating opportunities include the National Trust's historic Steam Yacht Gondola, Lakeland's most exquisite vessel, while hikers can tackle the iconic peak of the Old Man of Coniston. Beatrix Potter gets a look-in too at Yew Tree Farm, a guesthouse that is in some ways superior to anything on her formal tourist itinerary. And the Ruskin Museum in Coniston village expertly and engagingly pulls together all the disparate threads of geology, literature and world water speed records. Finally, a short drive south, just outside the National Park, is the pleasant market town of Ulverston, whose attractions include Quaker and Buddhist centres, England's shortest canal and an eccentric museum devoted to Hollywood comedy duo Laurel and Hardy.

CONISTON WATER

Coniston village & the western shore

From Ambleside, the A593 (the main route south to Broughton in Furness) passes Skelwith Bridge and cuts through the pretty valley of Yewdale, past the sprawling drop of White Gill waterfall and picturesque Yew Tree Farm (*see p68*). Once owned by Beatrix Potter, it's now a working farm with rooms and one of the loveliest places to stay in the Lakes. From here it's a couple of miles to Coniston village, on the north-eastern tip of Coniston Water. The main road continues down the western side of the lake and can be linked with the minor road on the eastern shore – so it's easy to make a circuit of the whole lake.

Straddling Churchdale Beck and Yewdale Beck, Coniston is the main settlement in the area. It has assorted places to stay, a handful of shops and cafés and three pubs – and easy access to Coniston Water itself. Unlike cutesy Hawkshead, it has a down-to-earth, working air. Apart from farming, it was built on copper, first dug out by pioneering German miners in the 16th century. By the 19th century the mines were the biggest and most profitable in the north of England, with tunnels leading down to deep, rich seams at the Bonsor and Paddy End workings.

The friendly, community-run Tourist Information Centre (015394 41533, www.conistontic.org) is in the main car park on Ruskin Avenue in the centre of the village. Next door is St Andrew's Church, where a Celtic cross of local green slate in the north-east corner marks the grave of John Ruskin. It's carved with interlacing patterns and symbols in illustration of Ruskin's belief that everything connects. Donald Campbell's modest gravestone, also in local slate and with a bluebird motif, is in the cemetery behind the Crown Inn. Nearby, the Ruskin Museum (*see p60*) is amply stocked with material and information on every aspect of Coniston past and present, especially the triumvirate of Ruskin, Ransome and Campbell, and is definitely worth a visit.

To reach the shore of Coniston Water, head down Lake Road – a ten-minute walk from the village. Here, you can hire boats from the Coniston Boating Centre (*see p68*) or pick up the Steam Yacht Gondola (*see p69*) and the Coniston Launch (*see p68*). Once on the lake you soon understand how this long, straight stretch of water (five miles long, half a mile wide) invited continued attempts on world water speed records. You can also appreciate the serene beauty that so attracted Ruskin and Ransome.

There's little of interest immediately south of Coniston, though you can sometimes make out the disused rail bed of the Coniston & Furness Railway, which finally packed up with Beeching in 1962. It was designed not for passengers, but to replace carts and barges in freighting the iron ore, copper and slate from the fells above Coniston, the real business of these parts before the arrival of mass tourism. A turn-off to the west leads to the Tranearth Mountaineering Hut underneath the Old Man.

At Torver, the A5084 splits off the A593 to head south-east to the southern tip of the lake and on to

Coniston Old Man

Coniston Water

Places to visit

Brantwood

CONISTON WATER

Brantwood ★

Brantwood, East of the Lake, LA21 8AD (015394 41396, www.brantwood.org.uk). Open Mid Mar-mid Nov 11am-5.30pm daily. Mid Nov-mid Mar 11am-4.30pm Wed-Sun. Admission House & gardens £6.30; £1.35-£5 reductions; £13.15 family. Gardens (incl Severn Studio) £4.50; £1.35-£3.60 reductions; £8.60 family.

'A mere shed of rotten timbers and loose stone' is how John Ruskin described the house he bought unseen in 1871, but he reckoned that any house overlooking Coniston Old Man 'must be beautiful'. And so it is. Ruskin restored, enlarged and transformed the rotten timbers into a beautiful house and garden, and spent the rest of his life there. Today it is an essential stop in the southern lakes, not least because Ruskin himself has never seemed so relevant. As poet, artist and critic, he was precocious and prolific; by the age of 24 he had published the first of five acclaimed volumes of *Modern Painters*. As a conservationist, he was already predicting his version of the 'greenhouse effect'. As a social reformer, he proposed free state education, social security, housing for the elderly and the poor, public transport and a European trading community, long before they became reality. He inspired such diverse talents as Oscar Wilde, Frank Lloyd Wright and Gandhi. All the work took its toll and in his later years he suffered from depression. In 1888 he suffered a mental breakdown in his turret bedroom and could never sleep there again. He died at Brantwood in 1900, aged 81.

The house is large but not grand, and contains plenty to reflect Ruskin's life and interests (although the Turners and Gainsboroughs he so lovingly collected were sold by later owners). There are rocks, stones and shells from his geology collection; the wallpaper he designed; the silk purse in the drawing room annexe in which he kept the letters from Rose la Touche, the love of his life, who died aged 29. There is the celebrated turret bedroom, which he built to provide a panoramic 180° view along the lake, and the seven-arched Venetian-style window in the dining room. The lovely gardens include terraces, dappled walkways with ferns and foxgloves, herbaceous borders, and the Moorland Garden that leads on to the fell. Combined with the Jumping Jenny café (*see p65*) and the Severn Studio art gallery, it all makes for a great excursion. Arrive on the Coniston Launch or, better still, the Steam Yacht Gondola, both of which stop at the Brantwood jetty. And to truly immerse yourself in Ruskin, hire the Eyrie (*see p66*) on the upper floor.

Ruskin Museum

Yewdale Road, Coniston, LA21 8DU (015394 41164, www.ruskinmuseum.com). Open Mar-mid Nov 10am-5.30pm daily. Mid Nov-Feb 10.30am-3.30pm Wed-Sun. Admission £5.25; £2.50 reductions; £14 family.

An excellent museum that combines plenty of human interest with ample scholarship to back it up – and curator Vicky Slowe is a tireless fund of local knowledge. There are displays on Coniston's geology, farming, lace, drystone walls, and copper mining and slate quarrying history. Local heroes include Bert Smith, who made violins for Yehudi Menuhin, and

John Usher, who created an enchanting model village (on show outside the museum) using Coniston slate. There is a solid collection of Ruskin material – paintings, prints and memorabilia – as well as Arthur Ransome's rowing boat *Mavis* (the *Amazon* of *Swallows and Amazons*). But for most visitors, Donald Campbell and the story of his ill-fated water speed record of 1967 takes pride of place. His silver helmet and blue flying suit and the remnants of his boat's engine are on show, alongside a fascinating photographic record of his speed attempts. A new Bluebird Wing has been built for the return (sometime in 2011) of his boat, *Bluebird K7*, which is currently being restored.

ULVERSTON

Conishead Priory

Ulverston, LA12 9QQ (01229 584029, www.nkt-kmc-manjushri.org). Opening times vary; phone or check website for details. Admission Temple & grounds free. House (guided tour) £2.50; free reductions.
A Christian priory in the 12th century, and since then variously a country house, a health spa and a miners' convalescent home, this is now the British 'mother centre' of the Manjushri Buddhist Community. The organisation bought the crumbling 19th-century Gothic Revival mansion in the 1970s and gamely restored its stained glass, decorative plasterwork, 160ft-long cloister and vaulted great hall to their former glory. Now the priory offers meditation, study courses and retreats. In 1997 a Kadampa World Peace Temple was built in the grounds, and both the priory and temple are open to the public. There's also a café and a gift shop, and 70 acres of gardens to explore.

Laurel & Hardy Museum

On Stage at the Roxy, Brogden Street, LA12 7AH, (01229 582292, www.laurel-and-hardy.co.uk). Open Feb-Dec 10am-5pm daily. Jan 10am-5pm Thur, Sat, Sun. Admission £4; £2 reductions; £8 family. No credit cards.
Founded by Bill Cubin and now run by his grandson, this museum to the silver screen comedy duo moved in 2009 to the former Roxy cinema, behind the Coro. It's less cluttered and less eccentric than in its previous incarnation, but remains a tribute to one man's passion. Laurel and Hardy movies run all day and among scores of press cuttings and photos of 'the boys' are the prize exhibits of Stan's bowler hat, cigarette case and razor, the piano from Stan's family home and the mangle from the washroom where he was shut in as a child.

Swarthmoor Hall

Swarthmoor Hall Lane, Ulverston, LA12 0JQ (01229 583204, www.swarthmoorhall.co.uk). Tours Mid Mar-mid Oct 1.30-4pm Tue-Fri. Admission £4.50; £3.50 reductions. No credit cards.
Swarthmoor Hall is considered the birthplace of Quakerism. Founder George Fox stayed here with the hall's owners, Thomas and Margaret Fell, in 1652 and it became the powerhouse from where the peaceful, non-hierarchical religious movement spread across the country and to Europe and the States. Eleven years after the death of her husband, Margaret Fell married George Fox. Today, the hall is a place of pilgrimage for Quakers from all over the world; afternoon tours of the historic rooms come with a guide or recorded commentary. Accommodation is also available (*see p72*).

Lowick and Ulverston. The Church House Inn (*see p65*) at Torver is worth noting – if you stay in the area for any length of time, you'll certainly want to eat and drink here. A mile further on, next to the water, is Sunny Bank, where the long-distance Cumbria Way footpath (www.thecumbriaway.info) kicks in. (If you fancy walking back to Coniston from here, it's a particularly scenic four-mile stretch, starting off on high ground skirting Torver Common then following the shore to the village.)

There are jetties at Torver, Sunny Bank and Lake Bank (the southernmost one), where you can pick up the Coniston Launch. To continue along the eastern shore, cross the River Crake at Water Yeat – the bridge was badly damaged in the 2009 floods, so check if repairs are still under way.

For a short walk of sharp contrasts, head north from Coniston on the A593 and turn left near Yewdale. A circuit of High Tilberthwaite, involving a combination of lanes and footpaths either side of High Yewdale Beck, combines ample charm in woodland, stream and crag, then delivers a startling high point as the Langdale Pikes appear ahead. Suddenly, the world turns grey-green and you are in the middle of the most enormous quarry: an eerie moonscape of slate waste and spoil heaps, a few sparse trees and some perilously deep pools and sheer drops.

Local heroes: Arthur Ransome

Time will tell whether Arthur Ransome will endure as a Lakeland literary giant as towering as Wordsworth or Beatrix Potter. Certainly, more than 40 years after his death, the 12 volumes of the *Swallows and Amazons* series are still in print. The Lake District sailing and island adventures of the Walker children present a picture of innocent childhood that still resonates (even if most modern parents would never allow their own offspring such freedom).

But Ransome did more than write children's books. His life was packed with adult intrigue and mystery. Born in Leeds in 1884, he dropped out of his chemistry degree to become a junior at a London publisher and start writing. After writing a book on Oscar Wilde, he successfully defended a libel writ from Lord Alfred Douglas over the latter's homosexual relationship with Wilde. Employed as a foreign correspondent during World War I, Ransome had a front seat at the Russian Revolution in 1917, befriending Lenin and having an affair with Trotsky's secretary, Evgenia Shelepina, who became his second wife. He was also suspected of being both a MI6 spy and a double agent.

As well as reporting upheavals in Russia and China, he settled in the Lake District, first in the Winster Valley, where he contributed 'Nature Notes' to the *Guardian* and illustrated his children's stories. Family holidays to Coniston Water fostered his devotion to sailing, fishing and natural history. The first book of *Swallows and Amazons* (published in 1930), reinforced by a TV dramatisation in 1962 and a film version in 1974, has always been the most successful. Of the 12 stories in the series, only five are actually set in the Lake District; the rest roam around England, the Outer Hebrides, the Caribbean and China. They were international successes too; like Beatrix Potter, Ransome remains hugely popular in Japan. His last home was in Haverthwaite. He and Evgenia are buried in St Paul's Church in Rusland, between the southern ends of Coniston Water and Windermere.

For devoted fans, *In the Footsteps of Swallows and Amazons* by Claire Kendall-Price features walks to key Lakeland locations in Ransome's life and work. The Arthur Ransome Society (TARS, www.arthur-ransome.org) organises forums, literary weekends and Lakeland sailing events in his memory. The Ransome Room at the Museum of Lakeland Life & Industry (*see p254*) in Kendal includes the author's desk, typewriter, original illustrations and some of his pipes.

Coniston Old Man ★

The high point of the Furness Fells that separate Coniston Water from the Duddon Valley, the Old Man lies a couple of miles west of Coniston village. At 2,634 feet, it's the 12th highest peak in England, with sterling views from the top to Duddon Valley and Dow Crag across Goat's Water tarn, and even as far as the Isle of Man and Blackpool Tower.

There are various trails to the summit. If you take the longer, gentler 'tourist route' by the anti-clockwise path around Levers Water, you will pass through Coppermines Valley. With its scarred landscape, pyramids of abandoned mine tailings, and a rocky, pot-holed track above Miner's Bridge, it has a touch of the Wild West after the gold rush. Mine enthusiasts explore the network of shafts and tunnels that lead down more than 1,000 feet, but the dangers of flood and collapse are such that expert guides are essential. At the head of the valley, in a grimly impressive setting, is the Coppermines Youth Hostel (*see p66*).

Above are waterfalls, yet more ruined workings (which provided slate for the roof of St Paul's Cathedral) and the summit of the Old Man – Kanchenjunga to those well versed in *Swallows and Amazons*. Occasionally, you'll see a Burlington Slate & Stone truck carrying slate from the quarry at Low Brandy Crag, which reopened in 1982. There is said to be a small seam of uranium ore within the mountain too. The Old Man is never quite exhausted.

Eastern shore

The minor road running along the eastern side of Coniston Water passes the two quintessential sights linked to Arthur Ransome and John Ruskin. Heading south from Coniston village, it's less than two miles to Bank Ground Farm, a working farm irresistibly set on a slope facing the lake and the Old Man. Ransome was inspired to write his 12-part children's adventure series *Swallows and Amazons* after spending summers here. The eponymous first book, published in 1930, went on to become a classic, although many probably best remember it as the 1974 film starring Virginia McKenna and Ronald Fraser, which was partly filmed at the farm. The cast stayed there too – and so can you, as it has been a guesthouse (*see p66*) for more than 50 years.

Church House Inn. See p65.

A mile further on is Brantwood (*see p60*), the home of Ruskin from 1872 until his death in 1900. Writer, artist, campaigner, philosopher, all-round Renaissance man and one of the greatest Victorians, Ruskin bought the house and its 250 acres of gardens as a near ruin, sight unseen, so convinced was he of the unbeatable location. It's one of the must-see destinations of the Lake District, kept open year round by the Ruskin Trust. Culture is enhanced by cooking in the form of the Jumping Jenny café/bistro (*see p65*), a rare oasis in Coniston's foodie desert.

South of Brantwood, buildings disappear as the road hugs the shoreline for long and pleasant stretches. Hemmed in by Grizedale Forest and broadleaf woods are a succession of handy parking spots at Machell's Coppice, Parkamoor, Dodgson Wood and Rigg Wood. To see the lake at its best, take a picnic out to a rocky promontory or dangle your feet from a wooden jetty with views to old boathouses, diminutive Peel Island, Fir Island, Torver Common and the ever-present Old Man. Alternatively, follow the footpath from Bank Ground, which runs the length of the lake just above the tree line.

Minor civilisation returns at the southern end of the lake at the hamlet of Nibthwaite, where Arthur Ransome spent his childhood summers sailing and befriending the local charcoal burners. Five miles south-east, in Bouth, is the White Hart Inn (*see p65*), an agreeable old pub with bags of local history, straightforward food and local real ales. From here it's a short drive to the bright lights of Ulverston, the nearest destination for anything more than basic shopping and eating.

Where to eat & drink

The Coniston area has only two notable eating spots: the Church House Inn (*see p65*) at Torver on the western side of the lake; and the Jumping Jenny (*see p65*) on the opposite shore, south of Brantwood.

Coniston village has a smattering of cafés, Our Plaice for fish and chips, a Spar grocery for basics, and assorted pubs. The Black Bull (Coppermines Road, 015394 41335, www.conistonbrewery.com) has a reputation for good, if expensive, beer; its on-site microbrewery, the Coniston Brewing Company, offers six real ales including Bluebird Bitter. The pub also claims connections with the usual suspects of Coleridge, de Quincey and Wordsworth. Rooms (£60-£90 double including breakfast) are available.

Located on the old packhorse route above the village, the Sun (015394 41248, www.thesun coniston.com) is the last pub before the climb up the Old Man, and a welcome stop on the way down. It has eight en suite rooms (£95-£110 double incl breakfast) in a separate extension. Both pubs are said to have been Donald Campbell's favourite; there seems little doubt that Coniston's publicans enjoyed a heyday of late-night partying when his entourage and associated TV crews were in town.

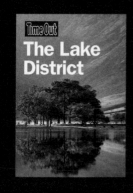

Bank Ground Farm. See p66.

Bluebird Café by the Lake

Lake Road, Coniston, LA21 8AN (015394 41649, www.thebluebirdcafe.co.uk). Open Mid Feb-Nov 10am-5pm daily. Dec-mid Feb 10.30am-4.30pm Sat, Sun.

This historic tin hut next to the pier, built in 1896 by the Furness Railway Company to house the gondola crews, is now part of the Coniston Boating Centre run by the National Park. The Bluebird connection is fully milked with postcards, stamps, T-shirts, prints and books on Donald Campbell and *Bluebird* – you can even buy a DVD of his final fateful trip. The menu offers soup, simple sandwiches, jacket potatoes with all the usual fillings, flapjacks and caramel slices. Your best bet is a well-filled 'bacon butty in a barmcake', enjoyed in the sunshine on the terrace overlooking the lake.

Church House Inn

Torver, LA21 8AZ (01539 441282 , www.church houseinntorver.com). Open noon-3pm, 5pm-midnight daily. Lunch served noon-3pm, dinner served 6-9pm Mon-Sat. Food served noon-9pm Sun. Reduced opening hours in winter; call for details.

The main road straggle of Torver is hardly a dream Lake District location, but this pub is well worth investigating. In fact, it's the best place to eat on the whole western flank of Coniston Water. The dining room is perfectly nice, but, if you can, bag a spot in the bar amid old oak barrels and chunky stonework to earwig the local farmers and enjoy some very good food. Tatie pot made from Herdwick lamb, belly pork, Cumberland sausage and colcannon mash, game pie, sticky toffee pudding with clotted cream ice-cream: it may read like regulation pub fare, but it's done with heart, soul and expertise – not surprising when you discover that the two main men in the kitchen used to work at the

renowned Drunken Duck (*see p49*). There are also five simple en suite rooms (£70 double incl breakfast), plus space for five caravans round the back of the inn.

Jumping Jenny

Brantwood, East of the Lake, LA21 8AD (015394 41715, www.jumpingjenny.com). Open Summer 11am-6pm daily. Winter 11am-5pm Wed-Sun.

Named after John Ruskin's rowing boat (now lovingly restored and in the adjoining carriage house), this licensed café and restaurant is set in the tastefully converted former stables at Brantwood. Independently run, it's a cut above the average stately home café. You can eat summer salads and smoked salmon on the terrace next to Coniston Water or take a rough-hewn table in the stalls inside – presided over by a log-burning stove in winter – and warm up with casserole or butternut squash and sweet potato soup. Co-owner Gillie Addison's delicious own-made cakes are available all year.

White Hart Inn

Bouth, LA12 8JB (01229 861229, www.whitehart-lakedistrict.co.uk). Open noon-11pm Mon-Sat; noon-10.30pm Sun. Lunch served noon-2pm, dinner served 6-8.45pm Mon-Fri. Food served noon-8.45pm Sat, Sun.

This 17th-century whitewashed inn between Coniston and Ulverston, stuffed with ancient industrial and farming implements, hunting prints and the odd trophy fox, echoes the days when Bouth was a bustling village on the route of the turnpike. In the 19th century it served the workers from the gunpowder works at Black Beck (now a caravan park), which was forced to close in 1928 after ten fatal accidents. Nothing so explosive shakes the White Hart now, but it caters quietly to holidaymakers and anglers with five rooms (£60-£90 incl breakfast) and hefty servings of gammon, egg and chips or steak baguette with onion, mushroom and hoisin sauce. Rehydrate with a pint of Coniston Bluebird or a quality guest ale (perhaps Jennings of Cockermouth, Yorkshire's Black Sheep or Timothy Taylor Landlord).

Where to stay

Most local pubs offer accommodation. The choice pick is the Church House Inn (*see p65*) in Torver, which also guarantees some of the best cooking and packed lunches in the area. There are two YHA hostels in Coniston: the 60-bed Holly How (Far End, 0845 371 9511, www.yha.org.uk), a few minutes' walk from the centre of the village, and the more isolated Coppermines (*see right*).

Self-caterers should contact Coppermines & Lakes Cottages (The Estate Office, The Bridge, LA21 8HJ, 015394 41765, www.coppermines.co.uk) in the centre of Coniston village. It offers scores of holiday homes, from country farmhouses to manor houses, throughout Coniston and the south Lakes. Some of the properties are in truly remote locations.

Bank Ground Farm
East of the Lake, LA21 8AA (015394 41264, www.bankground.com). Rates B&B £90-£110 double incl breakfast. Cottages £420-£3,750 per week.
The ultimate Arthur Ransome destination. This handsome farmhouse on Coniston's north-eastern shore has a persuasive claim to being the place that inspired Ransome to write *Swallows and Amazons*, and was the model for the lakeside home (Holly Howe) of the fictional Walker family. The next-door neighbours had a dinghy called *Swallow*, and the 1974 film of the novel was partly shot here too. Throughout, the working farm has been home to the Batty family. It's some package: fantastic views to Coniston Old

Man and the Yewdale Fells, half a mile of lake frontage, a boathouse and ample opportunity for modern, wholesome family adventures, including swimming and fishing for trout, charr, pike and eel. The seven bedrooms (five en suite), breakfast room and sitting room, decorated in a mix of period styles, have lots of charm. Five self-catering cottages next to the farmhouse sleep between two and 16; from November to Easter the farmhouse is also let out on a self-catering basis. The tearoom, serving snacks and own-made cakes, is open weekends from Easter and every day in summer.

Coppermines Youth Hostel
Coniston, LA21 8HP (0845 371 9630, www.yha.org.uk). Rates from £17.95 per person; £13.50 reductions.
The Coppermines YHA hostel occupies a wild and spectacular setting at the foot of the Old Man, just over a mile on foot from Coniston village. If you're driving, turn off at the Black Bull and test the limits of your car's suspension on the heavily pot-holed road. The white building has just five rooms and a total of 26 beds.

Eyrie at Brantwood ★
Brantwood, East of the Lake, LA21 8AD (015394 41396, www.brantwood.org.uk). Rates £750 per week.
A true one-off: the chance to sleep in Brantwood, in a self-catering apartment on the upper floor of John Ruskin's former home. The accommodation is simple – a double bedroom, kitchen-diner and drawing room – but offers great views across the lake. When the sightseers have left, you can wander the gardens in peace and stroll down to the little harbour built by Ruskin.

Lakeland House Guest House
Tilberthwaite Avenue, Coniston, LA21 8ED (015394 41303, www.lakelandhouse.co.uk). Rates £60-£80 double incl breakfast.

Local heroes: Donald Campbell

It was shortly after dawn on 4 January 1967. Donald Campbell launched his blue-painted *Bluebird K7*, the latest of his futuristic-looking hydroplanes, at Pier Cottage in a bid to break 300mph in an attempt on the world water speed record – and get back to London that night. He needed to average 300mph across two runs of Coniston Water's measured mile. The first run, north to south, was timed at 297mph. Campbell turned smartly, not refuelling as arranged or waiting for the wash to settle. The world's press and TV were watching. Speed records were big news in those days; the pilots were heroes.

As Campbell recrossed the start of the course he was doing 320mph. The boat, a beautiful streamlined icon of 1960s British design, was flying. No one knows for sure what went wrong, but the unforgettable monochrome footage shows the boat suddenly lifting, then flipping over, crashing and plunging down into the lake. Then stillness. Campbell must have died instantly.

It was the filming of Campbell's death that made him and Coniston Water imperishably famous. The moment has virtually become the motif of Coniston. It plays on a permanent loop in the village museum. Every other pub has the freeze-frame newspaper photograph above the bar. You can take home a

DVD and hear Donald Campbell's last words on a crackly intercom – 'I can't see a thing... I'm going... oh.' It's macabre yet compelling.

Fewer people recall that Campbell had set the water speed record two years earlier on Ullswater. He and his father Malcolm broke some 13 land and water speed records between them. Probably fewer still recall that Sir Henry Segrave captured the water speed record on Windermere in 1930. His boat hit a log and he regained consciousness long enough to be told that he'd broken the record, and then died.

The *Bluebird* crash site was soon located by navy divers, but they failed to find Campbell's body. It wasn't until 2000, 33 years after the crash, that engineer and diver Bill Smith located his remains 60 yards from the wreck of the boat. Donald's wife Tonia and his daughter Gina gave permission for both the wreck and the body to be brought to the surface for burial in Coniston village. But his sister Jean stayed away, claiming it was Donald's wish that 'skipper and boat' remain together.

Bill Smith and his team are currently restoring *Bluebird K7* (www.bluebirdproject.com) before bringing it to its new home, the Bluebird Wing of Coniston's Ruskin Museum (*see p60*), which is scheduled to open 2011. The mystique endures.

A budget B&B in the centre of Coniston village, catering to walkers. The ten rooms (all en suite) are decorated in a straightforward, contemporary style. Daytime meals and packed lunches are available in Holland's Café at the front of the building. Internet access, a bike store and a drying room are also provided.

No 1 Silverbank
Coniston, LA21 8HW (07810 091008, www.no1 silverbank.com). Rates £750-£1,295 per week.
Luxury self-catering keeps redefining itself: at the end of a little terrace five minutes from the centre of Coniston, this whitewashed retreat is in the forefront of rural chic. Leather sofas meet oak floors; Bose CD player and Wi-Fi sit alongside a traditional log fire. In the kitchen, Shaker-

style cabinets rub against Smeg appliances, along with wine, chocolates and breakfast basics. Climb the modish spiral staircase to reach the high-spec bedrooms (two double, one single/twin), equipped with sleigh beds, Egyptian cotton bedding, White Company towels, and a roll-top bath. Romantic and glamorous? Of course. And pretty expensive.

Pier Cottage Caravan Park
Lake Coniston, LA21 8AJ (015394 41252). Open Mar-Oct. Rates £16 for two people. No credit cards.
With a beautiful and peaceful setting next to the lake on Coniston's north-west shore, Pier Cottage is the ideal spot for touring caravans and campervans (tents aren't allowed). The facilities are pretty simple – there are no

Yew Tree Farm. See p68.

electric hook-ups, and a basic shower and toilet block – but it's perfect for dinghy owners and fishing fans. This is where Donald Campbell launched *Bluebird K7* and where the Steam Gondola ties up for the night. It's a ten-minute walk into Coniston village.

Waterhead Hotel
Hawkshead Old Road, Coniston, LA21 8AJ (015394 41244, www.waterhead-hotel.co.uk). Rates £119 double incl breakfast.
This traditional country house hotel on the north-western tip of Coniston Water, just outside Coniston village, has 24 en suite rooms of varying sizes, some with views of the lake (for which you pay extra). Lawns lead down to the water, but there's no access along the shore to the ferry jetty and Gondola Pier; you have to go back inland first.

Yew Tree Farm ★
On the A593, LA21 8DP (015394 41433, www.yewtree-farm.com). Rates £104-£124 double incl breakfast.
There can hardly be a finer setting or farmhouse than this National Trust property, sitting pretty beneath Holme Fell, two miles north of Coniston village. The exterior spinning gallery, historic wooden farming implements, and muscovy ducks waddling around the farmyard create a scene straight out of Beatrix Potter. Indeed, the farm once belonged to her. Her ornaments, pictures and oak dresser are still in the house, and the farm had a starring role in the Renée

Things to do

Steam Yacht Gondola

CONISTON WATER

Coniston abounds with activity centres and companies teaching outdoor pursuits, so there are plenty of opportunities to push yourself to the limit on mountain, rock or water. If you fancy learning about kayaking, abseiling, gorge scrambling or just walking safely on the fells, Summitreks (Lake Road, Coniston, 015394 41212, www.summitreks.co.uk) has a session to suit. It also runs British Hill-Walking Leadership Certificate (BHLC) courses, and has three outdoor equipment shops, in Coniston, Ambleside and Hawkshead.

Adventure 21 (01257 474467, www.adventure 21.co.uk) runs events around Coniston throughout the year. Family and group day and half-day adventures include gorge scrambling, canoeing and raft building.

Two-hour guided walks from the Ruskin Museum (*see p60*) covering Coniston village, John Ruskin and Donald Campbell take place on selected Thursdays between April and October. For annual events, including the Coniston Water Festival in July, *see pp11-15.*

Coniston Boating Centre
Lake Road, Coniston, LA21 8EW (015394 41366, www.lakedistrict.gov.uk/index/visiting/coniston boatingcentre.htm). Open 10am-4.30pm daily (later in midsummer).

Half a mile out of the village, at the end of Lake Road next to the Gondola Pier, is the National Park's boating centre. You can hire rowing boats, canoes, kayaks, sailing dinghies and electric motorboats, and also enrol on sailing lessons, two-day RYA sailing courses and powerboat courses. It's also the place to launch your own craft.

Coniston Launch
Lake Road, Coniston, LA21 8AN (01768 775753, www.conistonlaunch.co.uk). Open all year; weekends only Dec-mid Feb. Tickets Northern cruise £8.90; £4.95 reductions; £22 family. Northern cruise plus Brantwood admission £14.70; £6.20 reductions; £34.15 family. Southern cruise £12.50; £6.25 reductions; £27.50 family. Southern cruise plus Brantwood admission £18.30; £7.50 reductions; £39.15 family.
Coniston Ferry Services run two solar-powered wooden launches, the ML *Ruskin* and the ML *Ransome*, stopping at seven jetties on both sides of the lake. You can hop off at any jetty and catch a later sailing home. The northern service stops at Waterhead Hotel, Torver and Brantwood; the southern service at Torver (boarding only), Water Park, Lake Bank, Sunny Bank and Brantwood. The lakeshore walks between Torver

Zellweger film *Miss Potter*. But this is no Hollywood fantasy; it's a real working farm where Jon and Caroline Watson rear Herdwick sheep and belted Galloway cattle as well as providing a magical B&B experience. The oldest part of the house dates from 1690, and it shows in the ancient oak panelling, traditional door latches, and walls and floors that bow and lean. There's nothing old-fashioned about the three bedroooms, though, which feature craftsmen-made beds (two are four-posters), goose down quilts and luxurious bathrooms. The guest lounge features games, books and an open fire in winter. Breakfast is sourced from the farm: Herdwick haggis, home-cured bacon, Yew Tree sausages and eggs. Passers-by can purchase the Watsons' Heritage Meats from the farm shop.

and Sunny Bank both have pleasant picnic spots. Extra excursions in peak season include a two-hour *Swallows and Amazon* cruise visiting locations that helped inspire Beckfoot, Holly Howe and Wild Cat Island in the book, while the 75-minute Campbells on Coniston cruise relates (yet again) Donald Campbell's fatal world-speed record attempt. In 2001 the ML *Ruskin* carried Donald Campbell's coffin from the crash site to Coniston graveyard for burial.

Steam Yacht Gondola ★
Pier Cottage, LA21 8AJ (015394 41533 weather check 015394 41288, www.nationaltrust.org. uk/gondola). Open Easter-Oct 10.30am-4.15pm daily. Rates Regular cruise £8.50; £4.50 reductions; £21.50 family. Gondola Explorer Cruise £18; £9 reductions; £45 family. Wild Cat Island Cruise £15; £7.50 reductions; £37.50 family.
The National Trust's wood-burning, steam-powered gondola is the superstar attraction on Coniston Water. The sumptuously upholstered vessel was built in 1859 for the Furness Railway Company for visitors who had travelled to the Lake District on the railway. It sailed daily until 1936, when it became a houseboat; it was totally rebuilt by the NT in the 1970s. Now you can sit in the first-class saloon or out on deck as the gondola glides silently across the lake. Carrying 86 passengers, it runs from Coniston Pier (on the western shore) to Brantwood (one the eastern) and Monk Coniston (at the northern tip – where there's a popular walk through Monk Coniston estate to Tarn Hows). Sailings are every half hour and you can't pre-book. Special cruises (book tickets in advance at the Coniston TIC) include the 90-minute Gondola Explorer Cruise along the length of the lake (departing 1.15pm Mon, Thur); and the new 75-minute Wild Cat Island Cruise (departing 11am Sun). For ultimate showing-off and seclusion, private bookings start at £390 per hour.

ULVERSTON

Lanternhouse International
The Ellers, LA12 OAA (01229 581127, www. lanternhouse.org). Open 10am-5pm Mon-Fri; call or check website for evening and weekend opening. Admission free.
The town's progressive arts centre stages an eclectic year-round mix of events, workshops and exhibitions from film shorts to the fandango.

ULVERSTON
Fourteen miles south of Coniston village, just beyond the National Park boundary, Ulverston is a solidly old-fashioned market town. The centre, cheered up by brightly coloured Georgian buildings and the quirky Laurel & Hardy Museum (*see p61*) hasn't, thankfully, been swamped by chain stores. The town also lays claims to England's shortest, widest canal and the invention of the sport of pole-vaulting. More spiritually, it is also a major place of pilgrimage for both Buddhists and Quakers. And it's handy for rail enthusiasts, who can join the Furness Line (which connects with the spectacular Cumbrian Coast line at Barrow), and for walkers: Ulverston is the start of the Cumbria Way (www.thecumbriaway.info), the long-distance path that runs the length of the Lake District National Park to Carlisle.

Arriving from Coniston, you can't miss the Hoad Monument, a 100-foot limestone tower perched atop Hoad Hill on the edge of town, and a replica of Smeaton's Eddystone lighthouse off Devon – but without the light. Erected in 1850 and properly called the Sir John Barrow Monument, it honours the 18th-century naval man, born in Ulverston, who supported attempts to find the North-West Passage and wrote the standard text on the mutiny on the *Bounty*. It reopened in 2010 following extensive restoration, and visitors can climb to the top for panoramic views over Ulverston and its surroundings; a flag flies when it's open. There's no road access, so the only way to the tower is a slog up Hoad Hill.

In Ulverston itself, equip yourself with town trails and local knowledge at the Tourist Information Centre (01229 587120, closed Sun) on the ground floor of the 'Coro': the cream-pillared Coronation Hall that's now the town theatre. Outside is a statue of the Hollywood comic duo Stan Laurel and Oliver Hardy, unveiled by Ken Dodd in 2009; the skinny one, Stan, is Ulverston's most famous son. He was born Arthur Jefferson at 3 Foundry Cottages (now Argyle Street) in 1890 and died 190 films and 75 years later in a Los Angeles hotel. The Ulverston connection might have faded were it not for local fan Bill Cubin, who began sticking pictures of his heroes on his basement walls in the 1970s. The hobby gradually grew into a chaotic collection of memorabilia open to the public; Cubin died in 1997, but the museum continues, under the care of his daughter and grandson.

When the pleasures of Stan and Ollie wane, take refuge in Ulverston's varied shopping scene. The indoor market is cheap, cheerful and traditional. The outdoor market dominates the area around the Market Square on Thursday and Saturday, with the added bonus of Women's Institute baking at the Coro on Thursday morning. The best independent shops are found at the bottom end of Market Street; Brambles sells chichi gifts, Olive specialises in funky clothes and jewellery, and the Tinners Rabbit is, aptly enough, a warren of a bookshop. At Irving's butchers you can buy handmade pies and hot roast chicken to take out.

Ulverston bills itself a festival town, and hosts all manner of annual events celebrating everything from beer to classical music, walking and Buddhism. Carnival Day is held at the beginning of July, while the Dickensian Festival (www.dickensian festival.co.uk) is on the last weekend in November. One of the best is the Lantern Procession, in mid September, which parades a 'river of light' through town, ending up at Ford Park.

Ulverston Canal

The essential local walk is along the towpath of the Ulverston Canal. The shortest (one and a half miles), widest (66 feet), deepest (15 feet) and straightest canal in England saw ocean-going ships from Morecambe Bay come into the centre of town until the canal was finally abandoned after World War II. Don't buy the tale that pole-vaulting was invented as a way to cross the canal; it originated at the football club's sports day in 1879.

From Canal Street, turn south by the Canal Tavern and follow the towpath, crossing a disused railway line along the way. Ignore the sprawling factory of GlaxoSmithKline. At Canal Foot, the lock gate and pier open up a fine panorama of Ulverston Sands and Morecambe Bay. To the left is the Leven railway viaduct with 49 spans across its 500-yard length. To the right, tiny Chapel Island once contained a church and a house built by the monks of Conishead Priory as a shelter for fishermen. A light burned at night to guide travellers across the dangerous sands; now it's just a mass of impenetrable brambles. When the mist lies low over the silent silver sands and the Lake District fells are just distant outlines, the spot has something of the eerie beauty of a Venetian lagoon. Turning left past the public toilets, cross the fields and stiles and go under two railway bridges to return to town.

More dedicated walkers congregate at the modern conical sculpture in the Gill, which marks the start of the Cumbria Way. The cairn inside the sculpture contains all the minerals found in the Lake District along the 70-mile route north to Carlisle.

Where to eat & drink

Bay Horse Hotel & Restaurant

Canal Foot, LA12 9EL (01229 583972, www.the bayhorsehotel.co.uk). Open 7am-12.30am daily. Lunch served noon-2pm, dinner served 7.30pm for 8pm daily.

This hefty coaching inn stands guard over Morecambe Bay by the entrance lock of the old Ulverston Canal. Before the arrival of the railway, this was a staging post for the horse-led coaches racing the tide across the sands. Thick with beams, horse brasses and log fires, it delivers food well above pub fayre expectations. Lunch dishes include hot and cold poached salmon sandwiches with spiced cucumber, smoked chicken with curry mayonnaise and toasted coconut, and hot smoked pork loin on caramelised

Gillam's. See p72.

apple, apricot and shallots. Conservatory dining makes the most of the estuary views, while chef Robert Lyons makes the most of Cumbrian produce with the likes of Waberthwaite belly pork and Lakeland lamb shank. There's a vegetarian menu too.

Gillam's ★
64 Market Street, LA12 7LT (01229 587564, www.gillams-tearoom.co.uk). Open 9am-5pm Mon-Sat; 10am-4pm Sun.

With proper leaf tea, a classy coffee selection (all organic and Fairtrade), delicious cakes and scones and a friendly, no-rush vibe, this daytime-only café has got it right. Enjoy lunch – perhaps butternut squash risotto or mushrooms stuffed with stilton and redcurrants – by the old range in the cosy downstairs room or upstairs, where there are high beams, Moroccan lanterns and a marble fireplace. There's also a cute back garden. Winter brings warming winter cordial and mulled wine. Children are well looked after with miniature tea-time trays.

Rustique
Brogden Street, LA12 7AJ (01229 587373, www.eatat rustique.co.uk). Restaurant Dinner served 7-9pm Tue-Sat. Deli Open 10am-3pm Mon, Tue, Thur-Sat; 10am-2pm Wed.

Ulverston's most bijou restaurant is hidden away down an unmarked alley off Brogden Street. The decor at Rustique is contemporary and the dinner-only menu nicely balanced, offering the likes of gravadlax and soda bread, followed by duck leg confit with garlic potatoes and coriander carrots, and lemon panna cotta. Around the corner, at no.3, Rustique's smart new deli sells salad boxes, bespoke hampers and sandwiches with a Mediterranean twist, good for a picnic lunch.

World Peace Café
5 Cavendish Street, LA12 7AD (01229 587793, www.worldpeacecafe.org). Open 10am-4pm daily. Lunch served 11.30am-2.30pm daily.

Run by the Manjushri Buddhist Community, based at Conishead Priory (*see p61*), this vegetarian and organic café is indeed a peaceful spot. Settle on a sofa inside or find a spot in the conservatory or garden. Tuck into such flavoursome dishes as savoury sweetcorn fritters and mixed bean salad, aduki bean burgers with potato wedges, or just good coffee and a slice of own-made lemon and poppy seed cake. Prices are enticingly low, with main dishes costing just £5.90. On Friday evenings, you can join a meditation class followed by communal supper, for £12.

Where to stay
The Bay Horse Hotel & Restaurant (*see p70*) has nine simple en suite rooms (£90-£120 double incl breakfast), of which six enjoy mesmerising views across the Leven Estuary.

Swarthmoor Hall
Swarthmoor Hall Lane, Ulverston, LA12 0JQ (01229 583204, www.swarthmoorhall.co.uk). Rates vary; call for details. No credit cards.

Simple, clean, cheap self-catering accommodation is available in a modern barn conversion in the grounds of the impressive 16th-century Swarthmoor Hall. It may be the birthplace of Quakerism, but there are no religious obligations for anyone staying here. Three units sleep four, five or six people, and one has wheelchair access. Guests help themselves to cereals, fruit, eggs, toast and coffee in a shared kitchen. B&B (£64 double incl breakfast) is available when the units are not being used for self-catering.

World Peace Café

Ambleside & Waterhead

Set close to the head of Lake Windermere, Ambleside is one of the great crossroads of the Lakes – which means everybody pitches up here sooner or later. Although it has some delightful attributes and excellent nearby excursions, it's not the prettiest town in the Lake District. Instead, it is best embraced as the most well equipped and cosmopolitan centre that the National Park has to offer, with a plethora of pubs and restaurants, and an embarrassment of outdoor equipment shops. With the beating heart of a market town and an industrial past that runs deep, there's a lot more to Ambleside than meets the eye from the viewpoint of a summer traffic jam.

A mile outside town, Waterhead stands on Windermere's shore: from here, you can catch a steamer from the pier or hire a smaller boat to make your own exploration.

AMBLESIDE

If you fancy a respite from the wholesome virtues of the outdoor life and all that honest, local food, Ambleside is the place to guiltily catch a good movie and consume a Thai green curry. Impressively, for a town of just 2,600 permanent residents, it has two independent cinemas, three proper bookshops, (again, all independent) and the widest array of pubs, wine bars, cafés, delis and restaurants in Lakeland. Its university campus also means the average age is lower than that of nearly any other location in the Lakes.

Throw in a clutch of art galleries and pottery studios that range from the excellent – the Armitt Collection (*see p84*) – to the horribly commercial, and you might forget that you came to the Lakes for walking and wonderful scenery. But then you start to notice that Ambleside seems to have rather a lot of shops selling walking and climbing gear. Fifty years ago, there was only one; 25 years ago, a guidebook thought it remarkable that Ambleside had five. Today there are no less than 23, so there can be no excuse for leaving town without all the right equipment for the fells.

Plenty of familiar names jostle for position, but a local, family-run business probably trumps the lot. Gaynor Sports ★ (Market Cross, 015247 34938, www.gaynors.co.uk) sprawls over five floors, with a magnificent array of walking boots, fleeces and waterproofs, plus a collection of maps that runs from a town guide of Ambleside to an ascent of Annapurna. Gaynor's second outpost (Market Place, 015394 32062) is devoted to camping, with 40 ready-pitched tents on display and a wall of rugged-looking rucksacks.

Look up as you walk out with your new waterproof and you'll see Loughrigg Fell to the west, Wansfell Pike to the east and the Fairfield Horseshoe to the north. Before you head for the hills and start climbing, though, Ambleside has some worthwhile distractions at ground level.

The town's main shops and restaurants are situated around Lake Road and Compston Road. Running north-south through town is the main A591,

called Rydal Road to the north and Lake Road to the south. Approaching from the south you will be sucked round the one-way system, which eases pressure on Ambleside's heavy through traffic.

The Town Trail leaflet (available from the tourist office) provides a circuit of Ambleside's most historic locations, giving you a feel for the long-lost industries of charcoal making, corn milling and paper manufacture, as well as the timber mills for bobbin making. Although summer visitors might struggle to believe it, looking at the water levels, Stock Ghyll beck, which runs east-west through the middle of town, once powered 12 mills. The most spectacular relic is the Old Corn Mill, now home to shops and cafés. A mill has stood on this site since 1335, and although the impressive old wooden waterwheel no longer turns, the wheel at the Glass House Restaurant (Rydal Road, 015394 32137, www.theglasshouserestaurant.co.uk), 50 yards downstream, is still in working order.

Across the main road, most visitors stop to photograph the tiny, 17th-century Bridge House, which straddles Stock Ghyll; even Turner was impressed enough to paint it. According to popular legend, the one-up, one-down abode was built by a Scotsman angling to dodge land taxes. Other stories relate that it was home to a family of six, or even eight – or that it was simply an apple store. A group of locals bought the house in the 1920s and gave it to the National Trust: it became their first information office (015394 32617, closed Nov-Easter) and is the smallest property on the NT's books.

Blue plaque spotters should swing by the Old Stamp House on Church Street. Here, Wordsworth fulfilled his duties as Distributor of Stamps for Westmorland, a government post that earned the former radical an easy £400 a year and the scorn of Robert Browning for taking the government shilling ('Just for a handful of silver he left us'). Another town landmark is the 19th-century St Mary's Church, on Vicarage Road. Topped by a distinctive spire, it is the work of Sir George Gilbert Scott, whose Gothic revivalist works

Ambleside. See p73.

included London's Albert Memorial and Foreign Office; inside, a side chapel is dedicated to Wordsworth. This is also the scene of July's time-honoured rushbearing ceremony, depicted in a striking 1940s mural on one wall.

In addition to its Wednesday market at King Street car park, Ambleside is well supplied with food and wine shops. The pick of the crop is Lucy's Specialist Grocers (Compston Road, 015394 32223, www.lucysofambleside.co.uk). Along with fancy jams and jellies to take home, it has a stellar range of regional cheeses, breads and cakes, own-made pâtés and more; there's also an in-house café. On Market Place, the diminutive Granny Smiths (015394 33145), selling wholefoods and organic produce, is also handy for self-catering supplies and picnic provisions. Bear your bounty to Rothay Park, an appealing spot bordered by Stock Gyhll and the River Rothay, with ancient footbridges leading across the water.

Tucked away but deserving a detour, Organico (Fisherbeck Mill, Old Lake Road, 015394 31122, www.organi.co.uk, closed Mon, Sun) claims to be Britain's first dedicated organic wine store, with

Things to do

AMBLESIDE

Biketreks
Rydal Road, LA22 9AN (015394 31245, www. biketreks.net). Open 9am-5.30pm daily. Rates £20 per day.
All things cycling-related come together in one of the north-west's biggest and best bike centres. As well as selling all sorts of cycles and associated gear, and offering repairs, it has mountain bikes to hire (and one tandem). On Tuesday and Thursday evenings, experienced staff lead night rides on roads and fell trails; routes are between ten and 25 miles, with the promise of a pub stop or two on the way back. The course isn't too ferocious, and is set up according to who turns up; nonetheless, the fells at night are no place for the unfit novice.

Zeffirellis
Compston Road, LA22 9AD (015394 33845, www.zeffirellis.com). Open Cinema times vary, check website for details. Café 10am-4.30pm, restaurant 5.30-10pm daily. Tickets £5-£8; £4-£6 reductions.
The four screens at this independent cinema show a pleasing mix of mainstream hits and arthouse movies, with a good sprinkling of children's films. It also incorporates a jazz bar, with performances most Fridays and Saturdays. Vegetarian pasta and own-made pizzas are the mainstays of the restaurant menu – including some inventive toppings such as roasted butternut squash with thyme and dolcelatte – while the café menu offers snacks, spuds, panini and antipasti, along with more substantial mains. For a similar combination of films and veggie food, check out its newer sister operation, Fellinis (*see p79*).

WATERHEAD

Low Wood Watersports Centre
Low Wood, LA23 1LP (015394 39441, www.elh.co.uk/ watersports). Open Easter-Sept times vary, phone for details. Lessons from £15. Hire from £16/2hrs.
Pretty much every variety of messing about on the water is covered at this centre on the eastern edge of Windermere, attached to the Low Wood Hotel. Options include wakeboarding, wakesurfing, kneeboarding, canoeing, kayaking and dinghy sailing, and tuition is available. The centre still offers waterskiing, despite the new Windermere speed limit of ten knots; fine for learners, but not quite so much fun for the proficient. Rowing boats and motorboats (again, note the speed limit) can also be hired for a turn around the lake.

Zeffirellis

more than 100 wines and all sorts of tastings. Ambleside Wine Stores (Compston Road, 015394 34558) is also of interest, thanks to its 100-strong selection of malt whiskies and shelves of local bottled beers.

The town's trio of independent bookshops – Fred Holdsworth (Central Buildings, Market Cross, 015394 33388, www.fredontheweb.co.uk), Henry Roberts (Waveley House, Market Place, 015394 33264) and Wearing's (Lake Road, 015394 32312) – are all within a stone's throw of Market Cross, and have strong local sections. The Hub tourist office (Central Buildings, Market Cross, 015394 32582, www.amblesideonline.co.uk) can also supply local books, maps, walking guides and brochures; handily, it incorporates a post office.

Around Ambleside

Half a mile north of town on Rydal Road is expansive Rydal Park ★, where you can watch a few overs at Ambleside Cricket Club (015394 33313); *Wisden Cricketer* described it as the most beautiful ground in England. On the last Thursday in July, the park hosts Ambleside Sports, where hotly contested events include Cumberland and Westmorland wrestling, hound trails and children's races.

Heading south on Lake Road towards Waterhead, garden enthusiasts will inevitably be drawn to Hayes Garden World (015394 33434, www.hayesgarden world.co.uk). In fact, you can't miss it. Family-run for some 200 years, this sprawling garden centre is undeniably popular, and a major local employer. Nonetheless, its glass galleries are something of a blot on the landscape. Permission has been granted for a sizeable expansion, including an airport terminal-like building (due for completion in 2012), crazy golf and a 460-seater terrace.

Ambleside is a great jumping-off point for Coniston, the Langdale Pikes, Thirlmere and Derwent Water, but the most spectacular exit is the high road to Ullswater, heading north-east from the top of town. Not even listed as a B-road, it is heavily pot-holed and ominous signs warn of danger in winter, when the road is regularly cut off by snow. Its historic nickname of the Struggle, now formally adopted by the roadsign, is highly appropriate, given the alarming one-in-four gradient at the road's steepest point. High up to the left is the working slate quarry under Red Screes. Gradually the road winds up to the Kirkstone Pass – at almost 1,500 feet, the highest of all the Lake District passes.

At the very top, as you join the Windermere to Ullswater road (A592), pause for a breather at the Kirkstone Pass Inn (015394 33888, www.kirkstone passinn.com, closed Tue winter). The highest inhabited building in Cumbria, its foundations date from the 15th century; sit outside to drink in the heady view back over Windermere.

Nearby walks

Refresh your spirits with a visit to Stock Ghyll Force, an impressive 70-foot waterfall just east of town, reached via a well-trodden route starting at the Old Market Hall. The footpath meanders through sun-dappled woodland, dotted with daffodils in spring, while the waterfall tumbles down mossy rocks set among the trees.

For a longer walk, consider the standard four-and-a-half-mile circular climb of Loughrigg ★. At 1,101 feet, the hill is modest by Lake District standards, and the web of footpaths reflects its popularity. Still, there are gorgeous vistas over Rydal Water, Grasmere and Windermere, and you can survey a fantastic range of peaks from the top: Skiddaw and Helvellyn to the north, the Langdale Pikes and Crinkle Crags to the west. An easy detour takes in Loughrigg Tarn. From the west, its uncluttered beauty is framed by Loughrigg Fell, with two whitewashed farmhouses reflected in the water. Wordsworth named it 'Diana's Looking Glass', after a Roman fable, when he stopped at an opening in the road and saw 'Within the mirror's depth, a world at rest'. A gap in the moss-covered roadside wall still reveals a tranquil view of the scene.

The Coffin Trail – until 1821, the route that coffins were carried along between Ambleside and the nearest consecrated ground at Grasmere – makes for another enjoyable, relatively undemanding walk. Join the public footpath to the right shortly after Scandale Bridge, on the northern edge of town, and make a circuit around Rydal Water or, more energetically, Grasmere (which has countless refreshment options).

Where to eat & drink

The quality of food in Ambleside is definitely on the up. Indeed, apart from the Michelin-starred hotel kitchens of Windermere and the swanky gastropubs of the Lyth Valley, this is probably the all-round

Waterwheel. See p81.

Loughrigg Tarn

TEN CUMBRIAN FOODSTUFFS

Charr
A Lakeland rarity, the Arctic charr is a trout-like fish that was stranded in the deep, cold waters of Windermere when the waters receded at the end of the last glacial period. The fish was popular in the 17th century, when it was spiced and preserved in butter-topped pots, then shipped to London. Overfishing and netting led to its decline, but up to a dozen part-time fishermen still catch charr on Windermere, with long lines and spinners trailed from a moving rowing boat. Also found in Wastwater, Buttermere, Ennerdale and Crummock Water, the fish still occasionally turn up on restaurant menus, served potted or grilled.

Cumberland ham
The indefatigable Mrs Beeton wrote about curing hams 'in the Westmorland way' in her *Book of Household Management*, and Woodall's (*see p111*), based in Waberthwaite, has been curing them to the same recipe since 1828. The hams are air-dried for a month with salt and saltpetre, then matured for two months. Today, the firm holds a royal warrant for supplying bacon, sausage and hams to the Queen, and is a byword for quality on scores of Lakeland menus.

Cumberland rum nicky
Look out for this sweet tart at farmers' markets, bakeries and farm shops. The pastry case is filled with chopped dates, preserved ginger, butter, sugar and rum; in the 18th century, the more exotic ingredients would have been imported at Whitehaven. A lattice pastry top is the finishing touch – sometimes the edges are cut, or nicked, hence the name.

Cumberland sausage
This well-spiced pork sausage is sold in a long coil, from which the butcher will cut off the required quantity. Cranston's of Penrith (*see p212*) makes a splendid version. Alas, the Cumberland pig breed became officially extinct in the 1960s, so that succulent semi-circle on your plate, teamed with gravy, onions and mash, is probably Gloucester Old Spot pork.

Damsons
These small, tart-tasting members of the plum family flourish in the Lake District, particularly in the Lyth and Winster valleys. Orchards and hedgerows once bloomed with white damson blossoms in spring, and the fruit was piled up on carts in Kendal market for Damson Saturday in late September; until the trade died out during World War II, bushels of damsons were sent south to be made into jam. A modern revival of interest has seen

foodie capital of the Lakes. Options range from Thai, Indian and Chinese restaurants and takeaways to homely restaurant/tearoom Sheila's Cottage (The Slack, 015394 33079) and daytime café/bakery Apple Pie (Rydal Road, 015394 33679, http://applepieambleside.co.uk). Luigi's (Osborne Villa, Kelswick Road, 015394 33676, www.luigis-ambleside.co.uk) is a traditional Italian, while Zeffirellis (*see p75*) and Fellinis (*see right*) have a more contemporary feel.

There is plenty of pub life: the Churchill Inn (Lake Road, 015394 33192, www.churchill inn.co.uk) offers big-screen sports, darts, pool and accommodation; the well-kept ales at White Lion (Market Place, 015394 39901) include award-winning Hawkshead bitter; the Unicorn Inn (North Road, 015394 33216) is a homely horse brass and black-beamed local with folk music. For a more urban vibe and cocktail chic, the Lake Road Café/Wine Bar (12-14 Lake Road, 015394 33175, www.lakeroadwinebar.co.uk) is open to midnight or beyond, offering mocha lattes, open mic nights and early evening happy hours.

If one person could be said to have brought real change to Ambleside, it has be Lucy Nicholson, founder of Lucy's. Arriving from London in 1989 she launched something of a foodie revolution, bringing modern sensibilities to a clapped-out food scene by championing quality and regionality. Today, her company's outposts run from a deli (*see p75*) and cookery school to the relaxed, all-day café Lucy's on a Plate (*see right*), and wine bar/bistro Lucy4 (*see p80*).

Not surprisingly, such empire building has attracted some carping, not least when the North West Development Agency helped prop it all up with a £250,000 loan in 2009. The relentless, folksy self-promotion and menu patter about how

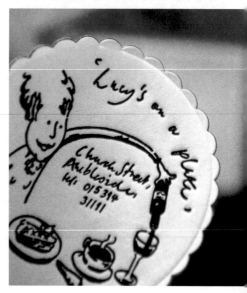

everything is 'blissful' and 'delicious' can sometimes grate, and service – as elsewhere in the Lake District – can be sloppy. Nonetheless, Lucy's is still the best deli in town, and it's hard to resist the easygoing appeal of the café and wine bar.

Another dinner option is the Log House (*see p80*), which offers a polished, seasonally changing menu; if it's slightly beyond your budget, a cheaper three-course menu is served 5-6.30pm.

Fellinis ★
Church Street, LA22 0BT (015394 33845, www.fellinis ambleside.com). Dinner served 5.30-10pm daily.
Independent cinema, café, pizzeria and jazz bar Zeffirellis (*see p75*) is an Ambleside institution. Its owners have now opened Fellinis – a similar set-up, incorporating an arthouse cinema and an inviting restaurant. Here, the emphasis is on more ambitious, Mediterranean-influenced vegetarian food: shallot and thyme tarte tatin to start, perhaps, followed by radicchio, walnut and pear 'cannolli' with poached pears and gorgonzola sauce. Both establishments offer film and dinner deals; check online for details.

Golden Rule
Smithy Brow, LA22 9AS (015394 32257).
Open 11am-midnight daily. No credit cards.
This cracking local pub is set in the back lanes, off the tourist trail. Inside you'll find a rabbit warren of rooms, comprising a cosy mish-mash of beams and brass, china dogs, period paintings and photos. There's Robinson's and Hartley's ales on tap, but no cooked food; instead, drinkers fill up on no-nonsense pork pies and filled rolls.

Lucy's on a Plate
Church Street, LA22 0BU (01539 432288, www.lucys ofambleside.co.uk/on_a_plate/index.html). Open 10am-9pm daily. Lunch served 10am-5pm, dinner served 6-9pm daily.

Lucy's on a Plate

the planting of new orchards, and the launch of Damson Day in April. Look out for jams, jellies, wine, beer and dense, sweet fruit 'cheese' at shows, farm shops and roadside stalls.

Grasmere Gingerbread
Half cake, half biscuit, Sarah Nelson's Grasmere Gingerbread (*see p87*) has been baked in the same little cottage since 1854. The recipe is thought to have been inspired by Whitehaven's spice trade, and the ginger imported from the West Indies. The slabs of gingerbread, sold in old-fashioned wrapping, are best eaten very fresh, while they are still soft.

Herdwick lamb & mutton
A hardy native breed that can survive in the most difficult terrain, these white-legged, white-faced, grey-coated sheep were once found across the Lake District. These days, they are confined to the central and western dales. Beatrix Potter helped to maintain the breed, and left her farms and flocks to the National Trust on condition that Herdwicks were kept on the land in perpetuity. Herdwick lamb and mutton can be bought in butcher's shops, at farmers' markets and direct from farms, including Yew Tree Farm (*see p68*) near Coniston. It can also be sampled on menus across the area.

Kendal Mint Cake
Not a cake at all, but a slab of white or brown candy flavoured with peppermint oil, Kendal Mint Cake was famously supplied to Edmund Hillary's expedition to the summit of Everest in 1953, and has been giving climbers an energy boost ever since. Three companies in Kendal still produce mint cake: Romney's, Quiggin's and Wilson's. Romney's is the most famous and ubiquitous brand, its wrapper little changed since the formula was inadvertently discovered in 1869.

Sticky toffee pudding
You'll find this stickily sumptuous baked sponge pudding on menus and food counters the length and breadth of the Lake District. The Sharrow Bay Hotel on Ullswater claims to have invented the dish in the 1960s, as does the Cartmel Village Shop (*see p262*) – which was probably the first company to sell it in foil trays to warm up at home. The recipe is, however, probably much older, and part of Britain's proud steamed pudding heritage.

Tatie pot
This lamb stew, topped with sliced potatoes, is really a Lakeland variation on classic Lancashire hotpot. Made with Herdwick lamb or mutton and black pudding, it requires long, slow cooking; the end result is wonderfully warming and tasty. It's a regular on the menu at the Church House Inn, Torver (*see p65*).

Golden Rule. See p79.

This snug café segues from breakfasts (anything from yoghurt-topped warm fruit compote to hearty cooked breakfasts), brunches and lunches to candlelit dinners. In between, there are crumpets, cakes and various little savoury somethings. You can sit in the conservatory, but the essence of the place is best captured by the homely main room with its worn floorboards, newspapers, chapel chairs and blackboard. If the substantial, laminated menus remind you that this is a proper, hard-sell business too, then at least it's held together with good taste and largely dependable cooking. Daytime grub is all about superior comfort food: potato rösti with bacon and cheese, say, or own-made lasagne with salad. In the evening, chirpily named main courses such as Cider with Piggy and Wellbred, Fellbred Filly (beef, not horse) combine local sourcing with global influences. Puddings are a speciality, so save some room.

Lucy4 Wine Bar & Bistro
St Mary's Lane, LA22 9DG (015394 34666, www.lucys ofambleside.co.uk/lucy4/index.html). Open/food served 5-10.30pm Mon-Fri; noon-10.30pm Sat; noon-10pm Sun.
When you don't want to fork out for another pricey restaurant meal or can't face another pub Cumberland sausage, this laid-back tapas and wine bar should fit the bill. Tucked down a narrow alley, it occupies a clever split-level conversion with brightly painted tables and walls and intimate lighting. The menu runs from olives and dips to antipasto platters and tapas: dolcelatte-stuffed figs with balsamic syrup, perhaps, or spiced coconut mussels (avoid the crudely battered calamares). Rather impressively, nearly 90 wines are available by the glass. There's also a franchise in Bowness.

Rattle Gill Café
2 Bridge Street, LA22 9DU (015394 34403). Open 10am-5pm Mon, Thur-Sun.

Blessed with an unrivalled hideaway location, this charming café has an outdoor terrace beside Stock Ghyll as it tumbles under stone bridges and past an old wooden waterwheel. Although the address is Bridge Street (formerly Rattle Gill), no car could possibly access this ancient cobbled walkway. Eat inside or out from a vegetarian menu. The soups, sandwiches, veggie chilli, baked potatoes and paninis are deservedly popular, as are the scones, victoria sponges and carrot cakes (all baked on the premises); not surprisingly, the neighbours are fond of this place too, as leftovers are given away at the end of the day.

Where to stay
You can't visit Ambleside without being struck by the profusion of Victorian guesthouses, B&Bs and timewarp country house hotels. With a few exceptions, though, it's best to carry on through: the town may be great for stocking up on books, provisions, maps and outdoor gear, but the fells and lakes are the views you want to wake up to.

One nearby option to consider is the Drunken Duck inn and restaurant (*see p49*), set in the hills above town: after a drink in the snug, oak-floored bar, and a superb dinner, retire to one of the delightfully appointed rooms.

If you're struggling to find a bed for the night, the helpful staff at the Hub tourist office can fix you up with accommodation, for a £3 booking charge.

Log House
Lake Road, LA22 0DN (015394 31077, www.loghouse. co.uk). Rates £80-£90 double incl breakfast.
A five-minute walk south of the town centre, this rustic log cabin looks slightly incongruous amid all the slate and local stone. Nonetheless, the building has a rich heritage, as the

studio of Lakeland's favourite Victorian watercolourist, Alfred Heaton Cooper, who had the cabin shipped over from the Norwegian fjords. It's now a restaurant/bar serving an upmarket Modern European cuisine, and also has three double rooms furnished in a contemporary style: think neutral colours, White Company toiletries, free Wi-Fi and flatscreen TVs.

The Oaks
Loughrigg, LA22 9HQ (015394 37632). Rates £54 double incl breakfast. No credit cards.
This lovely, cream-painted old farmhouse stands on the delightful back road that climbs from between Clappersgate and Skelwith Bridge to take in Loughrigg Tarn and High Close. It's perfectly positioned for walks through the unspoiled countryside or fell climbing to Grasmere and Rydal; at the same time, it's only a mile (as the crow flies) from Ambleside. Run by Dorothy Wrathall for nearly 40 years, it feels like an idyll from a different age. There are three double bedrooms, two bathrooms (not en suite) and a residents' lounge.

Waterwheel
3 Bridge Street, LA22 9DU (015394 33286, www. waterwheelambleside.co.uk). Rates £85-£100 double incl breakfast.
If you're after a romantic little B&B, this place should tick all the boxes. It's a 300-year-old, Grade II listed cottage perched above Stock Ghyll, with three guest bedrooms. The decor is traditional without resorting to frills and chintz; Rattleghyll, with a Victorian claw-foot bath, is particularly lovely. Beds are comfortable, and thoughtful extras include a tot of port to send you to sleep. In the morning, refuel with a textbook full English breakfast or smoked kippers.

WATERHEAD
A mile south of town is Waterhead. Leaving aside arguments as to whether or not Waterhead belongs to Ambleside (if nothing else, they are umbilically joined by a string of B&Bs), this is the northern tip of Windermere.

Windermere Lake Cruises (*see p26*) make drop-offs and pick-ups at the charming mock-Tudor pier at Waterhead; you can use their charming old steamers and launches to travel to the Lake District Visitors Centre at Brockhole (*see p34*), Wray Castle Gardens (*see p44*) and Bowness. Alternatively, hire a boat at Low Wood Watersports Centre (*see p75*).

On dry land, watch the comings and goings on the lake from Ambleside Youth Hostel (*see p84*), which enjoys a priceless setting. Take in the view from the lawn, which is lapped by the lake, keeping your back to the hideous 1960s café where you just bought your ice-cream. The Wateredge Inn (Borrans Road, 015394 32332, www.wateredge inn.co.uk) also welcomes non-residents for tea or a tipple in its lakeside garden.

Next door is Borran's Field, a public park with thoughtfully positioned benches and a gateway to the Roman fort of Galava, founded in AD 79 and redeveloped under Hadrian in the second century. It's hard to imagine it as a mighty fort of empire as little is left beyond a grid of foundations; it's best appreciated from Loughrigg Fell on a clear day. Still, the 200 conscript soldiers who wintered here would have found it a soft option compared to the isolated hilltop fort at Hardknott Pass (*see p105*). Ambleside's Armitt Collection (*see p84*) has a worthy stab at bringing it all to life.

For romance, make the brief, stiff climb 200 or so yards to Jenkyn's Crag. Take the footpath opposite the Waterhead Hotel up through Skelghyll Woods until you reach a rocky outcrop set amid towering fir trees. From here, there's a chocolate-box view of Windermere, Claife Heights and Wray

Lucy4 Wine Bar & Bistro

Waterhead. See p81.

Castle. According to Cumbria Tourism, this is the Lake District's most popular spot for Valentine's Day marriage proposals (Aira Force came second, and Catbells third).

Next to Skelghyll Woods is the National Trust's Stagshaw Garden (015394 46027, www.national trust.org.uk/main/w-stagshawgarden), open daily from April to June and by appointment from July to the end of October. A small woodland garden on the hillside, it packs in rhododendrons, azaleas, magnolias, camelias and a tremendous show of bluebells in the spring, with little waterfalls and more fine views thrown in. Payment of the £2.50 entrance charge is, rather sweetly, deposited in an honesty box at the entrance.

Where to eat & drink

The café at Ambleside Youth Hostel (*see right*) serves snacks and simple lunches. If you want something smarter, the pricier Bay Restaurant & Bay Bar at the Waterhead Hotel (Lake Road, 015394 30708, www.elh.co.uk) combine lovely views with the closest thing to cutting-edge decor and food to be found in Waterhead. To really splash out, Windermere's Michelin-starred Holbeck Ghyll (*see p33*) and Samling (*see p35*) are a short hop down the eastern shore of the lake.

For a wider range of options, Ambleside's cafés and restaurants are only 15 minutes' walk away.

Where to stay

Ambleside Youth Hostel

Waterhead, LA22 0EU (0845 371 9620, www.yha.org.uk). Rates £15.95 for 1 person.
The youth hostel is set on the shore of Lake Windermere, with stunning views over the water. It's an imposing-looking building, with 257 beds and a good array of private and family rooms, along with a café-bar and plenty of self-catering facilities.

Places to visit

AMBLESIDE

Armitt Collection ★
Rydal Road, LA22 9BL (015394 31212, www.thearmittcollection.com). Open 9.30am-5pm Mon-Sat. Admission £2.50; £1 reductions.
The star exhibits at this small but exemplary museum are Beatrix Potter's exquisite watercolours of fungi – she was a pioneering mycologist – and the finds from Ambleside's Roman fort. Also worth investigating is the permanent exhibition on influential German avant-garde painter and collage artist Kurt Schwitters, who settled in Ambleside after the Nazis denounced him as 'degenerate'. Visitors can also read about Wordsworth's unsuccessful battle against the Kendal-Windermere railway, and learn about other local luminaries such as anti-slavery campaigner and early feminist Harriet Martineau.

Upstairs is a superb library of Lakeland literature. The enthusiastic staff will reveal such treasures as the first guide to the Lakes, written by Thomas West in 1778, and the original prints of 19th-century photographer Herbert Bell, who lugged his hefty Victorian camera up to the peaks, and also recorded the Roman bridges at Thirlmere before they were swallowed up by the Manchester Corporation reservoir. The museum is staffed by volunteers, so opening times can be erratic; call ahead.

The Homes of Football
100 Lake Road, LA22 0DB (015394 34440, www.homesoffootball.co.uk). Open Summer 10am-5pm daily. Winter times vary, phone for details. Admission free.
Prompted by the Hillsborough stadium disaster of 1989, photographer Stuart Clarke began to document the nation's football stadiums and fans. Having found an unlikely permanent home in Lakeland (where there has never been an English league club), his pictures are a treat, capturing with an original and often playful eye the agony and the ecstasy of our national obsession. Football fanatics can purchase pictures of virtually every English league ground, ranging from 50p postcards to pricey limited-edition prints.

The Homes of Football

Grasmere & Rydal

Grasmere sits almost at the centre of the National Park, at a natural dividing line between north and south Lakeland. The setting of Grasmere Lake and its slightly smaller adjoining sister, Rydal Water, is utterly beautiful – from the swans posing on the water to the stunning backdrop of Helm Crag, with the Lion and the Lamb outcrop and Dunmail Raise. Although its endlessly varied vistas have inspired the likes of Turner and Constable, Grasmere owes its international fame not to art but to poetry. Samuel Taylor Coleridge, Thomas de Quincey and Robert Southey were among the literary greats inspired by the area, but it is William Wordsworth, above all, whose name is linked with that of Grasmere. The Cumbrian-born Romantic poet lived and wrote here, and is buried in the village he described as 'the loveliest spot that man hath ever found'.

Grasmere

Although Wordsworth would doubtless be appalled by the steady procession of coaches crawling around the bends of the A591 from Ambleside to Grasmere, he himself helped draw the tourist hordes: his immensely popular *Guide to the Lakes* was published in 1810, aimed, as he explains, at 'Persons of taste, and feeling for Landscape'.

So don't feel too guilty about joining the queue for Dove Cottage (*see p92*), just south of Grasmere and the magnetic centrepiece of all the fuss – and certainly don't be so snobbish as to bypass it. Go early in the day if you can; even in a multinational crush, though, the half-hour tour through the low-ceilinged rooms is wonderfully atmospheric, as you take in the chaise longue where Wordsworth composed, the ice-skates on which he sped over Esthwaite Water, or the opium scales that preoccupied his friend Thomas de Quincey.

The Wordsworths – William and his sister Dorothy and then also his wife Mary and three of their children – lived here from 1799 to 1808, later moving a mile downstream to the larger Rydal Mount. While there is a tense little contest between the two houses as to which was the poet's best-loved home, there can be no doubt that he produced some of his finest verse at Dove Cottage.

In the centre of Grasmere village stands the 13th-century St Oswald's Church – more interesting than its unprepossessing rendered exterior might suggest, with splendid oak timbers and a marble Wordsworth memorial over the choir stalls. Wordsworth and his wife lie beneath a modest headstone in the south-eastern corner of the graveyard, under the shadow of Rydal Fell; three of their children are buried nearby, as is Dorothy Wordsworth. Just beyond the graveyard is the burgeoning Wordsworth Daffodil Garden, where individuals can sponsor daffodils to raise money for local charities.

The village is heavily geared towards the tourist pound, with a proliferation of cloying gift shops and dinky tearooms; that said, you'll find plenty of organic and Fairtrade foods. Sam Read's

Grasmere

(Broadgate, 015394 35374) is an excellent independent bookshop. Duck your head as you enter Sarah Nelson's Gingerbread Shop (015394 35428, www.grasmeregingerbread.co.uk), housed in the converted schoolroom by the churchyard gate where Wordsworth once taught. Here, pinafore- and bonnet-clad staff dispense slabs of the spicy confection, baked on the premises to a recipe supposedly so secret that it's kept in a bank vault in Ambleside. The packaging, certainly, looks as if it hasn't changed since Sarah Nelson began selling the gingerbread in 1854.

Works by four generations of the Cooper family are exhibited at the Heaton Cooper Studio (015394 35280, www.heatoncooper.co.uk). Pieces range from prints and original watercolours of the fells and lakes by Victorian landscape painter Alfred Heaton Cooper and his son William to striking modern landscapes and studies by William's son Julian.

A true Grasmere original is tucked away opposite the churchyard and gingerbread shop: Taffy Thomas's magical Storyteller's Garden (see p94). On the northern side of the lake, at Red Bank Road, Faeryland has rowing boats for hire in summer. It may sound insufferably twee, but the little wooden hut and tea garden above the reeds are charming, and the leaf tea selection is first-class.

Around Grasmere

Wordsworth compared Grasmere to the hub of a wheel, with the dales radiating outwards like spokes, and there are superb walks in all directions. It's a simple uphill stroll to either White Moss Common or Loughrigg Terrace, on either side of the divide between Grasmere and Rydal Water, for classic panoramas of the lakes, woods and fells. The more adventurous, meanwhile, can take up the challenge of Helm Crag, described by Wainwright as 'an exhilarating little climb'. Look out for the distinctive outcrop of rocks known as the Lion and the Lamb at its southern end.

Another popular detour from Grasmere is Easedale Tarn. Don't waste time looking for anywhere to park on Easedale Road, the dead-end lane that branches off west at the top end of the village: you can't. Instead, follow the lane on foot until a bridge crossing sends you along Sour Milk Gill and the ascent to the tarn. It's a well-trodden route, less than four miles there and back; although most of it is mundane by Lake District standards, the final stretch of extended waterfalls and the amphitheatre of the glacial tarn is stunning. For superior refreshments along the way, try the Lancrigg Vegetarian Country House Hotel (see p93).

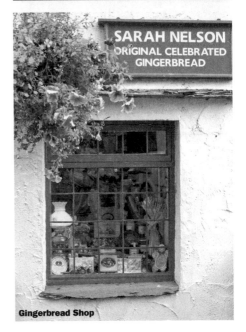

Gingerbread Shop

Rydal

Less than half a mile downstream of Grasmere, along the rocky River Rothay, is Rydal Water ★. Although the village of Rydal lacks a defined centre, it has a pub, a church, an enormous estate and religious retreat, and some highly individual places to stay, all in an idyllic setting.

The village's main draw, though, is Rydal Mount (see p92), Wordsworth's home for 37 years. The stately, 16th-century pile reflects the poet's

Dove Cottage, Wordsworth Museum & Art Gallery. See p92.

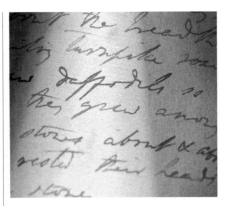

FIVE WORDSWORTH READS

Collected Poems,
William Wordsworth
Tintern Abbey, The Prelude, 'I Wandered
Lonely as a Cloud'... Wordsworth's poetry
is branded on to the national psyche. If
he never soared like Coleridge, he is the
English master of nature and nostalgia;
enduring and accessible.

Grasmere Journal,
Dorothy Wordsworth
In her letters, diaries and poems, Dorothy
penned a vivid record of her life, from
nature walks with her brother to their talks
with the literary luminaries of the age.
Overshadowed by her famous (and male)
sibling, Dorothy had her own – largely
unsung and unexploited – talent: guess
who first thought of daffodils dancing in
the breeze?

Guide to the Lakes,
William Wordsworth
A fascinating first-hand account of
Wordsworth's thoughts on the Lake
District, this is his 'Guide or Companion
for the *Minds* of Persons of taste, and
feelings for Landscape'. It offers a route
up Scafell and pungent side-swipes
against 'new settlers' and 'the country
disfigured'. It was long better known
than his poetry.

William Wordsworth, Hunter Davies
This accessible Wordsworth biography
was written by Hunter Davies, who lives
in Loweswater and knows the territory
backwards. However, the scholar's
benchmark text on the poet remains
Stephen Gill's *Wordsworth – A Life.*

Wordsworth: A Life, Juliet Barker
Barker's well-rounded, well-written
biography looks at both the man and
his work, with tremendous attention to
detail and enlightening excerpts from
family letters and diaries.

Rydal Water. See p87.

enhanced status, and was large enough to accommodate his many visitors. The gardens, which Wordsworth helped design, have barely changed: terraces above the main lawn afford spirit-lifting views to Rydal Water and Lake Windermere, and the rustic summer house is enchanting.

Halfway up the hill to Rydal Mount is the grand, early 19th-century Rydal Hall (015394 32050, www.rydalhall.org), now a religious retreat and conference centre. Non-residents are welcome to explore the elegantly landscaped formal gardens (£2.50 voluntary contribution) in front of the hall; to the rear, woodland paths lead to a walled organic garden and an orchard, planted with 30 or so traditional apple varieties. Other features include an 18th-century ice house, a grotto overlooking Rydal Falls and the appealing Old School Room Tea Shop.

At the bottom of the road is St Mary's Church, built in 1824. Wordsworth worshiped here, as did the Arnold family; a window commemorates Thomas Arnold, headmaster of Rugby School. Wordsworth planted the neighbouring Dora's Field with daffodils, after the death of his daughter in 1847. Now run by the National Trust, it's free to enter and at its loveliest in March and April, when a sea of bluebells follows the daffodils.

Of the 16 official lakes in the National Park, Rydal Water is one of the smallest, measuring just three-quarters of a mile long and a quarter of a mile wide, and with two little islands. Follow the lane from Pelter Bridge car park, past Cote How, until the road turns into a path. Suddenly, the lake is unveiled at Wordsworth's Seat, fringed by woodland and framed by a ring of fells. Look out too for red deer, which sometimes swim out to Heron Island.

Footpaths lead to Rydal Caves (the no entry sign barring access to the lagoon in the higher cavern must be the most ignored notice in all Lakeland), the higher reaches of Loughrigg Fell and the belvedere at Loughrigg Terrace. But for a quintessential introductory circuit of Rydal, drop down through the woods, cross the Rothay, climb up to White Moss and follow the ancient Coffin Route back to Rydal Mount. As the name suggests, it was the path used to carry Ambleside's dead to Grasmere for burial. Keen walkers may prefer to tackle the ten-mile Fairfield Horseshoe; a classic six-hour trek, it takes in the high-level Grisedale Tarn and Fairfield – at 2,864 feet, the area's dominant peak.

Where to eat & drink

Laminated pub grub menus are all too common in the further flung corners of the Lake District, so the quality options around Grasmere make for a pleasant change. Although some joints are out to clip the tourists, with uninventive food at premium prices, operations such as the vegetarian restaurant at the Lancrigg (*see p93*), which is also open to non-residents, show a genuine passion for good grub.

Grasmere isn't much of a drinker's village, but decent real ales are to be found at the Lamb Inn (015394 35456, www.grasmereredlionhotel.co.uk)

and Tweedies (015394 35300, www.tweedies bargrasmere.co.uk) in the centre, and Traveller's Rest (015394 35604, www.lakedistrictinns.co.uk/travellers_welcome.cfm) on the main road north of the village. In Rydal, the Badger Bar (015394 34500, www.theglenrothay.co.uk) at the Glen Rothay Hotel serves solid pub food, including fish and chips and own-made lamb hotpot.

Green's Café & Bistro
College Street, Grasmere, LA22 9SZ (015394 35790). Food served Summer 10.30am-6pm Mon-Wed, Fri-Sun. Winter 10am-5pm Mon, Tue, Fri-Sun.
As its name suggests, this agreeable set-up tends towards organic, local and Fairtrade supplies 'wherever possible'. It serves speciality teas, Farrer's of Kendal coffee and organic ice-cream, along with wraps, baguettes, toasted ciabatta, salads and baked potatoes. In summer, head for the patio.

Jumble Room ★
Langdale Road, Grasmere, LA22 9SU (015394 35188, www.thejumbleroom.co.uk). Lunch served noon-2.30pm Sat, Sun. Dinner served 5-10pm Mon, Wed-Sun.
Tucked away on a back lane and an enduring favourite with locals, this informal eaterie is the safest bet in Grasmere. Its two cosy dining rooms are decorated in eclectic, exuberant style; space is limited, so book ahead. The menu runs from spiced parsnip and apple soup to catalan fish stew and roast Goosnargh chicken, while desserts include a sumptuous own-made brown bread ice-cream. Good wine, a homely vibe and decent value for money knocks Grasmere's more pretentious eateries into a cocked hat.

Jumble Room

Places to visit

Dove Cottage, Wordsworth Museum & Art Gallery ★

Grasmere, LA22 9SQ (015394 35544, www. wordsworth.org.uk). Open Mar-Oct 9.30am-5.30pm daily. Feb, Nov, Dec 9.30am-4pm daily. Admission £7.50; £4.50 reductions; £17.20 family.

Unmissable, of course. This beautiful 400-year-old property has been immaculately preserved by the Wordsworth Trust. Before the poet moved here in 1799, with his sister Dorothy, the cottage was the Dove & Olive inn – and it must have been a wonderfully cosy boozer. It has been a museum since 1891, and its atmospheric interior is pretty much as Wordsworth left it, mutton-fat candles and all. There is the corner chair where he wrote – or dictated – his finest work; his French passport, recording his height and weight; and his still-working cuckoo clock. A sprig of poppies is wryly placed under the portrait of opium-eating Thomas de Quincey, who took over the Dove Cottage tenancy, along with his opium scales and a vial of Kendal Black Drop – a potent mix of laudanum, red wine and opium with which de Quincey, Coleridge and occasionally Wordsworth treated their 'headaches'. Sir Walter Scott and William Hazlitt were among the luminaries who visited. The cottage is only accessible by guided tour, but what you lose in freedom you gain in fascinating detail.

Set in a tasteful modern slate building, the adjoining Wordsworth Museum is full of treasures: almost all of Wordsworth's manuscripts and notes, Dorothy's evocative *Grasmere Journal* and the manuscript of de Quincey's *Confessions of an English Opium Eater*. Look out too for Edward Lear's Lake District drawings on the staircase. The Trust runs regular (and usually free) musical and literary events here, and the shop is mercifully free of museum shop tat. The Jerwood Centre is open by appointment for more scholarly research into the Lakes poets and the Romantic movement.

Rydal Mount & Gardens

Rydal, LA22 9LU (015394 33002, www.rydalmount. co.uk). Open Mar-Oct 9.30am-5pm daily. Feb, Nov, Dec 11am-4pm Wed-Sun. Admission £6; £2.50-£5 reductions; £15 family.

Rydal Mount was Wordsworth's last home and he lived here for 37 years until his death, on the stroke of midnight, in 1850. The 16th-century house was a social step up for the Wordsworths after little Dove Cottage, and their brief stays at Allan Bank and the Old Rectory in Grasmere, where two of Wordsworth's children died. Here, the poet's admirers could be entertained in the spacious drawing room, simply but elegantly furnished and with magnificent views over Rydal Water and Windermere. Something of a rebel in his youth, Wordsworth settled into comfortable middle age at Rydal, writing in his attic study and working in the lovely gardens, which he was largely responsible for designing. By this time he had become a national celebrity – invited, in 1843, to become Poet Laureate. A letter to Queen Victoria declining the position hangs in his study, although he was eventually persuaded to take up the post, on the rather extraordinary condition that he didn't actually have to write any poetry. Rydal Mount is still owned by descendants of the family: as the guides are quick to point out, this is a family home as well as a museum, and silver-framed family photographs of the present-day Wordsworths adorn the drawing room table.

Through a gate at the bottom of the garden (or via St Mary's churchyard) is Dora's Field, a plot of land on which Wordsworth planned to build a house for his daughter. When Dora died of tuberculosis, her father was inconsolable. He never wrote another line of poetry, but he and Mary planted the field with daffodils in memory of their daughter.

Rydal Mount & Gardens

Cote How Organic Guest House & Tea Room

Where to stay

As a tourist honeypot, Grasmere has a number of large hotels – and at the height of the season, it's not unusual for every bed to be taken. Book well ahead at the more characterful places, such as Cote How B&B.

Cote How Organic Guest House & Tea Room ★

Rydal, LA22 9LW (015394 32765, www.cotehow.co.uk). Rates £45-£80 double incl breakfast.
This superior B&B is one of only three Soil Association-registered organic guesthouses in the UK, where everything from the beer to the baking powder is organic. Breakfast involves muesli, granola, fruit, and fry-ups (as meaty, vegetarian or vegan as you wish), while room rates include afternoon tea with freshly baked scones and cakes. The three bedrooms are decorated in elegantly traditional style. The Rydal Suite features a kingsize bed and cosy bathrobes; the roll-top bath offers a view of Rydal Water and the fells. The sitting room has a piano, games, books and an honesty bar, but no TV. Instead, enjoy the abundant birdlife in the grounds, keeping an eye out for roe deer, or borrow a kayak from the old boathouse: Cote How has the sole boating rights on Rydal Water. A tearoom opens at weekends, with seats by the river. Note that the guesthouse only allows over-12s.

Full Circle Luxury Lake District Yurts

Rydal Hall, LA22 9LX (07975 671928, www.lake-district-yurts.co.uk). Rates £380-£500 per week.
Warm, watertight and comfortable, these four Mongolian yurts are the real deal – and a remarkably comfortable way

to camp. Each yurt contains a double bed and two singles, with room for a couple of extra camp beds; wooden floors, a wood-burning stove, lanterns and a gas hob and grill are among the other home comforts. Outside, there's a decked picnic area with a barbecue, and the shower block and toilets are a mere 100 yards away. Guests have access to Rydal Hall's lovely grounds and a children's adventure playground, and the limpid pools of nearby Rydal Beck are perfect for wild swimming. Weekend, midweek and week-long bookings are available all year, but the place gets booked months in advance for the school holidays – you could consider an autumn or winter visit instead.

Grasmere Independent Hostel

Broadrayne Farm, Grasmere, LA22 9RU (hostel 015394 35055, www.grasmerehostel.co.uk; cottages 015394 32321, www.heartofthelakes.co.uk). Rates Hostel £19.50 per person. Cottages £305-£657 per week.
A mile north of Grasmere, this friendly independent hostel is pretty luxurious for a bunkhouse. It's clean, warm and carpeted, with 24 beds spread across five rooms (most of which have en suite showers and views to the outlying fells). Facilities include a well-equipped kitchen, a lounge, a laundry and drying room, and even a sauna. The hostel is particularly good for families on a budget and for groups, who can book the entire place; there are three self-catering farm cottages on site too, sleeping from two to four people.

Lancrigg Vegetarian Country House Hotel

Easedale, nr Grasmere, LA22 9QN (015394 35317, www.lancrigg.co.uk). Rates £110-£170 double incl breakfast.

Things to do

Storyteller's Garden

Church Stile, Grasmere, LA22 9SW (015394 35641, www.taffythomas.co.uk). Open varies, check website for details. Admission £5; £3 reductions; £12 family. No credit cards.

The Storyteller's Garden belongs to Taffy Thomas, MBE, one-time thespian, puppeteer, retired fire eater and Britain's first Storyteller Laureate. Taffy and his wife Chrissy have created a beguiling garden, with rustic seating, willow pigs and hidden fairies; when he's not touring the country in a campaign to keep oral storytelling traditions alive, Taffy runs events here – or, in bad weather, in the quaint cottage. Ring in advance; if he's at home, Taffy will tell you a story, or show you the river and lakeside trail. Other events take place seasonally, and to tie in with Grasmere's summer music festival. At Christmas, Taffy dons his embroidered 'tale coat', the garden is warmed by braziers, and stories, songs, mince pies and wassail cup bring festive cheer.

Wordsworth Trust Events

015394 35544, www.wordsworth.org.uk.

Based at Dove Cottage, the Wordsworth Trust arranges events throughout the year. In addition to highly regarded talks and poetry readings, there are regular workshops (which in the past have ranged from beadwork and embroidery to making your own leather-bound notebook) and special children's activities during the school holidays. Mid January, meanwhile, brings the annual Arts & Book Festival, a scholarly weekend of talks, readings and workshops.

Taffy Thomas of the Storyteller's Garden

This venerable country house hotel is the perfect base for forays around Easedale Tarn and Helm Crag; and what's more, your hosts will send you out with the healthiest packed lunch around. Bedrooms are pastel-hued and of the four poster and quilt variety; Silver Howe, with its wonderful views, brass bed and sprigged wallpaper, is particularly charming. The hotel's organic café and restaurant serves the likes of root vegetable rösti topped with mushrooms and Cumbrian rarebit, or tofu burger with paprika wedges, chargrilled veg and salad. Non-residents are welcome to explore the hotel's woodland estate and the terraced walk that William and Dorothy Wordsworth once strolled. According to Dorothy Wordsworth, it was their 'favourite haunt' – and since the Wordsworths probably equalled Alfred Wainwright's mileage as a walker, that's high praise indeed.

Nab Cottage

Rydal, LA22 9SD (015394 35311, www.rydalwater.com). Rates £60-£68 double incl breakfast.

When it's not fully occupied in its summer incarnation as a language school, there can be few more seductive B&Bs in the Lake District than the 16th-century Nab Cottage. Just behind the road on the banks of Rydal Water, it is steeped in history. Coleridge's wayward son Hartley lived here for a time, but its best-known resident was Thomas de Quincey: the room where he took his opium most voraciously and also deflowered the local farmer's daughter is preserved in suitably decadent red velvet. Write your postcard home on the desk where he edited the *Westmorland Gazette* or indulge in more New Age enlightenment; all sorts of dance, yoga, music and painting courses take place in the adjoining barn.

Rothay Garden Hotel

Broadgate, Grasmere, LA22 9RJ (015394 35334, www.rothaygarden.com). Rates £190-£295 double incl breakfast.

This lovely, old-school establishment has just been given an impressive £2.5m makeover by its energetic owner, Chris Carss, and certainly raises the bar for upmarket lodging in and around Grasmere. The overall feel is more modern plush than boutique minimalism, with upmarket touches (vast beds, flatscreen TVs, five loft suites) and a polished finish. Most rooms overlook the River Rothay or have views towards Loughrigg Fell. The Conservatory Restaurant is run along similar lines, with a menu that might include ballotine of quail and foie gras with truffle port jus to start, followed by roasted Lakeland venison with dauphinois potatoes, then sticky toffee pudding with gingerbread ice-cream. The hotel is just far enough out of Grasmere to escape the summer swarm, but close enough to stroll in for an evening meal.

White Moss House

Grasmere, LA22 9SE (015394 35295, www.white moss.com). Rates £88-£110 double incl breakfast.

This traditional, ivy-covered establishment doesn't look as if it's changed much over the years, but unlike too many Lakes hotels it doesn't need to. The five rooms are sweetly old-fashioned (albeit with flatscreen TVs and DVD players), and a welcoming log fire crackles in the lounge. Breakfasts are splendid: expect oatmeal porridge cooked on the Aga overnight, Fleetwood kippers and distinctly superior sausages and smoked bacon.

Lancrigg Vegetarian Country House Hotel. See p93.

Elterwater & the Langdales

Starting at the little hamlet of Skelwith Bridge, a clockwise circuit of Elterwater, Little Langdale and Great Langdale brings a succession of beautiful landscapes, taking in lakes and tarns, rivers and waterfalls, packhorse bridges and rocky mountain highs. Little wonder that this area is so well loved – and, as the first obvious excursion from the busy towns of Windermere and Ambleside, so well visited. The appeal is particularly strong for walkers and rock climbers. 'No mountain profile in Lakeland arrests and excites the attention more than that of the Langdale Pikes,' wrote Wainwright, and their craggy summits, looming over Great Langdale, are among the best known and respected peaks in the Lake District. It's not a matter of height (none exceeds 2,500 feet) – more their sheer, bulky presence. Whether you contemplate them at a distance, from Windermere, or stand encircled by them at Stickle Tarn, they exert an irresistible pull.

Skelwith Bridge to Elterwater

Skelwith Bridge, a few miles west of Ambleside on the A593, is the natural starting point for explorations. The combination of an old stone bridge and a picturesque riverbank picnic spot was always ripe for commercial exploitation, and it has duly become quite an oppressive honeypot. There's a swish café, Chesters by the River (see p103), and an adjoining shop, selling upmarket knick-knacks and local slate products. It's usually packed; if you're struggling to park outside, there's a pricey public car park some 500 yards north.

The river is the Brathay, and it's well worth following its bonny banks upstream to Elterwater – it's less than a mile, along a stretch of the Cumbria Way. En route you pass Skelwith Force, where the river compresses between two boulders to create a frothing, 16-foot spurt. The smallest of the Lake District's 16 lakes (some consider it three linked tarns rather than one lake), Elterwater is only half a mile long and has a delightfully serene quality. Its name derives from the old Norse for 'swan lake'; appropriately, there is a resident swan population, joined by whooper swans from Siberia in winter. Frustratingly, the footpath leaves the shore almost immediately; apart from the woodland stretch belonging to the National Trust, Elterwater's surrounds are privately owned, so its reeds and swans are mainly glimpsed from a distance. The stylishly revamped Eltermere Inn (see p103) has exclusive fishing and boating rights on the lake.

Elterwater village is seductively framed by a backdrop of the Langdale Pikes and Loughrigg Fell. An ancient maple shades the village green; behind it stands the 16th-century Britannia Inn (see p103). Parking is next to impossible in peak season – and often out of season too.

The village was once a centre for charcoal production, made from the juniper bushes that thrive here, and for gunpowder, which it exported round the world. It was also the birthplace of Ruskin lace. Art critic and social reformer John Ruskin encouraged a cottage industry of spinning and embroidery, based around Elterwater and Skelwith Bridge, with Ruskin lace mats being sent to Liberty and Heal's in London before the fashion faded in the 1920s. Samples of the intricate needlecraft are on display at the Ruskin Museum (see p60) in Coniston.

Little Langdale

Heading south from Elterwater, the road runs through leafy woodland and past moss-covered walls. Just after the turn for Little Langdale is the access point for Colwith Force, marked by a National Trust sign. It's a half-mile stroll through the curiously named Tongue Intake Plantation, a verdant wood of oak, birch, rowan and hazel, coppiced centuries ago for charcoal smelting and gunpowder production at the Elterwater Works. A rocky footpath bordered by rustling trees leads to a precipitous viewing point for the waterfall, while steps cut into the hillside climb to a higher vantage point. The Force itself is a 55-foot outpouring of the Brathay, dividing into two broad torrents and dropping into a deep, clear pool at the base. The ladder and pumping station on the opposite bank are tempting but inaccessible.

Little Langdale Valley opens up on the climb out of the woods, with a scattering of farmsteads and whitewashed cottages, and the scenery becomes bigger and bolder at every turn in the road. There's real ale refreshment at the Three Shires Inn (see p104), named after the nearby three-way border of

Britannia Inn. See p103.

the former counties of Cumberland, Westmorland and Lancashire. From the pub, stroll across Slaters Bridge ★, a 17th-century packhorse bridge, and head to Cathedral Cavern. A lengthy tunnel system in the huge, disused slate quarry above Moss Rigg Wood, its centrepiece is a 40-foot-high cave with a startling central pillar. The National Trust, which runs the site, asks that groups attend a safety briefing (015394 41197); private individuals may enter at their own risk. It's safe enough, although torches, helmets and a plan of the cave are highly advisable. Better still, bring a guide (try Mike Wood on www.mikewoodmountain.co.uk, or visit the National Park's website, www.lakedistrict.gov.uk).

Back on the road, Wetherlam and High Tilberthwaite guard Little Langdale Tarn ★ – inaccessible by public footpath, but still a fine sight. Beyond the tarn, the road forks. To the left is the wonderfully located Fell Foot Farm (*see p104*) and the start of the daunting ascent to Wrynose Pass and Hardnott Pass (*see p105*). A National Trust board also marks the Ting Moot, the site of a Viking open-air parliament. To the right, a narrow lane rises from pasture to moorland alongside Lingmoor Fell to Side Pike and the looming summits of the Langdale Pikes. After a mile, you'll come to a small car park; from here you can follow an easy, half-hour circuit around atmospheric Blea Tarn, with its wildflower meadow, spring show of wild rhododendrons and a fringe of conifers producing photogenic reflections in the water.

Langdale Pikes & Great Langdale

After Blea Tarn, at the cattle grid marking the top of the pass between Little Langdale and Great Langdale, the Langdale Pikes unfold in all their glory. A hike to the rocky summit of Side Pike (1,187 feet) will afford even lovelier vistas. Both Langdale valleys and the Mickleden valley are laid out below, and the skyline sweeps round from Crinkle Crags, Bowfell and Pike o' Blisco to the Langdale Pikes – most notably Pike o' Stickle, Harrison Stickle (the highest) and Pavey Ark. Ghylls and waterfalls tumble down the mountainsides; catch it all on a sunny day, and this is undoubtedly one of the great Lake District views.

The steep road from the pass bottoms out at the National Trust's Great Langdale Campsite (*see p104*) and the Old Dungeon Ghyll Hotel (*see p103*). The hotel is so much a part of Langdale history that it seems only right and proper that it was the historian GM Trevelyan who bought the property in the early 1900s and promptly gave it to the National Trust. Fortify yourself in the Walkers' Bar, and plan an adventure in the Pikes. Leaving aside experts-only rock climbing – and Langdale abounds with some of the best routes in Britain – and assuming reasonable fitness and sure-footedness, there is one essential climb to make. Taking in the twin spectacles of Dungeon Ghyll Force and Stickle Tarn, it brings you to the very heart of the Langdale Pikes, with options to traverse their peaks and beyond.

Set off from the NT car park at the New Dungeon Ghyll Hotel (*see p100*). It's a straight, unrelenting, rocky climb alongside the tumbling falls of Stickle

Ghyll. There's no sign of Stickle Tarn for an hour or so, until you suddenly – and breathtakingly – come upon it some 1,550 feet up. It is a bleak and powerful sight; Pavey Ark towers directly over one side, while the eastern face of Harrison Stickle dominates the other.

Tough nuts head straight up to the top of Pavey Ark; softer types circle round the back for the easier path to the top of Harrison Stickle. Beyond Harrison Stickle, a footpath continues to Pike o' Stickle – the extraordinary, high-level site of a Neolithic axe factory, where primitive man cut, shaped and polished the hard volcanic rock into tools. Langdale axe heads have been found across Britain, from Cornwall to Scotland.

The detour for Dungeon Ghyll Force can be tricky. The 50-foot waterfall is buried deep in a cleft, and to get close invites a cold shower. The reward, though, is dramatic. Wordsworth, who visited in 1800, described the scene in *The Idle Shepherd-Boys*. 'Into a chasm a mighty block/Hath fallen, and made a bridge of rock:/The gulf is deep below;/And, in a basin black and small,/Receives a lofty waterfall.'

Langdale Pikes

Countless others have since followed in his footsteps. The Stickle Tarn path has been re-routed once because of erosion and also given a stone staircase in places, but continuing wear means it may need to be re-routed again. As with popular footpaths across Lakeland, scores of volunteers from Fix The Fells (www.fixthefells.co.uk) work with the National Park Authority to repair and maintain the routes. It's a longstanding problem, with the first complaint about a damaged track to Old Dungeon Ghyll recorded in 1819.

Vehicles are also problematic, with the two main car parks at Old Dungeon Ghyll and Stickle Ghyll filling up from early morning in summer. There is only one access road through Great Langdale to the Pikes, much of it single track with tight stone walls and passing places, and no one enjoys reversing in convoy. Unless you're staying overnight, there's a lot to be said for catching the 516 Langdale Rambler bus, which departs from Kelsick Road in Ambleside and runs to the Old Dungeon Ghyll Hotel.

Inevitably, after the high drama of the Pikes, the rest of the Great Langdale valley is a bit of a let-down. The next settlement is Chapel Stile, a former slate-mining village whose modern estate seems designed to prove that architects can't make good-looking, affordable housing. At the other end of the economic spectrum is the somewhat controversial Langdale Estate, a hideaway hotel and timeshare establishment on the site of the former gunpowder works, done up like a private gated village. Scores of Scandinavian-style wooden lodges are dotted around a winding woodland road, amid a network of cleverly arranged streams and ponds; although the concept appears oddly out of place in the Lake District, it's worth a look. The pool and spa at the Langdale Hotel (*see p104*) are open to day members, and has tie-ins with several local guesthouses. The holiday resort originated in the 1930s, when gunpowder was superseded by dynamite and a local entrepreneur purchased the site and erected the first cabins.

Chapel Stile's other attraction is the two-acre mountain garden at Copt Howe, just north of the village. Set against the imposing backdrop of the Langdale Pikes, the garden contains a superb collections of acers, camelias, rhododendrons, azaleas, rare shrubs, trees and unusual perennials.

20 LAKE DISTRICT PUBS

A popular poster on sale around the Lake District displays its pubs in mimicry of the famous London Underground map. There aren't quite as many pubs as tube stations, but it would take a determined crawl to visit them all. It would be fun trying too, since Lakeland is doubly blessed with the quality of its pubs – invariably in a fine old building in a fantastic setting – and the quality of its beer. Here, combining famous inns with personal favourites, are Time Out's top 20 Lakes pubs.

Bitter End
Cockermouth. *See p200.*

Blacksmiths Arms
Broughton Mills. *See p120.*

Britannia Inn
Elterwater. *See p103.*

Brown Horse
Winster. *See p249.*

Church House Inn
Torver. *See p65.*

Drunken Duck
Barngates. *See p49.*

George & Dragon
Clifton. *See p241.*

Golden Rule
Ambleside. *See p79.*

Howtown Hotel
Ullswater. *See p217.*

Kirkstile Inn
Loweswater. *See p160.*

Mardale Inn@St Patrick's Well
Haweswater. *See p242.*

Masons Arms
Strawberry Bank. *See p249.*

Old Crown
Hesket Newmarket. *See p207.*

Old Dungeon Ghyll Hotel
Great Langdale. *See p103.*

Pheasant Inn
Bassenthwaite. *See p191.*

Punch Bowl Inn
Crosthwaite. *See p249.*

Three Shires Inn
Little Langdale. *See p104.*

Tower Bank Arms
Near Sawrey. *See p51.*

Wasdale Head Inn
Wasdale Head. *See p132.*

Wheatsheaf
Brigsteer. *See p250.*

It is open to the public on selected dates, under the auspices of the National Gardens Scheme (www.ngs.org.uk).

Finally, back at Elterwater, you can retrace your steps to Skelwith Bridge or take the steep but beautiful back road over High Close to Grasmere.

Where to eat & drink

In Chapel Stile, the Co-op is the place to stock up on food basics. It's also home to Brambles Café (015394 37500), serving hot drinks, light lunches (quiche, toasties, own-made soup) and picnic packs; you can get your flasks filled here too. The village is also home to Wainwright's Inn (015394 38088, www.langdale.co.uk); formerly the Langdale, the pub was rather opportunistically renamed after Arthur Wainwright's death. It's a dependable choice for a selection of real ales from Lakeland's finest microbreweries, an alluring riverside beer garden, a smoky log fire from autumn onwards, and much flagstone and modern slate. But, rather like its renaming, it somehow lacks authenticity, and the food has attracted mixed reports of late.

Alongside the Stickle Barn Tavern (*see p104*) is the New Dungeon Ghyll Hotel (015394 37213, www.dungeon-ghyll.co.uk). Inevitably a slightly poorer relation to the iconic Old Dungeon Ghyll

Stickle Barn Tavern. See p104.

Colwith Force. See p96.

River Brathay. See p96.

Hotel, it provides comfortable rooms and another Walkers' Bar, where food runs along the familiar lines of steaks, burgers and scampi.

Britannia Inn

Elterwater, LA22 9HP (015394 37210, www.britinn. net). Open 10.30am-11pm daily. Food served noon-9.30pm daily.
This delightful-looking inn on Elterwater village green has been a classic stop for generations of motorists heading out of Windermere for the Langdale Pikes. Inside, there are oak settles, honest beers and sturdy enough pub food; on a quiet evening, when you've nabbed a rocking chair by the fire, you can understand all the fuss. On a busy lunchtime, though, it can be too popular for its own good. Nine compact B&B rooms (£60-£118 incl breakfast) offer the chance to enjoy Elterwater after the crowds have evaporated.

Chesters by the River

Skelwith Bridge, LA22 9NJ (015394 34711, www. chestersbytheriver.co.uk). Food served 10am-5pm daily.
This daytime café presses all the right buttons (proper baking, sustainable fish, Fairtrade coffee). Along with excellent cakes, there's a seasonal lunch menu that might run from summer salads to more wintery cottage pie or white bean and chorizo cassoulet. However, being packed out virtually round the clock, year-round, does little for its soul. If you can, negotiate your way through the throng, bag a table on the veranda perched on the River Brathay and appreciate the stellar location. Adding to the jostle is the adjoining, semi-posh interiors shop. The owners also run the acclaimed Drunken Duck inn and restaurant (*see p49*) at Barngates crossroads.

Eltermere Inn ★

Elterwater, LA22 9HY (015394 37207, www. eltermere.co.uk). Open noon-11pm daily. Food served Bar noon-9.30pm, dining room 7-9pm daily.
A stylish makeover has transformed this 400-year-old property. The public rooms (look out for the stuffed Elterwater swan) exude a clean-cut chic, and the bar is as warm and enfolding as vintage claret. The bar menu ticks all the boxes of Modern British cooking: posh fish cakes, ham hock terrine, pork belly and slow-cooked duck leg. The dining room is even smarter, with a three-course set-price menu. The refurbishment of the hotel's 15 bedrooms (£100-£200 double incl breakfast) should be finished by the end of 2010. Muted colours, white linens and sleek bathrooms are the order of the day; those at the front of the building have hypnotic views over the lake. The hotel has exclusive fishing (pike, perch and trout) and boating rights on Elterwater, with a rowing boat available to guests. Staff are happy to suggest walking routes; alternatively, enlist the service of mountain guide Mike Wood for a more testing outing in the fells.

Old Dungeon Ghyll Hotel

Great Langdale, LA22 9JY (015394 37272, www.odg.co.uk). Open 11am-11pm daily. Lunch served noon-2pm, dinner served 6-9pm daily.

The Walkers' Bar in the ODG (as old hands know it) is so steeped in Lakeland lore that it comes as a shock to discover it was only created in 1949. Before then, the bar was a shippon, or cowshed; indeed, black iron stalls still divide the roughly whitewashed interior. Its fame comes from the roll-call of great mountaineers and climbers who have route-planned, lectured and drank here: Sir John Hunt, Chris Bonnington, Joe Brown and Don Whillans among them. Bill Birkett's black and white mountaineering photos evoke the past, while the collecting box for the local mountain rescue team brings it all up to date. The bar's glory days as the 'base camp' of post-war British climbing may be behind it, but a trip through Great Langdale wouldn't be complete without dropping in for a pint. Match the unpretentious bar food with a pint of real ale, then take the 516 Langdale Rambler bus back to civilisation. Alternatively, B&B rooms are available.

Stickle Barn Tavern

Great Langdale, LA22 9JU (015394 37356). Open 10am-11pm Mon-Sat; noon-10.30pm Sun. Lunch served noon-2.30pm, dinner served 5-9pm Mon-Thur. Food served noon-9.30pm Fri, Sat; noon-9pm Sun.
Conveniently located for a climb up Stickle Ghyll and the peaks of the Langdale Pikes, this friendly pub sits just beyond the NT car park. It's the favoured spot for outdoor types straight off the fells, thanks to its selection of real ales and lively musical performances at weekends. At the front is a spacious patio perfect for sunset viewing; at the back is a bunk barn (£13 per person). Dependable pub grub includes chilli, Cumberland sausage, and steak and Guinness pie.

Three Shires Inn

Little Langdale, LA22 9NZ (015394 37215, www.three shiresinn.co.uk). Open 11am-10.30pm Mon-Thur, Sun; 11am-11pm Fri, Sat. Lunch served noon-2pm, dinner served 6-8.45pm daily.
Perched high up in Little Langdale, this old coaching house is a welcome refreshment stop for hikers and bikers. Hearty food (chunky baguettes or beef and ale pie for lunch, and pricier Lakeland lamb or local trout for dinner), great beers and winter fires create an air of convivial contentment in Slaters Bar – named in honour of the long history of local slate, and generations of thirsty quarrymen. In summer, sup your pint on the veranda facing Great Intake and Wetherlam Fell, and map your circular route to Cathedral Cavern and back. Ten pleasantly appointed bedrooms (£88-£116 double incl breakfast) offer fine views to the front.

Where to stay

Almost all the pubs and inns listed above have rooms of dependable quality, ranging in style (and price) from boutique best to cheap and cheerful barn. There are also two fine – though very different – youth hostels. On the winding road high above Elterwater, Langdale Youth Hostel (0845 371 9748, www.yha.org.uk) is a grandiose Victorian mansion; set amid lush gardens, it's a great starting point for Loughrigg Fell and Grasmere, as well as Great Langdale. A mile away, down in Elterwater village, Elterwater Youth Hostel (0845 371 9017, www.yha.org.uk) occupies the oldest farmhouse in the village and its barn. Rates at both start at a mere £13.95 per person.

Fell Foot Farm ★

Little Langdale, LA22 9PE (015394 37149, www.fellfootfarm.co.uk). Rates B&B £50-£60 double incl breakfast. Self-catering £280-£560 per week. No credit cards.
Impeccably located at the head of the Little Langdale Valley and at the foot of Wrynose Pass, Fell Foot is a Grade II-listed 17th-century farmhouse and working farm. Here, Isaac and Kerrie Benson breed and show Herdwick sheep as well as providing B&B, with substantial breakfasts cooked on their Rayburn. The farm has two crisp white double bedrooms (one en suite), a two-bedroom self-catering cottage, and wonderful views in every direction to wake to.

Great Langdale Campsite

Great Langdale, LA22 9JY (015394 63862, www.nationaltrust.org.uk/campsites/lakedistrict). Rates Camping £7.50-£20 per person. Pods £25-£45.
This large, well-organised site occupies a pretty copse at the head of Great Langdale, below Side Pike, and is immensely popular with walkers and climbers. Open all year, it has all the facilities you'd expect from a National Trust site, including a drying room for wet gear and a children's play area. Camping pods – basic, bow-roofed wooden shelters, which sleep a maximum of two adults and one child – were being trialled at the time of writing, and there are two fully equipped Mongolian-style luxury yurts with fairy lights and stoves (www.long-valley-yurts.co.uk). No cars are allowed on site, but a quick stroll over the beck takes you to the car park and the Old Dungeon Ghyll.

High Hallgarth & Low Hallgarth Cottages

Little Langdale (0844 800 2070, www.nationaltrust cottages.co.uk). Rates High Hallgarth £354-£732 per week. Low Hallgarth £329-£674 per week.
'Bracingly rustic' is the NT's description of High Hallgarth, a picture-perfect whitewashed cottage overlooking Little Langdale Tarn that sleeps seven. There's no vehicle access, so be prepared for a short but steep walk up a slate track from Low Hallgarth. Play at *Withnail & I* with a tin bath and an earth closet dunny in an outbuilding. Low Hallgarth is an equally pretty 17th-century cottage, whose water supply runs straight off the fell. Part of a little terrace of three cottages, it has two bedrooms (one double, one with bunk beds), a kitchen, a sitting room and – unlike High Hallgarth – a shower and indoor toilet. A telephone, shared by the two properties, is out in the woodshed.

Langdale Hotel

Langdale Estate, Great Langdale, LA22 9JD (015394 37302, www.langdale.co.uk). Rates £125-£175 double incl breakfast.
At the heart of the 35-acre Langdale Estate is this 57-bedroom hotel, with all the trimmings of a luxury retreat: a pool, sauna, spa and pricey restaurant. Rooms are decorated in a sleek modern style, with Egyptian cotton bedding, the odd stretch of statement wallpaper, flatscreen TVs and tasteful colours. The Ultimate Rooms feature deluxe flourishes (a pair of freestanding baths, say), while the Waterside Rooms have pole position, with a balcony over a fast-flowing stretch of Great Langdale Beck, which liberates you from the enclosed feel that pervades much of the compound. Up to 100 self-catering apartments and Scandinavian-style lodges can be rented when not in use by timeshare owners; call for details.

Eskdale & the High Passes

Fasten your seatbelt for the most thrilling drive in the Lake District, up and down one of the steepest roads in England. For centuries, the route that the Romans called the Tenth Highway, linking the forts at Ambleside, Hardknott and Ravenglass, was nothing more than a packhorse trail. Although a tarmac surface was laid after World War II, it remains a twisting, numberless, single-track road. Nonetheless, it is the only way through from the heart of the Lakes to Eskdale, Ravenglass and the Cumbrian coast, with two exhilarating high passes at Wrynose and Hardknott, a series of engaging diversions and a dramatic mountain fort that must have been one of the most godforsaken postings in the Roman Empire.

Stretching down from the mountains to the coast at Ravenglass, where the River Esk meets the sea, Eskdale is one of the loveliest landscapes in Lakeland. Even Wainwright was awed by its beauty, declaring it to be 'the finest of all valleys for those whose special joy is to travel on foot'.

Wrynose & Hardknott Passes

Ideally – and most likely – you'll be arriving from the east and the Langdales. From Fell Foot Farm on the floor of the Langdale valley, close to Little Langdale Tarn, the road branches west. Shifting downwards through the gears, the landscape changes from whitewashed farmhouses and gentle meadows to increasingly rugged, remote terrain. Although the drystone walls never quite disappear, these are wild and lonely fells, with only circling buzzards for company – or, if you're lucky, peregrines.

At the top of Wrynose Pass (1,282 feet) is the Three Shires marker stone. Before the 1974 boundary changes, it stood at the apex of three counties (Westmorland, Cumberland and Lancashire), and there are stunning vistas back to Little Langdale and beyond. From here, the road dips through the two-mile-long, starkly beautiful Wrynose Bottom, a high-level valley with a footpath on the right tracking the Roman road.

At the arched stone bridge at Cockley Beck you'll find a working sheep and cattle farm, owned by the National Trust, along with an ultimate get-away-from-it-all holiday cottage (see p121). Here, at the road junction, it's time to make your choice; follow the River Duddon through the Duddon Valley (see p117) or, having paid due attention to the roadside warnings of severe bends and one-in-three gradients, press onwards and upwards to Hardknott Pass ★. At 1,292 feet, it may be only marginally higher than Wrynose, but at the top it feels like the difference between a hill and a mountain. This is the steepest road in England, equalled only by Yorkshire's Chimney Bank.

You wouldn't want to attempt it in icy conditions or in anything bigger than a minibus, especially when you see the descent on the other side – a vertiginous drop, punctuated by alarming hairpin bends. Add oncoming traffic into the equation, and it's a cool driver who doesn't emerge from the experience with clammy hands and a racing heart.

Passengers, meanwhile, can enjoy a series of spectacular vistas. Spread out ahead to the west lies Eskdale and the distant sparkle of the Irish Sea; south is Harter Fell, a Wainwright favourite; and north lies the Scafell range and Scafell Pike, the highest peak in England. Whether the fells are bathed in sunlight or swept by storm clouds, the views are as vast as they are magnificent.

At the Eskdale end of the pass are the striking ruins of Hardknott Roman Fort ★. Standing some 800 feet above sea level, the fort (known as Mediobogdum) was built to guard the supply routes between Ravenglass and Galava Fort (see p81) at Ambleside. It covered three acres, housed 500 men and was an extraordinary undertaking, even by the uncompromising standards of Roman building. Although the walls are now only a few feet high – most of the stones having been filched by farmers centuries ago – the remains are impressive. Information boards mark the sites of the barracks, watchtowers, parade ground and substantial bath house. Standing at the edge, contemplating the silent, empty Eskdale valley far below, it's not difficult to imagine how cold and far from home the Roman soldiers, conscripts from the Dalmatian coast, must have felt in this wild and hostile place.

If the high passes are closed by bad weather, the alternative longer route to Eskdale is via the A595 coast road. Don't be too frightened by Hardknott Pass, though; so long as your brakes work it's not dangerous, and it is a truly memorable drive.

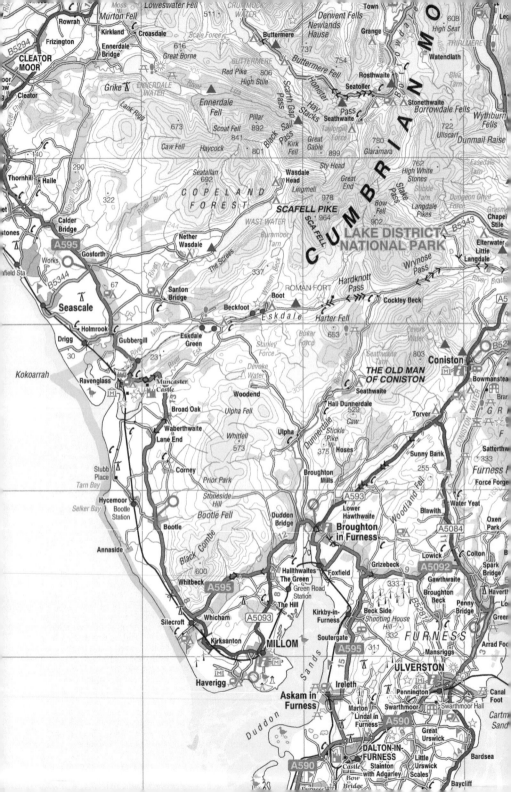

Hardknott Roman Fort. See p105.

Narrow route severe bends

30%

Road suitable for cars and light vehicles only

Unsuitable for all vehicles in winter conditions

Hardknott Pass. See p105.

Meet and bleat

You can't go far in the Lake District without meeting sheep. Rough Fell, Swaledale and Herdwick are the main Cumbrian breeds, but it is the Herdwicks that are the most distinctive, with their grey coats, sturdy legs and white faces. While the other breeds are found all over the Lake District, Herdwicks are concentrated among the central and western fells, where they have evolved to cope with the inhospitable terrain, sparse vegetation and high rainfall; their dense fleeces dry out more rapidly than those of other breeds. The dark wool is difficult to dye, though, and worth little more than sixpence a kilo to the farmer.

Life may be tough for farmer and sheep, but Cumbrian lamb is exceptionally tender, fine grained and lean. You can buy it from local butchers, Booth's supermarkets and direct from farms such as Yew Tree Farm (see p68) near Coniston, High Wallabarrow Farm (see p121) in the Duddon Valley, and Yew Tree Farm in Rosthwaite (see p187). The National Trust owns 91 farms in the Lake District, a number bequeathed to it by Beatrix Potter, who stipulated that Herdwicks should be kept on her farms in perpetuity. These 'landlord' flocks stay with the farm even when there is a change of tenant.

Herdwicks live out on the fells year round, and the flavour of the meat is attributed to their foraged diet of lichen, heather and bilberries. The lambs inherit or learn a homing instinct from the ewes, so that they always return to the 'heaf' (grazing area) where they were reared. A 'heafed' or 'hefted' flock is crucial in the Lake District, where farms are separated by high fells; a lost sheep can mean a tedious journey by road. The culling of sheep during the 2001 outbreak of foot and mouth disease threatened the hefted flocks, but farmers are slowly rebuilding numbers.

Sheep do sometimes stray into neighbouring fells, and in the days before mobile phones and quad bikes farmers would get together to exchange lost sheep at annual shepherd meets. Such gatherings still go on now, although their function is more social: an opportunity to show prize breeds, compare notes over a pint or three and worry where the next generation of shepherds will come from to uphold the old traditions. Meets and agricultural shows take place throughout the summer, varying in size and ambition, but all based around the showing and judging of livestock. Some also involve sheepdog trials, hound trails, Cumberland wrestling and fell running; others incorporate craft shows and tractor demonstrations, along with myriad agricultural trade stalls.

The most important Herdwick show in Cumbria – and, for that matter, in England – is the Eskdale Show, (www.eskdale.info) held on the field outside the George IV Inn in Eskdale on the last Saturday in September. Others include the Loweswater Show at Lorton (www.loweswatershow.co.uk) and Borrowdale Shepherd's Meet at Yew Tree Farm in Rosthwaite.

Eskdale to Ravenglass

The valley of Eskdale follows the course of the River Esk down to the sea at Ravenglass. Wainwright captures the essence of the landscape in his pocket guide Walks from Ratty, describing how the valley 'descends from the highest and wildest mountains in the district to the sands of Ravenglass, in a swift transition from bleak and craggy ridges to verdant woodlands and pastures watered by a charming river'.

Those interested in exploring Eskdale's untamed upper reaches, over which loom Scafell, Scafell Pike, Esk Pike, Bowfell and Crinkle Crags, can tackle the challenging, 18-mile Woolpack Walk (www.eskdale.info/walks.html) – for experienced walkers only. For gentler terrain and a tentative return to modern civilisation, continue down into the valley to the mid and lower reaches of the valley: a gloriously scenic slice of the Lake District that is home to the pleasant settlements of Boot and Eskdale Green.

The stone-built hamlet of Boot contains a pretty packhorse bridge, two pubs and the splendid Eskdale Mill (see p114). Occupying a converted barn, the Fold End Gallery (01946 723316, closed Nov-early Mar) sells crafts, gifts, and pieces by local artists. Just outside Boot, Dalegarth station is the last stop on the picturesque, narrow-gauge Ravenglass & Eskdale Railway (see p116), aka La'al Ratty, built in the 19th century to transport iron ore from the mines above the village at Nab Gill to the coast at Ravenglass. There's also a charming walk from the station to Stanley Ghyll Force (see p116), one of the loveliest waterfalls in the Lakes.

The railway also stops at Eskdale Green, a few miles south-west of Boot. In the centre of the village, opposite the shop, diminutive St Bega's Church houses an exhibition on Eskdale and its history. The village is also home to the Gatehouse, a grandiose, late 19th-century mansion built for Lord Rea, a Liverpool coal and shipping magnate. Half castle, half stately home, its scale is wildly out of proportion to the local buildings; the plan was to outdo nearby Muncaster Castle. The house is now owned by the Outward Bound Trust and used as a conference centre, but visitors are welcome to explore the Japanese garden and Potteresque-sounding Giggle Alley wood (see p114).

From Eskdale Green, a road leads south to the village of Ulpha and the Duddon Valley, over Birker Fell (bleak or beautiful, depending on the weather). A short bridleway links the road with Devoke Water,

Eskdale Campsite. See p113.

Pennington Hotel. See p112.

a long, lonely tarn. Despite being one of the highest tarns in the Lakes, it is also one of the most accessible, and the old stone boathouse incorporates a refuge. While it looks as if no human has ever settled here, the surrounding moorland is studded with ancient cairns and barrows.

Just over five miles downriver from Eskdale Green, the magnificent, pink granite Muncaster Castle (*see p114*) stands guard over the Esk. Set in 77 acres of grounds, its attractions include stately interiors, an owl centre, a 'meadow vole maze' and – if legend is to be believed – the odd unquiet spirit.

A mile further on, Ravenglass is the only coastal village within the National Park, built around a natural harbour. It seems inconceivable that this rather sleepy backwater, home to a few yachts and lobster boats, was once one of England's most important ports, shipping iron ore from Eskdale. The Romans kept a garrison here for 300 years, and a strategically important route led over Hardknott Pass to Ambleside and north to Hadrian's Wall. Little remains of the garrison today, but a stroll to the edge of the village beyond the caravan park (on a road marked 'private') leads to the remnants of a Roman Bath House (0870 333 1181, www.english-heritage.org.uk/ravenglass). With walls 12 feet high, the ruins are among the tallest surviving Roman structures in Britain; it's just about possible to make out the rooms and the niches for statues.

Most people come here, though, for a jaunt on the Ravenglass & Eskdale Railway. The station complex incorporates a compact museum, which explains how today's photogenic little train has a hard-working history. There's also a café and shop, while the Victorian station house has become the Ratty Arms pub (01229 717676). Ravenglass is also a halt on the main Cumbrian Coast Line, which runs from Carlisle to Barrow-in-Furness.

It's worth taking a stroll along the waterfront and down the broad main street, which narrows at each end to contain the animals that were once brought here to market. There's a quaint jumble of houses of different styles and periods, with archways and alleys leading off the main drag. At the far end lie a shingle beach and the vast mudflats of Ravenglass estuary, created from the confluence of the Esk, Mite and Irt rivers.

Beyond, forming the last barrier to the sea, Drigg Dunes is a remote nature reserve with black-headed gulls and natterjack toads, where sea holly and sea bindweed flourish. A few miles north along the coast, the village of Drigg is home to the nation's creepiest dump. Entombed by concrete and guarded by police is the low-level radioactive waste from the Sellafield nuclear reprocessing plant nine miles up the road.

As well as having suffered pollution from Sellafield, the long, deserted sandy beach on either side of the mouth of the Esk estuary is also part of the Ministry of Defence's Eskmeals Firing Range. Nature may have the last laugh, though, as coastal erosion is threatening the only road to the range. Meanwhile, call 01229 712245 to check if there is firing on the day of your visit.

Where to eat & drink

Filling, familiar Lakeland standards prevail over pretension in Eskdale: you'll never want for a Cumberland sausage or a steak and ale pie hereabouts. Even in these no-nonsense outposts, though, cooking standards are steadily rising, and the local beers are superb. New owners had just taken over the Woolpack Inn (019467 23230, www.woolpack.co.uk) in Boot when we went to press. Changes are expected, though we hope they stick with the emphasis on local produce in the kitchen and the pub's own-brewed Hardknott ales, made with the distinctive, peaty local water. Call to check opening times and to find out if B&B accommodation is still provided.

For take-home or self-catering comestibles, make a detour to Richard Woodall ★ (Lane End, Waberthwaite, 01229 717237, www.richard woodall.com, closed Sun), whose Cumberland sausages, air-dried hams and traditionally cured bacon are among Cumbria's most celebrated delicacies. The family began curing bacon in 1828 from their little shop in Waberthwaite, just off the coast road between Millom and Ravenscar. Eight generations later, they're still there; you can also pick up stamps for your postcards home as the shop doubles as the village post office.

Boot Inn

Boot, CA19 1TG (01946 723224, www.bootinn.co.uk). Open 11am-11pm daily. Lunch served noon-4pm, dinner served 6-9pm daily.
Darts, pool, quiz nights and a log fire set the tone at this classic Eskdale inn, with a less traditional conservatory for sunny days. At the heart of this historic hamlet, the pub promises own-made food with minimal food miles (free-range eggs come from Penny Hill Hens, while beef and sausages are bought at Bewley's). There are nine comfortably old-fashioned B&B rooms (£90 double incl breakfast), with substantial breakfasts to set you up for a day's fell-walking.

Bower House Inn

Eskdale, CA19 1TD (01946 723244, www.bower houseinn.co.uk). Open 11am-11pm daily. Lunch served noon-2.30pm, dinner served 6-9pm Mon-Fri. Food served noon-9pm Sat, Sun.
A whitewashed 17th-century coaching inn, just beyond Eskdale Green, Bower House offers a fine line in Cumbrian ales, and has a pleasant beer garden. The restaurant menu promises the likes of onion and blue cheese soup to start, followed by Woodall's pork belly with black pudding mash. There are 29 clean, comfortable rooms (£70-£90 double incl breakfast), housed in the main building, the garden annex and an adjacent barn conversion.

Brook House Inn

Boot, CA19 1TG (01946 723288, www.brookhouse inn.co.uk). Open 9am-11pm daily. Food served 9am-8.30pm daily.
This dependable all-rounder is probably the pick of the current Eskdale crop. Cosier and friendlier inside than its roadhouse exterior suggests, it serves excellent real ales and a stellar array of malt whiskies. Seasonal ingredients from local producers and butchers take pride of place on the

Brook House Inn. See p111.

menu, which runs from lunchtime ploughman's to blackboard specials and good vegetarian options. Upstairs are seven nicely appointed en suite rooms (£95 double incl breakfast), with glorious views.

Millstones Farm Shop
The Byre, Bootle, LA19 5TJ (01229 718757, www. millstonesbootle.co.uk). Open Summer 9am-5pm Tue-Sat. Winter 9am-4pm Tue-Sat.
Just north of Bootle, Millstones is a handy roadside halt, with plenty of parking. The licensed café, housed in the old cow byre, offers tea, coffee and simple meals – think soup, ploughman's lunches or pork and apple loaf with own-made chutney. For take-home edibles and souvenirs, there's a bakery, a farm shop and deli, and an arts and crafts centre.

Pennington Hotel ★
Ravenglass, CA18 1SD (01229 717222, www. penningtonhotels.com). Breakfast served 7-9am, lunch served noon-5pm, dinner served 5-9pm daily.
The Penningtons of Muncaster Castle have done a fine job of upgrading this white-painted inn on the seafront at Ravenglass. It's now the best place to eat in town – though competition, it must be admitted, is limited. The modern bar, with its potted palms and moody monochrome photographs, serves superior pub food (Thai fish cakes, smoked salmon platters and the like) all day; the more polished menu in the Estuary Restaurant next door might feature rocket and beetroot risotto, garlic marinated scallops and passionfruit panna cotta. The hotel's 21 rooms (£110-£130 double incl breakfast) are also in an inoffensively contemporary vein, with neutral tones, free Wi-Fi and flatscreen TVs.

Where to stay
Don't expect boutique hotels or luxury spas in this part of the world. This is walking country, and after a day spent tramping across the fells, most visitors are content with a proper pint, a plate of hearty food and a clean, warm place to lay their head. Unless you're camping or caravanning, a farmhouse B&B or a pub with rooms (all those listed above provide accommodation) is the best bet. There's also the Pennington Hotel (*see left*) in Ravenglass.

Fisherground Farm Camping (01946 723349, www.fishergroundcampsite.co.uk, closed Nov-Feb) is another option. A quiet, family-friendly site with a 10.30pm curfew, it allows campfires and has an adventure playground and a pond with rafts.

And if you're in a large group, consider Eskmeals House (01229 717151, www.eskmealshouse. co.uk), a good-looking country house set in seven-acre grounds near the Ravenglass estuary. It has nine bedrooms and can sleep up to 21 people (rates from £850 for three nights). The decor is delightfully old-fashioned: creaking floorboards, wood-panelled baths and homely patchwork quilts.

Coachman's Quarters
Muncaster Castle, Ravenglass, CA18 1RQ (01229 717614, www.muncaster.co.uk). Rates B&B £80 double incl breakfast. Self-catering from £3,080 per week.
Set around the castle's stable yard, in a renovated stone building, ten rooms are available in various combinations of twin, double and family rooms. Visitors can stay on B&B basis, with breakfast served in Creeping Kate's café – or hire

at least eight rooms and cater for yourself. All the rooms are clean and comfortable, although the bland decor creates a somewhat institutional feel. Rates include free entry to the gardens and owl sanctuary, and discounted entry to the castle – though check seasonal opening times first.

Eskdale Campsite

Boot, CA19 1TH (01946 723253, www.campingand caravanningclub.co.uk/eskdale). Rates £7.50-£16 per pitch. Camping barn £110. Pods £40.

Tents, motorhomes, a camping barn and pods all fit comfortably into this well-groomed site, admirably organised by the Camping & Caravanning Club. Two level fields are set among the trees, along with a car-free strip for backpackers, reached via a slate bridge across the beck. The facilities are splendid, with power showers, a modern toilet block, a laundry room, playground and shop – plus the all-important drying room for damp walking gear. Ten wooden camping pods (sleeping two to four) are an enticing alternative to snoring under canvas; you'll need to bring camp beds or inflatable mattresses. The camping barn (which sleeps eight) has a lovely stone-flagged kitchen, a wood-burning stove and central heating.

Eskdale Youth Hostel

Blea Beck, Holmrook, CA19 1TH (0845 371 9317, www.yha.org.uk). Rates from £15.95 per person.

Set well back from the road as it passes over Blea Beck, this purpose-built hostel has a splendid setting in front of Kepple Crag, with its own nature trail and wildlife garden (look out for red squirrels). There are 49 beds in total in a series of two- to eight-bed rooms, plus all the usual hostel facilities (including a common room, cycle store and drying room). If you don't want to self-cater, reasonably priced breakfasts and evening meals can be provided on request.

Stanley House

Eskdale, CA19 1TF (01946 723327, www.stanleyghyll-eskdale.co.uk). Rates £75-£120 double incl breakfast.

Conveniently located opposite Beckfoot station, on the Ravenglass & Eskdale Railway line, this striking black and white house also has two picturesque waterfalls (Gill Force and Stanley Force) just around the corner. It's a relaxed, family-friendly place, with two inviting sitting rooms, a communal Playstation, free Wi-Fi and a DVD library. The 12 en suite bedrooms are comfortable and individually decorated, with a couple of linked family rooms and larger deluxe rooms; dogs are allowed in the ground-floor rooms. Breakfast is served in the large, sunny dining room, overlooking the leafy garden and Whillan Beck.

Wha House Farm

Boot, CA19 1TH (019467 23322, www.whahousefarm. co.uk). Rates £50 double incl breakfast. No credit cards.

The first farm on the left as you drop into Eskdale from Hardknott, this is as authentic a hill farm (and B&B) as you could wish for. Owned by the National Trust, it is run by David and Marie Crowe, who keep seven working sheepdogs. Downstairs, guests gather round one big table for breakfast, and there is a residents' lounge with an open fire and a library of books on the Lakes and local wildlife. Upstairs, clean, simple rooms are grouped around the bathroom. The setting is tranquil, and there's a huge telescope for gazing at the uncontaminated night sky and spotting mountain rescue teams training on Hare Crag.

FIVE SCENIC RAILWAYS

For obvious geographical reasons, the Lakes were a great challenge to Victorian railway builders, although they were rarely daunted if there was profit at the other end. Nowadays, Cumbria is cobwebbed with disused lines, but here are five survivors that bring fun and a fresh perspective to touring the Lakes.

Cumbrian Coast line
From Carnforth to Carlisle this Northern Rail line is a winding, coastal spectacular of viaducts, mudflats, estuaries, the Irish Sea and the Solway Firth. Unless you want a close-up view of Sellafield, the best stretch is from Arnside to Ravenglass.

Lakeside & Haverthwaite Railway
This former industrial line that once carried timber and iron out of the Lakes has, happily, been rescued from the British Rail scrapheap. Arrive by steam train at Lakeside, at the bottom end of Windermere, then cross the lake on an equally vintage launch. *See p26.*

Oxenholme to Windermere (Northern Rail)
The branch off the West Coast mainline that Wordsworth and Ruskin never wanted. But today, by leaving the car behind and travelling by train, then using bikes and public transport, you can enjoy the moral high ground as well as the mountains.

Ravenglass & Eskdale Railway
The ever popular La'al Ratty, saved and run by steam enthusiasts, takes visitors on a seven-mile adventure between the coast and the heart of Eskdale. It feels like a toy train, but is steeped in mining history. *See p116.*

Threlkeld Quarry & Mining Museum
Sir Tom, a sturdy little saddletank loco, puffs its way into the heart of one of the Lake District's biggest quarries. It's not a pretty ride, but it's as true to the Lakes as daffodils and sticky toffee pudding. *See p171.*

Places to visit

Eskdale Mill
Boot, CA19 1TG (019467 23335, www.eskdale mill.co.uk). Open Apr-Sept 11.30am-5.30pm daily. Admission £1.50; 75p-£1.25 reductions; £3.75 family. No credit cards.
Built in 1547, this magnificent Grade II-listed corn mill was powered by the waters of Whillan Beck, rushing down from Scafell. Now run by a heritage trust, it is the last working mill in the Lake District. You can take a guided tour, led by the miller, to see the old wooden machinery, hoppers, hoists and grindstones, and a demonstration of the milling process.

Giggle Alley
Eskdale Green, Holmbrook, CA19 1TE (019467 23281, www.forestry.gov.uk). Open 24hrs daily. Admission free.
The land attached to the Gatehouse (which is closed to the public) includes the delightfully named Giggle Alley: a small area of woodland, set on a granite spur. Long neglected, the wood is now being lovingly restored by the Forestry Commission and local community groups. Amid the trees is a Japanese garden; planted with bamboo, magnolia and vibrant red acer trees, it was laid out by Thomas Mawson, Lakeland's most prominent and prolific garden designer, in 1914. A guide to the woodland and garden is available from Eskdale Green post office.

Muncaster Castle ★
Muncaster Castle, Ravenglass, CA18 1RQ (01229 717614, www.muncaster.co.uk). Open Castle Mar-Oct noon-4.30pm Mon-Fri, Sun. Dec 1-3pm Sun. Gardens Mar-Oct 10.30am-6pm daily. Feb, Nov, Dec 11am-4pm daily. Admission Castle & Gardens £11; free-£7.50 reductions; £32 family. Gardens only £8.50; free-£6 reductions; £27 family.
This pink granite castle was built in the 1860s around a 13th-century pele tower, constructed to protect the English from marauding Scots. These days the invaders are tourists, who flock to admire the castle's sumptuous interiors, its bedroom for visiting royals and its impressive paintings (including works by Gainsborough and Reynolds). Keep an eye out for ghostly goings-on: all sorts of spooky apparitions have been reported here, and intrepid visitors can book ghost tours or sleepovers in the Tapestry Room. The Pennington family has resided here since 1208: Patrick Gordon-Duff-Pennington provides the recorded commentary for the house tour, while Peter Frost-Pennington grows his whiskers to lead the candlelit Victorian tour at Christmas when the house is festooned with decorations and lit by candles.

The castle's 77 acres of gardens and woodland, criss-crossed by paths, include magnificent displays of azaleas and rhododendrons. Younger visitors will make a beeline for the Meadow Vole Maze and the World Owl Trust headquarters, home to 40 species of owl. Meet the Birds talks take place at 2.30pm most days, while up to 20 wild herons silently congregate in the trees outside the castle entrance for their 4.30pm feed. Special events run from medieval re-enactments to a five-day Festival of Fools in early summer and a winter sound and light show in the grounds. Note the castle's strictly seasonal opening times.

Muncaster Castle

Things to do

Ravenglass & Eskdale Railway ★
*01229 717171, www.ravenglass-railway.co.uk.
Open varies, check website for details. Tickets
Unlimited travel £11.20; free-£5.60 reductions;
£29 family. Single £6.60; free-£3.30 reductions.*
Opened in May 1875, La'al Ratty was England's first
narrow-gauge railway. It may look like a dinky model
railway, but it had a serious purpose, transporting
iron ore from the mine near Boot to the harbour at
Ravenglass, some seven miles down the dale. The
mine closed in 1877 and the line in 1913, though it
was resurrected a couple of years later to serve local
quarries and remained operational until the mid 1950s.
It's now a heritage railway. For more on its history,
visit the small museum at Ravenglass station.

Today, Ratty takes passengers on a sublime 40-
minute steam- or diesel-powered jaunt through some
of Cumbria's loveliest countryside. From Ravenglass,
the route skirts the tidal reaches of Barrow Marsh,
passes the charming old Muncaster watermill (closed
to the public, sadly) and rattles along under Muncaster
Fell. Quaint Miteside Halt is nothing more than an
upturned boat; next up, Irton Road is the only original
station on the line, serving the village of Eskdale Green
– a good starting point for walks in the Eskdale valley.
After climbing Hollinghow Bank, it takes in a request
stop at Fisherground Campsite, before ascending
though Beckfoot Wood and terminating at Dalegarth
station, near Boot, as the lofty Scafell range looms
ever closer. At Dalegarth, you'll find a children's play
area, a café and a gift shop.

Stanley Ghyll Force
www.english-lakes.com/stanley_ghyll_force.htm.
The short, signposted walk from the car park at
Dalegarth station to this 60-foot waterfall, tumbling
down a narrow ravine, is delightful. Vivid green ferns
and wild rhododendrons grow on the damp ledges,
while little wooden bridges cross the beck and
mossy boulders below.

Ravenglass & Eskdale Railway

Duddon Valley & the Copeland Peninsula

Nowhere in the Lake District is undiscovered. Every road, bridleway and footpath has been well trodden and recorded, and there are no secrets – merely degrees of popularity and crowdedness. Perhaps because it has no lake, no famous scenery and no obvious top-of-the-bill attractions, the Duddon Valley is not a household name. That, though, is its strength. Beautiful, unspoiled and comparatively forgotten, it is for many aficionados the very best of the Lake District. No hotels. No petrol station. One shop. Two pubs. Fifty footpaths. Exploring it from top to bottom is a simple matter of following the River Duddon. It will take you on a richly varied journey, from the wind-blown heights of Wrynose and Harter Fell to the spooky, deadly sandbanks of the Duddon Channel.

To the west of the Channel, and just beyond the small market town of Broughton in Furness, lies the Copeland Peninsula. It's a quiet place, well off the tourist trail: the main human settlement is the former mining town of Millom, while terns and wading birds flock to the freshwater lagoon at Hodbarrow.

DUDDON VALLEY

Wordsworth was so captivated by the River Duddon that he devoted 34 sonnets to it. 'Still glides the stream, and shall forever glide,' he wrote – and so it does. But it also delivers rocky canyons, exciting stretches of waterfall, and a tough final journey for salmon and sea trout, making their way from the Irish Sea to their spawning ground at Dale Head. For centuries, the 15-mile waterway also marked the border between Lancashire and Cumberland.

Fast and furious when in spate, the river also offers tremendous conditions for whitewater kayaking in winter, when water levels are high – though only experienced paddlers need apply (www.ukriversguidebook.co.uk). In the international water grading system (grade 1 is easy; grade 6 is a real risk to life), the Duddon is classified grade 3 below Ulpha and grade 4 above Ulpha, progressing to a scary grade 5+ at Wallowbarrow Gorge and Troutal Farm. You'll find information on river levels and great pictures at www.rainchasers.com.

Despite its peaceful appearance, the Duddon Valley has a ripe history of smuggling, cockfighting and rioting, along with an industrial heritage of mines and iron furnaces, which were constructed at either end of the dale.

Cockley Beck to Seathwaite

The natural place to join the valley is at its northern end, at Cockley Beck bridge, beside the solitary farmhouse between the two thrilling high passes of Hardknott and Wrynose (*see p105*). The first surprise is a plateau of farmland; soon, though, the valley narrows as the woodland and the bulk

of Harter Fell, to the west, and the Old Man of Coniston range, to the east, loom over the road.

Stop at the Forestry Commission car park to visit Birks Bridge ★ (not the plain structure at the car park, but the more ancient edifice some 100 yards down the lane), the most photogenic of a series of stone bridges that cross the River Duddon. The water is a curious clear green colour, refracted from the rocks on the riverbed; although it looks serene enough, the holes in the superstructure of the bridge are to let the water through when the trickle turns to a torrent.

Birks Bridge is also a popular starting point for an ascent of Harter Fell (2,128 feet), a mountain that Wainwright himself, in a rare concession, called 'beautiful'. Follow the footpath to Brandy Crag and it's a straight route to the peak, where the eye can sweep from Scafell Pike to the Duddon Estuary and the Irish Sea. It's around four miles there and back, and quite a climb; set aside three to three-and-a-half hours. Across the dale sit the Seathwaite Fells, where Richard '*Watership Down*' Adams wrote and set much of his novel *Plague Dogs*.

Approaching the village of Seathwaite – not to be confused with the infamously rainy Seathwaite in Borrowdale – is an excellent six-mile walk to Fickle Crag and Wallowbarrow Gorge. Shortly before a cattle grid, turn right on to a path that drops down to the Fickle Steps: an exciting river crossing via large and slippery stepping stones, made safe only by a steadying cable and quite impossible when the Duddon is in spate. Turn left, follow the riverbank path through the beautiful, rocky gorge, then cross a stone stile next to a huge boulder in the river and take the little RAF bridge back over the river. The

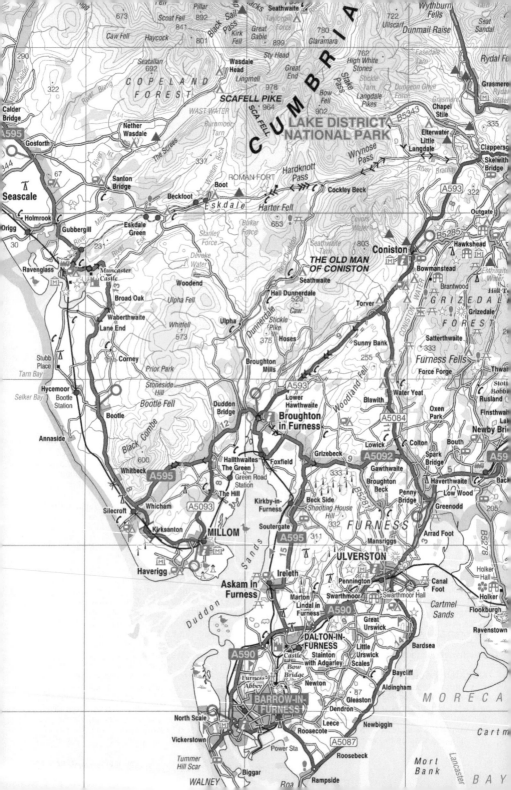

Cockley Beck bridge. See p117.

winding path brings you out opposite Seathwaite church. Late May is best; it might still be muddy, but you can smell the sap rising from the birches, and the woods are carpeted in bluebells.

As the first – and rare – chance of refreshment in the valley, the 16th-century Newfield Inn (*see p121*), obligingly open all day and all year, is a must. Note the spectacular floor of local Walna slate, with its distinctive white stripes. A framed newspaper report in the darts room tells the story of the Seathwaite Riots of 1904, when a group of navvies who had been working to dam the Seathwaite reservoir went on a wrecking spree, after landlord Tom Dawson refused to serve them any more beer. They stoned the vicarage, the church and the school; as they returned to the pub, the landlord let loose with his shotgun, killing three of the men. Dawson's canny defence to the murder charge was that he was protecting Crown property, since the inn also acted as the post office, and he was acquitted.

The windows of the church, Holy Trinity, have long since been repaired. Look out for the shearing stone that commemorates the life of 18th-century curate Robert Walker, who served here for 67 years. He was known as 'Wonderful Walker'; besides being the parson, he taught the village children, sheared sheep, wove his own cloth, worked as an unofficial lawyer, inspired Wordsworth and even ran an ale house in the parsonage, though he reputedly never touched a drop himself. His church stipend was a mere £24 a year, but when he died, aged 94, Walker left his family £2,000, worth some £200,000 today. He was hailed in the parish register as 'a man singular for his temperance, industry and integrity' – though the feisty Victorian writer Mrs Linton, less sentimentally, called him shrewd and thrifty.

Hall Dunnerdale to Duddon Bridge

A mile downstream at Hall Dunnerdale, another bridge and bend in the river and a 'no through road' sign mark the turn-off to High Wallabarrow Farm (*see p121*), an idyllic 18th-century farmhouse with a camping barn, bunkhouse and self-catering cottage. The farm sits in the impressive shadow of Wallowbarrow Crag, with a rock face straight out of a John Ford Western. Rock climbers can choose from routes of varying difficulty; strollers can choose a simpler (when sober) footpath to and from the Newfield Inn, via more stepping stones and some magical woodland. There is parking at the farm, and an honesty box, with the proceeds going to local charities.

The spur road south-east climbs sharply through Dunnerdale to the hamlet of Broughton Mills. The road passes the volcanic rock of Stickle Pike and the ruins of lime kilns, but there is a more pressing reason to take this detour: the Blacksmiths Arms (*see p120*). With its gas lighting, magnificent range, ancient timbering and splendid beer and food, it's a slice of living history.

Back by the river, on the main road, Ulpha is a tiny settlement with a post office and general store (the only one in the valley). The small, whitewashed church of St John the Baptist has a lychgate, hefty oak beams and fragments of 18th-century frescoes. The backdrop of farmland, fell and forest provides one of the prettiest settings for a church in the

Blacksmiths Arms

Lake District. In the graveyard, look for the touching memorial to 17-year-old James Crosbie Jenkinson, who perished in a 'pelting pitiless storm' on Birker Moor on New Year's Day 1926.

For the last leg of the Duddon Valley, the road splits in two. The road to the east is the more scenic, but the western route has better diversions. Follow the bridleway to the forlorn, wonderfully evocative ruins of Frith Hall – over the years, a deer-hunting lodge for the gentry, an inn for packhorse drivers and a smugglers' rough-house for brandy- and rum-runners from the coast, with at least one fatality to its name. One day in 1730, when it was an inn, the local vicar rustled up 17 couples from the valley who were living in sin and married them en masse. It later became a sheep farm, before finally being abandoned to the elements.

Further along the road stands the imposing Duddon Hall, with a public footpath running through its grounds. Now divided into apartments, it was built in the 18th century by Major John Cooper, a huntsman and notorious gambler. The circular folly-cum-chapel (now a private home) was where he and his chums prayed on Sunday mornings, then held cockfights on Sunday afternoons.

Just outside Duddon Bridge is the extraordinary Duddon Furnace ★. Built in 1736, it was one of eight charcoal-fired furnaces in the area, used for smelting iron ore transported here from West Cumbria. The furnaces were fired up day and night for 30 weeks at a time, devouring ten acres of coppiced wood every week. The Furnace operated until 1866, then slid slowly into dereliction. It has been beautifully restored by the National Park and English Heritage, and the slate and stone complex, with its exceptional casting arch, is one of the finest examples of industrial archaeology in all Lakeland. It is something of an unsung treasure, so you'll probably have the place to yourself.

Duddon Bridge effectively marks the end of the 15 miles of the Duddon Valley, although the tantalising glimpses of the estuary and coast afforded by its higher reaches will tempt you onwards to the Copeland Peninsula. Another option is to take a break in Broughton in Furness, one of the most unspoilt, attractive towns in the National Park.

Where to eat & drink

With a couple of notable exceptions, your best bet is to have a hearty breakfast at your B&B, then stock up with some prime local produce and assemble a picnic – or to opt for self-catering digs. Pubs are few and far between; restaurants that can be safely recommended are even thinner on the ground.

Blacksmiths Arms ★

Broughton Mills, LA20 6AX (01229 716824, www.theblacksmithsarms.com). Open July-Sept 5-11pm Mon; noon-11pm Tue-Sat; noon-10.30pm Sun. Jan-June, Oct-Dec 5-11pm Mon; noon-2.30pm, 5-11pm Tue-Fri; noon-11pm Sat; noon-10.30pm Sun. Lunch served noon-2pm, dinner served 6-9pm Tue-Sun.

Built in 1577, this cracking country pub started life as a farmhouse. By the 18th century it incorporated an inn, a farm and a blacksmith's, giving the pub its name. Inside, the stone-flagged floors are worn smooth from centuries of use, the beams are blackened, and an ancient range occupies one wall. Low ceilings, wonky walls and benches thickened by countless coats of black gloss paint ooze atmosphere. Order a pint of Mothbag (from the Barngates microbrewery), then take a seat in the tiny, one-table bar. There's a fire on winter evenings, and trestles outside on sunnier days. Food is served in three cosy room; if you're booking, ask for the front room nearest the bar. For all the rustic surrounds, the menu is remarkably on trend: roast pigeon breast with apple and black pudding, belly pork with the crispest of crackling, or Flookburgh potted shrimps in a pot of melting, spiced butter.

Newfield Inn
Seathwaite, LA20 6ED (01229 716208, www.newfield inn.co.uk). Open 11am-11pm daily. Food served noon-9pm daily. No credit cards.
This whitewashed watering hole dates from the 16th century. Wordsworth drank here (although his main tipple was water), as have generations of walkers and climbers. The pub was the start and finish point of the Duddon Valley Fell Race – a gruelling, 20-mile slog up hill and down dale – until the growing number of competitors meant they had to set off from the field at Wallabarrow Farm instead. Runners and spectators still gather here afterwards. Truth be told, it's nothing fancy: a typical British darts-and-pork-scratchings boozer. On the menu there's Cumberland sausage, egg and chips, steak and chips, bread and cheese, and sticky toffee pudding, with Jennings, Theakstons and Barngates on tap. There's also a beer garden, and two self-catering flats, sleeping a maximum of four and six people (a mere £35 and £45 per flat per night, respectively).

Where to stay
Never mind country house hotels: there's scarcely a guesthouse or a B&B to be found in the Duddon Valley. Self-catering is probably the best bet for a protracted stay; otherwise it's camping, the barn or the bunkhouse. The Duddon Valley website (www.duddonvalley.co.uk) has a list of holiday cottages; Sally's Cottages (01768 779445, www.sallyscottages.co.uk) also offers a selection of properties in the western lakes.

Cockley Beck Farm
Seathwaite, LA20 6EQ (01229 716480, www.cockley beck.co.uk). Rates £325-£375 per week. No credit cards.
This working fell farm has a truly stunning location at the top of the Duddon Valley, beneath Hardknott Pass, on a National Trust-owned estate. Next to the 19th-century farmhouse stands a two-bedroom self-catering cottage, which will appeal to committed walkers: there's little else to do. The Scafell range, Harter Fell and Crinkle Crags beckon, and it's a couple of miles to the nearest pub at Seathwaite. The cottage itself is simple but comfortable, with its own patio area and garden, and beautiful views over the fells.

Dower House
High Duddon, LA20 6ET (01229 716279, www.dower house.biz). Rates B&B £64-£72 double incl breakfast. Self-catering £210-£385 per week.

Accessed via a winding, wooded road next to Duddon Furnace, Dower House perches high above the river, amid six acres of wooded grounds. Don't expect any modern flourishes; this place offers solid, traditional values inside and out, as befits a house built for a dowager. There's a residents' lounge with a wood-burning stove, along with four suites (available for self-catering stays or B&B). Chimneys is the largest, with a twin and a double bedroom, along with a lounge, bathroom and kitchen.

High Wallabarrow Farm ★
Ulpha, LA20 6EA (01229 715011, www.wallabarrow. co.uk). Rates Barn £8.50 per person. Bunkhouse £7.50 per person. Cottage £300-£500 per week. No credit cards.
A rustic, single-track lane leads to this National Trust-owned hill farm, where Liz Garner and Chris Chinn grow organic vegetables, make charcoal and rear Galloway beef cattle and Herdwick sheep, who fearlessly scale Wallowbarrow crags. In the clean, warm 17th-century barn, ten guests can bed down on mattresses in the eaves (bring your own bedding and towels). Downstairs, the kitchen has a woodburning stove, slate flooring and wooden pews; the turf-roofed toilet and shower room are in a separate building, so don't forget your torch. The separate wooden bunkhouse has a sleeping platform for up to four people, and basic cooking facilities. For more comfort, opt for the sweet two-bedroom cottage beside the farmhouse. There's plenty of room to roam, with hay meadows, and walks through Wallowbarrow Woods and the heather-covered crags. Children can watch the sheepdogs at work, pick bilberries and make friends with pet rabbits, guinea pigs, lambs and a spotty pig called

Places to visit

COPELAND PENINSULA

Millom Folk Museum
Old Station Building, Station Road, Millom, LA18 5AA (01229 772555, www.millomfolkmuseum.com). Open 10.30am-3.30pm daily. Admission £4; £1-£3 reductions; £9 family. No credit cards.
Along with displays on the town's mining heritage (including the cage in which the men descended into the depths, and a re-creation of the cosy, cramped interior of a miner's cottage), the Folk Museum's eclectic collection runs from World War II ration books and gas masks to railway memorabilia. The work of Millom's most famous son, poet and writer Norman Nicholson, is also celebrated here; Nicholson wrote beautifully about the Lakes, but also recorded the hardships endured by the local miners and steelworkers, and their suffering when the industry collapsed.

RSPB Hodbarrow
Off Mainsgate Road, Millom (01697 351330, www.rspb.org.uk). Open 24hrs daily. Admission free.
The freshwater lagoons here draw herons, terns and merganser ducks, but the star turn is the great crested grebe, which was hunted almost to extinction by Victorians in search of feathers with which to adorn ladies' hats. In spring, the birds lay on a balletic courtship display, emerging from the water in unison and brandishing a beakful of waterweed.

High Wallabarrow Farm. See p121.

Things to do

DUDDON VALLEY

Lake District Sheepdog Experience
Troutal Farm, Seathwaite, LA20 6EF (01229 716235, www.lakedistrictsheepdogexperience.co.uk). Open Mon-Fri; advance bookings only. Price £40 1hr, £60 2hrs, for up to 4 people. Solo tutoring £10 extra. No credit cards.

In a smart form of rural diversification, Troutal Farm offers a 'one man and his dog' day, training visitors in the art of shepherding, and offering an unusual insight into life on a Lakeland sheep farm. Working with border collies, you'll learn the commands, then attempt to round up a flock and send them into a pen; it's harder than it looks. Wear wellies or stout shoes.

COPELAND PENINSULA

PH Watersports
Haverigg, LA18 4LG (01229 772880, www. phwatersports.moonfruit.com). Open Apr-Oct. Rates £15 per session; £30 20min lesson.

With water speed limits firmly set across the main public lakes, the purpose-built lake at Haverigg's Caravan Park is dedicated to powerboat adrenalin, offering both wakeskating and wakeboarding. Wakeboarding is to waterskiing what snowboarding is to conventional skiing, while wakeskating is more akin to skateboarding on water; the videos on the website show you what these sports involve and demonstrate how to stomp your kickflip.

Duddon Valley. See p117.

Penelope; adults can negotiate the stepping stones to and from the Newfield Inn. You can buy lamb, beef and eggs from the farm, along with Lakes Ice-Cream.

Turner Hall Camp Site

Turner Hall Farm, Seathwaite, LA20 6EE (01229 716420, www.duddonvalley.co.uk). Rates £12 for 2 people. No credit cards.

This farm-based campsite offers no-frills camping all year round in a drop-dead gorgeous location. The showers and toilets are relatively basic, but the pay-off is that you get to stay in a secluded corner just north of Seathwaite, with clear starry skies. Children are welcome, campfires are allowed and there's plenty of space, even in high season. There are easy walks to the Newfield Inn and the waterfalls, crags and gorges around Wallowbarrow, along with more challenging routes to Seathwaite Tarn and the Old Man of Coniston.

COPELAND PENINSULA

Broughton in Furness

Set on the southern edge of the National Park, Broughton in Furness lies just north of the Duddon Estuary and the Copeland Peninsula. Pink and yellow houses cluster round the market square, whose 19th-century obelisk commemorates George III's Golden Jubilee. Here too is the Information Centre (Old Town Hall, the Square, 01229 716115, www.lakedistrictinformation.com, closed Sun) – a good resource for local history and a detailed exploration of the Duddon Valley and the coast.

Broughton was once an important market town, and still hosts a market on Thursdays. In the square, look out for the ancient slabs of slate on which fish were once displayed, along with the old stocks. A handful of reasonable cafés, pubs

TEN OUTDOOR THRILLS

As a self-styled 'adventure capital', the Lake District offers a huge number of heart-pumping challenges, plus experts ready to guide you through them. Destination Cumbria (015397 36006, www.destinationcumbria.co.uk) and Activities in Lakeland (015395 35999, www.lakesactivities.co.uk) co-ordinate activities, and can organise and book them at no extra charge. Here are some options, not in order of difficulty.

Birds of prey days
07500 956348, 07733 366748, www.predatorexperience.co.uk.
Professional falconers Dee Mitchell and Daniel Ashman of Predator Experience, based near Grange over Sands, offer a variety of interactive encounters with birds of prey. Spend a day on the fells with your own personal falconer; walk the woods with hawks; fly owls on the shores of Windermere or – most exciting – experience the thrill of a golden eagle on your glove.

Canyoning
Slide, jump and abseil down spectacular mountain gorges and waterfalls – the opposite to gorge scrambling. Mere Mountains (015395 35030, www.mere mountains.co.uk) runs half-day courses for adults and teenagers (minimum age 16), plus numerous other activities, from archery to zipwires. Most take place within a half-hour drive of Kendal or Ambleside.

Climbing Helvellyn
Along with Great Gable, Helvellyn is the quintessential Lake District peak to scale and England's third highest point, at 3,117 feet. The classic route (*see p230*) is via Striding Edge, an exhilarating mile-long ridge bordered by crags and scree, followed by the rocky column of the Chimney. Anyone not confident with a map and compass can join one of the many guided walks.

Go Ape!
0845 6439215, www.goape.co.uk.
Go Ape!'s ropes, cargo nets, Tarzan swings, wobbly bridges and long, long zipwires through the forest canopy have taken the country by storm. It has two sites in the Lake District, at Grizedale (*see p54*) and Whinlatter Forest Park (*see p201*).

Hot-air ballooning
Just you, a balloon and a wicker basket gliding over Windermere, with a bucket of champagne to steady the nerves. It's a unique way to see the Lake District. High Adventure (015394 47599, www.high-adventure.co.uk) offers flights

Broughton Village Bakery. See p128.

(including the Manor Arms; *see p128*) and craft shops are dotted around the square, but the town's two standout foodie outlets are on Princes Street. Melville Tyson (nos.1 & 3, 01229 716247, www.melvilletyson.co.uk, closed Sun) is a one-stop shop for top-quality meat (including Herdwick mutton), fruit and vegetables, along with cooked deli items, wines and spirits. Next door, own-baked goodies and a charming little café make the Broughton Village Bakery (*see p128*) an enticing retreat. Fresh bread and muffins, old-fashioned iced cinnamon buns, almond slices and fluffy meringues are temptingly arrayed, and it's a lovely spot at which to while away an hour by the fire.

Copeland Peninsula
The A595 marks the boundary of the National Park as it skirts the Duddon Estuary and the North Sea. It is scarcely a resort coastline, but it is a potent one, with vast sandbanks, superb birdwatching and long-distance sea views, culminating in the dunes and beaches of Haverigg.

In an area rich in standing stones and megaliths, Swinside stone circle is worthy of particular note – and deserves to rank alongside the much more popular Castlerigg, just outside Keswick. It's easy to reach: take a right turn off the A595 a mile west of Duddon Bridge on a minor road signposted to Broadgate, park at the farm, then walk along the

for £179 per person; trips are weather-dependent, but the conditions are usually best early morning or evening.

Human bowling
Rookin House Farm, Troutbeck, CA11 0SS (017684 83561, www.rookinhouse.co.uk).
Strap yourself into a giant bowling ball, then get your mates to aim you at the pins. Go-karts, quad bikes and amphibious army vehicles are among the other activities available at this outdoor centre, four miles north of Ullswater.

Mountain biking
Whinlatter Forest Park, Whinlatter Pass, Braithwaite, CA12 5TW (017687 78469, www.forestry.gov.uk).
Altura is an 11-mile technical trail for experienced mountain bike riders in Whinlatter Forest. Enjoy switchbacks, berms, humps and jumps and, if you've time to look, views of Braithwaite, Derwentwater, Catbells and Grisedale Pike. There's also the shorter, and easier Quercus trail. *See p196.*

Mountain boarding
Raines Hall Farm, Sedgwick, LA8 0JH (07740 861019, www.surf-the-turf.co.uk).
Skateboarding on turf rather than tarmac. The Lake District's only mountain boarding centre, near Kendal, offers a three-hour learn-to-ride session for £25. You get an hour on the bunny slope, then move on to the fells for rollers, burns and ramps.

Ridge scrambling
Experienced fell walkers looking to raise their game can have a go at ridge scrambling – a cross between walking and rock climbing, using hands, feet, ropes and harnesses. For gorge scrambling, just add water. Two-day courses, with prices starting at around £170 per person, are offered by More than Mountains (07984 410230, www.morethan mountains.co.uk) and Climb 365 (015397 39186, www.climb365.net).

Via Ferrata
Honister Slate Mine, Honister Pass, Borrowdale, CA12 5XN (017687 77230, www.honister-slate-mine.co.uk).
Honister Slate Mine's Via Ferrata (*see p161*) is a safe but nerve-racking rock climb for novices. Traverse the face of Fleetwith Pike on steel ladders attached to ropes and a permanent cable, then ride the zipwire home. Definitely not for vertigo sufferers. Prices start at £25 for adults, £20 for 10-15s and £85 for a family.

track for a mile. There, in a farmer's field, are 55 prehistoric stones, set in a 90-foot-diameter circle. Raven Crag and Black Combe form a dramatic backdrop. Although it is private land, the stones are clearly visible from the footpath. Nearby are the remains of two other Bronze Age circles, at Lacra and the mounds that constitute the Ash Wood House circle – but with a dozen stones between them, these sites are strictly for the converted.

As for the 1,896-foot Black Combe, which dominates the peninsula, Wainwright snorted that it could be climbed in slippers. That may be so, but it still offers what Wordsworth described as 'the amplest range of unobstructed prospect that British ground commands'. On a clear day, you can supposedly see from its summit some 14 counties, the Isle of Man and the mountains of Mourne, Scafell, Snowdon and Ingleborough.

Millom & Haverigg
From the A595 it's a few miles down the A5093 to the former iron and steel town of Millom. The town's past is immortalised in a statue of a scutcher – the man whose job it was to halt the heavily laden carts of iron ore with a thick metal rod. Made from a mixture of resin and iron ore dust, the sculpture is reddish in hue: the miners were known as 'red men', because of the colour of the dust that coated them.

The story of how iron ore was discovered at nearby Hodbarrow in 1855, and how the town prospered and then failed, is recounted in Millom Folk Museum (*see p121*), which doubles as the tourist office. There are re-creations of corner shops and old parlours, but the most telling exhibit is a two-wheeled Victorian mortuary cart, used to stretcher away the bodies of those who had miscalculated the shifting quicksands and tides of the Duddon estuary. On nearby Holborn Hill, meanwhile, a stone above the door of the former Pilot Inn, dated 1745, reminds visitors to call there to be guided across the treacherous sands.

Duddon Sands are just as dangerous today, and although the Ordnance Survey maps indicate a public right of way across the Duddon Channel to Askam in Furness, you would be mad to attempt it without proper guidance. Cedric Robinson, the officially appointed Queen's Guide to Morecambe Bay sands, occasionally leads parties across (01524 582808, www.grangeoversands.net, May to Sept only).

What is perilous for humans is paradise for birds, and the sands provide a year-round spectacle of gulls, terns and all sorts of waders. On the edge of Millom, where the River Duddon meets the sea, is the weird, wonderful and rather eerie Hodbarrow Lagoon. This was once the site of Hodbarrow Mine, with its mighty ironworks, bustling railway yards and massive, ore-carrying ships, protected from the Irish Sea by a mile-long sea wall. The mine fell into a slow decline after World War I, closing for good in 1968. Now, only the sea wall remains – it makes for a good circular walk, or a rough, pot-holed drive – along with a ruined windmill, an unmanned working lighthouse and an RSPB bird reserve (*see p121*) and hide beside the lagoon.

Gazing out across the estuary is a curiously mesmeric experience, as sea, sand and sky meet against a panoramic backdrop of fells. The sun makes strange patterns on the untouched sandbanks, while across the bay in Barrow-in-Furness looms the giant, metal-clad Devonshire Dock Hall, where Britain's nuclear submarines are built.

Millom and the lagoon merge into the village of Haverigg, where there is a safe, sandy beach. The beach café, opposite the children's playground, is handy for snacks and shelter, while paths through the dunes extend to the point. Overlooking the beach is *Escape to Light*, a weighty sandstone sculpture by Josefina de Vasconcellos, dedicated to Britain's inshore rescue teams.

The road continues to the modest RAF Millom Aviation & Military Museum (01229 777444, www.rafmillom.co.uk), which displays RAF equipment and memorials to aircrews that fought in World War II. Set in an old Clarks shoe factory, it's one for the hardcore enthusiast, with more aircraft engines than actual aircraft on show. Unless you're heading up the coast to Ravenglass, the last sights on the peninsula are rather bleak: a wind farm (currently threatened with replacement by a nuclear power station) and the perimeter fences of HM Prison Haverigg.

Where to eat & drink

Broughton Village Bakery ★
4 Princes Street, Broughton in Furness, LA20 6HQ (01229 716284, www.broughtonvillagebakery.co.uk). Open 9am-5pm Tue-Sat.
This friendly establishment is the very model of a small-town bakery and café. The bread is baked daily, using organic flour from the Watermill at Little Salkeld, and there are splendid custard tarts, walnut- and white chocolate-studded brownies and tasty 'scrolls' (white bread dough wrapped around savoury fillings such as sweet chilli and cheese). The small, elegant café serves goodies from the bakery, along with Fairtrade and organic teas and coffees; come lunchtime, there are club sandwiches, BLTs and various own-made soups and stews. There's free Wi-Fi if you spend a minimum of £2, which should not present a problem.

Manor Arms
The Square, Broughton in Furness, LA20 6HY (01229 716286, www.manorarmsthesquare.co.uk). Open noon-11pm daily. Food served noon-10pm daily.
Commanding a strategic corner of Broughton's fine Market Square, the Manor Arms was once the pub of choice for *Watership Down* author Richard Adams, and the place retains a soft spot for writers and artists. The cosy bar makes for a warm winter retreat, while in summer everyone takes their drinks outside to congregate around the town centre obelisk.

Prince of Wales
Foxfield, LA20 6BX (01229 716238, www.prince ofwalesfoxfield.co.uk). Open 2.45-11pm Wed, Thur; noon-11pm Fri, Sat; noon-10.30pm Sun. No credit cards.
A mile or two south of Broughton in Furness, the village of Foxfield is a request stop on the scenic Cumbrian Coast railway line. Opposite the station, this popular roadhouse has ales from its own Foxfield Brewery, along with a Belgium or German beer on draught, and an ever-changing list of scrumpy ciders. To soak it all up, order one of the sturdy, no-nonsense Cumbrian pasties. There's music most Wednesdays, and assorted traditional bar games (dominoes, bar billiards and the like). The pub also has four en suite double rooms (£48 incl breakfast).

Where to stay

Bank House Farm
Broadgate, Hallthwaites, LA18 5JU (01229 777193, http://bankhousefarm.wordpress.com). Rates £75 double incl breakfast.
It's well worth bumping your way up the long farm track off the A595 to reach this gem. Two nicely decorated en suite rooms (a twin and a double) occupy a converted hay barn beneath White Combe. Each has its own sitting area, with a flatscreen TV and a DVD/CD player. On weekdays, guests are provided with a breakfast basket of ham, cheese, bread, yoghurt, fruit compote and freshly laid eggs; at the weekend, a full English breakfast is served in the farmhouse kitchen. Easy footpaths lead to Baystone Bank reservoir and Swinside stone circle, with show-stopping views over the Duddon Estuary.

Wasdale & Wastwater

Home to England's highest mountain and deepest lake, Wasdale is the Lake District at its most primal, most inaccessible and most thrilling. The only road approach to the valley is from the west; from the A595 take the road to Santon Bridge, which runs straight as an arrow from sea level to the heart of a mountain range in less than ten miles. Spread out from west to east are the looming peaks of Pillar, Great Gable and, biggest of all, Scafell Pike – a truly spectacular sight. By the time you reach the shores of Wastwater at Wasdale Hall, though, the most imposing feature is not Scafell, now obscured by its foreground peak of Lingmell, but the Screes, the great wall of rock that dominates the lake's south-eastern flank. Almost sheer from 2,000 feet down to the water, the precipitous black rock fans out its grey scree for more than a mile.

Wastwater & Wasdale Head

Described by Wordsworth as 'long, narrow, stern and desolate', Wastwater ★ is a striking sight: three miles long, almost half a mile wide and 260 feet deep, it is England's deepest lake. From the north-western shore, the scale of the Screes on the opposite side is breathtaking; close up, the thousands of individual boulders are disturbingly large (and still occasionally tumble down the fellside). Above are the summits of Whin Rigg and Illgill Head. Even on the sunniest of days, the Screes has a sinister feel.

Wastwater is also indelibly associated with the 'Lady in the Lake' murder. In 1976, Margaret Hogg was strangled by her husband, who then drove some 300 miles from Surrey to Wasdale, rowed out on to the lake and tipped her body into its depths. There she remained for eight years, until divers hunting for a missing French climber found her remains on a ledge 100 feet down. The icy waters had preserved her body well enough for friends to identify her, and she was still wearing her inscribed wedding ring. Peter Hogg was put on trial, and convicted of manslaughter.

No one would have seen Peter Hogg in his dinghy, along the three-mile lakeside road there is just one solitary farm. Around a bend, the large word 'INN', painted in black on a whitewashed gable end, announces the end of the road and the arrival of the famous Wasdale Head Inn (*see p132*) – worthy of inclusion on anyone's shortlist of the Lake District's most iconic pubs.

The tiny community of Wasdale Head is an ancient one, with prehistoric field systems and a stunning inheritance of drystone walls. The beams in the little church dedicated to St Olaf (*see p131*) are said to have come from a Viking longboat; Norse farmers colonised the valley in the ninth and tenth centuries. The place has scarcely changed since Wordsworth reported 'a little chapel and half a dozen neat dwellings scattered on a plain of meadow'. And it's remote: the nearest settlement is Seathwaite in Borrowdale, six miles away as the crow flies, but almost 40 miles by road.

The hamlet is the starting and finishing point for the Lake District's most exacting and exciting climbing. This is the place where restless Victorian gentlemen first turned rock climbing into a sport, and four of the seven English mountains that soar over 3,000 feet are within reach. Even so, the dominant peak is the pyramid of Great Gable ★, standing at just under 3,000 feet but as definitive a summit as any in the Lakes. It's said that you can see every peak in Lakeland from Gable's summit. There are numerous ascents to the top from numerous valleys, but it is most closely associated with Wasdale; the views back down over Wastwater are sensational, whether you follow the Sty Head route or detour to 'thread' Napes Needle, stopping to admire the climbers from the safe distance of the Dress Circle. If you want to be alone on the summit, avoid Remembrance Sunday, when 500 climbers make the pilgrimage to lay wreaths and poppies at the peak's war memorial.

In Scafell (3,163 feet) and Scafell Pike (3,209 feet), the Scafell massif has England's two highest summits. But size isn't everything, and compared to the wow factor of Great Gable or Helvellyn, ticking off Scafell Pike is less inspirational. The simplest and most popular ascent is from Wasdale Head, but there are plenty of alternative routes for purists. Advice, route maps, ropes, weather reports, porters, guides, Kendal Mint Cake, waterproof clothing,

Things to do

Carolclimb Outdoor Adventures
Little Ground House, Wasdale Head, CA26 1EU (019467 26424, www.carolclimb.co.uk). Rates vary, check website for details.
Carol Emmons and Richard Sagar offer a wide range of adventures, including bivouacking and birdwatching, fell walking and rock climbing, canyoning and ghyll scrambling, canoeing and kayaking and much more, all with as much ecological and naturalist background as you want. Richard Sagar, a former ghillie, also teaches coarse and fly fishing.

Great Gable. See p129.

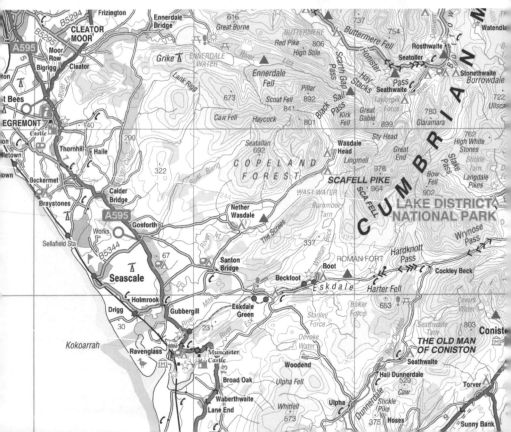

Wainwrights and all the other essentials for a sensible climb and safe return are available at the the Barn Door Shop & Campsite (see p135), next door to the Wasdale Head Inn.

If you have no head for such heights, it is perfectly possible to circumnavigate Wastwater by foot, notwithstanding the daunting Screes, and to ponder a scene carved by Ice Age glaciers. There is little underwater life in the dark waters, save the Arctic charr – an ancient relative of the salmon that lives landlocked in the lake's chill depths. Motor and sailing boats aren't permitted on Wastwater; rowing boats and canoes are, but you'll have to bring your own as none are for hire.

Nether Wasdale to Sellafield

Wastwater and Wasdale Head are so compelling that it is hard to advocate spending much time in the surrounding area, and the scenery soon mellows once the screes and high fells are behind you. At the south-western end of Wastwater, Nether Wasdale centres on a village green and the tiny, 16th-century St Michael's Church, and is home to two commendable pubs, the Screes Inn and the Strands Inn & Brewery (for both, see p132).

A few miles to the west is the much larger village of Gosforth. Its church, St Mary's, dates from Norman times, although it was rebuilt in the late 19th century. Inside, it houses the tombs of two tenth-century Norse chieftains, a Norse stone depicting a fishing boat, and a Chinese bell seized from a naval raid up the Canton River in 1841. A remarkable, carved 14-foot Viking cross towers over the ancient gravestones in the churchyard. Look out too for the venerable cork tree, planted in 1833 and the most northerly of its kind in Europe.

Gosforth Hall Inn (019467 25322, www.gosforth hallhotel.co.uk) is the place for a pint and a pie with mushy peas; overnight guests can also drink in the history of a 17th-century building with a priest's hole, a spiral stone staircase and beams that – not uniquely in the Lake District – are said to have come from ships wrecked on the Cumbrian coast. There are three more pubs huddled around the crossroads in the centre, and the Gosforth Bakery (Meadow View, 019467 25525, closed Mon, Sat, Sun) bakes all its bread, pies and cakes on site.

Gosforth is a dormitory village for Sellafield, long Britain's most controversial nuclear site. Formerly known as Windscale, the vast complex – it employs 10,000 people and the perimeter fence measures eight miles – manufactured weapons-grade plutonium for Britain's nuclear warheads in the 1950s; the Windscale fire of 1957 was Britain's worst nuclear accident. Today, the plant continues to reprocess nuclear waste and is decontaminating (at enormous cost to the taxpayer) its outdated plant. The Irish and Norwegian governments have also expressed grave concerns over its history of radioactive discharges into the Irish Sea, and a study exploring the cluster of childhood leukaemias found in the nearest village, Seascale, stirred up further controversy in 1990.

South-east of Gosforth – where the road splits for Wasdale or Eskdale – is the hamlet of Santon

Places to visit

Tourist attractions are limited in these parts, with most visitors out tramping the fells or recovering in front of a pub fire.

St Olaf's Church
Wasdale Head, nr CA20 1EX (www.visitcumbria.com/wc/chc2.htm). Open 24hrs daily. Admission free. All but hidden by yew trees, slate-roofed St Olaf's is said to be the smallest church in England. The low-slung exterior is plain, but it's an evocative, poignant spot. In the little churchyard you'll find the grave of an 18-year-old climber who 'fell asleep' on Scafell Pike one New Year's Day, along with a monument to a five-man expedition lost in the Himalayas in 1959. The south window is a memorial to the members of the historic Fell & Rock Climbing Club who died in World War I, and is engraved with an image of Napes Needle and an inscription from Psalm 121: 'I will lift up mine eyes unto the hills from whence cometh my strength'. The massive roof beams, meanwhile, certainly look their age (at least 1,000 years); it seems likely that they were salvaged from a Viking ship, as local lore recounts.

Bridge. A single-arch bridge spans the River Irt, and the Bridge Inn is where the annual World's Biggest Liar contest (*see p136*) is held.

Where to eat & drink

Unpasteurised sheep's and cow's milk Wasdale cheeses are sold by the roadside at Murt Camping Barn (*see p135*), between Nether Wasdale and Wastwater; on the same road, the Cumbrian Goat Experience (019467 26246, www.cumbrian-goat-experience.co.uk) has a farm shop selling meat, dairy, and free-range duck's and hen's eggs.

Screes Inn

Nether Wasdale, CA20 1ET (019467 26262, www.the screes.co.uk). Open 11am-11pm Mon-Fri; noon-11pm Sat, Sun. Lunch served noon-2.30pm, dinner served 6-9pm daily.

With a row of tankards hanging above the bar, a crackling fire and a fine line-up of Cumbrian real ales, the bar at the Screes Inn oozes good cheer; in summer, decamp to the beer garden to make the most of the magnificent views. The menu sticks to tried-and-tested classics (scampi and chips, steak and kidney pie, local lamb with mint gravy). Upstairs are five simple en suite bedrooms (£65 double incl breakfast).

Strands Inn & Brewery

Nether Wasdale, CA20 1ET (019467 26237, www.strandshotel.com). Open 4-11pm Mon; noon-11pm Tue-Sun. Lunch served noon-2pm Tue-Sat. Dinner served 5.30-8.30pm Mon-Sat. Food served noon-7.30pm Sun.

Standing directly opposite the Screes Inn, the Strands is another handsome, upstanding old hostelry. Beer aficionados can sample the efforts of the in-house microbrewery, whose offerings include the light, hoppy Errmmm bitter; they launched their first beer festival in 2010. There's a casual bar menu at lunchtime and smarter food come the evening, featuring the likes of herb-crusted salmon, slow-braised lamb shank with parsnip purée or butternut squash and pea risotto. The inn also has 14 bedrooms (£79 double incl breakfast) of varying sizes.

Wasdale Head Inn ★

Wasdale Head, CA20 1EX (019467 26229, www. wasdaleheadinn.co.uk). Open 11am-11pm daily. Food served Summer noon-9pm daily. Winter noon-8pm daily.

For climbers, Ritson's Bar is almost as much a place of pilgrimage as the crags of Great Gable, which loom above. The inn has been hailed as the birthplace of rock climbing, since the intrepid Walter Parry Haskett-Smith first scaled the standalone pinnacle of Napes Needle – solo and without ropes or spikes – in 1866. Since then, a *Who's Who* of British

Search and rescue

'Cragfast' is a Cumbrian expression for being stuck on a fell, and it's a term that the 12 mountain rescue teams covering the Lake District National Park know only too well. Together, they get more than 450 call-outs a year. Some are tragic, many are frightening and plenty are unnecessary. Every team has its own tales of cragfast craziness – the elderly man in wellies and a shoulder bag who had somehow managed to wander up Napes Needle and had to be lowered 150 feet on a rope, say, or the woman who went up the fells in city sandals.

Scafell Pike, England's highest mountain, is on the patch of Wasdale Mountain Rescue Team. According to team leader Julian Caradice: 'We get a lot of people who just want to be guided off the mountain. That's not what we're there for. We are not guides.' Last year he climbed Scafell 32 times, out of the 85 calls that his team attended.

However, Caradice acknowledges that there's a fine line between being cold, wet and lost on a fell, and just wanting to be shown the way down. 'I'm a climber, that's my hobby, and sometimes I push myself too far and do something silly. Everybody does and that's what we're there for. I want to help like-minded people who enjoy the fells.'

Mountain rescuers all live locally. They must have excellent fitness, a good knowledge of the fells and, Caradice says, a streak of madness. Teams have regular practices and get paramedic training, but they're all unpaid volunteers – hence the collection boxes on the bar of just about every pub in the Lake District and the year-round fundraising events.

At one time the only people who went out on the fells were people who worked on them – shepherds, farmers and quarrymen – all of whom had to look after themselves. The increasing popularity of the fells as a leisure destination changed that. The Scafell Tragedy of 1903, when four roped climbers fell to their deaths on the mountain, was the impetus for the early first-aid posts and the eventual development of a mountain rescue service in the 1930s. Today, the teams have a range of sophisticated equipment, search and rescue dogs that are trained to locate bodies, and can call for the assistance of RAF helicopters. In 2008, 31 people died on the fells.

Call-outs continue to rise. Mobile phones have changed everything. While it means the mountain rescue teams can locate people sooner, it also means more people call at the first sign of trouble. Think ahead, says Caradice: 'When the weather turns and things look bad, make a decision to come down early. The mountain will always be there; pick another day.'

For advice on walking in the fells, *see p180*.

Wastwater Screes. See p129.

mountaineers have supped here and hung their helmets and carabiners from the ceiling. Old maps and faded photos adorn the warren of panelled rooms and alcoves; in winter, fires and hot toddies revive half-frozen walkers. The bar is named after the pub's first landlord, Will Ritson, whose tall stories were legendary: he once managed to persuade a group of gullible tourists that the local turnips grew so big that they could be hollowed out and used as sheep shelters. Staff dispense excellent real ales (including Loweswater Gold, Hawkshead Brodie's Prime and Black Sheep Best) and solid Lakeland dishes, such as steak and ale pie, Cumberland sausage, and lasagne. There's plenty of accommodation too: ten B&B rooms (£118 double incl breakfast) and nine self-catering apartments (£370-£470 per week for two people), most set in the converted barn next door.

Woodlands Tea Rooms
Santon Bridge, CA19 1UY (019467 26281, www.santonbridge.co.uk). Open 10am-5pm daily.
With its modern decor, this bright little café makes a refreshing change from the dark, wood-panelled local pubs. Home-cooked blackboard specials complement sterling breakfast fry-ups and simple lunchtime fare (toasted sandwiches, baguettes, jackets and salads); alternatively, pop in for tea and a hot buttered crumpet or a slice of lemon drizzle cake. The cutesy gift shop next door brings a rare intrusion of sheepskins, teddy bears and Beatrix Potter branding to this end of the Lakes.

Where to stay
Climbers and walkers have a range of options around Wastwater, including a National Trust campsite, a classic lakeside youth hostel, no-frills bunkhouses and unpretentious B&Bs. As the landscape becomes more genteel, so do the guesthouses.

Gosforth Hall (see p131), Screes Inn, Strands Inn, Hotel and Wasdale Head Inn (for all, see p132) offer rooms. Just opposite the latter is a camping field, run by the Barn Door Shop (019467 26384, www.barndoorshop.co.uk). It's very basic but very cheap (only £2.50 per person), and can't be booked in advance. In Nether Wasdale, the Murt Camping Barn (01946 758198, www.campingbarns.co.uk) is a converted hayloft and byre, with very basic amenities and room for up to eight people.

For more luxurious outdoor living, two yurts are for hire at Rainors Farm (019467 25934, www.rainorsfarm.co.uk), halfway between Nether Wasdale and Gosforth. Each sleeps five, and has proper beds and a wood-burning stove; toilet and shower facilities are separate and breakfast is served in the farmhouse. Simple B&B and self-catering accommodation is also available.

Bowderdale Farm
Wasdale Head, CA20 1EX (019467 26113, www.wasdaleweb.co.uk). Rates B&B £50 double incl breakfast. Self-catering £350-£550 per week.
A steep track up the fell beside Netherbeck Bridge leads to this sheep farm – the only building on the stretch of road between Wasdale Head and Wasdale Hall. The white-painted farmhouse has high views over Wastwater, and

Wastwater YHA. See p137.

Wasdale Head Inn. See p132.

A LIKELY STORY

One of Britain's oddest events, the World's Biggest Liar competition (www.biggestliar.co.uk), has been held in Wasdale for more than 100 years. It all began with 'Auld' Will Ritson, the landlord of the Wasdale Head Inn (*see p132*), who made quite a name for himself by teasing hapless drinkers with ever more incredible yarns about the Lake District. One particularly ingenious tale recounted how he solved the valley's fox problems by taming a golden eagle and then mating it with a foxhound, thus creating a brood of winged foxhound pups that could pursue their prey over the highest of drystone walls.

Now held at the Bridge Inn (019467 26221, www.santonbridgeinn.com) at Santon Bridge, the event has become an annual institution, taking place in November. Recent years have drawn 200-strong crowds, and glib-tongued contestants from as far away as Australia and South Africa.

Comedian Sue Perkins was the first woman to storm this male bastion in 2006, winning the title with an elaborate tale about the ozone layer being damaged by the farting of Herdwick sheep. If you're considering entering, watch out for local farmer John 'Johnny Liar' Graham, whose seven victories make him an all-time great to rival Ritson himself. Previous winners have triumphed with strange tales of giant cod and U-boats in the lakes, while legend has it that the Bishop of Carlisle romped to victory one year simply by pronouncing 'I have never told a lie'. Politicians and lawyers are, of course, banned from entering. First prize, quite a coup for a Lakeland sheep farmer, is typically a date with a Hollywood starlet. Honest.

there's a choice of two straightforward, good value B&B rooms or a self-catering stay in a converted hay barn (sleeping up to seven) with impressive old beams.

Burnthwaite Farm B&B
Wasdale Head, CA20 1EX (019467 26242, www.burnthwaitefarm.co.uk). Rates B&B £54-£64 double incl breakfast. Self-catering £300-£450 per week. No credit cards.
In addition to a knock-out location at the head of the valley, below Great Gable and Styhead Pass, this seven-room B&B is irresistibly picturesque. The traditional whitewashed exterior is set against the fells, while the beamed, low-ceilinged rooms have an old-fashioned charm. Note that only two of the bedrooms are en suite. Morning brings a sturdy farmhouse breakfast, and packed lunches can be assembled on request. There's also a self-catering apartment at the end of the main farmhouse that sleeps four.

Hermons Hill B&B
Wasdale Road, Gosforth, CA20 1ER (019467 25008, www.hermonshill.co.uk). Rates £70 double incl breakfast. No credit cards.
If you're in retreat from more rugged living conditions and scenery, this 18th-century farmhouse could be just the ticket. It is set just outside Wasdale, amid 20 acres of neatly tended gardens and farmland, with the Screes and Scafell safely on the horizon. There are three quaint, comfortable rooms, with

sloping ceilings, quilts and plenty of character – none are en suite. Downstairs is a homely breakfast room and a delightful residents' lounge, warmed by a wood-burning stove.

Lingmell House
Wasdale Head, CA20 1EX (019467 26261, www.lingmellhouse.co.uk). Rates £70 double incl breakfast. No credit cards.
Now a three-bedroom B&B, this Victorian vicarage is devoid of any conspicuous modern development: no TV, no radio, no awkward en-suite conversions. It's a splendid location: you can look straight back down the dale from the front door, and Great Gable towers over the back. If you get into trouble on the fells, proprietor Tim Brooks might be the man to fetch you down: he's a leading light in the Wasdale mountain rescue team.

Old Post Office Campsite
Santon Bridge, CA19 1UY (019467 26286, www.theoldpostofficecampsite.co.uk). Open Mar-Oct. Rates £6 per adult. No credit cards.
Bordered by the River Irt, this is a delightfully pretty, peaceful spot at which to camp. It's a small-scale affair, with five hardstanding pitches with electric hook-ups, plus a sheltered, grassy expanse for tents and motorhomes. Facilities include clean toilet and shower facilities, and a laundry room; barbecues are allowed, although campfires, alas, are not.

Wasdale Head Campsite ★
Wasdale Head, CA20 1EX (019467 26220, www. nationaltrust.org.uk). Rates Camping £7.50-£11 per pitch. Pods £30-£40.
The National Trust run some superbly located campsites around the Lakes, and this is no exception. Tucked away at the north-eastern head of Wastwater and reached via a bridge across Lingmell Beck, the large, level camping field is surrounded by trees, beyond which loom the mountains. The site is much loved by climbers and campers, whose compact tents lend the place a spacious feel; cars must be parked away from the main field, and facilities are simple but perfectly adequate. On one side of the field, three unfurnished wooden pods insulated with wool offer a solid roof for the night (phone to check these are still in operation). For a pint and down-to-earth pub grub, it's a 20-minute walk to the Wasdale Head Inn. The campsite is open all year.

Wastwater YHA ★
Wasdale Hall, Wasdale, CA20 1ET (0845 371 9350, www.yha.org.uk). Rates from £13.95 per person.
From the outside, this half-timbered 19th-century mansion could be mistaken for a stately home or a grand country house hotel. The woodland location, with lawns running down to the south-west shore of Wastwater, is matchless. Add home-cooked food, served in the panelled dining room, and delightfully friendly staff, and this is another star in the YHA's extraordinary Lake District firmament.

Ennerdale & the Coast

Anyone interested in exploring the Lake District by car should avoid Ennerdale. At the western end of Ennerdale Valley, the roads run out and travelling around Ennerdale Water and further into the valley is only feasible on foot, bicycle or horseback. The reward for such effort comes with the disappearance of the crowds, proper wilderness walking and a passport to some of Lakeland's most awesome peaks – Steeple and Pillar, Haycock and Scoat Fell, Kirk Fell and Great Gable. This is also the site of England's most remote and evocative youth hostel, the shepherd's bothy known as Black Sail Hut.

For a complete contrast, head west and out of the National Park towards the coast, where you'll find sandy beaches and the fascinating port of Whitehaven, which has a painful history of mining disasters, connections to the rum and slave trades and a singular architectural heritage. St Bees is the start of the Coast to Coast Walk.

ENNERDALE

Ennerdale Water

Only Wastwater can compare to Ennerdale Water as the least visited and most remote of the lakes. It's pretty spectacular too: two-and-a-half miles long, half a mile wide and framed by ever-rising peaks. Bowness Knott and Crag Fell form an entrance gate at the western end, while the pinnacles of Pillar Rock and Steeple menacingly guard the eastern end. It's the only lake in the National Park where cars cannot drive its length, a protection that has been fiercely guarded ever since a Victorian plan to build a railway was defeated. (Another

Things to do

ENNERDALE

Bradley's Riding School
Low Cock How, CA13 3AQ (01946 861354, www.theultimategavin.co.uk/bradleys/trekking.htm). Open 11am-3.30pm daily. Rates £21/hr. No credit cards.
Ennerdale Valley is ideal for horse riding, and Bradley's offers just about every combination for all ages and all abilities (including disabled riders). You can spend just half an hour or a whole day trekking on the fells, in groups of up to 15. Back at the farm there's B&B and bunkhouse accommodation for 12.

C2C Cycle Way
www.c2c-guide.co.uk.
Whitehaven marks the start of the 190-mile, trans-Pennine cycle route to the North Sea at Tynemouth or Sunderland. For details, see p213.

Wild Ennerdale
01946 816940, www.wildennerdale.co.uk.
Assorted events and activities around Ennerdale, from April to October. Typical options are a guided walk with one of the project officers to Pillar Rock, canoeing on the lake and horseback treks; details on the website.

defeat came in 1973, when a young Arkansas law student unsuccessfully proposed marriage here to his girlfriend. Hillary Roddam later relented and married Bill Clinton.)

With Great Borne (2,021 feet) hovering above, back roads take you to a choice of two dead-end car parks: Bowness Knott on the north-western shore and Bleach Green on the west shore. The former is the start of a straightforward cycle route to the eastern end of the lake and over the Irish Bridge to Ennerdale Youth Hostel (see p141). Walkers have a 20-mile network of paths, starting with the red-waymarked Smithy Bridge Forest Trail. Beyond Bowness Knott, only forestry vehicles can continue along the shore into Ennerdale Forest. One of Cumbria's most extensive plantations, it was set up amid much controversy in the 1930s. Regular felling of conifers will see replanting with native broadleaf trees under the Wild Ennerdale initiative to restore the valley to a wild and natural state.

Ennerdale has – like so much of the Lake District – a long history of mining. There's evidence of a medieval settlement, with longhouses and a bloomery (smelting furnace), near Smithy Beck. And if you arrive at Ennerdale Water from the north-east, on the road from Loweswater via Lamplugh, you pass the embankment and cuttings of the Rowrah & Kelton Fell Mineral Railway, which transported iron ore from Ennerdale's mines until the 1920s. Human activity is much scarcer now.

Set aside three to four hours for the seven-mile circuit of the lake. From Bowness Knott, follow the track on the north shore to the lake's eastern end, where you can cross the River Liza by footbridge or ford. Continue next to the shore (along a section of the Coast to Coast Walk; see p145) to Anglers Crag. This is the one intimidating section as Crag Fell drops steeply to the lake and some rock scrambling is required. The simpler alternative of going over Anglers Crag has the added bonus of fantastic views across to Great Borne and down the length of the lake. After Anglers Crag, it's plain sailing at low level around the gentle western shore.

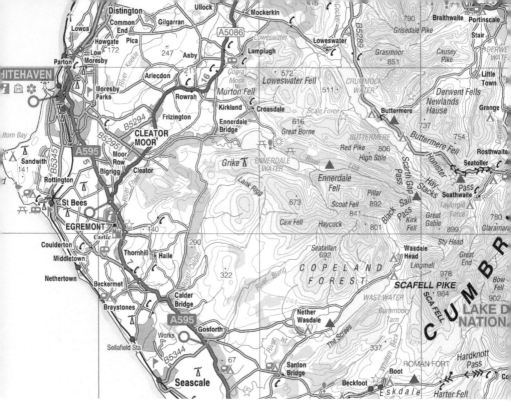

At the start of the River Ehen by the Bleach Green car park is a salmon ladder, and England's last major breeding habitat for freshwater mussels. The bivalves can live to 120 years; one produced a black pearl for Queen Victoria. Everyone from the Romans to 19th-century poachers used to pick them, but it's now illegal to interfere with them in any way, backed up by a £2,500 fine.

By the track to How Hall Farm, a landscaped plot contains a bench dedicated to the former owners of the Anglers Inn. The pub was demolished in 1960 as part of a plan to raise water levels, in order to allow increased water extraction for the industries of Whitehaven and Sellafield and to supply more drinking water for the population of West Cumbria. Planning battles continued for 20 years until Michael Heseltine, then environment minister, finally blocked the scheme. The pub, in its priceless location, had been needlessly destroyed. The remains of its slipway can be seen, as can the wooden piers of its old jetty when water levels drop.

You're unlikely to see much activity on the lake. Now owned by United Utilities, Ennerdale is designated a 'quiet' lake, so only rowing and canoeing are permitted; no sailing, no motorboats, no swimming. It's also a Site of Special Scientific Interest for its flora and fauna, including a fragile population of Arctic charr. As with most of the lakes, the use of live bait is forbidden to protect endangered species.

Ennerdale Valley

Beyond the eastern end of Ennerdale Water, the valley follows the course of the River Liza through another four miles of forest, with unmetalled forestry roads on either bank. Wild Ennerdale (a partnership of the National Trust, United Utilities and the Forestry Commission; *see left*), is committed to developing the valley as 'a unique wild place allowing natural forces to become more dominant in the shaping of the landscape and the ecology' and has several laudable initiatives and educational programmes in support of their mission statement. For practical enjoyment, stay at Low Gillerthwaite Field Centre (*see p141*), which offers guests a wealth of activities, from night walks and building willow 'wigloos' for kids, as well as all the usual rock climbing and canoeing options.

Low Gillerthwaite is the first of three cut-price accommodation options, followed further up the valley at High Gillerthwaite by Ennerdale YHA and its adjacent barn (*see p141*) and, when you finally emerge from the forest on to the fells, the fondly lionised Black Sail (*see p140*).

Here, when the forest finally ends, the Liza rises under the twin peaks of Green Gable and Great Gable, another mile and half away. This is serious fell walkers' country. For climbers, Pillar Rock, a bulbous outcrop on the north side of Pillar with sheer faces overlooking Ennerdale Valley 2,000 feet below, is of special significance. First made famous by Wordsworth in his poem 'The Brothers', it was then thought impossible to scale. Its first ascent in 1826, by a local shepherd, John Atkinson of Crowfoot, is cited as the first recorded rock climb in the Lake District. Walter Parry Haskett-Smith, who pioneered Napes Needle on Great Gable, conquered the north face in 1891.

Another great summit is the well-named Steeple, next to Great Scoat Fell. You don't need to be a mountaineer, but a head for heights helps as a rocky scramble takes you to a peak with more sensational 360-degree views. Committed walkers can follow one of Lakeland's highest stone walls to Haycock and Caw Fell before dropping down to the eastern end of the lake. And for the truly hardcore, there's the Ennerdale Horseshoe Fell Race, held every June. One of the so-called 'classics', the 23-mile route involves 7,500 feet of climbs and goes round Ennerdale clockwise via all the peaks on both sides, plus Green Gable for good measure.

Where to eat & drink

There are no pubs or cafés around Ennerdale Water, and nothing special about the two pubs in Ennerdale Green, so it's best to push on towards the coast and the town of Whitehaven.

Where to stay

Simplicity is the order of the day in the Ennerdale Valley. Without a single guesthouse, pub or B&B from one end of the lake to the other, the options are youth hostels, bunk barns or camping. But if you're going to rough it anywhere, then do it here – preferably in Black Sail, the YHA's shepherd's bothy at the far end of the valley, with Haystacks and Great Gable for company.

Black Sail Youth Hostel ★
Black Sail Hut, Ennerdale, CA23 3AY (0845 371 9680, www.yha.org.uk). Rates £17.95 adult.

Local heroes: Alfred Wainwright

When the shy, solitary (and, according to some, rather grumpy) Alfred Wainwright began to chart his ascents of Lakeland's fells, he didn't even have a publisher. Who could have imagined that almost 20 years after his death, he would have become a household name (among households with a penchant for walking, at any rate) – and that his handwritten 'Pictorial Guides' would have sold over two million copies worldwide? His acolytes are legion: the Wainwright Society is thriving, while the Wainwright Baggers gamely endeavour to climb the 214 fells described by their hero.

Born to a working-class Lancastrian family in 1907, in the industrial town of Blackburn, Alfred Wainwright left school at 13 to become an office boy at the borough council, studying at night school to work his way up through the departments. In 1930 he went on a week-long holiday to the Lakes with his cousin. Arriving in Windermere, the pair climbed Orrest Head, and looked out across the fells. 'It was a moment of magic, a revelation so unexpected that I stood transfixed, unable to believe my eyes,' Wainwright would later remember. 'Those few hours on Orrest Head cast a spell that changed my life.'

He returned to the Lakes whenever he could, mostly by bus at weekends. He walked in his shirt, tie and 'third best suit', with only a spare pair of socks as back-up. In 1940 he took a job at Kendal Town Hall, to be nearer his beloved fells. The contentment he found while walking the fells was in sharp contrast to his home life; he had married at 24 and had a son, but both he and his wife admitted it was a long and unhappy marriage.

Wainwright recorded his many visits to the Lakes in obsessive detail, and as the notes piled up he embarked on an ambitious plan to map and describe every major Lake District peak. He began work on what would become the seven-volume *Pictorial Guide to the Lakeland Fells* in late 1952: every spare moment took him on to the fells, and he finished the last volume on schedule in 1965.

The books are astonishing. Meticulously handwritten and accompanied by beautiful indian ink drawings, they cover 214 of the Lake District's fells. The level of detail is truly remarkable, covering routes, maps, skylines, ascents, views, summits, natural features and descents. What's more, the author's personal observations and dry humour are there too – and a far remove from the somewhat curmudgeonly face he often presented to the world. Wainwright himself may have been a loner, taciturn to the point of rudeness, but his personality comes alive in the books that he described as a 'love letter' to the landscape. 'The one thing he got wrong was to call them guides – they were much more than that,' enthuses Eric Robson, chairman of the Wainwright Society. 'Poetry, philosophy, conversations… I don't know what the right word would be. They were unique, and they still are.'

In 1966 Wainwright retired from his full-time job and separated from his wife; he went on to write a further 50 books, including the famous *A Coast to Coast Walk*, whose epic 192-mile route ran from St Bees, on Cumbria's west coast, to Robin Hood's Bay in North Yorkshire. He knew that the guides would need revising as the landscape, footpaths, forests and buildings changed, and before he died in 1991, he decided on the man to do it. So, in a heroic effort worthy of AW himself, cartographer Chris Jesty spent five years updating all seven volumes, walking and recording all 214 fells and subtly amending the text. Only the photo on the cover and the routes printed in red distinguish the new guides from the originals.

After his death in 1991, Wainwright's wife Betty McNally (whom he'd married in 1970) scattered his ashes on his favourite summit, Haystacks. AW described it in his usual inimitable style: 'Haystacks stands unabashed and unashamed in the midst of a circle of much loftier fells, like a shaggy terrier in the company of foxhounds. For a man trying to get a persistent worry out of his mind, the top of Haystacks is a wonderful cure.' A fitting final resting place, then, for the man who found such solace – and such joy – out on the windswept fells. He himself chose the spot, by Innominate Tarn, 'where the water gently laps the gravelly shore and the heather blooms and Pillar and Gable keep unfailing watch. A quiet place, a lonely place. I shall go to it, for the last time, and be carried.'

Ennerdale Water. See p138.

The address is superfluous. Black Sail is possibly the YHA's most famous hostel. It may only get one star for facilities, but, apart from Skiddaw House (*see p193*), there's nothing in the YHA portfolio to match it for beauty and remoteness. The hostel is located six miles from Bowness Knott car park out on the fells at the farthest end of the Ennerdale Forest. As well as being on the Coast to Coast walking route, this old shepherd's hut is on the crossroads of some outstanding footpaths, with trails fanning out to High Stile, Haystacks and Buttermere to the north; Great Gable to the east; and Kirk Fell, Pillar, Steeple and down to Wasdale Head to the south. There are three dorms (two with four beds, one with eight), a self-catering kitchen and a common room. Rather wonderfully, staff can provide meals (if given plenty of notice) and keep a range of bottled beers and wine. Otherwise, this is the ultimate mountain hostel. Note that from November to Easter it's not open for individuals; you have to book the whole place.

Ennerdale Barn

High Gillerthwaite, CA23 3AX (01629 592700, www.yha.org.uk). Rates £9 per person.

Near the Ennerdale Youth Hostel, the YHA's High Gillerthwaite camping barn accommodates 14 people in three sleeping areas in a converted 16th-century barn. You can book the whole place for £126. There's a toilet, shower, stove and electric lighting, but no sockets. Evening meals can be provided with advance notice.

Ennerdale Youth Hostel

Cat Crag, Ennerdale, CA23 3AX (0845 371 9116, www.yha.org.uk). Rates £17.95 adult.

An updated and refurbished forestry cottage on the edge of Ennerdale Forest. It's a welcome stop for walkers on the Coast to Coast and for cyclists on the Whitehaven to Ennerdale route; there's a drying room and a cycle store. A combination of six- and four-bed dorms can sleep 26, and there's a restaurant as well as the standard self-catering kitchen. Electricity only came to the valley in the 1980s, but the hostel is powered by its own hydro-electric turbine.

Low Gillerthwaite Field Centre

Ennerdale, CA23 3AX (01946 8629899, www.lgfc.org.uk). Rates £13 adult. No credit cards.

Black Sail Youth Hostel. See p140.

Mostly used by schools and youth groups, but also available for groups of friends, families and Coast to Coasters and individuals. The centre – set up with the aim of 'encouraging a love and respect for wildlife and wild places' – can sleep up to 40 in five dormitories of varying size. Bring your own sleeping bag and pillowcase. There's a self-catering kitchen, two sitting rooms and a dining room. A group of 26 can have the place in its entirety. Camping is also possible (advance notice is usually required); you won't have use of the centre's facilities, but you can enjoy an unforgettable pitch with views to Pillar under one of the darkest night skies in England. Plenty of pre-booked activities are available, including canoeing, climbing and orienteering – check the website for more information.

WHITEHAVEN & THE COAST

The landscape promptly flattens out at the western end of Ennerdale Water. Ennerdale Bridge is the first stop on the Coast to Coast Walk (*see right*), so the Shepherds Arms and the Fox & Hounds do a reasonable trade, but the village is thin beer after the thrills of Ennerdale Valley and its mountain surrounds. Collectors of stone circles should head south on the fell road to Kinniside, where there's a ring of 11 stones whose magic is rather tarnished by some of them being concreted into position.

Just outside the National Park boundary, the straggle of Cleator Moor, an old ore mining community, is where the road divides for Whitehaven or St Bees. A few miles to the south, the industrial town of Egremont has the last remaining deep iron ore mine in western Europe. Here, a handful of miners extract haematite for jewellery and cosmetic products. Sadly, the Florence Mine Heritage Centre, which offered underground tours, has closed because of flooding.

Egremont's other claim to fame is its annual Crab Fair and the accompanying World Gurning Championships. The story goes that gurning hails from 1297, when Henry II gave the crab apple fair a royal charter and the bitter taste of the apples made people grimace. Traditionally, the contorted faces of contestants are presented through a horse collar, with the elderly and toothless at an advantage because of their greater facial flexibility. Egremont Castle, or what's left of it, stands on a mound by a bend of the River Ehen just south of the town centre. Built in the 12th century and now cared for by English Heritage, it has a semi-ruined gatehouse and walls; entrance is free.

Whitehaven

The most interesting and attractive town on the Cumbrian coast, Whitehaven has splendid Georgian architecture befitting its prosperous past. In the 18th century it was England's most important port after London and Bristol. Such wealth came at a cost, though – fortunes were built on the backs of coal miners and slaves – and most was pocketed

St Bees beach. See p149.

Coast to Coast Walk ★

This is one of Britain's – and the world's – finest long-distance treks, voted ahead of the likes of the Inca Trail and the Himalayan hike to Everest. The 192-mile route, devised by Alfred Wainwright for his 1973 pictorial guide *A Coast to Coast Walk*, classically begins at St Bees beach and finishes at the bottom of the slipway at Robin Hood's Bay. Walkers then dip their toes in the water, add a Cumbrian pebble to the Yorkshire coastline and repair to the Wainwright Bar of the Bay Hotel for a celebratory pint. Along the way the route crosses three National Parks – the Lake District, the Yorkshire Dales and the North York Moors – crossing the roof of England amid almost unfailingly glorious scenery for the entire journey. It can, of course, be done in the opposite direction, from east to west.

Although unofficial and mainly unsignposted, the walks follows public rights of way. Wainwright intended it to be done in 13 stages, averaging about 15 miles a day (to fit into a fortnight's holiday, with a rest day). But he was not dogmatic. By cutting down the mileage to around 11 miles a day, it can be stretched out over a more leisurely three weeks, allowing for greater contemplation and fewer blisters. The route's popularity, assured from the start, has risen to 10,000 walkers a year (numbers will no doubt soar following the BBC TV series hosted by Julia Bradbury).

It's been an economic boon to pubs and cafés along the way and quite an industry has sprung up around it, offering luggage deliveries stage by stage, guesthouse bookings, route maps, GPS systems and shopping orders. There are 13 youth hostels en route.

Of course, the best guide is the original – so long as you get the most recently revised edition; the walk is regularly updated to note path erosion and changes to rights of way. The chosen route is unashamedly demanding, though some easier options are possible. You should be walking fit before you start; you certainly will be by the end.

The Ramblers Association (www.ramblers.org.uk) recommends four companies for carrying luggage and booking accommodation:

Brigantes Walking Holidays
Rookery Cottage, Kirkby Malham, BD23 4BX (01729 830463, www.brigantesenglishwalks.com).

Coast to Coast Holidays
60 Durham Road, Redcar, TS10 3RY (01642 489173, www.coasttocoast-holidays.co.uk).

Coast to Coast Packhorse
Chestnut House, Crosby Garrett, CA17 4PR (017683 71777, www.c2cpackhorse.co.uk).

Sherpa Van Project/Sherpa Expeditions
29 The Green, Richmond, DL10 4RG (0871 520 0124, www.sherpavan.com).

Whitehaven lighthouse

Places to visit

WHITEHAVEN & THE COAST

The Beacon ★
West Strand, Whitehaven, CA28 7LY (01946 592302, www.thebeacon-whitehaven.co.uk). Open Summer 10am-4.30pm daily. Winter 10am-4.30pm Tue-Sun. Admission £5; free-£4 reductions.
It has the look of an old harbourside lighthouse, but this is an admirable, purpose-built museum on four floors (all wheelchair accessible) with well-organised exhibitions. Start at the top where windows fill a semicircle of the tower and telescopes provide superb views to the Solway Firth. The lower floors explain the area's involvement in salt production, fishing and farming and tell the story of the Lowthers and the slave trade. The history of coal and iron mining and its tragedies are thoroughly covered, and room sets show how rich and poor lived. The basement Wellington Café has a prime position overlooking the harbour.

Haig Colliery Mining Museum
Solway Road, Kells, Whitehaven, CA28 9BG (01946 599949, www.haigpit.com). Open daily in summer; call for opening times. Admission free.
Found to be unworkable after the Miners' Strike, Haig Colliery finally capped its last shaft in 1986, thus ending a history of local coal mining going back to the 13th century. Part of the mine was turned into an industrial park; the rest was purchased for £1 in 1993 by the volunteer Haig Pit Restoration Group. Visitors aren't allowed underground, but can tour the surviving buildings, notably the winding engine house that stands resplendent on a clifftop over the Irish Sea. There are workshops (containing engines under renovation) and displays on Whitehaven's remarkable mining history.

The Rum Story
Lowther Street, Whitehaven, CA28 7DN (01946 592933, www.rumstory.co.uk). Open 10am-4.30pm daily. Admission £5.45; £3.45-£4.55 reductions; £16.45 family.
The Rum Story is located off Whitehaven's main street, in the original courtyard and bonded warehouse that belonged to the Jefferson family, 18th-century rum importers. More theme park than museum, with its elaborate sets filled with mannequins, it provides a reasonably atmospheric re-creation of the triangular trade involving West Indian rum and African slaves. The bowels of a slave ship with full-size models of the human cargo and eerie sound effects might send a shiver; handling an actual slave's shackle certainly should. Best of all are the unchanged rum cellars and the fusty Dickensian office of the Jeffersons, complete with big old ledgers on big old desks. A free tot of rum at the end of the tour will take some of the sting out of the price of a family ticket.

Saltom Pit
www.whitehavencoast.co.uk/saltom. Open 24hrs daily. Admission free.
Set on the shore at the southern end of the harbour, 18th-century Saltom Pit was abandoned to the mercy of the Irish Sea until a local campaign forced the council and English Heritage to step in and safeguard its future. It's now a scheduled Ancient Monument, and it's safe to explore the surviving surface buildings. Saltom was the first mine to tunnel beneath the sea (to a depth of 456 feet) and also pioneered underground explosives and safety lamps. The site is part of the Whitehaven Coast project, a scheme to regenerate the coastal area of Whitehaven.

The Rum Story

Fleatham House. See p149.

by Cumbria's biggest landowning family, the Lowthers (*see p240*). They bought up land for coal seams and sank pits; built the harbour and engaged in the slave trade; and laid out the town in its distinctive grid formation.

The stain of slavery is indelible. Whitehaven was one corner of a triangle of trade whereby goods were shipped to Africa and traded for slaves. The slaves were taken to the plantations of the West Indies and America, where they were auctioned for the rum, sugar, tobacco and coffee that was imported through Whitehaven. The town was also key to the country's shipbuilding industry. As the rum and slave trade declined, coal mining thrived – but it exacted a terrible toll. Before nationalisation, the Whitehaven mines had the worst safety record in Britain, and explosions were common. Estimates of the number of men, women and children killed in the district's mines range from 500 to 1,200. In the worst single disaster, 136 died at Wellington Pit in 1910.

John Paul Jones, 'The Father of the American Navy', first went to sea on a Whitehaven slave ship. He travelled to America and returned an ardent colonist in 1778 during the American War of Independence, leading a seaborne raid of Whitehaven. The cannons of two forts were disabled and some colliers in the harbour were set alight – though some of Jones' men simply repaired to a local pub (thought to be today's Pier House). All escaped unscathed, but Jones became public enemy no.1, and the skirmish is popularly referred to as the last invasion of English soil. Whitehaven has forgiven him with a statue.

Three museums vividly recount this potent history. The Rum Story (*see left*) on Lowther Street has adapted the rum cellars of the Jefferson importers to recreate their trade, while not shying away from the slaves who oiled its wheels. The Beacon (*see left*) at the south end of the harbour is an excellent all-round municipal museum. And a ten-minute walk south on the coast path takes you to the remains of Saltom Pit (*see left*), the first place to introduce undersea mining. You can then climb a grassy slope to the Haig Colliery Mining Museum (*see left*). The pit here, the last of the Whitehaven district's 70 mines, closed in 1986. The winding gear and engine house standing proudly on the clifftop, with spectacular views across the Irish Sea to Scotland and the Isle of Man, is an eloquent memorial to the lost jobs in the pit village behind and the lost lives beneath the sea below.

Modern Whitehaven can hardly compete with such a poignant past. In the town centre a clutch of independent shops and cafés take on the chain stores on Lowther Street and its side streets. Look out for Cumbria's biggest and best-loved second-hand bookshop, Michael Moon's (19 Lowther Street, 01946 599010, closed Wed, Sun Jan-Easter, Sun Easter-Dec). Some 25,000 volumes are housed in a wriggle of crammed rooms and rickety staircases. Its regional specialism runs to reprints of old guides and monographs.

Although the harbour appears mainly given over to a yachting marina, a revival in the fishing fleet has seen more landings, with a local speciality in prawns and scallops. You can walk out on West Pier to imagine the harbour's heyday, and there's still a salt tang to the warehouses on Strand Street and King Street. The regeneration of the waterfront includes the Whitehaven International Maritime Festival, held over a weekend in June.

Lowther House

Students of Georgian architecture will find plenty of impressive examples around town, especially Whitehaven Castle, designed by Robert Adam and once the home of Sir John Lowther, the town's founder and principal planner; the building is now divided into private apartments. St James's Church, on the High Street, was described by Nikolaus Pevsner as having the finest Georgian church interior in the country.

St Bees

Five miles south of Whitehaven the cliffs run out and the road sweeps down the valley into the old-fashioned seaside resort of St Bees. It has one of the best beaches on the Cumbrian coast; at high tide it's all shingle and groynes, but as the water recedes a long wide stretch of yellow sand opens up. Two major caravan sites on either side of the car park do little for the aesthetics, but they're invisible from the beach.

Buy a traditional Hartley's ice-cream from the beach shop and café and watch hang-gliders launch off South Head, or intrepid walkers go through the ritual of wetting their boots and pocketing a pebble as they set off on the Coast to Coast Walk. Before the path turns east for the Lake District, it follows a clifftop route for a couple of miles – with a possible detour down to the beach at Fleswick Bay – to St Bees Head, where an unmanned lighthouse on the promontory marks the westernmost point of Cumbria. The RSPB reserve at St Bees Head (www.rspb.org.uk) has the largest colony of nesting seabirds on the west coast, including England's only breeding black guillemots.

Where to eat & drink

La'al Tattie (38 Strand Street, 01946 592929) is the nicest little takeaway in Whitehaven. It's nothing fancy, just baked potatoes with good-quality fillings: meatballs, garlic mushrooms, hot and spicy chilli, chicken tikka and more.

Café West

56 King Street, Whitehaven, CA28 7JH (01946 598960). Open 9.30am-3pm Mon-Sat.
This community café was set up to support people with learning disabilities; students gain an opportunity to learn new skills and gain work experience. There's nothing amateur about the set-up. With bare-brick walls, wooden floors, modern furnishings and a mix of tables and sofas, it's an easy place to relax, and free internet access is available too. The food – soups, sandwiches, cakes and scones, plus such dishes as cheese flan and salad – has similar simple, honest value. It's also possibly the only place in the UK to offer hot Vimto.

Vagabond

9 Marlborough Street, off Strand Street, Whitehaven, CA28 7LL (01946 693671). Open 11am-3pm, 5-11pm daily. Lunch served 11am-2pm, dinner served 5-9pm daily.
There's a picture of Bob Dylan on the pub sign and while it would be a stretch to compare this likeable bolthole to a New York folk club, it has a dark wood, hideaway vibe and

regular music sessions. Located in a side street just behind the harbour, it's the sort of place John Paul Jones' mutinous crew might have jumped ship for. The short gastropub-style menu includes fresh fish and is good value; top Cumbrian ales are served.

Zest

Low Road, Whitehaven, CA28 9HS (01946 692848, www.zestwhitehaven.com). Food served 6.30-9.30pm Wed, Thur; 6.30-10pm Fri, Sat.
Head out of town for Whitehaven's best restaurant (though there's not much competition in the three-course category). Start with salmon fish cake on mushy pea purée, or goat's cheese and caramelised onion tart. For mains, try slow-cooked lamb, teriyaki salmon fillet or haggis-stuffed chicken breast wrapped in Woodall's streaky bacon. Local and British produce are to the fore, and there are vegetarian and gluten-free options throughout. Celebrity diners have included Tony Blair and Abi Titmuss, though presumably not together.

Zest Harbourside

8 West Strand, Whitehaven, CA28 7LR (01946 66981, www.zestwhitehaven.com). Open 11am-11pm Mon-Sat; noon-11pm Sun. Food served 11am-9pm Mon-Thur; 11am-9.30pm Fri; noon-9.30pm Sat; noon-9pm Sun.
The hipper and cheaper offshoot of Zest, set in a converted fish warehouse on the harbourside. A long menu offers casual tapas-style eating, and attempts to cover all bases from bacon butties to caesar salad, not to mention meat balls in tomato sauce, spanish omelette, cajun prawns and fish stew. Note that bookings aren't accepted. It's also a stamping centre for the start of the C2C cycle ride.

Where to stay

Fleatham House

High House Road, St Bees, CA27 0BX (01946 822341). Rates £90 double incl breakfast.
The address is fitting for a tall house on top of a high drive, overlooking St Bees and the coast. The building's red stone matches the sandstone cliffs of South Head. Fleatham House had a moment in the spotlight in 2002 when Tony Blair took a family holiday here in an effort to support Lake District tourism a year after the foot and mouth epidemic. There are three doubles and three singles, and the front rooms with big bow windows, including the dining room, have sunset views over the Irish Sea. The decor suits an upstanding Victorian residence. You can breakfast on eggs from their own hens and local smoked haddock; evening meals are available for guests from Monday to Thursday.

Lowther House

13 Inkerman Terrace, Whitehaven, CA28 7TY (01946 63169, www.lowtherhouse-whitehaven.com). Rates £80 double incl breakfast.
Three elegantly furnished double rooms are available in this large Victorian merchant's house located high above Whitehaven, including one with views of the Solway Firth. All are spacious and gracious, with gorgeous French beds and huge modern bathrooms, one with striking blue and white sailing boat tiles. Host Trevor Lloyd calls himself an 'ambassador for Whitehaven' and can fill you in on the history of the town, as well as where to go and what to do.

Loweswater, Crummock Water & Buttermere

Like three pearls held together by a single string, these three beautiful lakes follow one another in quick succession. Each is mercifully unspoiled, and each has terrific mountain backdrops. This is what the Lake District is all about; no wonder that Wainwright chose to have his ashes scattered here. Loweswater, Crummock Water and Buttermere are linked by a single, scenic through road – one of the most cherished routes in Lakeland. Its location, however, affords some protection against being overrun with visitors; the north-west corner of the National Park may not be as inaccessible as Wastwater and Ennerdale Water, but it's too far for most day-trippers and coach tours.

The three lakes are a walker's paradise. Paths wind all the way around their shorelines, and there are high-level trails to challenge even the hardiest of hikers: Mellbreak, Red Pike, High Stile and Haystacks are celebrated names in the fell walker's lexicon. Quieter pleasures include taking a rowing boat out on tranquil waters where motorboats and even sailing dinghies are banned.

At the southern end of Buttermere, the great bulwark of Fleetwith Pike marks the start of the Honister Pass leading into Borrowdale; not the highest pass in the Lakes, but one of the most inspiring. At its summit, the Honister Slate Mine is not only still excavating slate from this most inhospitable of mountaintops, but offers visitors a remarkable adventure, in the shape of its underground tours and vertiginous Via Ferrata.

Loweswater

The westernmost of the three lakes is also the smallest, gentlest and least disturbed. It's surrounded by forests and rolling countryside rather than moorland and precipitous fells; nonetheless, it is the gateway to proper mountains. Arriving from the west, the highest peak in frame is in the middle distance: Grasmoor, standing at 2,795 feet.

An easy, three-mile circular walk runs around the lake, which is a mile long and never more than half a mile across. Set off from the car park at Loweswater Hall, at the northern corner, or from the little car park at Maggie's Bridge, close to the southern end.

On the western shore, the path follows an old coffin route that leads to St Bees Abbey, on the Cumbrian coast, and passes through the National Trust-owned Holme Wood – a mix of Scots pine and native broadleaf, and a stronghold for red squirrels. At the top of the woods, a footbridge crosses Holme Force, with its succession of cascades. At the bottom is a windowless stone bothy, which can be rented from the National Trust as a primitive but rather magical holiday home, Holme Wood Bothy (*see p161*).

Swimming in Loweswater is discouraged because of the algae. Instead, hire one of the old-fashioned rowing boats, acquire a fishing permit (*see p155*) and drift out to the middle of the lake to see what's biting. Maybe brown trout; maybe perch. Nothing save another of the handful of rowing boats can possibly interrupt the idyll, so sit back and idly consider climbing Mellbreak. There's no need to hurry in Loweswater, and in the evening there's nowhere better to discuss the one that got away than the Kirkstile Inn (*see p160*), over a pint of the pub's own-brewed ale.

Crummock Water

Three miles long and wholly owned by the National Trust, Crummock Water is gloriously undeveloped. At one end, rising straight out of the western shore, is the soaring, isolated cone of Mellbreak (1,680 feet); north of Mellbreak is the cosy hamlet of Loweswater, which is closer to Crummock Water than its namesake lake.

To drive along Crummock Water's shore, take the road from Loweswater, which heads north-east into Lorton Vale before doubling back for the approach to the lake, as the B5289. It's a fine, freewheeling stretch for cyclists, under the screes of Grasmoor; look out for the sign at Langthwaite that reads 'Tek Care, Lambs On't Road'. From here to Rannerdale Farm, there's no interruption to the scenery save a couple of car parks – unless you count a boathouse and a fish ladder. After the farm, there's nothing again until the end of the lake.

Crummock Water

Loweswater. See p150.

Buttermere. See p154.

Honister Pass

In winter, the landscape looks rugged and wild. By late spring, though, the Rannerdale Valley shimmers with bluebells. If Mellbreak still looks too daunting, then Rannerdale Knotts (1,165 feet) is an easier option, with a sharp, straight hike up from Hause Point to a summit commanding both Crummock Water and Buttermere. It's a tranquil view: motorboats and sailing boats are banned on all three lakes, and nothing bigger than a rowing boat or canoe can take to the water. For boat hire and fishing permits apply to Wood House (*see p162*), which is set on the isthmus that separates Crummock Water from Buttermere.

Any low-level circuit of Crummock Water should take in the half-mile detour up Scale Beck gorge to the highest waterfall in the Lake District. Scale Force consists of a single, narrow drop for 150 feet – like a bath tap pouring uninterrupted – and several smaller drops. It's a steep climb, but you can carry on from here to the top to join the so-called Buttermere Round.

Buttermere

Buttermere is as lovely as it sounds. Just over a mile long, it's fringed by forest, meadow and mountain. The village of Buttermere lies just north of the lake, while at its southern end, the 'Buttermere Pines' are reflected in the still water

– an idyllic scene captured by countless paintings and tourist photographs.

At the edge of the village stands the little chapel of St James, whose south window looks out across to Haystacks (1,959 feet). A slate plaque set into the sill reads: 'Pause and remember Alfred Wainwright. Fellwalker, guide book author and illustrator who loved this valley. Lift your eyes to Haystacks, his favourite place. 1907–1991.'

Indeed, Wainwright's ashes were scattered high on Haystacks, by the shores of Innominate Tarn, which has become a place of pilgrimage. In his *Memoirs of a Felllwanderer*, AW drily noted: 'And if you, dear reader, should get a bit of grit in your boots as you are crossing Haystacks in years to come, please treat it with respect. It might be me.' Many boots have been wistfully checked in the intervening years.

Running north-west from Haystacks and its cluster of tarns are the three higher peaks of the Buttermere Round; High Crag (2,443 feet), High Stile (2,644 feet) and Red Pike (2,476 feet) – the last aptly named, given the red tinge of the exposed ground and well-trodden footpath. Even without its Wainwright connections, this would be one of Lakeland's essential walks: to have four such peaks within three miles, with superb views across to Ennerdale, Pillar and Great Gable as well as back down Buttermere and Crummock Water, is truly glorious. The much easier four-mile shoreline circuit is also extremely popular, and includes a damp and rather unexpected tunnel, cut through solid rock at the Hassness promontory.

As with Loweswater and Crummock Water, there are no shops at Buttermere. In summer, though, walkers can bless those friendly farms that provide refreshments for the weary. Croft Farm and Syke Farm – which makes its own ice-cream and has a simple 40-pitch campsite (*see p161*) – are at the village end of the lake; Gatesgarth Farm is at the south-eastern end, under Fleetwith Pike. There are also two pubs in the village.

Leaving Buttermere is almost as exciting as discovering it. From the village, one road runs straight up to the Newlands Hause pass and on through the Newlands Valley towards Keswick. Better still, at the southern end of the lake is the start of the dramatic Honister Pass.

Honister Pass

The stretch of the B5289 from the Gatesgarth end of Buttermere up to the Honister Pass is nothing less than awesome. Fleetwith Pike is a domineering presence on the right, while the canyon floor is strewn with giant Ice Age boulders. On the final approach to the Hause (1,167 feet), there's the humbling knowledge that higher still, under the black crags, men risked their necks every day on the precipitous footpaths to the slate mines and quarries at the summit.

This remains the site of England's last working slate mine. It closed in 1986, after 250 years of

Row your boat

'Believe me, my young friend, there is nothing – absolute nothing – half so much worth doing as simply messing about in boats.' Such was the opinion of Ratty, in Kenneth Grahame's classic children's tale *Wind in the Willows*, and it's hard to disagree. And while the Lake District offers abundant opportunities for taking to the water, Loweswater, Crummock Water and Buttermere are some of the best spots at which to do it, thanks to the 'quiet lake' policy in operation across all three lakes. What this means, in practice, is that there are tight restrictions on what kinds of boats are allowed: namely, no motorboats or yachts. Instead, you can paddle a rowing boat out on the water and drift in blissful, lazy solitude.

The National Trust has four traditional-looking rowing boats for hire on Loweswater – made from fibreglass, sadly, rather than varnished wood. The boats are moored at Watergate Farm at the south-eastern end of the lake, where bookings can be arranged through the warden (01946 816944, Easter-Oct), or at the other end of the lake, through Waterend Farm (01946 861465). No other boats are allowed on Loweswater.

Another six NT-owned rowing boats are moored at the eastern end of Crummock Water, where hire is arranged via Wood House (*see p162*). There is no slipway on Crummock Water, but visitors can hand-launch kayaks, canoes, dinghies and windsurfing boards, with a limit of ten crafts at any one time. There are no boats for hire on Buttermere; again, visitors are allowed to launch their own small boats, with the same restrictions on numbers.

All three lakes provide good seasonal fishing for brown trout, pike and perch, with the occasional sighting of charr. Fishing permits (£8 a day), which also cover a mile stretch of the River Cocker as it leaves the top of Crummock Water, can be bought at Wood House. Over-12s also need a rod licence, available from post offices, the Environment Agency (www.environment-agency.gov.uk) or by phone (0844 800 5386); a one-day licence costs £3.75-£8.

Places to visit

Honister Slate Mine

Honister Slate Mine ★

Honister Pass, CA12 5XN (017687 77230, www.honister-slate-mine.co.uk). Open 9am-5pm daily. Admission free. Tours £9.75; £4.75 reductions.

High up in the crags of Fleetwith Pike, Honister Slate Mine is a fascinating place. In its heyday, tramways, railways and dizzying aerial runways ran up and down the mountainside, as its valuable green slate was mined and carried away. Over 11 miles of subterranean tunnels remain; various tours are available, all involving helmets, miners' lamps and guides, who adroitly counterbalance amusing anecdotes with the stark human history of the mine. The Kimberley tour covers the essentials, leading visitors through narrow, stooping tunnels that open up into the lofty caverns where the best slate was extracted. In one, an enormous vertical incline, used to lift slate from the six working levels to the surface, is still operational. In another, the acoustics are so good that it's been used as an experimental music recording studio; when the lights are switched off, the darkness is absolute. The Edge tour, meanwhile, takes in a mountainside stretch that is not for those prone to vertigo – though not quite as hair-raising as the Via Ferrata (*see p161*). Back at the mine offices, there's a café and a shop with all manner of slate products, from coasters to hand-cut roof slates.

Paradigm. See p162.

The Maid of Buttermere

It was all the fault of a guidebook. In 1792, Joseph Palmer's *A Fortnight's Ramble in the Lakes* rhapsodised about the beauty of the barmaid at Buttermere's Fish Inn. She was the publican's daughter, 15-year-old Mary Robinson; so extravagantly did Palmer praise her long brown hair, her full eyes, her lily cheeks and red lips that she became a veritable tourist attraction – a beauty spot in her own right. Wordsworth and the Lakeland poets passed by and enthusiastically confirmed her innocent, unspoiled beauty as embodying the very ideals of the Romantic movement.

The tourists kept turning up to see her – and so, presently, did Colonel Alexander Augustus Hope, an MP with aristocratic connections. After a swift romance, the colonel and the maid were married at Lorton Church in 1802, and Samuel Taylor Coleridge wrote it all up for the newspapers. However, the *London Sun* quickly realised that the real Alexander Hope MP was abroad. Poor Mary had married John Hatfield: an imposter and – worse still – a bigamist, jailbird and bankrupt. Hatfield was arrested, but managed to escape, stowing away at Ravenglass and staying on the run until the Bow Street Runners caught up with him near Swansea. He was returned to Cumbria, where Carlisle assizes sentenced him to death by hanging for bigamy and for the greater offence of masquerading as an MP.

Mary Robinson went back to her former position behind the bar at Buttermere, pursued by even greater fame and notoriety. Eventually, she married a farmer from Caldbeck; on her death in 1837, she was buried as Mary Harrison, and lies in St Kentigern's graveyard in Caldbeck village. Wordsworth described her as 'the artless daughter of the hills' in *The Prelude*, and was moved by the 'cruel mockery of love and marriage bonds' she endured. Successive generations of dramatists and novelists have also borrowed her poignant story. In 1988 Melvyn Bragg's novel *The Maid of Buttermere* became a bestseller, and is apparently about to be made into a big-budget Hollywood film starring Catherine McCormack and Colin Firth.

mining, but was saved after helicopter pilot Mark Weir flew over it with his grandfather, who had worked in the mine. Weir decided there and then to buy the mine, and set it to work once again. It re-opened in 1997; as well as the slate mining business (buy your gravestone or kitchen worktop here), the site has become a significant tourist attraction thanks to its exciting underground tours (*see p157*) and even more thrilling Via Ferrata (*see p161*), which takes participants on the Lake District's ultimate high-wire act.

From the wild heights of Honister Hause and Fleetwith Pike, the road winds more gently down into Seatoller and beautiful Borrowdale.

Where to eat & drink

Unless you're lucky enough to have found a guesthouse or hotel with a good in-house cook, the Kirkstile Inn is the eternally popular first

TEN REMARKABLE CHURCHES

Dotted around the Lake District are some of England's smallest, oldest, most remote and most appealing churches. Invariably they are still used for services, and left open for visitors.

Holy Trinity, Grange
The startling black dogtooth beams on Holy Trinity's white ceiling look disconcertingly like rows of sharks' teeth, and are as worthy of the 'Jaws of Borrowdale' moniker as the 'steep fells outside. Look out, too, for the slate window settings and the unusual perimeter wall, made of tombstone-like slabs. *See p182.*

Keld Chapel, Shap
This one-storey stone chapel was a medieval chantry for the monks of Shap Abbey, where prayers for the dead were supposed to be said in perpetuity. Used as a private dwelling in the 17th century, it was given to the National Trust in 1918, and preserved inside and out in its bare, unadorned stone and oak simplicity. *See p240.*

St Bega, Mirehouse
This exquisite little Norman church has stood beside Bassenthwaite Lake for some 900 years, and possibly longer; parishioners of old used to get to church by boat. St Bega's splendid solitude inspired the lakeside chapel described in Tennyson's *Morte d'Arthur:* 'A broken chancel with a broken cross/That stood on a dark strait of barren land/On one side lay the ocean, and on one/Lay a great water, and the moon was full.' *See p190.*

St Cuthbert, Kentmere
Although the current building is Victorian, the roof beams are 16th century and the 1,000-year-old yew outside suggests there's been a place of worship here for aeons. The plain, white-walled interior is enlivened by colourful tapestry kneelers, decorated with birds, floral sprigs and rural scenes. A plaque by the pulpit honours Bernard Gilpin, the Protestant reformer and famous preacher known as the 'Apostle of the North', born in Kentmere in 1517. *See p245.*

St James, Buttermere
Most famous for its window-sill plaque to Alfred Wainright – 'Lift your eyes to Haystacks, his favourite place' – this small Victorian church on the edge of Buttermere village postdates the one that moved Wordsworth. Look out for the charming wrought-iron gate to the porch, depicting a shepherd with a crook, a ewe and a lamb. *See p154.*

choice. If that's booked up, it's worth trying the Wheatsheaf Inn (*see p197*) or Winder Hall (*see p198*) in Lorton Vale.

Bridge Hotel
Buttermere, CA13 9UZ (017687 70252, www.bridge-hotel.com). Open noon-9pm daily. Dinner served 6.30-8.30pm daily.
Under the same ownership for more than 30 years, the Bridge's formula attracts faithful returnees for its traditional, well-mannered approach. 'No less than smart casual attire' must be donned to sample a dinner menu typified by cream of broccoli soup, and avocado and prawn terrine by way of starters, followed by classic, meaty mains. Well-kept real ales and simpler grub are dispensed in the bars. The furnishing and fabrics in the 21 spick-and-span bedrooms (£130-£140 double incl breakfast) evoke the unbending Lakeland tradition. The hotel also lets out six self-catering apartments (from £355-£655 per week for two people) above Mill Beck, which are simpler and more modern in style.

Fish Hotel
Buttermere, CA13 9XA (017687 70253, www.fish-hotel.co.uk). Open 10.30am-10.30pm daily. Food served noon-2.30pm, 6-9pm daily.
With an idyllic position on Mill Beck, and unruffled by changing fashions in food or design, the Fish has welcomed walkers and tourists since 1790. It has 12 bedrooms (£96 double incl breakfast) and pub grub, both cheaper and more basic than its more upmarket neighbour, the Bridge, although both are highly traditional in their own ways. We won't pass comment on the beauty of the bar staff. The last time a guidebook did that it ended up in a hanging (*see p159*).

Kirkstile Inn ★
Loweswater, CA13 0RU (01900 85219, www.kirkstile.com). Open 10.30am-11pm daily. Lunch served noon-2pm, dinner served 6-9pm daily.
With Mellbreak towering above and Crummock Water and Loweswater on either side, this Lakeland favourite scores ten out of ten for location. It has stood here for some 400 years; inside, old photographs reflect a different way of life but unchanged scenery. The inn's own Loweswater Brewery turns out award-winning beers, while the food (Mellbreak lamb hotpot, steak and ale pie, baguettes packed with Cumberland sausage and carmelised onions) is gusty and generous; one or two more unusual options are generally chalked on the blackboard. The place is deservedly popular, so book ahead. There are also ten bedrooms (£93 double incl breakfast), including a family suite, which are neat, clean and good value.

Where to stay
In terms of sheer colour and variety, the three lakes offer exceptional accommodation. Options run from 'stone tent' basics at the National Trust bothy (*see right*) on the shores of Loweswater to lottery-winner luxury at Paradigm (*see p162*). There's a sophisticated guesthouse at Wood House (*see p162*), timeless character at the Kirkstile Inn (*see above*) and, for a more rugged retreat, the youth hostel (*see p162*) at the top of Honister Pass.

In summer, arrive early if you plan to pitch your tent at the tiny Syke Farm Campsite (017687 70222) in Buttermere village; set behind the Fish Hotel, it's a simple, hilly site with no-frills facilities. No advance bookings are taken.

Buttermere Youth Hostel

Buttermere, CA13 9XA (0845 371 9508, www.yha.org.uk). Rates £15.95 adult.
Set back from the road above Buttermere village, this well-equipped, 70-bed YHA hostel is conveniently located for forays to Buttermere and Crummock Water. The house iself is a slate Victorian pile with a garden. Family rooms are available, and facilities include a drying room, a cycle store and a licensed restaurant.

Cragg House Farm

Buttermere, CA13 9XA (01687 70204, www. buttermerecottage.co.uk). Rates Camping barn £7-£8 per person. Self-catering £250-£280 per week.
This unfussy holiday cottage and camping barn are set on a working sheep farm at the head of Buttermere village. The cottage sleeps four: the interior is simple, the garden delightful. It's self-contained, except for a staircase shared with owners John and Vicki Temple. John is the farmer, Vicki a vet, and with their knowledge of local wildlife they can tell you where otters have been sighted within ten minutes of the farm, and help you to identify all manner of passing birds. The barn has a sink and kitchen area but no stove, a gas fire (50p per night), a coin-operated shower and a toilet. Upstairs, the sleeping area has mattresses for eight. To book it, contact Lakeland Camping Barns (01946 758198, www.lakelandcampingbarns.co.uk).

Enzo's Escape

Stone Barns, Mockerkin, CA13 0ST (01946 862818, www.enzosescape.co.uk). Rates £350-£535 per week. No credit cards.
An ultra-cool, one-bedroom hideaway, Enzo's occupies part of a barn conversion next to the village green in Mockerkin, a few miles north-west of Loweswater. Underfloor heating, a walk-in shower, a roll-top bath and a Danish wood-burning stove all bring a touch of urban luxury to this rural outpost. The well-equipped kitchen leads to the sitting room and bedroom, where a porthole window provides views all the way to the Solway Firth. On a rainy day, make the most of the sleek line-up of gadgets, including a plasma TV, home cinema system and iPod docks.

Holme Wood Bothy

Loweswater (015394 63862, www.nationaltrust.org.uk). Rates £160-£245 per week.
Standing in a forest clearing on the edge of Loweswater, this stone bothy looks like a woodcutter's cottage in a fairytale: a sturdy, diminutive, windowless construction, with a wisp of smoke rising from the chimney. Formerly a fish hatchery hut, the building is now owned by the National Trust and rented out as the ultimate back-to-basics accommodation. There's a wood stove and a gas cooker, room for ten sleeping bags, a cold tap (the water's not for drinking, mind), a compost loo and the use of a shower at a nearby warden's hut (from 5pm to 8pm). The rest is up to you. Get a permit and catch a brown trout for supper, and don't forget the essentials (sleeping bags, torches, toilet paper, matches and cutlery).

Things to do

Via Ferrata ★

Honister Slate Mine, Honister Pass, CA12 5XN (017687 77714, www.honister-slate-mine.co.uk). Open 9am-5pm daily. Rates from £25; £20 reductions.
The via ferrata ('iron road') is a mountain crossing technique pioneered in the Dolomites by Italian soldiers during World War I. The iron in question consists of cables, bridges and ladders, stapled into the mountainside to scale otherwise impassable terrain. In 2008, Honister Slate Mine built a Via Ferrata up the side of Fleetwith Pike, to give an insight into how generations of slate miners scrambled up primitive rockface staircases to get to work. For good measure, its Via Ferrata adds in sections with sheer drops of 1,000 feet, vertiginous ladders and a zip-wire; it's scary but safe, thanks to qualified guides and a double clip-on carabiner system. A reassuring letter in the visitors' book from Gamblesby Women's Institute confirms how their party went out in wind, mist and rain and all returned safe and sound. Nevertheless, it cannot be recommended for anyone remotely nervous of heights. Participants must be over ten years old, and weigh less than 20 stone.

Via Ferrata

TEN CHURCHES continued

St John the Baptist, Ulpha
The stark outline of the fells rises up beyond this diminutive, Grade II-listed church, with its whitewashed exterior, slate roof and little bell turret. Inside are fragments of 18th-century wall paintings, rediscovered in 1934 when a coat of whitewash was removed; outside, the grassy churchyard is dotted with weathered, lichen-clad gravestones, including a memorial to a 17-year-old local lad who died out on the moor in 1926. *See p119.*

St John's in the Vale, Keswick
Set on a remote pass between High Rigg and Low Rigg, where the road comes to an end, this one is all about location. The church itself is an unremarkable mid 19th-century construction that replaced the 16th-century church that once stood on the site – but just imagine being married here. *See p165.*

St Martin, Martindale
A church has perched above Howtown since the 13th century; this 16th-century successor is delightfully basic, with no electricity, hefty beams spanning the roof, plain glass windows and well-worn pews set against the massy stone walls. It's said that the font was once a Roman altar; it also served as a tool sharpening stone for a time, and still bears the scars. *See p215.*

St Olaf, Wasdale Head
It's said that St Olaf's is the smallest church in England, and that its beams were salvaged from a Viking longboat. Whatever the truth, it's a wonderfully atmospheric place, in the shadow of Great Gable and Wastwater – and made all the more poignant by its many memorials to long-dead climbers and mountaineers. *See p131.*

Wythburn Church, Thirlmere
Behind a simple slate and whitewashed stone exterior, there are treasures to be discovered: stained glass windows depicting seventh century Celtic saints and bronze pieces by artists from the Keswick School of Industrial Art. The church is particularly poignant, given its history: the community it once served was swallowed up by the Thirlmere reservoir, just across the road. *See p165.*

Honister Hause Youth Hostel
Seatoller, CA12 5XN (0845 371 9522, www.yha.org.uk). Rates from £15.95 per person.
The location of this 26-bed YHA hostel, on the wind tunnel summit of Honister Pass, is as unforgiving as it is spectacular. Occupying a converted quarry workers' building, it looks straight over the backyard of the Honister Slate Mine and provides easy access to central Lakeland's greatest peaks: Scafell Pike, Great Gable and Pillar. This is a true walkers' hostel, geared towards providing food and warmth: breakfast, packed lunches and evening meals can be rustled up, but facilities are decidedly low key.

Paradigm
Mosser, CA13 0SS (01900 825011, www.discover paradigm.com). Rates £1,000-£1,200 per week per property.
Champagne, an open-air jacuzzi, a helicopter flight over the Lakes – it's a mighty seductive package at these two luxury holiday lets, a couple of miles north of Loweswater. The champagne comes in the welcome hamper of Cumbrian goodies, while the jacuzzi sits in six acres of orchards and woodland. And the helicopter ride – weather permitting – comes courtesy of Mark Weir, Paradigm's owner, taking in Loweswater and Crummock Water before landing at Honister Slate Mine, which Mark also owns. The renovated farmhouse and hay barn each have two double bedrooms, and are gorgeously appointed, with rich fabrics, polished antiques and up-to-the-minute technology (flatscreen TVs, Wi-Fi, Bang & Olufsen sound systems). Thoughtful little extras include the use of two mountain bikes, and home-cooked meals can be provided on request. Call for short break availability (£600-£800).

Swallow Barn Camping Barn
Waterend Farm, Loweswater, CA13 0SU (01946 758198, www.lakelandcampingbarns.co.uk). Rates £7-£8 per person.
Simplicity reigns supreme at this 17th-century barn, which has four separate sleeping areas (mattresses provided) taking up to 18 people. Bed spaces can be booked individually; more often, though, the barn is booked in its entirety. A gas heater, hot water, toilets and coin-operated showers are among the creature comforts, while fishing permits and boat hire are available from the farm.

Wood House ★
Buttermere, CA13 9XA (017687 70208, www. wdhse.co.uk). Rates B&B £110 double incl breakfast. Self-catering £390-£590 per week. No credit cards.
It would be hard to better Wood House's location, between two lakes. In fact, it stands almost exactly where a rainbow touches the ground in Turner's painting of Crummock Water and Buttermere that hangs in Tate Britain. The house is delightfully elegant, the antiques refined and the six en suite bedrooms uniformly tasteful. It's all very hospitable – though not a place to be careless with muddy boots or tearaway kids. Judy McKenzie will prepare four-course dinners and packed lunches (at extra cost), both excellent investments given the dearth of quality dining options nearby. Also available is Wood House Cottage, a traditional stone cottage with a beamed, snug interior and three bedrooms for self-caterers. Wood House is also the place to hire rowing boats (£20 a day) for Crummock Water and to buy fishing permits (£8 a day).

Keswick, Derwentwater & Borrowdale

Keswick and Derwentwater, town and lake, are the cornerstones of the northern Lake District. Keswick has culture, literature and history in spades, much of it packed into an eclectic array of museums, while Derwentwater, 'the Queen of the Lakes', is for many the most beautiful lake of them all. Touched by the mystery and magic of Castlerigg Stone Circle and the grit of old mines and quarries, they are also the twin launch pads for two exceptional journeys into Newlands Valley and Borrowdale. There are famous waterfalls at Lodore and Moss Force, picture-postcard scenes at Ashness Bridge and Watendlath Tarn, and an abundance of wildlife in the sky, the oak woods and even underwater. Above all, though, visitors are dwarfed by the mountains and fells whose names are indelibly associated with the Lake District – Skiddaw, Helvellyn and Catbells among them. And once you're swallowed up by the craggy Jaws of Borrowdale, the soaring peaks of Great Gable and Scafell Pike await.

KESWICK & AROUND

Keswick ★

In the 19th century, John Ruskin – a man rarely given to understatement – pronounced Keswick 'almost too beautiful to live in'. No one could dispute its peerless location, with Derwentwater at its front door and the vast bulk of Skiddaw (3,054 feet) overlooking its backyard, but some might beg to differ over the beauty of the town itself. Ruskin did not live to see the jumbled development on the outskirts, the sprawling car park that divides the town centre from the lake, or some of the tired shops and takeaways. In Ruskin's day, Keswick was a bustling market town, whose rich local mineral reserves fuelled an economic boom in Victorian times. Its thriving literary culture, meanwhile, was embodied by Greta Hall (*see p173*) – home to both Robert Southey and Samuel Taylor Coleridge.

The Market Place, whose charter dates from 1276, remains the epicentre of Keswick. A market is held here every Saturday; at the centre of the broad, pedestrianised space is the Moot Hall, with its one-handed clock. Once a courthouse and prison, it is now a National Park Information Centre (01768 772645, www.keswick.org), with an accommodation booking service (note the £4 fee) that will probably send you to the grid of Victorian streets to the east of the town centre, with their countless guesthouses in matching grey slate.

The principal shopping streets fan out from the Market Place: Main Street and its side streets; Station Street, which continues north to Fitz Park and the Keswick Museum (for both, *see p171*); and Lake Road, home to some of the best cafés and restaurants in town, which leads south to Hope Park and Derwentwater. If you play nine

holes of pitch and putt in the park, with the mountains all around, doff your cap to Sir Percy Hope, who donated this priceless piece of real estate to the town in 1927; look out too for the ornamental gardens that once belonged to his wife.

While Keswick's fortunes have always fluctuated, and it was badly hit by the 2009 floods, life here has rarely been dull. When the railway arrived from Penrith in 1865 it came with a flourish; the imposing Keswick Hotel was built next to the station, and Fitz Park was laid out between the hotel and the River Greta. Visitors flooded in – not least for the annual Keswick Convention, which, since 1875, has brought 12,000 Christians to fill the town's guesthouses and B&Bs for three weeks. Regrettably, the railway closed in 1972; the station is still in good repair, and there's a campaign to restore the line, but it would require considerable investment. In the meantime, a few surviving stretches of track have found new life as footpaths and cycleways.

Although Keswick isn't living in the past, it does have a remarkable number of museums. The Keswick Museum provides the glass-case basics on the area's wildlife, geology and cultural history, but with an endearing oddball charm and some genuinely weird exhibits – not least its musical stones. The Cumberland Pencil Museum (*see p170*) and the Keswick Mining Museum (*see p171*) are both packed with unexpectedly fascinating details, bringing two significant local industries to life.

For lighter entertainment, the Puzzling Place (Museum Square, 017687 75102, www.puzzling place.co.uk) will fill a rainy hour or two with its optical illusions, visual trickery and marvellous anti-gravity room. The Cars of the Stars Motor Museum (Standish Street, 017687 73757, www.carsofthestars.com) houses various famous vehicles, from the A-Team's van to a clutch of

Batmobiles. Its sister establishment, the Bond Museum (Southey Hill Trading Estate, 017687 75007, www.thebondmuseum.com) has a shiny collection of 007-related transport, including skiddoos and Aston Martins.

Keswick also has a growing foodie reputation. Thomason's (8-10 Station Street, 017687 80169, closed Sun) is a superior butcher's with swish premises, quality meat and an enterprising range of cooked dishes; while Fond Ewe Fine Cheeses (9 Packhorse Court, 017687 73377, www.fond ewe-cheeses.co.uk) supplements a substantial selection of cheeses with oils, vinegars and olives. Ye Olde Friars of Keswick (6-8 Market Square, 017687 72234, www.friarsofkeswick.co.uk), opened in 1927, provides the town with such old-fashioned sweets as violet creams, fondant brazils and cinder toffee; and family-run Luchinis (1 Tithebarn Street, 017687 73668, closed Dec, Jan) has been producing its own Italian ice-cream since it was founded in Cockermouth in 1901. Big-name supermarkets do no favours to towns like Keswick, but the small, northern chain of Booth's (Tithebarn Street, 017687 73518, www.booths-supermarkets.co.uk) honourably supports local produce, including Brysons' plum bread.

There are enough stores dealing in walking, climbing and outdoor gear to rival Ambleside. Commanding a corner of Lake Road, George Fisher (017687 72178, www.georgefisher.co.uk) is deservedly pre-eminent. Founded half a century ago by local rock climber George Fisher, a founding member of the Keswick Mountain Rescue Team, it sells all the leading outdoor brands and offers ski repair and boot hire; staff will even check whether your waterproofs really are waterproof. Upstairs is Abraham's Tearoom (see p168). Hardcore climbers will find their proddlers and an ice-screw sharpening machine at Needle Sports (56 Main Street, 017687 72227, www.needlesports.com). If you can't find the required map, try friendly independent Bookends (66 Main Street, 017687 75277) or the Lake District Trading Company (48 Main Street, 017687 75127), which also has an internet café.

Other diversions include the historic Alhambra Cinema and the splendid Theatre by the Lake (for both, see p178). It is to the lake itself, though, that all roads lead before too long – see p173.

Threlkeld

Two miles east of Keswick is Cumbria's Stonehenge, where 40 weathered, rough-hewn boulders make up the remarkable Castlerigg Stone Circle (*see p170*). It is one of the most impressive henges in Britain, and an essential on the Lake District checklist. Its setting, on a raised brow with a 360-degree mountain panorama, is pure theatre in almost any weather, bar pouring rain.

Just outside Threlkeld village, the Threlkeld Quarry & Mining Museum (*see p171*) comprises a packed little museum, an open-air collection of vintage cranes and diggers, and a narrow-gauge railway that takes you into the heart of an old granite quarry. Another worthwhile turn-off leads up over a cattle grid and through a gate to the little church of St John's in the Vale, which serves the valley of the same name that joins Threlkeld to Thirlmere. It is dramatically set, high on the remote pass between High Rigg and Low Rigg, where the road effectively peters out for cars. The 16th-century church that once stood here was almost completely rebuilt in 1845; the building is unremarkable, but the location spectacular.

Thirlmere

Most visitors speed past Thirlmere on the A591 between Keswick and Ambleside – and with just cause. It is a reservoir, not a natural lake, and United Utilities owns both the lake and the surrounding land. Most of its three-and-a-half mile length is uniformly planted with thousands of acres of conifers; at best, it looks like a Scandinavian fjord that has been mistakenly transplanted. The water is so glacial that swimming is banned, although there is open access for dinghies, canoes, kayaks and sailboards.

New reservoirs were as controversial in the 1890s, when Thirlmere was created, as they are today. Ruskin led the opposition, but parliament eventually bowed to the need for clean drinking water in rapidly expanding Manchester. There's an almost triumphalist air to the grandiose plaque at the northern end of the reservoir, erected by the Manchester Corporation Waterworks to mark the start of construction; Dale Head Hall, now a hotel, was commandeered as the summer residence of the Lord Mayor of Manchester until it was sold in 1985.

Two small lakes, Leatheswater and Brackmere, were dammed to form Thirlmere; the villages of Ambroth and Wythburn were submerged in the process, and a Roman bridge was also lost. Nonetheless, it was – and remains – an impressive feat. The aqueduct to Manchester is 95 miles long and carries 55 million gallons a day; the water, powered by nothing more than gravity, takes a day to make the journey.

On the eastern shore, shortly after the venerable King's Head coaching inn (*see p167*) at Thirlspot, the first sight of Thirlmere is from the Swirls viewpoint car park – although possibly more eye-catching is the soaring vista of Helvellyn, England's third highest mountain at 3,117 feet. The classic route to Helvellyn's summit is via Striding Edge from Ullswater, but Thirlmere offers a handful of shorter, if steeper, climbs. The other main attraction is the area's population of red squirrels. United Utilities has erected squirrel reserves around Thirlmere, and a nature trail leads from Swirls to a woodland hide. The long-term plan to replant the shoreline spruce and larch with native woodland is a laudable project.

Further south at Whelpside Gill is another car park. Stop here to visit Wythburn Church, a half-

Ye Olde Friars of Keswick

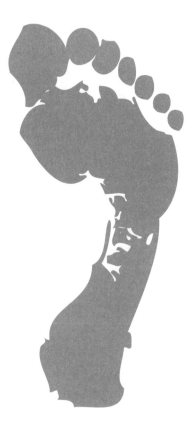

Whatever your carbon footprint, we can reduce it

For over a decade we've been leading the way in carbon offsetting and carbon management.

In that time we've purchased carbon credits from over 200 projects spread across 6 continents. We work with over 300 major commercial clients and thousands of small and medium sized businesses, which rely upon our market-leading quality assurance programme, our experience and absolute commitment to deliver the right solution for each client.

Why not give us a call?

T: London (020) 7833 6000

whitewashed, half-slate building dating from 1620 and described by Wordsworth as a 'modest house of prayer'. Inside are stained-glass windows depicting Celtic saints, and work by artists from the Keswick School of Industrial Arts. Outside are the gravestones of a community that no longer exists, the hamlet of Wythburn having been long lost beneath the reservoir.

Alternatively, explore the western shore. At the north end of the reservoir, you can drive across the 855-foot-long dam, 100 feet above St John's Beck. The road is narrow but scenic, with intermittent views of the wooded islands of Deergarth How and Hawes How. Armboth car park is a good place to access the water, and the starting point of a two-mile footpath that passes Cockrigg Crags and can be followed over the top via High Tove to Watendlath and Borrowdale.

Further south, Hause Point is the narrowest point of the reservoir; the Helvellyn Screes dominate the view across the water. At nearby Dob Gill, a path leads from the car park through woodland and past a series of waterfalls to Harrop Tarn – an enchanted little pool, fringed by tall firs, where you may glimpse buzzard, red deer or red squirrels.

Where to eat & drink

Lake Road is Keswick's best hunting ground, with options running from light lunches at the Good Taste Café (*see p168*) to more ambitious dinners at Morrels (*see p168*).

Abraham's Tea Rooms. See p168.

On Station Road, No XVII Emporium (no.18, 017687 71171) is a gift shop and daytime café (croissants, panini and other light lunches) that turns into an affordable bistro in the evening; the compact menu might run from own-made vegetarian pâté or pan-fried brie to start, followed by Scottish salmon with lemon butter sauce or Lakeland rump steak. Temporary Measure (74 Main Street, 017687 75254, www.temporarymeasure.co.uk), which sells photographic canvases, handmade books and cards, also has a quirky little tearoom at the back, serving own-made pear crumble, plum cake and cherry and pistachio flapjacks.

Ethnic eateries are concentrated at the bottom of Main Street: good options include Thai food at the Star of Siam (no.89, 017687 71444, www.starofsiam.co.uk) and Indian at Lakeland Spice Cuisine (no.81, 017687 80005). Casa Bella (24 Station Street, 017687 75575, www.casabellakeswick.co.uk) is the standout Italian, with child-friendly staff and modest prices.

For drinking, steer away from the rather soulless Market Square and Main Street pubs and plump for the Square Orange Café Bar, the Dog & Gun or the Pheasant Inn (for all three, *see p168*). All serve decent food, but are chiefly dedicated drinking spots.

The only pub between Keswick and Grasmere is the 17th-century King's Head Hotel & Inn (017687 72393, www.lakedistrictinns.co.uk) at Thirlmere. Motorists drop by for real ales, bar meals or three-course sit-downs in the restaurant.

Abraham's Tea Rooms,

George Fisher, 2 Borrowdale Road, Keswick, CA12 5DA (017687 71811, www.georgefisher.co.uk). Food served 10am-5pm Mon-Fri; 9.30am-5pm Sat; 10.30am-4.30pm Sun.

Tucked away in the rafters above three floors of outdoor gear, in the old Abraham's photography shop and studio, is one of the best tearooms in Keswick. Abraham's pays tribute to brothers George and Ashley Abraham, pioneering mountain photographers and rock climbers of the early 1900s. Their stunning images adorn the walls, while the self-service café offers the likes of smoked fish pâté, open sandwiches, Cumberland rarebit, toasted teacakes and chocolatey fell-walkers' slab. Despite its Victorian shell, the ambience is light and modern.

Brysons

42 Main Street, Keswick, CA12 5JD (017687 722257, www.brysonsofkeswick.co.uk). Food served 9am-5.30pm daily.

It's hard to imagine that Brysons' bakery counter has changed much in 60 years. There's a fine array of scones, cakes and muffins, including spiced plum bread and deliciously dense fruit cake. Upstairs is a café filled with pine tables, where waitresses serve own-made lasagne, sausage with herby mash, baked potatoes, hot Keswick rarebit and Cumberland cream teas.

Café Bar 26

26 Lake Road, Keswick, CA12 5DQ (017687 80863, www.cafebar26.co.uk). Open 11am-11pm daily. Lunch served noon-2.30pm daily. Dinner served 6-8.30pm Thur-Sat.

The lower end of Lake Road is as cool as it gets in Keswick, as the stout Victorian stone exteriors are injected with a succession of lively shops and cafés. The wide-ranging lunch menu here roams from cod and chorizo fish cakes to ciabatta topped with bacon and melted brie, along with cakes, crumpets and apple crumble. Pushchairs have to be folded down or left at the door, and it's grown-ups only come the evening, when cocktails and champagne by the glass are served. Above the bar are four smart bedrooms (£60-£75 double incl breakfast) for over-14s only.

Dog & Gun

2 Lake Road, Keswick, CA12 5BT (017687 73463). Open noon-11pm daily. Food served noon-9pm daily.

This well-loved, low-beamed, dog-friendly boozer fits the centre of town like an old glove. Expect a fire in the grate, Keswick ale on tap and a filling menu that includes Hunters' chicken, lasagne, bangers and mash, vegetable moussaka and the pub's trademark goulash, which loyal locals never tire of recommending. Children are welcome 9pm.

Good Taste Café ★

19 Lake Road, Keswick, CA12 5BS (017687 75973, www.simplygoodtaste.co.uk). Food served 8.30am-4.30pm Mon-Sat. No credit cards.

Peter Sidwell is something of a celebrity chef around Keswick, with a couple of books, a cookery school, a catering company and a consultancy service to his name, so it's a surprise to find that he runs his empire from this compact deli/café on Lake Road. Of course, size doesn't matter a jot when he can produce food of this quality. Sandwiches are stylishly presented on a slate tile, while soft, doughy focaccia, filled with melting onions, is served with hot and spicy moroccan soup in a mug. The sweet-toothed have tempting slabs of flapjack, millionaire's shortbread and chocolate brownies, plus excellent coffee. Stock up for a picnic, or head upstairs to a relaxed space with pine tables and chairs, squashy leather sofas, shelves of cookery books and piles of newspapers and magazines.

Lakeland Pedlar

Hendersons Yard, Bell Close, Keswick, CA12 5JD (017687 74492, www.lakelandpedlar.co.uk). Food served Summer 9am-5pm daily. Winter 9am-4pm daily.

It doesn't get much more wholesome than this: a vegetarian restaurant combined with a cycle shop. The Pedlar may be hidden down an alley on the edge of the town centre, but plenty of fans find their way here. The all day-menu kicks off with excellent breakfasts (muffins with cheese, beans and scrambled eggs; full-scale veggie fry-ups) before moving on to soups, salads, three-bean burritos, nachos, chilli, afternoon teas and an ever-changing array of cakes.

Lakeside Tea Gardens

Lake Road, Keswick, CA12 5DJ (017687 72293). Food served Summer 9.30am-6pm daily. Winter 10am-5pm daily. No credit cards.

This timeless institution is set right on the waterside by the landing stages, serving morning coffees, light lunches and afternoon cream teas. There's a Pianola, and the whole place is virtually unchanged since 1928. Its days may be numbered if the Theatre by the Lake's expansion plans go ahead; best call ahead before visiting.

Morrels

34 Lake Road, Keswick, CA12 5DQ (017687 72666, www.morrels.co.uk). Food served 5.30-9pm Tue-Sun.

Pale wood floors, high-backed suede chairs and linen napkins set the tone for Keswick's most urbane night out. Morrels is handy for pre-theatre suppers and good-value Sunday lunches, while the à la carte concentrates on uncontroversial bistro fare: sea bass with buttered spinach, say, or ribeye steak with lyonnaise potatoes; there are always several vegetarian choices too. Two self-catering apartments (£370-£650 per week), one with two bedrooms, one with three, aspire to similar sophistication.

Pheasant Inn

Crosthwaite Road, Keswick, CA12 5PP (017687 72219). Open Summer noon-11pm daily. Winter noon-2.30pm, 5.30-11pm daily. Lunch served noon-2pm, dinner served 6-9pm daily.

Not to be confused with the Pheasant at nearby Bassenthwaite, this bird is perched on the edge of Keswick and is generally reckoned to produce the best pub food in town. It has a changing blackboard menu, and although it can't claim gastropub status (and probably wouldn't want to), it's not without ambition. Think cod and chorizo fish cake with cajun yoghurt dressing, or roast loin of pork wrapped in parma ham, with warm chocolate brownie or rhubarb and raspberry frangipane for afters.

Square Orange Café Bar

20 St John's Street, Keswick, CA12 5AS (017687 73888, www.thesquareorange.co.uk). Food served 10am-11.30pm Mon-Thur; 10am-midnight Fri, Sat; noon-3pm Sun.

Good Taste Café

Places to visit

KESWICK & AROUND

Castlerigg Stone Circle ★

Chestnut Hill, Keswick (www.english-heritage.org.uk/castleriggstonecircle). Open 24hrs daily. Admission free.

There's no pay-and-display car park on this hillside plateau above Keswick, no admission charge, no one to stop you touching or even clambering over the stones, no tearoom and no intrusive interpretative displays. In fact, there's no explanation whatsoever of the 40 enigmatic, unhewn boulders that make up the prehistoric standing stone circle of Castlerigg. The circle may not be as big as Stonehenge – its largest stones are a mere 16 tons – or as romantically remote as Callanish in the Outer Hebrides, but Castlerigg enjoys an unparalleled setting. There's nothing but the weather to interrupt a fabulous circular backdrop featuring three of England's highest peaks: Blencathra, Helvellyn and Skiddaw.

Castlerigg has not given up its secrets, and probably never will. One theory is that it was a meeting and trading place for the Neolithic axe makers of Great Langdale; another possible function was as a royal mourning site for dead kings. Others have found alignments suggesting astro, solar and lunar significance, while UFO-spotters claim sightings of strange white lights going back to 1919. Most concur that the stones were erected in around 3,200 BC, making Castlerigg one of Europe's earliest circles.

Cumberland Pencil Museum

Southie Works, Keswick, CA12 5NG (01768 773626, www.pencilmuseum.co.uk). Open 9.30am-5pm daily. Admission £3.25; £1.75-£2.50 reductions; £8.25 family.

Don't scoff at this museum, set in part of the old Derwent pencil factory. There's more to this place than the world's biggest pencil (25ft long), and it's not just for kids. This is about black gold. The museum tells the story of graphite, which was discovered in Seathwaite in the 16th century and used by Borrowdale farmers to mark their sheep; industrially mined, it became so valuable that thieves stole it, leading to the term 'black market'. In the Victorian boom times, the cottage industry expanded until Keswick was home to no less than 14 factories. Features include a recreation of the original Seathwaite mine, a drawing zone for children, and a fine array of specialist arty workshops. The shop is a treasure trove for all those who covet a nicely sharpened pencil or a box of Lakeland crayons.

Castlerigg Stone Circle

Fitz Park
Station Road, Keswick, CA12 4NF (017687 73607).
Open 24hrs daily. Admission free.
Fitz Park's charms include a bowling green, an 18-hole putting green, a children's play area and a cricket ground with a handsome old pavilion. Plans are afoot to add a floodlit, all-weather games area and a tennis court. Relax by the riverbank or wander through the arboretum; the park is also conveniently close to the admirable Keswick Museum & Art Gallery.

Keswick Mining Museum
Otley House, Otley Road, Keswick, CA12 5LE (017687 80055, www.keswickminingmuseum.co.uk). Open 10am-4pm Tue-Sun. Admission £4; free-£1.50 reductions. No credit cards.
As befits a mining museum, this establishment is small, dusty and a little cramped; nonetheless, it is a gem. Its owner, creator and curator is the charismatic Ian Tyler – the author of 11 books on mining in Cumbria. Having photographed and surveyed every mine in the Lake District, Tyler has amassed a remarkable archive of mining memorabilia. Packed floor to ceiling with rocks, fossils, tools, explosives equipment and hundreds of press cuttings and photographs, the museum recounts the history of

Cumbria's mines. It's the human stories that make the place so evocative, along with the battered relics: the leather hats worn by early miners, and the tallow candles that lit their way. Most touching of all are the stories of mining disasters. The William pit in Whitehaven had the worst record, with 181 men, women and children dying in four separate accidents; it's thanks in large part to Tyler that we still remember them.

Keswick Museum & Art Gallery ★
Fitz Park, Station Road, Keswick, CA12 4NF (017687 73263, www.allerdale.gov.uk). Open Apr-Sept 10am-4pm Tue-Sat. Admission free.
Once voted the third strangest museum in the world, this is an extraordinary place. Among the weird and wonderful objects on display are Napoleon's tea cup, a spoon made from sheep's bone and a man trap. The natural history collections run from the mummified, 664-year-old remains of a cat to a vendace (Britain's rarest fish), pickled in a jar. The star exhibit, however, is the geological piano. While walking on Skiddaw in 1785, local eccentric Peter Crosthwaite noticed that tapping one of the slate stones produced a perfectly pitched musical note. Chipping away at more stones for different notes, he created a stone xylophone. In 1848, the Skiddaw stones were played for Queen Victoria, and taken on nationwide tours. Today, visiting children are encouraged to have a go at coaxing a tune out of the stones.

You'll also find Victorian cabinets of curiosities and stuffed birds, and some fine paintings and delicate metalwork pieces by the Keswick School of Industrial Art (set up in 1884 by Canon Rawnsley, a close friend of John Ruskin). There are manuscripts and letters written by Hugh Walpole and Keswick's own Lakeland poet, Robert Southey – including the latter's first transcription of the story of *The Three Bears*. Wordsworth is here too, still moaning about the railways and the working classes – 'I do not wish them to see Helvellyn when they are drunk.'

Threlkeld Quarry & Mining Museum
Threlkeld, CA12 4TT (017687 79747, www.threlkeld miningmuseum.co.uk). Open Mar-Oct 10am-5pm daily. Admission Underground tour £5; £2.50 reductions. Museum £3; £1.50 reductions. No credit cards.
There's nothing remotely sophisticated about this museum, with its hand-painted signs and Portakabin tearoom. For an authentic taste of the tough industrial past of the Lake District, though, it's hard to beat. Located in the fells above Threlkeld village, the museum is based around a large quarry, where stone was once smashed for concrete. The enthusiasts who have taken over the site have relaid a narrow-gauge rail track to take visitors half a mile into the heart of the quarry, with the saddleback engine 'Sir Tom' the pride of their loco collection. What looks to the untutored eye like a giant scrapyard is actually (take their word for it) the largest collection of working vintage excavators in Europe. The little museum is a crammed repository of mining- and quarrying-related artefacts, from displays on explosives to evocative photographs of the site in its heyday, when 300 locals worked the quarries. You can also take a 45-minute underground tour of a reconstructed mine.

Howe Keld

OPENGOWAN

Is this Amsterdam, Paris or Keswick? This café/bar has a tiled floor, original art on the walls, a wonderful teak bar with shelves of bottles stretching to the ceiling, and a winning mix of French accents, Belgian beers, German gluhwein, Spanish chorizo and stone-baked Italian pizza. Jazz, Irish folk and roots music provide a suitably international soundtrack, with musicians playing on Thursday evenings.

Treeby's Gallery Café
12 Lake Road, Keswick, CA12 5BX (017687 72443, www.treeby-bolton.co.uk). Food served 10.30am-5pm daily.
This newly refurbished café is at the back of the Treeby & Bolton china, glass and jewellery shop. Pop in for a cup of proper leaf tea, coffee or a light lunch. The menu includes seasonal salads, daily specials, crêpes and omelettes made with eggs 'from hens we know personally', and platters of local fish, meat and cheese.

Where to stay
With a basic population of 5,000, Keswick more than trebles in size when its hotels and guesthouses put out their 'no vacancies' signs in high season. You won't find much cutting-edge design in these parts, but clean, good-value B&Bs are in ready supply in the area between Ambleside Road and the river. Parking can be tricky, but once you've found a spot you can forget the car; everything you need in town is within walking distance.

Borrowdale House
Eskin Street, Keswick (017687 80894, www.borrowdale house.co.uk). Rates £395-£995 per week. No credit cards.
Located on a tranquil residential street in Keswick's historic heart, with fine views across to Latrigg, this is a stylish self-catering option. Behind a slate-clad Victorian frontage, the interior is beautifully decorated and pleasantly spacious: four good-sized bedrooms; a cream-painted, chandelier-lit living room with an open fire; a dining room; a modern kitchen; and a lovely bathroom, complete with an elegant Victorian roll-top bath and a swish separate shower room. Check the website for details of their three- to four-night short breaks.

Greta Hall ★
Main Street, Keswick, CA12 5NH (017687 75980, www.gretahall.net). Rates from £300-£460 per week for 2 people. No credit cards.
Set high above town, Greta Hall is a stunning Grade I-listed Georgian house with commanding views over Skiddaw, Latrigg, Grisedale Pike, Borrowdale and Derwentwater. The house has impressive literary connections: Samuel Taylor Coleridge and Robert Southey lived here (though not at the same time), and the latter claimed it to be 'the finest spot in England'. Visitors included Wordsworth, Byron, Keats and Shelley. Over the last ten years, Jeronime and Scott Palmer have gradually brought the house back to life, and created three lovely self-catering apartments. The two-floor Coleridge Wing has pride of place, with three double bedrooms and a sitting room with huge sash windows, a cast-iron fireplace and comfy sofas. At the back, the Old Wash House is now a cosy bolthole for two, kitted out with

exemplary good taste. The third – and largest – apartment is the detached Coach House, with a vast upstairs sitting room, four double bedrooms and one triple.

Howe Keld ★
5-7 The Heads, Keswick, CA12 5ES (017687 72417, www.howekeld.co.uk). Rates £90-£130 double incl breakfast.
This 14-room guesthouse, handily located between the town centre and the lake, has been comprehensively upgraded to an impressive standard. The bedroom furniture was made by a local craftsman, while Herdwick wool rugs dot the natural wood and Kirkstone slate floors. The beds, with goosedown quilts and Egyptian cotton sheets, are inviting, and the bathrooms gorgeous. The charming attic room has views across Derwentwater to Catbells and Causey Pike, while the ground-floor room will suit guests with mobility problems. Valerie Fisher used to work for vegetarian restaurant chain Cranks, and knows how to dish up a delicious breakfast: expect home-baked organic bread, free-range eggs, dry-cured bacon, a smoothie of the day, porridge, and pancakes with maple syrup.

Lynwood Guest House
12 Ambleside Road, Keswick, CA12 4DL (017687 72081, www.lynwood-keswick.co.uk). Rates £74 double incl breakfast.
Lynwood sets the standard for the myriad B&Bs that cluster in the residential streets around Ambleside Road. With boundless good cheer and enthusiasm, Gerry and Elsie Empson offer six immaculately clean, sizeable bedrooms, traditionally furnished and all en suite. There are generous breakfasts, internet access and assorted maps and walking guides, and it's just five minutes' walk to the centre of town or down to the lake.

DERWENTWATER ★
Just five minutes walk from the centre of Keswick, Derwentwater stretches below the town like a beautiful teardrop. No other lake in the National Park can compare to it in terms of the variety of its surrounding mountains, while its shore is broken up by a series of beautiful coves and promontories. Around the lake, trails and footpaths alternate between magical oak woodlands and open vistas.

The lake is three miles long and a mile and a half wide, and surprisingly shallow, averaging just 15 feet in depth. It's the first to freeze in winter – usually just at the water's edge, but in January 2010 it froze completely, and to the horror of the authorities, people took to the ice en masse on foot and on skates. They were merely following a long tradition; a Victorian painting in the Keswick Museum (*see p171*) shows hundreds of skaters gliding across the lake. In 1879 the ice was more than ten inches thick, and within living memory locals can recall a coal lorry using the frozen lake as a shortcut to Portinscale.

It's in spring and summer that Derwentwater comes alive. Rowing boats and dinghies appear, and the Keswick Launch ★ (017687 72263, www.keswick-launch.co.uk, closed Mon-Fri Dec-Feb) runs every half hour from the Keswick Boat Landings, alternating clockwise and anti-clockwise

Derwentwater. See p173.

Derwentwater by boat

A circuit of Derwentwater aboard the Keswick Launch (*see p173*) takes 50 minutes, and you can hop on and off the elegant wooden boats as you please. Keswick Boat Landings is the main stop, with a ticket office; at the others, you pay on board. Clockwise from Keswick, the landings are as follows:

Ashness Gate
At the head of Borrowdale, Ashness Gate is the starting point for walks to three celebrated beauty spots: picturesque Ashness Bridge; Surprise View, looking over Derwentwater to Bassenthwaite; and Watendlath and its tarn. Rock climbers will head straight for Shepherd's Crag, one of the most historic, popular and occasionally fatal challenges in the Lake District.

Lodore
This jetty's main draw is the famous Lodore Falls, behind the Lodore Hotel (the falls are on the hotel's land, so there's an honesty box). Watching Watendlath Beck crashing over 100ft of large boulders is a sight to behold, especially after rainfall, and moved Southey to verse. In a dry summer you might want your money back. There are lovely woodland walks, with the treat of tea and cakes at the crag rats' rendezvous of Shepherd's Café (*see p185*) at High Lodore Farm. Canoes and kayaks are available to hire from Platty+ (*see p178*) on the shore.

The newly restored Chinese Bridge crosses the Derwent at the southern end of the lake, and new decking made from recycled plastic bottles now allows pushchairs and wheelchairs to cross Lodore Marsh to the western shore, where there are further landing stages. The area by the bridge is also a popular swimming spot, while the marsh and reedbeds provide one of the best birdwatching spots on Derwentwater, with a resident kingfisher on the river, and snipe and tawny owls at dusk.

High Brandlehow
High Brandlehow is the first stage on the western shore. There are trees for kids to climb, and pleasant lakeshore footpaths through Manesty and Brandlehow Parks. A climb up to the Portinscale road brings you to Brackenburn, the former home of Hugh Walpole, which he called his 'little paradise under Catbells' and where he kept a library of 30,000 books. The views to Bleaberry Fell and High Seat are delightful.

Low Brandlehow
The jetty at Low Brandlehow is an alternative stop for Brandlehow Park's 100 acres of oak woodland and wetlands. You might spot red squirrels and deer among the trees; look out too for John Merrill's sculpture, *Entrust* – a pair of cupped hands, carved from oak to mark the centenary of the National Trust. It's a fitting location, as this was the first piece of land bought by the NT. When Brandlehow was put up for sale in 1902, the great fear was that Derwentwater would follow Windermere and have its prime lakeside land snapped up by voracious northern cotton kings. But it was saved after a public appeal raised the necessary £6,500, and Octavia Hill, NT co-founder, proclaimed: 'It belongs to you all, and to every landless man, woman and child in England.' Now, much of Derwentwater's shores and the lake itself are secure in the Trust's hands.

Hawse End
Hawse End jetty marks the start of the ever-popular route up Catbells ★. There's very little parking round here, so you'll be glad you arrived by launch. Catbells is only 1,481ft high, and it's less than two miles there and back; Wainwright described it as a place 'where grandmothers and infants can climb together', although some may run out of puff on the steeper stretches. Inevitably, there has been significant footpath erosion and re-routing, and on the busiest days there are actually queues to scale the summit. Nonetheless, there is no finer short climb in the northern lakes. The pay-off is a perfect panorama of Derwentwater, Skiddaw, Borrowdale and the Newlands Valley. Arrive early or late to avoid the crowds, but don't miss out.

Nichol End
At Nichol End Marine (017687 73082, www.nichol endmarine.co.uk) you can hire rowing boats for a jaunt under your own power or self-drive motorboats, or just have a cup of tea in the upstairs café overlooking the water. Half a mile along the north shore, there's access to the lake from Derwentwater Marina (017687 72912 www.derwentwatermarina. co.uk) with kayaks, canoes, dinghies, windsurfers and rowing boats for hire. A short walk leads into Portinscale, which can feel more like a well-off suburb of Keswick than an independent village. It's a five-minute journey on the launch to Keswick Boat Landings, or you can walk to town over the little suspension bridge.

routes around the lake and stopping at six other jetties (see left). Catching the boat is a pleasingly low-tech affair, according to the offical instructions: 'Stand on the jetty and wave when you want the launch to stop.'

Derwentwater contains various islands. The largest is Derwent Isle, owned by Fountains Abbey in medieval times and home to Cistercian monks; in the 16th century, the German workers at Keswick's copper mines lived here. In the 18th century the island was bought by Joseph Pocklington, who built an Italianate house and gardens – which Wordsworth detested as heartily as he hated the Round House on Windermere's Belle Isle. Today, the island and house are privately let by the National Trust, with only a few public days a year; such is the demand that entry is by timed ticket, booked in advance via the NT website.

Close to the eastern shoreline, Lord's Island was once home to the medieval Earls of Derwentwater, and had a drawbridge to the mainland; these days, you have to land by rowing boat. The ruins marked on the Ordnance Survey map consist of little more than the vaguest of foundations, and a couple of herons now inhabit the place.

In the middle of the lake, you can fight your way through the thickets of St Herbert's Island in search of the stones that mark the site of the old hermit's cell. The Venerable Bede's writings confirm that Herbert was 'the hermit of Derwentwater,' settling here in the seventh century to devote himself to 'unceasing mortification and prayer'. He chose a good spot. Each year, the local Catholic parish celebrates a Mass on the island in his memory.

Rampsholme Island is famous for its wild garlic, and is also home to a colony of cormorants. In the southern shallows, the phenomenon of a 'floating island' also occasionally appears. It pops up in exceptionally dry weather, when marsh gases drive a tangle of vegetation to the surface, and can be as big as an acre; don't try to land on it, though.

The lake's other curiosity is the vendace, Britain's rarest freshwater fish. Often compared to herring, its origins can be traced to the Ice Age. The Finns eat vendace with blini, but it's a protected species in Britain.

On dry land, there are countless footpaths to explore across Derwentwater's hinterland. But to finish the day on the lakeside, head out from Keswick on the footpath that hugs the lake's eastern shore for most of the two miles to Broomhill Point, where you can take in the grandeur of the setting and admire Peter Randall Page's *Hundred Year Stone*, which stands on the shoreline. An enormous boulder of Borrowdale rock, split in two and carved with a circular pattern, it was commissioned to mark the National Trust's centenary in 1995.

Closer to Keswick, Isthmus Bay and Friar's Crag are both an easy ramble along well-marked paths from Keswick's Boat Landings. At Friar's Crag, the scene memorably embraces the Jaws of Borrowdale, the islands, Catbells and beyond.

A monument to John Ruskin recounts that a visit with his nurse to Friar's Crag was his earliest memory; later in life, he would describe the view here as one of the three best in Europe.

Where to eat & drink

For cafés and restaurants, head back to Keswick. If you're picnicking, there are any number of gorgeous spots easily accessible by footpath on Derwentwater's bays and coves.

Where to stay

On the northern tip of Derwentwater, two miles from Keswick, the upmarket village of Portinscale has several guesthouses, along with the traditional-looking Derwentwater Hotel (0844 556 0880, www.coastandcountryhotels.com), set in 18-acre grounds overlooking the lake. The same company runs the Derwent Manor self-catering apartments; see the website for details.

Derwent Bank
Nr Portinscale, CA12 5TY (0845 470 7558, www.hfholidays.co.uk). Rates vary, phone for details.
Enviably located on the north-western tip of Derwentwater, this 32-bedroom guesthouse has charming gardens running down to a private jetty. It belongs to HF Holidays, which runs walking-based breaks across the UK. Graded and guided walks are arranged each day, ranging from a six-mile valley stroll to strenuous trips up Helvellyn. Accommodation is clean and basic, with furnishings tending towards the pastel-coloured and old-fashioned. The atmosphere is sociable, so don't book a place if you're not prepared to join strangers at dinner. Talks and quizzes are arranged in the evening; alternatively, retreat to the bar. Phone or check the website for details of designated family weeks.

Derwentwater Youth Hostel
Barrow House, CA12 5UR (0845 371 9314, www.yha.org.uk). Rates £17.95 adult.
Yet another stellar location secured by the YHA. Set on the eastern side of the lake, this handsome white mansion was built in 1790 for Derwentwater's rich eccentric, Joseph Pocklington, who also built a house on Derwent Isle. He created a waterfall in the grounds, although his attempt to install a hermit for the amusement of tourists thankfully never happened. The hostel is equally well sited for the Keswick Launch, risking your neck on Shepherd's Crag, walking in Watendlath or simply listening for woodpeckers in the wooded grounds. There are 88 beds, plus a full range of facilities, including a laundry and drying room, a games room and a licensed dining room.

NEWLANDS VALLEY

A couple of miles west of Keswick, just off the A66, is the village of Braithwaite. From here, beautiful, unspoilt Newlands Valley runs south-west for seven miles, leaving the western side of Derwentwater between Catbells and the 2,090-foot Causey Pike. The minor road through the valley rises up to Newlands Hause (1,093 feet), through terrain that becomes ever more sparsely populated, before dropping sharply down to Buttermere. There are few distractions from serious, high-level walking in the north-western fells; there's not so much as a pub after Swinside, and as you climb out of the valley on the three-mile Newlands Pass you're on the sort of wild mountain road where they shoot away-from-it-all car commercials.

Braithwaite, whose old heart is huddled around Coledale Beck under the fells, is a three-way junction with a couple of decent pubs – the Royal Oak and the Coledale Inn (for both, see right) – which are worth considering if you don't want to stay in one of Keswick's B&Bs.

Forget the car if you want to see Force Crag Mine – until its closure in 1991, the last working metal mine in the Lake District. From Braithwaite, it's a three-mile hike or cycle ride up the Coledale Valley

to a scarred, grey moonscape under the crags. Now owned by the National Trust, it's an Ancient Monument and Site of Special Scientific Interest. The mine buildings, a crude collection of structures with corrugated iron roofs, which already look as if they belong to another era, can be visited on pre-booked tours (017687 74649). The tunnels are closed to the public. You can extend the hike with the more ambitious nine-mile Coledale Horseshoe, a tough-ridge walk.

Heading into Newlands Valley, the road divides at Little Braithwaite; take the left-hand fork for a detour to the Swinside Inn (017687 78253, www.theswinsideinn.com), which serves ales from Jennings Brewery and has a beer garden facing Barrow fell. The next settlement is Stair, which is home to the Newlands Adventure Centre (see below). The village is also the starting point for an

Things to do

KESWICK & AROUND

Keswick Bikes
Southey Hill, Keswick, CA12 5ND (017687 75202, www.keswickbikes.co.uk). Open 9am-5.30pm Tue-Sun. Hire from £16/day.
This ever helpful and knowledgeable cycle hire outfit includes a bike workshop. There are discounts for group and multi-day hire discounts, and helmet and toolkit are provided. Note that they don't have children's bikes, buggies or tagalongs, though, and ID and a credit card are required.

Keswick Climbing Wall
Goosewell Farm, Keswick, CA12 4RN (017687 72000, www.keswickclimbingwall.co.uk). Open 9am-5pm Mon, Fri-Sun; 9am-9pm Tue-Thur. Admission varies, phone for details.
Part of the Newlands Adventure Centre, with a 300sq m indoor climbing wall and a sizeable bouldering area. Competetent adults can climb unsupervised, while novices can book lessons and one-on-one instruction. It's set in a converted barn, off the A5271 close to Castlerigg Stone Circle, with inspiring views across to Helvellyn.

Lonsdale Alhambra Cinema
St John's Street, Keswick, CA12 5AG (017687 72195, www.lonsdalecitycinemas.co.uk/keswick). Tickets £4.50-£5.50; £3.50-34.50 reductions; £14 family.
Opened in 1913 and run by a group of enthusiasts, this is one of the country's oldest surviving cinemas. It has a predominantly mainstream programme, but broadens its repertoire to take in foreign-language and independent films on Monday nights. On Sunday evenings in winter, the Keswick Film Club run its own screenings (non-members pay an extra pound to attend).

Theatre by the Lake ★
Lakeside, Keswick, CA12 5DJ (017687 74411, www.theatrebythelake.com). Open Box office 9.30am-8pm daily. Tickets vary, phone or check website for details.
This lottery-funded, 400-seat theatre was built in 1999, and is irresistibly situated just outside town

on Derwentwater's shore. It runs a year-round programme, ranging from musicals, comedy, operetta and talks through to crowd-pleasing farces and challenging contemporary drama. The theatre also hosts the Keswick Film Festival, the Jazz Festival, the Mountain Festival and Words by the Water – a ten-day literary festival whose 2010 line-up included Martin Bell, Brian Keenan and Penelope Lively.

DERWENTWATER

Platty+
Lodore Boat Landings, Derwentwater, CA12 5UX (017687 76572, www.plattyplus.co.uk). Open Mar-Oct times & rates vary, check website for details. No credit cards.
This family-run watersports business offers equipment hire and tuition for canoeing, kayaking, sailing and more; groups can view the lake from a dragon boat or even a replica Viking longboat, the Gift of the Gael. Rowing boats are also available for hire, for one- to six-hour sessions.

NEWLANDS VALLEY

Newlands Adventure Centre
Stair, CA12 5UF (017687 78463, www.activity-centre.com). Open & rates vary, phone or check website for details.
Canoeing, ghyll scrambling, high ropes and zip-wires, mountain biking and walking are on the agenda at this well-established outdoor adventure centre in the Newlands Valley. There are residential courses and individual activity days for adults and children.

BORROWDALE

Glaramara Outdoor Centre
Seatoller, CA12 5XQ (017687 77222, www.glaramara.co.uk). Open 8am-10pm daily. Rates vary, phone or check website for details.
Another comprehensive and experienced outdoor sports centre. Located in the fells, its offerings include gorge crossing, kayaking, underground abseiling into the Plumbago graphite mine, or even the chance to land on a Derwentwater island in a Viking longboat.

ascent of Causey Pike (2,090 feet), beyond which looms the aptly named Crag Hill (2,749 feet), the second highest point in the north-western fells.

Another back lane detour takes you to the hamlet of Little Town, which was co-opted by Beatrix Potter for her *Tale of Mrs Tiggy-Winkle*. On summer Sundays, afternoon teas are served at pretty, whitewashed Newlands Church. The village marks the start of another classic 'horseshoe' walk: the ten-mile Newlands Round, taking in Maiden Moor, High Spy (2,143 feet), Dale Head (2,473 feet) and Hindscarth (2,385 feet). In summer, Low Snab Farm at Hindscarth also maintains the Lakeland tradition of serving afternoon tea to descending fell walkers.

Back on the valley road, after crossing Rigg Beck, there are no more detours en route to Newlands Hause. For years, the Newlands Hotel – better known as the Purple House, thanks to its brightly painted wooden exterior – was a famous landmark on this road. In its prime, it was a writers' retreat and a lodging house for climbers and for thespians performing at Keswick's Century Theatre; Ted Hughes, Victoria Wood and Tenzing Norgay, the conqueror of Everest, all stayed here. It gradually fell into disrepair and was sold in 2007. Plans to replace the building with a daring new design were thwarted by a colony of protected bats that had settled in the derelict house; then, in summer 2008, a mysterious fire reduced the property to ash and rubble.

At the summit of the pass at Newlands Hause, a car park sits under the impressive Moss Force waterfalls, which pour down from Robinson Crags in three great leaps. The two lower sections are easy to access via a footpath; the third is a scramble – and, if the water freezes in winter, a Grade III-rated ice climb.

Where to eat & drink

The Coledale Inn (*see right*) has an agreeable bar and an old-school menu (prawn cocktail, scampi, gammon and pineapple) – nostalgic or time-warp, according to taste.

Royal Oak

Braithwaite, CA12 5SY (017687 78533, www.royal oak-braithwaite.co.uk). Open noon-midnight daily. Lunch served noon-2pm, dinner served 6-9pm daily.
In the heart of the village, the Royal Oak is a solid all-rounder. Beyond its whitewashed exterior is a traditional, oak-beamed bar, with a good line-up of real ales. The menu resists newfangled flourishes in favour of time-honoured favourites: big bowls of soup with chunky wedges of bread; lamb and mash; steak, mushroom and ale pie; or fish and chips. The ten bedrooms (£80 double incl breakfast) range from traditional to modern.

Where to stay

Catbells Camping Barn

Low Skelgill Farm, Low Skelgill, CA12 5UE (019467 758198, www.lakelandcampingbarns.co.uk). Rates £7-£8 per person.

Sheltering in a superb location under the western flank of Catbells, this farmhouse and barn are thought to date from the 14th century. Happily, the barn's metered shower room, multi-fuel stove (for heating) and cooking facilities are more up to date. There's space for 12; mattresses are provided, but bring sleeping bags.

Coledale Inn

Braithwaite, CA12 5TN (017687 78272, www. coledale-inn.co.uk). Rates £78 double incl breakfast.
This friendly, straightforward country inn stands by Coledale Beck at the top of Braithwaite. The 20 bedrooms are comfortable rather than cutting-edge; try to book one at the front with a view of Skiddaw fells. The residents' lounge is a snug spot for board games by the fire.

Greta Hall. See p173.

FELL WALKING SAFETY TIPS

Of the 15 million annual visitors to the Lake District, about half arrive with the intention of going walking. But these are England's highest mountains and fastest changing weather conditions: to avoid being one of the 500 or so visitors who have to be rescued every year, this is the Lake District Mountain Rescue Service's advice for anyone heading on to the fells.

Preparation
Check the weather forecast and note when it begins to get dark, especially in winter. Charge your mobile phone. If you're walking alone, tell someone your route before setting off, and notify them of any changes.

Clothing
Wear suitable boots with adequate tread and ankle support, and colourful outdoor clothes – both windproof and waterproof. Take spare clothing: it's always colder on the tops.

Food & drink
Carry sweet snacks such as chocolate or dates, which restore energy quickly. Streams are generally safe to drink from, if they're fast-running over stony beds.

Equipment
Take a watch, map and compass (and make sure you can use them). If you have a GPS, know how to read your current position. Also carry a first-aid kit, a whistle, a torch and a spare battery.

Mobile phones
Don't rely solely on your phone; many areas have a poor signal or none at all. Be self-reliant and don't summon the Mountain Rescue Service at the first sign of trouble. Do call the service if someone is injured, or gets separated and you have made every effort to find them.

Emergencies
Turn back if conditions are against you. Report changes of plan to anyone expecting you. If you can't contact 999, make six whistle blasts or torch flashes and repeat every minute to signal an emergency. Don't allow anyone to become separated from the main group.

Calling the Mountain Rescue Service
Make a note of your location – a grid reference, if possible. Note the name, sex and age of the casualty and the nature of injury, the number of people in the party and the intended destination. Know the number of the mobile phone you're using. Dial 999 and ask for the Mountain Rescue; tell them you're in Cumbria. Don't change your position until you've been in contact with the rescue team.

Swinside Lodge

Grange Road, Newlands, CA12 5UE (017687 72948, www.swinsidelodge-hotel.co.uk). Rates £192-£232 double incl breakfast.
Since their arrival in 2009, Kath and Mike Bilton have been ringing the changes at this country house hotel at the foot of Catbells, about four miles from Keswick. As well as bringing the plumbing and heating into the 21st century, they have given the public rooms a thorough overhaul, and were working through the seven guest rooms at the time of writing. From the fresh fruit and flowers in the hall to the immaculate bedrooms, where your bed is turned back at night, the couple's background as Swiss-trained hoteliers shines through. It's all rather grown-up, with an elaborate four-course set menu every night, and no boisterous children allowed. Outside, the garden is alive with birds, and occasionally visited by red squirrels and deer. Make an early start and you could have Catbells to yourselves.

BORROWDALE

The B5289 runs down the eastern shore of Derwentwater and into the Borrowdale Valley, one of the best-loved corners of the Lake District. Quaint villages, ancient farmsteads and attractive whitewashed churches co-exist in easy harmony with a lovely stretch of the River Derwent, amid old oak forests and the enclosing fells. The valley unfurls from the village of Grange and the square mile of terrain that Wainwright considered the most beautiful in all Lakeland, through the Jaws of Borrowdale – the craggy gorge carved in the rock by the Derwent – and to the mountainous heart of the Lakes. Three enticing valleys, Watendlath, Stonethwaite and Seathwaite, make up Borrowdale.

Watendlath

Two-thirds of the way down Derwentwater, an easily missed minor road to the east climbs to the farm settlement of Watendlath and Watendlath Tarn ★. En route is Ashness Bridge, a small, charming humpback bridge over a rocky stream, with a delightful view back over Derwentwater and beyond to Skiddaw. It's so charming, in fact, that this is one of the most photographed views in the Lake District, reproduced on biscuit tins, coasters, playing cards, jigsaw puzzles and – of course – chocolate boxes. Climb a little higher along the road to the viewpoint at Surprise View for an even more dramatic vista along the length of Derwentwater and Bassenthwaite.

The single-track road narrows as it ascends to Watendlath, where it comes to an end. The car park here soon fills up; in any case, with such glorious scenery it's better to park at one of the lakeside parks or at Surprise View, then walk up. Watendlath might be a remote dead end on the map – and it didn't get a telephone line until the 1980s – but it was always too beguiling a spot to stay secret. Hugh Walpole chose it as the setting for *Judith Paris*, the second of his best-selling Cumbrian quartet, *The Herries Chronicles*. There's another packhorse bridge, a green and a farmhouse tearoom; a few rowing boats loll on the shore

Catbells. See p177.

of the tarn, waiting for a fly fisherman to tickle the trout. The whole place is owned, and lovingly cared for, by the National Trust.

Watendlath is also a significant crossroads for walkers, with routes branching out to High Seat for impressive views (via a potentially boggy trudge); to Blea Tarn, which feeds Watendlath Tarn and Beck; or for a variety of routes that lead down to Grange and Derwentwater.

Grange, Stonethwaite & Seatoller

Heading south from Derwentwater on the Borrowdale Road, you'll come to a road junction where a twin-arched bridge exploits a river island on the Derwent to hop across to Grange. It's a good-looking, albeit rather manicured, village, with plenty of holiday and retirement homes. An exploratory stroll should encompass visits to its two contrasting places of worship, the simple Methodist chapel and the flamboyant Holy Trinity Church, whose jagged crescents of black dogtooth decoration, set against the white ceiling, can make visitors feel as if they're being devoured by a succession of sharks. You can recover from

such excesses at the Grange Bridge Cottage Tea Gardens (*see right*), on the riverbank.

Recross the bridge and turn right for the Jaws of Borrowdale, a dreamy stretch where the Derwent, as clear as gin, winds between mossy woods, stony outcrops and high crags. Rocks and boulders are plentiful, but one has become a tourist attraction in its own right. Park in the National Trust's pay-and-display, in an old quarry entrance, and a short woodland walk will bring you to the Bowder Stone. Weighing some 2,000 tons, it's perched, seemingly precariously, on one corner; since it has balanced here since the Ice Age, it would be bad luck if it crushed you now. In 1789, the enterprising Joseph Pocklington enlarged a hole at the bottom and charged tourists to join hands through the stone, and also built the first 30-foot ladder to the top. You can still enjoy both experiences today – without charge.

As the valley opens up, you'll come to Rosthwaite – something of a social hub, with the Borrowdale Show and Borrowdale Fell Race by way of summer attractions. The Scafell Hotel (*see p186*) has an unpretentious walkers' bar and a more genteel

Ashness Bridge. See p180.

bar, both open year round. The Flock-In Tea Rooms (see below) is a favourite refreshment halt for ramblers in season. An enjoyable circular walk runs from here, up Bowdergate Gill to Watendlath Tarn and on to Dock Tarn, with its tiny island; it then takes in the exhilarating views across Stonethwaite valley, before the steep descent by Willygrass Gill.

Half a mile on, the road splits on either side of Borrowdale Fells. Along the smaller left-hand fork stands St Andrew's Church, with its slate roof and little bell tower. The pulpit came from Mardale Church, and was rescued when Mardale village was flooded to make way for Haweswater reservoir. Trend-setting fell runner Bob Graham (see p187) is buried here; so is Sarah Youdale, who lived to 100 and never left the valley. A third feature of the graveyard is Lucy's Loo, a spotless public convenience built by the fundraising efforts of churchwarden Lucy Bestley.

The road comes to an end at Stonethwaite, a classic hamlet with a red letterbox, a farm, the Peathouse Tearoom (see below) and the Langstrath Country Inn (see p186). Beyond, the Cumbria Way and the Coast to Coast footpaths run hand in hand, and there is sensational scenery between steep-sided canyons as Stonethwaite Beck dog-legs into the Langstrath Valley. Wild swimmers can leap into Black Moss Pot to cool off under the waterfall – although you may have rock climbers for company on its steep side. If you're leaving Borrowdale, longer-distance routes lead to Easedale Tarn and Grasmere, the Langdale Pikes or the Scafell massif.

Back at the fork in the road, follow the right-hand road to the village of Seatoller. This is the last stop before the steep climb out of Borrowdale for the Honister Pass and Buttermere. An old slate miners' village, Seatoller still has close connections with the Honister Slate Mine (see p157), which runs the information and bike hire centre at Seatoller Barn (017687 77714, closed Nov-Easter); the ancient Yew Tree Inn (see p185); and Honisters' Cottage (see p186) – a hang-the-expense romantic hideaway, next door to the inn.

Seathwaite & beyond

The third and final finger of the Borrowdale Valley, branching off just before Seatoller, sees the road end abruptly at a muddy farmyard at Seathwaite. Not to be confused with Seathwaite in the Duddon Valley, this Seathwaite is popularly cited as the wettest inhabited place in England. It averages 172 inches of rain a year, and on 19 November 2009 soaked up 12.28 inches in 24 hours – thought to be the rainiest day in Britain since records began in 1766. Seathwaite Farm serves teas in the summer, and is also the headquarters for Gnash Baxter and Michael Norbury of Keswick Mountain Adventures (017687 77832, www. keswickmountainadventures.co.uk), which offers guided walks, canoeing, rock climbing and ghyll scrambling. The pair also built the thrilling Via Ferrata (see p161) high up Fleetwith Pike.

Beyond lie some 30 square miles devoid of cars and people: the Lake District's biggest unpopulated

wilderness. This is the start and finish point for some of the region's ultimate ascents: Great Gable (2,949 feet), Pillar (2,927 feet), Scafell (3,162 feet) and the mighty Scafell Pike (3,210 feet). The Corridor route from here to Scafell Pike is longer than the route from Wasdale Head, but is generally considered more accessible. Either way, this is a long and demanding climb (allow eight to ten hours), not to be undertaken lightly or without expertise and proper preparation. The unforgiving Wainwright recommends a detour to Sprinkling Tarn, a lost and lonely tarn hidden deep in the fells, which has a rainfall record that exceeds even Seathwaite's. The final stretch to the summit of Scafell Pike is across a sea of boulders, and is uncomfortably rocky ('just as it should be', according to Wainwright). At the very top, add your rock to an ever-growing circular stone platform – the chimney pot on the roof of England.

Where to eat & drink

Out in the valleys, eating options are conventional. Hotel dining rooms, while dedicated to Cumbrian produce, are on the whole solid but unvarying; many rely on loyal customers who return year after year. The are no pubs in Borrowdale, only hotel bars.

In spring, though, a network of farms opens to provide tea, cake and light bites to weary walkers. They can be as remote as at Seathwaite Farm (see p187) and Low Snab Farm (see p179) in the Newlands Valley, or as sweet as the Peathouse (see below) and Flock-In (see below) in Borrowdale.

Flock-In Tea Rooms ★

Yew Tree Farm, Rosthwaite, CA12 5XB (017687 77675, www.borrowdaleherdwick.co.uk). Open Feb-Oct 10am-5pm Mon, Tue, Thur-Sun. Nov 10am-5pm Mon, Thur-Sun. No credit cards.
Now a gorgeous tearoom, the old stone barn in the yard at Yew Tree Farm (see p187) provides welcome respite for walkers. The 'men-ewe' to 'tempt-ewe' may amuse or exasperate; nonetheless, the friendly staff serve a lovely Herdwick pasty, stew or burger, along with cheese on toast with own-made chutney, generously sized scones, slices of carrot cake and buttered Borrowdale tea bread. Sit outside to admire the verdant views across the Borrowdale fells.

Grange Bridge Cottage Tea Gardens ★

Grange, CA12 5UQ (017687 77201).
Open Mar-Oct 10am-5pm daily.
This delightful cottage, built from local slate, is set in a riverside garden with views to Grange Crags opposite (there are tables inside too, in case of inclement weather). Lunch on carrot and coriander soup, sandwiches or one of the own-made daily specials, such as steak and ale pie, or drop by for a cup of tea and a wedge of cake.

Peathouse Tearoom

Stonethwaite, CA12 5XG (017687 77604).
Open varies, phone for details. No credit cards.
The little ice-cream sign in the tiny front garden is the first welcome sign of commercial life after ten miles slogging north on the Cumbria Way. Small but perfectly formed, Mrs

Jackson's cottage is generally open from 9.30am to 6pm in summer and on holiday weekends, and will also open for groups with advance warning. Order a slice of own-made fruit cake or local tea bread, or tuck into a bacon roll.

Shepherd's Café
High Lodore Farm, CA12 5UY (017687 77221).
Open Easter-Oct 9am-6pm daily. No credit cards.
Ever popular with rock climbers scaling Shepherd's Crag and walkers exploring the web of local footpaths, this place is a classic. Turn off the B5289 between the Lodore and Borrowdale Hotels for High Lodore Farm, where the café occupies one of the barns. It has indoor and outdoor seating, where customers can revive from their exertions with light meals, cakes and ice-cream, or power up for the climb ahead with a bumper breakfast (served until 11am).

Yew Tree Inn
Seatoller, CA12 5XN (017687 77230). Open Easter-Oct 10am-5pm Tue-Sun.
Although the Yew Tree's opening hours are more limited these days, it's still an enticing retreat after a blast on the fells. The interior is all beams and flagstone floors, while the beer garden skirts a bubbling beck that runs straight down from Honister Slate Mine, which owns and runs this 17th-century institution. The 'African by night' meals of the past have, sadly, gone, but staff still make a good job of soup, cakes, panini and hot drinks by the mug.

Where to stay
There may not be any superstar hotels here, but there's a rich mix of accommodation, from ever-improving country house hotels and honest pub bedrooms to some great farmhouse B&Bs, campsites and camping barns.

Borrowdale Gates Hotel
Grange, CA12 5UQ (017687 77204, www.borrowdale-gates.com). Rates £150-£240 double incl breakfast & dinner.
This place may have had its ups and downs with various changes of ownership, but it has always had devotees – and it's the pick of the three big, pricier hotels around Grange and the bottom of Derwentwater. A major refurbishment has left its 25 en suite rooms looking fresh and inviting, with muted colours and traditional home comforts (plump feather pillows, fresh flowers, fluffy towels). The setting is superb: under Maiden Moor on one side, and across to Grange Crags on the other. The restaurant plays it safe with fine local ingredients and classic combinations: pork belly with celeriac purée to start, perhaps, followed by braised spring lamb with minted peas and fresh broad beans.

Hollows Farm Camping
Grange, CA12 5UQ (017687 77298, www.hollows farm.co.uk). Rates B&B £64 double incl breakfast. Self-catering £250-£320 per week. Camping £6 per person.
Half a mile along a bumpy track running south from Grange village, and beautifully positioned beneath Maiden Moor, this working sheep farm is far removed from the madding crowd. The riverside Woodland field is a no-frills camping area with a toilet block and a cold water sink; showers are in a barn at the main farm, 400 yards away. The smaller

Honisters' Cottage. See p186.

Skiddaw. See p163.

second field caters for modest campervans. For 'glampers' there are two bell tents with lanterns, rugs and wood-burning stoves; book through Inside Out Camping (07791 184271, www.insideoutcamping.co.uk). There is also a cheery, one-bed self-catering cottage, and three B&B rooms in the 17th-century farmhouse.

Honisters' Cottage ★
Seatoller, CA12 5XN (019008 250111, www.honister-slate-mine.co.uk/honisters_cottage.asp). Rates £1,000-£1,200 per week.
Once a miner's cottage, Honisters' is now a romantic holiday hideaway. Its beams, sloping slate floors, tiny windows and heavyweight oak doors exude rustic charm, but are paired with a thoroughly modern design sensibility – and plenty of luxurious little extras. The kitchen/dining room features a fine old cast-iron range as well as the last word in shiny kitchen appliances; up the stone staircase are three double bedrooms with flatscreen TVs, iPod docks and glamorous bathrooms. The den, meanwhile, is equipped with more DVD, satellite TV and Xbox technology. There's a patio and garden at the back, on the banks of Hause Gill. The welcome hamper contains a bottle of bubbly and assorted Cumbrian specialities, running from local sausages and bacon to cake and handmade chocolates. If you still don't fancy cooking dinner, the owners will deliver a three-course meal to the door.

Langstrath Country Inn
Stonethwaite, CA12 5XG (017687 77239, www.thelangstrath.com). Rates £94-£114 double incl breakfast.
A seat outside the Langstrath Inn is inscribed 'In loving memory of a lovely day in Borrowdale', and memorable rambles across the fells are in plentiful supply; the inn stands by an intersection of the Cumbria Way and the Coast to Coast Walk. A whitewashed former miner's cottage, it has eight pleasantly furnished en suite bedrooms, a beamed residents' lounge and an inviting bar. Lunchtimes bring Welsh rarebit with fruit chutney or granary baguettes and potted brown shrimps; the evening menu might feature Herdwick lamb from Rosthwaite, Borrowdale trout, Newlands Valley sirloin steak and a couple of pleasingly inventive vegetarian options (bean, coriander and chilli cakes with spiced tomato chutney, perhaps, or lentil and tomato cottage pie).

Scafell Hotel
Rosthwaite, CA12 5XB (017687 77208, www.scafell. co.uk). Rates £76-£132 double incl breakfast.
Popular with walkers looking for somewhere a cut above the usual B&B, this is a friendly and well-run place. There are 23 comfortable bedrooms, public rooms full of old climbing photos and a cosy residents' bar. Eat informally in the bar, or sample the more elaborate restaurant menu.

One fell swoop

Just below Ashness Bridge, on the dead-end road to Watendlath, is a plaque to the memory of Keswick guesthouse owner Bob Graham. In 1932, Graham completed a circuit of 42 Lakeland fells, including the four highest peaks, in less than 24 hours. Wearing tennis shoes, long shorts and a pyjama top, he part-walked and part-ran through the day and night to cover 74 miles, starting and finishing at Keswick's Moot Hall. En route he climbed a total of 28,500 feet; just 500 feet less than Mount Everest

Graham – who modestly described himself as 'averagely fit' – set an extraordinary record that lasted for 28 years. He also gave his name to the Bob Graham Round, which has since seen ever more improbable feats by the Lake District's greatest fell runners. In 1982 Billy Bland completed the round in 13 hours and 53 minutes, while Mark Hartell scaled 77 peaks in 24 hours in 1997, setting a new record. Age seems to be no barrier: the Round was completed by 13-year-old Brian Squibb in 1992, and by 66-year-old Brian Leathley in 1998. In 2006 the most famous fell runner of all, Wasdale's Joss Naylor, managed 70 peaks in under 24 hours, at the age of 70.

Anyone thinking of having a go should probably give up their job and any significant others: the training schedule recommended by the Bob Graham Club (www.bobgrahamclub.org.uk), guardians of the event, involves up to six hours of running a day and weekly climbing levels of about 10,000 feet – that's the equivalent of Scafell Pike three times over. Alternatively, experience the challenge vicariously with Richard Askwith's book *Feet in the Clouds*, a brilliant account of the mad men and women of fell running.

The hotel runs weekend walking breaks that involve a full-day guided walk on Saturday, and a shorter ramble on Sunday; it also sponsors the 13-mile Borrowdale Fell Race, which sets off from the paddock opposite the hotel.

Seathwaite Farm
Seathwaite, CA12 5XJ (017687 77394). Rates £5 per person. No credit cards.
Home to a mountain rescue post and a very basic campsite, this sheep and cattle farm is a classic landmark for fell walkers. This is as far as the road – and creature comforts – go. If you don't fancy sharing a field with the Herdwicks as Seathwaite's infamous rains pour down, then you're welcome to doss down in the barn. There's also a much-loved tearoom, open during the summer.

Seatoller House
Seatoller, CA12 5XN (017687 77218, www.seatoller house.co.uk). Rates £122-£128 double incl breakfast & dinner.
This charming, 300-year-old farmhouse has been a guesthouse for more than a century. It is owned by Lake Hunts, which was set up in 1901 by three Cambridge students – including the illustrious historian GM Trevelyan. The purpose of the company was to administer the 'Man Hunt', a game of hare and hounds over the fells that was inspired by the man hunt in Robert Louis Stevenson's

Kidnapped; twice a year, its devotees still return to Seatoller House for a meet. There are ten nicely appointed rooms (with such names as Badger and Eagle) and a delightfully informal, hospitable atmosphere: make yourself a mug of tea, help yourself to a slice of cake, or crack open a beer from the honesty fridge. Supper is a no-choice four-course meal, with guests gathering around two large oak tables in the slate-floored dining room.

Yew Tree Farm
Rosthwaite, CA12 5XB (017687 77675, www. borrowdaleherdwick.co.uk). Rates £75 double incl breakfast. No credit cards.
This idyllic farm is the stuff of jaded urbanites' dreams. The Herdwick lamb raised here finds its way into the best restaurants, while the farmhouse B&B is fit for a king – or at least a prince, since Prince Charles stayed here for two nights when walking in the Lakes in 2003. He and his security men would have enjoyed a prim, whitewashed and cobblestone-walled cottage, bursting with carefully tended hanging baskets. Inside are three en suite bedrooms, with beautiful views and dainty, homely decor. 'Marvellously cosy,' was the prince's verdict. We also like the story of how landlady Hazel Relph told Kensington Palace that the B&B was fully booked, and he would have to wait until the rooms came free. Proper breakfasts set guests up for a day's fell-walking, and packed lunches can be provided.

Bassenthwaite

It's hard to fall head over heels in love with Bassenthwaite. Finding a way to the lakeshore, when so much of its four-mile length is privately owned, is tricky – and taking a boat on to its spacious waters still more so. It's also hard to ignore that both its shores are flanked by A-road thoroughfares. At the same time, it's easy to develop a lasting affection for Bassenthwaite, and its unique attributes. No other lake is dominated by so imposing a mountain as Skiddaw, England's fourth highest peak: rather like a portrait whose eyes seem to follow you around a room, it is a constant, inescapable presence. Nor does any other lake harbour such diverse and fascinating wildlife, including its magnificent ospreys, who return year after year. Here too is Mirehouse, one of the best-loved stately piles in all Lakeland, and the exquisitely located little church of St Bega's.

Bassenthwaite is also the starting point for some diverse excursions, and has some fine places to stay. In the Dash Valley, the waterfall of Whitewater Dash is a glorious sight, while Skiddaw House is one of the most isolated youth hostels in England. Then, of course, there is Skiddaw to scale. Whinlatter Forest Park is a vast adventure playground, with rugged mountain bike tracks and a high-wire adventure course set among its lofty conifers; it's also the passageway to the gentler delights of the Vale of Lorton.

Finally, to the north-west, is Cockermouth. The birthplace of William Wordsworth, it became synonymous with the devastating floods of 2009. With grit and hard graft, though, this delightful town is emerging from disaster, and has some excellent places to eat and drink.

BASSENTHWAITE & AROUND

The lake & western shore

The most northerly of the lakes, Bassenthwaite is also one of the biggest. Indeed, as pedants will soon tell you, it's the only true lake in the Lake District, since all the rest are 'meres' or 'waters'. Such definitions tend to be beside the point, however – as with the long-running debate about how many lakes there really are in the Lake District.

What's more important about Bassenthwaite is its marvellous wildlife, and the dominant presence of Skiddaw and, more negatively, the A66, which noisily follows the western shoreline for three miles. The road was built in the 1970s, much of it on the bed of the old Keswick railway line, and in the face of opposition from the National Park, the National Trust and no doubt the revolving remains of Wordsworth and Ruskin. The government overruled them all in the interests of improved access to a British Leyland bus plant in Workington, and a theory that it would reduce traffic pressure around Ambleside. The bus plant closed in 1993; the Ambleside traffic jams remain.

If you're arriving from Keswick and the south, it's worth dodging some of the A66 by following the backroad spur that starts at Braithwaite and leads through Thornthwaite village, home to assorted holiday cottages and Thornthwaite Galleries (017687 78248, www.thornthwaitegalleries.co.uk),

with has a changing exhibition of Lakeland arts and crafts, and a café. Towards the end of the spur is a white-painted rock in the cliff, named 'the Bishop' after the Bishop of Derry. En route to a boat for Ireland in 1793, the prelate stopped for refreshment at the nearby Swan Inn; suitably fortified, he offered to prove that God was on his side by riding his horse up the scree. Both steed and rider perished, and the rock has been religiously whitewashed by the pub landlord ever since – though now that the inn has been given over to self-catering, the rock's upkeep may be in doubt. Close by, another whitewashed boulder, 'the Clerk', is the supposed burial place of the bishop and his mount.

A footpath from here leads through Powterhow Wood and to the shoreline, via an underpass beneath the A66. A bird hide commands fine views of the southern end of the lake, where reeds and birch scrub provide a busy breeding ground for some 70 bird species. Even the most impatient amateur birdwatcher shouldn't have to wait long to see some interesting wildfowl, and the fortunate few may spot an otter or two.

Stroll along the shore to the two little promontories at Blackstock Point and Hursthole Point. There's no ignoring the thundering lorries on the A66, but you won't have to look at them during your waterfront picnic, or as you watch the ducks arrive at dusk.

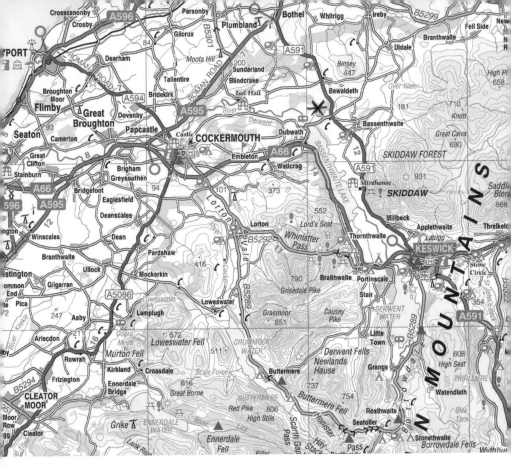

There's no further shoreline access until the upper north-west corner of the lake, as the A66 peels off to the west. At Dubwath Silver Meadows (017687 74785, www.bassenthwaite-reflections.co.uk), a 17-acre nature reserve has been developed, with a boardwalk and bird hide from which you might spot great crested grebes, red-breasted mergansers and golden-eye and tufted ducks.

The scheme is part of a lottery-funded regeneration project to improve the quality of the lake, prompted by a 2001 report revealing that sedimentation and high phosphate levels from agricultural overflow were damaging fish populations. It was too late for England's rarest fish, the vendace, whose last Lakeland home is now Derwentwater. Nevertheless, the lake is much improved. Both the River Derwent and Bassenthwaite Lake are Special Areas of Conservation (SACs) for Atlantic salmon and the much rarer sea lamprey. This prehistoric, eel-like creature, which lives by predatory bloodsucking of other fish, returns up the Derwent from the Atlantic to spawn and die, all well out of sight at the bottom of the lake.

Coarse and salmon fishing are permitted at Bassenthwaite, with day and month permits available from the National Park Information Centre (see p163) in Keswick. As for boating, the private Bassenthwaite Sailing Club (017687 76341, www.bassenthwaite-sc.org.uk) at Dubwath at the north-east end of the lake allows RYA members and affiliates to launch. No other craft are allowed on the water without a permit, and there are strictly enforced 'no boating' zones to protect wildlife habitats.

The other key attraction at this corner of the lake is the Pheasant Inn (see p191), happily bypassed by the A66 and an inviting retreat since well before the Bishop of Derry headed this way. It would take a stony soul to resist the chance to hunker down in its atmospheric old bar, or to stop for a pint in its gardens under Sale Fell.

After lunch, you can mix the sacred and the pagan with a walk to tiny St Barnabas' Church, and the remains of a nearby stone circle. The church has been hidden away in the woods in Cumbria's smallest parish, Setmurthy, since 1225; behind it, at the top of Elva Hill, are 15 stones. They lie around without much grandeur, leaving the circle sadly incomplete. As ever, lift up your eyes to see the mighty Skiddaw watching over the scene.

The village & eastern shore

At the time of writing, flood damage to the River Derwent crossings at Ouse Bridge and Isel Bridge at the northern end of Bassenthwaite had temporarily made a circuit of the lake difficult without major detours. Once across, the top of the lake is dominated by Armathwaite Hall (*see p193*), the biggest and grandest hotel in the northern lakes. It comports itself like a Scottish castle, but don't be intimidated by the length of the drive and the mounted tiger heads; staff are gracious about serving cups of tea, and letting visitors stroll down the lawns to the lakeside. For child-friendly fun, Trotters World (*see p195*) is just around the corner.

Rather than standing directly on the lake, Bassenthwaite village is set a mile inland. It has an attractive green, a row of limes and the tumbling Chapel Beck. The Sun Inn (017687 76439), oak-beamed and whitewashed in time-honoured Lakeland fashion, serves Jennings Ale from Cockermouth, along with solid bar meals.

For a spectacular excursion into the Back o' Skiddaw wilderness, head into the remote Dash Valley beneath Skiddaw Forest – not a forest, in fact, but an old hunting ground. A five-mile round hike will take you past Dead Crags to one of the Lake District's most sensational waterfalls, Whitewater Dash (aka Dash Falls), which lives up to its name with a 246-foot drop over a succession of falls. Three miles from the nearest road is Skiddaw House (*see p193*), a gloriously isolated youth hostel set on a crossroads of various long-distance walking routes, including a back route up Skiddaw.

The only way down the eastern shore of Bassenthwaite is via the A591 between Carlisle and Keswick, under the shadow of Skiddaw. It's not as speedy as the A66, but busy enough. One of the nicest detours is down to Scarness, where walkers can join a lakeside footpath called the Allerdale Ramble. It will take you from Scarness Bay and round a promontory with a cut inland before approaching Church Bay, and the exquisite Norman church of St Bega's ★, which has stood alone beside the lake for more than 900 years. Parishioners used to travel to church by boat, and even today need to leave their cars in the lane and walk through two fields, amid the sheep. The church's haunting, lonely beauty inspired Alfred Lord Tennyson, and the moonlit chapel that appears in the opening lines of his epic *Morte d'Arthur*.

Tennyson was staying at Mirehouse (*see p194*), a short stroll away, which is one of the Lake District's least stuffy and most enjoyable stately homes. It's owned by the Speddings, who have lived here for some 200 years; one of the family may well be at hand to greet you in the hall. A pianist plays in the music room, and the drawing rooms and libraries are a delight to explore. There are Victorian games to keep children amused, and adventure playgrounds and nature trails outside.

Across the road is the Old Sawmill Tearooms (*see right*), beneath Dodd Wood. In April, there's

a collective holding of breath as everyone wonders whether the ospreys, which arrived in 1997 and have returned every year since, will reappear once again. The pair that summer here are the first to nest in the Lake District for 155 years. The Osprey Viewpoint (*see p194*) is a ten-minute walk though the woods from the tearoom's car park. Even when there are no ospreys in residence, it's worth taking one of the trails through the trees – easy walks of between one and three miles to Sandbeg Gill, Skillbeck, the Douglas fir trail or to Dodd summit (1,647 feet), with its fine outlook over Bassenthwaite Lake.

More demanding is Dodd's very big brother, Skiddaw, the ever-present guardian of Keswick and Bassenthwaite. At 3,054 feet, it's England's fourth highest mountain. Climbing on from Dodd, rejoin the Allerdale Ramble path past little Carl Side Tarn before the final straight, steep finish to the summit plateau. Other routes begin at Underskiddaw, from Millbeck or High Side. The most popular ascent is the so-called 'tourist route' starting from Keswick, with parking at Gale Road car park. Or, more virtuously, start at Keswick's old railway station, going first via Latrigg and

then embarking on the easy, but unrelenting, climb to Skiddaw's summit. In 1815 William Wordsworth and Robert Southey climbed it with their families and a cauldron of rum punch to celebrate the victory at Waterloo. The modern-day summit greets climbers with the clutter of a trig point, a wind shelter, a viewfinder erected in 1977 to mark the Queen's Silver Jubilee, the occasional hang-glider, and truly fantastic views over the northern lakes and fells.

Where to eat & drink

Around Bassenthwaite, you're more likely to refuel in a leafy woodland setting than on a lakeside terrace, unless you assemble a picnic. Although there are worthy tearooms in Dodd Wood and Whinlatter Forest, there are no pubs or restaurants by the water – unless you count the handsome Pheasant Inn (*see right*), which is screened from the lake by trees. Still, it's always worth a pilgrimage to sit in its atmospheric old bar. For sheer pomp and circumstance, the Armathwaite Hotel (*see p193*) is a must for afternoon tea.

Old Sawmill Tearooms
Mirehouse, CA12 4QE (017687 74317, www.theold sawmill.co.uk). Open Mar-Oct 9am-5pm daily. Nov 9am-5pm Sat, Sun.
A wood-burning stove warms this atmospheric building of Cumbrian slate, while faded old photos and paraphernalia act as reminders of its days as a sawmill. It's handy for the Osprey Viewpoint and walks in Dodd Wood – especially after a descent from Skiddaw. Soups, sandwiches, quiche, salads and cakes are all made on the premises.

Pheasant Inn ★
Bassenthwaite Lake, CA13 9YE (017687 76234, www.the-pheasant.co.uk). Open 11.30am-2.30pm, 5.30-10.30pm Mon-Thur; 11.30am-2.30pm, 5.30-11pm Fri, Sat; noon-2.30pm, 6-10.30pm Sun. Lunch served noon-2.30pm Mon-Sat. Dinner served 5.30-10.30pm Mon-Sat, 6-10.30pm Sun.
A narrow corridor, lined with historic pictures, leads to the Pheasant's panelled tap room, where rows of malt bottles gleam behind the bar. Bag a settle with a frayed cushion and order potted Flookburgh shrimp, Cumberland sausage in red wine or a robust plate of ham, egg and chips. On summer days, the sunny lounge and garden open for lunch or afternoon tea (sandwiches, cakes and scones served with

Bassenthwaite. See p188.

Pheasant Inn. See p191.

jam and Cumberland rum butter). The dining room is more formal, with a smart three- or four-course menu, but can't compete with the patina of the bar. If you're staying over, there's a parquet-floored lounge and 15 well-appointed bedrooms (£146-£156 double incl breakfast) with quilted bedspreads and antiques. The more expensive rooms have half-tester beds and bigger bathrooms. Dog owners can book one of the garden rooms. Guests can also use the spa at Armathwaithe Hall.

Where to stay

For the best of Bassenthwaite Lake, easy access to Keswick's shops and museums, and the frisson of being on the slopes of Skiddaw, the interlinked hamlets of Underskiddaw have the best selection of upmarket accommodation. The Pheasant Inn (*see p191*) also has rooms.

Armathwaite Hall ★

Bassenthwaite Lake, CA12 4RE (017687 76551, www.armathwaite-hall.com). Rates £300-£370 double incl breakfast & dinner.
Those in search of super-sized grandeur should look no further than the 42-bedroom castellated Victorian pile of Armathwaite Hall. Forget understatement: the stuffed animal heads loftily surveying the hall are not fox or even deer from the hotel's 400-acre deer park, but buffalo, elk and big game from Africa, while the Victorian oils of Lakeland scenes are the size of double beds. The table d'hôte six-course dinner, meanwhile, is a feast of brandy cream, tians and tuile parcels. There's a sleek spa with a 16m infinity pool, a thermal suite and sauna, and much pampering with walnut oils, red algae and collagen masks. After a gym workout, relax in the outdoor hot tub, stroll down to the lakeside or play a frame of snooker in the sedate billiards room. Afternoon tea, served on squashy sofas in the lounge or on the gently sloping lawns, is a delight, with finger sandwiches, miniature cakes and scones arrayed on a tiered cake stand, accompanied by jam and clotted cream, a silver teapot and delicate bone china. Before booking, it's worth checking the hotel isn't hosting any big functions.

Dancing Beck

Millbeck, Underskiddaw, CA12 4PZ (017687 74781, www.dancingbeck.co.uk). Rates £72 double incl breakfast. No credit cards.
Dating from 1850, this brick-built Victorian schoolhouse has retained a pleasingly solid, well-turned out air. It's a mile from Bassenthwaite Lake and two miles from Keswick, with trails leading off into the surrounding forests. There are three nicely appointed bedrooms, a residents' lounge and a lovely garden, summerhouse and patio, where the western fells are spread out before you, and Skiddaw rises inexorably behind.

The Dash ★

Dash Valley, CA12 4QX (01697 371217, www. thedash.co.uk). Rates £570-£1,150 per week. No credit cards.
There are no neighbours, no shops and no pub close at hand at this thoroughly escapist self-catering property – just Whitewater Dash waterfall, sheep and the fells for company. Instead of a cottage or barn conversion, this is a Grade II-listed, 16th-century farmhouse, kitted out with sweetly

rustic antiques and modern essentials. There are three double bedrooms, a homely kitchen with an Aga, a sitting room with an open fire, and a dining room. Outside , the walled garden has a view to the waterfall that Wainwright reckoned to be Lakeland's finest. Kennelling is provided for dogs, and stabling can be arranged for visiting horses.

Highside Farm

Bassenthwaite Lake, CA12 4QG (017687 76952, www.highside.co.uk). Rates £70-£100 double incl breakfast. No credit cards.
Behind a 17th-century farmhouse exterior lies a decidedly luxurious B&B. Highside Farm is set just off the A591, a mile south of Bassenthwaite village, in an enviably elevated position: outside, 400 acres of traditional fell farmland spread from the foot of Ullock Pike almost to the north-eastern shore of Bassenthwaite. Downstairs, an inglenook fireplace and sturdy beams create a traditional atmosphere; upstairs, bedrooms combine big brass beds, tactile throws and cushions and charming attention to detail (home-made biscuits, binoculars for osprey-spotting) to great effect.

Millbeck Towers

Millbeck, Underskiddaw, CA12 4PS (0844 800 2070, www.nationaltrustcottages.co.uk). Rates £794-£2,709 per week.
This beautiful 18th-century house looks more like a German castle than the carding mill it once was. It has fairytale towers and turrets, enormous rooms and huge, curving bay windows. As with all National Trust holiday lets, it has been lovingly restored, and contains plenty of period furniture and detailing. The house sleeps 12 in six bedrooms; convene for a pre-dinner sherry in the gracious sitting room, or stroll the idyllic gardens, with their streams and fenced-off pond.

Ormathwaite Hall & Coach House

Ormathwaite, Underskiddaw, CA12 4PQ (017683 51875, www.ormathwaitehall.co.uk). Rates Ormthwaite Hall £1,500-£2,900 per week. Coach House £850-£1,650 per week. No credit cards.
A grand Georgian mansion at the foot of Skiddaw, the hall has three acres of gardens and a suitably noble aspect, with long-distance views to the Borrowdale Fells. Inside is country house heaven, with antiques, an Aga and some splendid art deco features. The building once belonged to scientist William Brownrigg, who in 1771 decanted olive oil into Derwentwater to demonstrate the theory of pouring oil on troubled waters. The main house offers superior self-catering for larger groups, with four doubles, one twin and a single. The stately looking Coach House has three doubles, along with a sofa bed in the lounge.

Skiddaw House Youth Hostel ★

Bassenthwaite, CA12 4QX (07747 174293, www.skiddawhouse.co.uk). Rates £16 adult. No credit cards.
Built for the gamekeeper of Cockermouth Castle as a grouse shooting lodge, then used as shepherd's cottage, this wonderfully isolated hostel offers peace, tranquillity and basic accommodation on the Cumbria Way. According to the YHA it's the highest (1,550 feet) and one of the most remote hostels in England; it's three miles beyond the end of the road at Whitewater Dash, so access is by bike or on foot. For star-filled night skies or a dawn walk to Skiddaw's summit, it's unbeatable. It sleeps 15 in ultra-basic, bothy-

Places to visit

BASSENTHWAITE & AROUND

Mirehouse ★

Underskiddaw, CA12 4QE (017687 72287, www.mirehouse.com). Open Aug 2-5pm Wed, Fri, Sat. Apr-July, Sept, Oct 2-5pm Wed, Sat. Admission House & Gardens £6.50; free-£3 reductions; £18 family. Gardens only £3; free-£1.50 reductions.
In comparison with Holker Hall or Muncaster Castle, Mirehouse may be a minor stately home, but then size isn't everything. With its relaxed demeanour, easy charm and 3,000 acres, stretching from Bassenthwaite's shore to Dodd Wood, this 17th-century manor house is many people's favourite Lakeland historic house. It has belonged to the Speddings since 1802; indeed, they still live on the premises. John Spedding was at school with Wordsworth, and the family amassed an impressive collection of literary and artistic friends, including Coleridge, Southey, Thomas Carlyle and John Constable. Tennyson, Wordsworth's successor as poet laureate, often stayed and wrote here, and even spent part of his honeymoon at Mirehouse. The house's rich heritage includes letters from Southey and Wordsworth, a drawing of Tennyson and a painting of Heath House by Constable; best of all, though, is the lack of fussy, keep-your-distance ropes. Children can ride the Victorian rocking horse, put the dolls in the cradle, climb into the hip bath, write on a slate and ring the servants' bells in the glorious 'bell passage' (in case the maids couldn't read, each bell sounded a different note). In Mirehouse's heyday, 25 to 30 staff looked after the family.

A one-mile circular walk through the gardens takes in woodland, the lake shore and lovely St Bega's Church. Elsewhere in the grounds, four play areas have been established; Squirrel Island has a tyre swing for under-11s, while the Forest Hazard Course for teenagers has an assault course of chain bridges, scramble nets and enough water in the beck for a serious soaking.

Osprey Viewpoint ★

Dodd Wood, CA12 4QE (017687 78469, www.ospreywatch.co.uk). Open Apr-Aug 10.30am-5pm daily. Admission free.
One day in April 1997, an osprey swooped from the sky, as if from nowhere, and flew over Bassenthwaite Lake – the first sighting in the Lake District in living memory. These enormous, majestic birds, which have a wingspan of up to five feet, winter in Africa, then return to the same nest to breed each spring. They were hunted to extinction by the 1840s in England, and by 1916 in Scotland; only in the '50s did they begin to recolonise Scotland. To encourage ospreys to return and breed in the Lakes, the Osprey Partnership erected a nesting platform in the woods above Bassenthwaite, and in 2001 a pair arrived and raised one chick – the first in 150 years. They've returned each subsequent spring, though it's never guaranteed. Ospreys usually lay two to three eggs between mid April and mid May, which then take around six weeks to hatch. The female adult leaves the nest in late summer, while the male teaches the young how to fish. By the end of August, all have made the long migration south for the winter.

During the birds' summer stay, the higher and lower viewpoints in Dodd Wood are open daily. They're three miles north of Keswick on the A591, and a ten-minute walk from the car park at the Old Sawmill Tearooms (see p191). Telescopes allow visitors to spy on the birds at their nest and fishing over the lake; bring your own binoculars, too, and bear in mind that visibility is often best in the morning. There are few more compelling sights in nature than a white-bodied osprey swooping to take a fish, and bearing it off in its talons.

The Osprey Bus runs at weekends, and daily in summer, from Keswick bus station; it travels round the lake, with stops at the Osprey Viewpoint and Whinlatter Visitor Centre (see p196), where there's an information point and a webcam.

Mirehouse

Trotters World of Animals

Coalbeck Farm, Bassenthwaite, CA12 4RD (017687 76239, www.trottersworld.com). Open Summer 10am-5pm daily. Winter 10am-dusk daily. Admission £7.50; free-£6.50 reductions.

This small, child-friendly zoo is just off the A591, at the top end of Bassenthwaite Lake: its owners, the Graves family, also run the adjoining Armathwaite Hotel. It's home to Odin, the only Canadian lynx in the UK, and Kali, a playful, plucky little Asian fishing cat. The family of mandrills, with their strange cheek pouches, are another highlight, as are the treetop-swinging, fast-moving gibbons. Activities include pony rides, animal handling sessions and daily hawk and falconry displays; indoor and outdoor play areas round off an enjoyable day out.

COCKERMOUTH

Castlegate House Gallery

Castlegate, CA13 9HA (01900 822149 www. castlegatehouse.co.uk). Open 10.30am-5pm Mon, Fri, Sat. Admission free.

Occupying a listed house with a secret garden hidden away behind Castlegate, this excellent commercial gallery specialises in works by established – and predominantly northern – artists. Winifred Nicholson, Elisabeth Frink, LS Lowry and Peter Quinn (who paints the buildings of Cockermouth) are among the leading lights. Owner Chris Wadsworth puts on a new exhibition each month, showcasing sculpture, jewellery and ceramics as well as paintings.

Jennings Brewery

Brewery Lane, Cockermouth, CA13 9NE (0845 129 7190, www.jenningsbrewery.co.uk). Open Shop July, Aug 10am-4pm daily. Jan-June, Sept-Dec 10am-4pm Mon-Sat. Tours vary, phone for details. Admission Tours £6; £3 reductions.

From humble, home-brewed beginnings in Lorton village in 1828, Jennings became a big player in the Cumbria

brewery scene, moving to its current riverside location next to Cockermouth Castle in 1874. It's now owned by Marston's, but still makes its beer the old-fashioned way. You can taste the results at the end of the guided tour; as well as its four main ales, Jennings has an array of seasonal ales including the wonderfully named Cross Buttock (a well-known Cumbrian wrestling throw) and the Wordsworth-inspired Golden Host.

Wordsworth House ★

Main Street, CA13 9RX (01900 824805, www.wordsworthhouse.org.uk). Open Mar-Oct 11am-5pm (last entry 4pm) Mon-Wed, Thur (school hols only), Sun. Admission £6.20; free-£3.10 reductions; £15.50 family.

William Wordsworth's father was the local agent for the Lowthers when they were Cumbria's most important landowners, so it's no surprise that the house where the poet was born in 1770 is rather special. Indeed, with its classical portico, sash windows and Main Street location, it's the most prominent house in town. The young Wordsworth lived here with his four brothers and sisters until the age of eight, when his mother died. He was sent to the Grammar School in Hawkshead (*see p46*), returning in the holidays; when his father died five years later, he left Cockermouth for good.

The National Trust present the property as an entertaining hands-on experience rather than a stuffy museum, recreating the interior as it would have been in 1777. A costume-clad cook invites visitors to roll the pastry, try the bellows in the stove, wash up with soft soap or sweep the kitchen floor. You can write a letter with a quill pen (William the manservant will put a seal on it), open drawers, play the harpsichord and practise with a whip and top, while special events might include ghost stories beside the kitchen range, demonstrations of Georgian cooking and harpsichord recitals. Severely damaged by the floods of 2009, the garden and lower floors have since been repaired and replanted, while the cellars now host an exhibition about the flood.

Whinlatter Forest

style dorms. A shop sells a few supplies for evening meals, though no fresh food, and there's a simple, help-yourself breakfast for a modest extra charge. It's staffed for most of the year, but call first to be sure of a place. From November to January, only group bookings are taken.

WHINLATTER PASS & THE VALE OF LORTON

From Braithwaite, west of Keswick, the B5292 runs up to the Whinlatter Pass through the Whinlatter Forest before pushing on to the Vale of Lorton. Here it splits for Cockermouth to the north, and Loweswater to the south.

At 1,043 feet, the Whinlatter Pass is modest by Lake District standards (certainly compared to the dramatic passes of Hardknott, Honister and Kirkstone); being enclosed by a 100-year-old conifer plantation also reduces the drama. But take a breather on the way up at the Noble Knott car park and drink in an alping view looking back down over the forest to Skiddaw, Dodd and Bassenthwaite Lake. Two waymarked circular walks up Grisedale Pike start here, or from the Revelin Moss car park.

The Whinlatter Forest Park Visitor Centre (017687 78469, www.forestry.gov.uk) at the top of the pass houses Siskins Café (*see right*) and a gift shop. The actively inclined can hire mountain bikes (*see p201*) and attempt the two purpose-built trails in the forest. The 11-mile Altura is the more technical trail, for experienced riders, graded red (difficult) with some black (severe) stages. The five-mile Quercus is moderate, with the opportunity to bypass some of the tougher sections. There are also 14 miles of walking trails, including a couple of gentler options for children.

A two-mile trek leads to Spout Force, which hurtles over a cliff for a straight, 40-foot drop into a rocky pool. There's an orienteering course and a Go Ape! high-wire course (*see p201*) through the treetops. You may not be lucky enough to spot the resident roe deer or badger, but there are red squirrels about, and between April and September the information centre has a live webcam link to the Osprey Viewpoint in Dodd Wood, on the opposite side of the lake.

As you leave the forest and head down the western side of the Whinlatter Pass, you enter the Vale of Lorton. Here, the landscape changes from forest to farmland, descending from moorland fells and into a lush, green valley of drystone walls and grazing sheep. At the bottom, the meandering River Cocker once supplied power to the local flour and flax mills. The sole reminder of the flood devastation it caused in the winter of 2009 are the stones from the riverbed that now scatter the adjoining fields.

High and Low Lorton are two prosperous-looking villages that stand side by side. Low Lorton has a superior dining pub in the Wheatsheaf Inn (*see below*), with a low-key caravan park and campsite looking out to Kirk Fell. Lorton Hall, with its 15th-century pele tower, is privately owned, but its semi-detached other half, Winder Hall (*see p198*) is a 16th-century manor house with four-poster beds, historic fireplaces and elegant dinners. More modest in its origins, but equally stylish, is New House Farm (*see p198*). In summer, lunches and afternoon teas are served in the converted cow byre next door, with views to Watching Crag, Wilderness Woods and Red How Crags. Beyond, the road heads on to Loweswater and Crummock Water, as the rising backdrop of Mellbreak, High Stile and Red Pike announces the end of Lorton's elysian vale, and the return of the Lake District's seriously big lakes and mountains.

Where to eat & drink

The dining room at Winder Hall (*see p198*) is open to non-residents.

Cottage in the Wood ★
Whinlatter Forest, CA12 5TW (017687 78409, www.thecottageinthewood.co.uk). Closed Jan. Lunch served noon-2.30pm, dinner served 6.30-9pm Tue-Sat.
Despite the forest surrounds of this aptly named restaurant with rooms, on the Bassenthwaite side of Whinlatter Pass, the ever-present Skiddaw fills the dining room windows. It's an engaging woodland hideaway, whose kitchen favours prime Cumbrian produce. Fish is landed at Maryport, while local farms supply fell lamb, Galloway beef and traditional Saddleback and Old Spot pork. Blackberries, bilberries, nettles and wild garlic add a Lakeland touch. The ten rooms (£96-£130 double incl breakfast) run from standard doubles to a deluxe attic with a skylight to the stars; stay during fungi season and there might be wild Whinlatter Forest mushrooms to accompany your sourdough toast. If not, sample the local damson jam.

Siskins Café
Whinlatter Forest Park, CA12 5TW (017687 78410, www.forestry.gov.uk). Open Apr-Oct 10am-5pm daily. Nov-Mar 10am-4.30pm Mon-Fri; 10am-5pm Sat, Sun.
The alpine feel of the setting at the top of the Whinlatter Pass doesn't quite stretch to raclette and gluhwein, although the soups, sandwiches and snacks includes some interesting cakes, such as beetroot or parsnip and lemon. Eat on the balcony, amid the mountains and the scent of Douglas firs.

Wheatsheaf Inn
Low Lorton, CA13 9UW (01900 85199 www.wheatsheaf innlorton.co.uk). Open noon-11pm daily. Lunch served noon-3pm Sat. Dinner served 6-8.30pm Mon-Sat. Food served noon-8.30pm Sun.
In the village where the Jennings Brewery was founded, this is, unsurprisingly, a Jennings pub (albeit one with guest beers too). Food is the best of British: beef and ale pie, slow-cooked lamb and whole Borrowdale trout. Sunny afternoons see everyone gathering around the picnic tables at the back, under Kirk Fell. Out of season, a wood-burning stove and cosy checked curtains warm up a cheery mix of locals, children, dogs and campers – behind the pub, a campsite, a field of static caravans and space for ten tourers are screened by firs (tents £6 per person, statics £140-£400 per week).

Squirrelled away

In Beatrix Potter's timeless tale, the naughty, russet-hued Squirrel Nutkin and his 'great many cousins' sailed across a lake – Derwentwater – on rafts made from twigs, using their tails as sails. When the story was first published in 1903, the red squirrel population was thriving; today it's in serious decline, and most children reading the story will probably never have seen a red squirrel.

A native species, red squirrels (*Sciurus vulgaris*) have been resident in Britain since the end of the Ice Age. In the late 19th century grey squirrels (*Sciurus carolinensis*) were brought over from the States, and the number of reds began to dwindle; now there are reckoned to be two and a half million grey squirrels in the UK, and fewer than 160,000 reds. It was thought the bigger, brutish grey variety competed with the red for food; recently, ecologists from the University of Stirling have suggested that a virus carried by the greys may be equally to blame. Greys have become immune to squirrel pox virus (parapoxvirus), but it's deadly to reds.

The Forestry Commission is working on various long-term conservation strategies, and the Lake District remains one of the few remaining strongholds for reds in England. Smaller than greys, with chesnut fur and long tufts on their ears, they are charming creatures and look remarkably like Beatrix Potter's illustrations. Red squirrels don't hibernate, and can often be spotted in woods during the day, foraging for seeds, nuts, berries, lichen and insects. You have a decent chance of spotting one if you're walking through Dodd Wood and Whinlatter Forest Park, near Keswick, the Threlkeld Railway footpath, the forests around Thirlmere, or at Holme Wood, Loweswater and Greystoke Forest near Penrith. And, of course, every self-respecting B&B will tell you that red squirrels visit their garden, so keep an eye out over breakfast.

For more information, visit the websites of the Save our Squirrels campaign (www.saveour squirrels.org), the Red Squirrel Survival Trust (www.rsst.org.uk) or the Penrith & District Red Squirrel Group (www.penrithredsquirrels.org.uk).

Castlegate House Gallery. See p195.

FIVE FILM LOCATIONS

Unsurprisingly, the Lake District's soaring hills, dramatic vistas and photogenic lakes have made it a prime filming location. All manner of cinematic and TV gems have been shot here over the years, from Ken Russell's *The Rainbow* to Karel Reisz's *The French Lieutenant's Woman*. Here are five of the best-known productions.

The Lakes (1997-99)

Somewhat controversial in its day, this BBC drama series brought a heady blend of sex, religion and murder to a Lakeland holiday hotel. Penned by Jimmy '*Cracker*' McGovern and starring John Simm, its key filming locations included the former Ullswater Hotel (now the Inn on the Lake; *see p224*), Patterdale, Glenridding and Ullswater itself.

Miss Potter (2006)

The Beatrix Potter phenomenon was booming even before this big-budget biopic; in its aftermath, the hordes of visiting fans redoubled. Renée Zellweger took the title role, while Ewan McGregor stepped in as her publisher and love interest, Norman Warne. Yew Tree Farm (*see p68*) in Coniston (once owned by Potter) stood in for her home, Hill Top, with Tarn Hows, Loughrigg Tarn, Derwentwater and Loweswater also appearing. The Jefferson rum office in Whitehaven's Rum Story (*see p146*) became the office of the man Potter eventually married, solicitor William Heelis.

Postman Pat (1981-)

The fictional village of Greendale in the *Postman Pat* animated television series was inspired by locations around author John Cunliffe's home in Kendal. The post office where Mrs Goggins sorts the letters is at Beast Banks; although it's now closed, there's a red plaque outside. The quiet valleys of Kentmere and the little arched bridge at Long Sleddale are also identifiable in the cartoon.

Where to stay

For stylish rooms and some superlative views, check in to the Cottage in the Wood (*see p197*).

New House Farm ★

Lorton, CA13 9UU (01900 85404, mobile 07841 159818, www.newhouse-farm.com). Rates £120-£170 double incl breakfast.
This archetypal, Grade II-listed Lakes farmhouse matches period features such as oak beams and flagged floors with rich fabrics, crisp linens and gorgeous bathrooms. The five double bedrooms are individually decorated – and for good measure, the owner cooks excellent Cumbrian dinners, exemplified by Silloth potted shrimps, pheasant casserole or salmon from the river Cocker, with puddings such as spotted dick and custard to finish. The lovely garden has a hot tub in which to soothe aching limbs and to meditate on the surrounding fells.

Winder Hall Country House

Low Lorton, CA13 9UP (01900 85107, www.winderhall. co.uk). Rates B&B £115-£185 double incl breakfast. Self-catering £650-£750 per week.
The walled-off neighbour to the 16th-century manor house and pele tower next door, this gorgeous old house still offers its guests plenty of country manor gravitas, and an impressive gravelled drive. The seven guestrooms are elegantly but relatively simply kitted out; Greystones has

window seats overlooking the walled garden and a Georgian four-poster bed, while Fellbarrow is tucked away in the old servants' quarters. Staff are delightfully welcoming, and the sauna and hot tub by the summerhouse are perfect for post-walk unwinding. The owners rear their own pigs and keep free-range hens for guests' breakfast bacon and eggs, and the kitchen has Slow Food and Fairtrade affiliations: dinner (open to non-residents) brings top-notch grub such as carpaccio of beef with Lorton beetroot, local lamb with minty pesto and ginger sponge with custard. It's also a lovely stop for afternoon tea, and a favourite with cyclists putting off the climb up Whinlatter Pass. Adjacent to the main drive, Packhorse Cottage (www.packhorse-cottage.co.uk) provides self-catering accommodation for five.

COCKERMOUTH

Whether you arrive from the top of Bassenthwaite Lake on the A66 or follow the River Cocker in from the Vale of Lorton, it's no hardship to step outside the National Park to explore the charming market town of Cockermouth. It has a broad main drag of attractive Georgian houses, many backed by burgage plots (long, narrow gardens), for which it was awarded 'gem town' status by the British Council for Archaeology. More gems can be found among its independent outlets: bookshops, toy and antique shops, old-fashioned hardware stores, a Monday market and an excellent gallery specialising in contemporary art.

Cockermouth has always been hard-working as well as good-looking, with a mill town history (cotton, linen, wool and leather) and a clutch of famous sons and daughters. William and Dorothy Wordsworth were born here, and their home on Main Street, Wordsworth House (*see p195*) conveys a vivid impression of bourgeois life in the late 18th century. Fletcher Christian, the mutineer on the *Bounty*, and John Dalton, the physicist who developed the atomic theory of matter, were also born nearby.

Cockermouth made headlines on 19 November 2009, when, after days of heavy rainfall, the Cocker and Derwent rivers overflowed. The town was engulfed in eight feet of floodwater: thousands were affected, houses made uninhabitable, businesses ruined and four bridges collapsed, wrecking the town's lifelines. Main Street bore the brunt. The staff at Wordsworth House rescued artefacts until the police told them it was too dangerous to continue, and householders had to be pulled from upstairs windows. Downstream, a policeman was swept to his death. When the waters finally subsided, every building in the centre was filled with stinking brown sludge, and the town was left heartbroken.

Scars remain, but the spirit of recovery has been impressive. Mitchell's the auctioneers threw open a warehouse so that local shops could keep trading; Wordsworth House reopened with a flood exhibition in its cleaned-up cellars. The stalwart Trout Hotel (*see p201*) was devastated, but should be up and running for drinks on the terrace. Jennings Brewery (*see p195*) is brewing

Swallows and Amazons (1974)
Arthur Ransome was inspired to write his wholesome, waterborne children's adventure series after spending a summer with the Altounyan family on the Coniston shoreline; the children sailed on the lake in two dinghies, *Swallow* and *Mavis*, and the germ of an idea was born. The book's classic status was reinforced by the 1974 film, which starred Virginia McKenna and Ronald Fraser as the grown-ups, and was partly filmed at Bank Ground Farm, which was where the Altounyans stayed. The film's cast kipped here too; so can you, as it's been a guesthouse for over 50 years (*see p66*).

Withnail & I (1986)
Bruce Robinson's cult classic sees two dissolute, out-of-work actors embarking on a rainy holiday in the Lake District. Uncle Monty's decrepit holiday cottage, Crow Crag, is in reality Sleddale Hall (*see p240*), in the aptly named Wet Sweddale. Semi-derelict for years, it was recently bought by a Kent architect and *Withnail* fan, who has pledged to restore it in keeping with the spirit of the film. For true devotees, the red telephone box from which Withnail rings his agent is in the nearby village of Bampton.

Bank Ground Farm

Quince & Medlar

again, and has restarted its twice-daily tours with free samples. On its doorstep is the Bitter End (*see below*), a pub and bistro that claims to be Cumbria's smallest brewery. The restaurants and bars of pedestrianised Market Place are back in business.

Up the hill from Market Place, Castlegate escaped the flood. The 13th-century Cockermouth Castle at the top is privately owned, and only open to the public on high days and holidays, when the vaulted underground chapel is worth a look. Opposite is the excellent Castlegate House Gallery (*see p195*). The former Wesleyan chapel on Market Street is now the town hall, and doubles up as the Tourist Information Centre (01900 822634, closed Sun Sept-June).

Where to eat & drink

Cockermouth has a handful of appealing bars in the town centre. Vegetarians should make a beeline for the acclaimed Quince & Medlar restaurant (*see right*).

Bitter End
15 Kirkgate, CA13 9PJ (01900 828993, www. bitterend.co.uk). Open noon-2.30pm, 6pm-midnight daily. Lunch served noon-2.30pm, dinner served 6-9pm daily.
This handsome real ale pub brews its own Bitter End ale. The flagship Cockermouth Pride is a fixture, with half a dozen other real ales on tap. The easy-going atmosphere in the trio of rooms is boosted by plenty of wood and a clutter of old photographs, while the bistro-style menu mixes

Lakeland standbys (Cumbrian lamb shoulder with dauphinois potatoes, say) with more creative concoctions, such as Chinese-style cod with crab and ginger sauce.

Castle Bar
14 Market Place, CA13 9NQ (01900 829904). Open 11am-11pm Mon-Thur; 11am-midnight Fri, Sat; noon-11pm Sun. Lunch served 11.30am-2.30pm, dinner served 5.30-8.45pm Mon-Thur. Food served 11.30am-7.30pm Fri, Sat; noon-8.45pm Sun.
An extensive makeover of the old Ship Inn has created something of a cross between a pub and a modern café-bar, more attuned to lager than real ale. The Georgian exterior gives way to three rambling floors of exposed stone, oak floors and wood-lined walls, with high stools at the bar and banquettes in the mezzanine. Upstairs is a spacious dining room, where lasagne, spaghetti carbonara, game pie, Hungarian goulash and filled potato skins set the tone for the menu. On clement days, head for the outdoor terrace.

Quince & Medlar
13 Castlegate, CA13 9EU (01900 823579, www.quince andmedlar.co.uk). Dinner served 7-9.30pm Tue-Sat.
Small but very prettily formed, this well-established vegetarian operation occupies two red-hued rooms. It cleverly marries homeliness and sophistication in the setting and service, as well as on the plate. Colin and Louisa La Voie may have trained at Ullswater's famous Sharrow Bay (*see p217*) in its heyday, but the menu they have evolved is all their own – from a lip-smacking wild mushroom pâté with own-made oatcakes via butternut squash and broad beans wrapped in vine leaves to sharp lemon tart or hot raspberry flapjack. A predominantly organic wine list confirms the all-round wholesome vibe.

Where to stay

Six Castlegate
Castlegate, CA13 9EU (01900 826786, www.six castlegate.co.uk). Rates £65-£75 double incl breakfast.
This elegant, Grade II-listed Georgian townhouse, set halfway up the hill on one of Cockermouth's oldest streets, would need only minimal set dressing to be a location in a Jane Austen adaptation. The six immaculate bedrooms are decorated in soothing tones of white and cream, with smart contemporary bathrooms and soft towels; flatscreen TVs and Wi-Fi add a contemporary edge. Come breakfast, guests can enjoy a full English while admiring Castlegate through the tall, shuttered windows.

Trout Hotel
Crown Street, CA13 0EJ (01900 823591, www.trout hotel.co.uk). Rates £110-£205 double incl breakfast.
Set on the banks of the Derwent, this traditional Cockermouth favourite was badly hit by the 2009 floods. Its restoration, set for completion by early summer 2010, promises a smart, contemporary makeover for its 49 bedrooms and front-of-house areas – expect a cool neutral palette, with vibrant splashes of colour. Request a room in the main building, which is the oldest part of the inn, for sloping ceilings, original features and quirky nooks and crannies. There's an à la carte restaurant and a more casual all-day bar and bistro; the gardens and heated terrace are a popular spot for a leisurely afternoon tea.

Things to do

BASSENTHWAITE & AROUND

Calvert Trust ★
Little Crosthwaite, CA12 4QD (017687 72255, www.calvert-trust.org.uk). Open by arrangement only. Admission varies, phone for details. No credit cards.
The Calvert Trust was founded in 1978 by John Fryer-Spedding, the present incumbent of Mirehouse, to enable young people with disabilities to enjoy the great outdoors. He donated Little Crosthwaite House, overlooking Bassenthwaite, to the trust, which now has two other centres at Kielder and Exmoor. Activities include canoeing, kayaking, sailing, climbing, abseiling, riding and trap driving, hill walking and much more. Visitors can attend as part of a group, or accompanied by family members or friends, with accessible accommodation provided on site. Facilities include a small hydrotherapy pool, a tuck shop, a sensory garden, a bird hide and a picnic area.

Food & Company
Garden Hall, Mirehouse, CA12 4QE (016974 78634, www.foodandcompany.co.uk). Open Apr-Nov. Times & rates vary, check website for details. No credit cards.
For a change from fell walking, sisters Joan Gate and Margaret Brough run day-long cookery courses in a converted 16th-century barn, in the refined setting of Mirehouse. Afternoon teas, simple and seasonal dinner party dishes and easy Thai cooking are among the courses offered, with regular appearances from appropriate guest experts. It's all very civilised, with coffee, a demonstration, a glass of wine and a light lunch. Prices vary, but expect to pay £40 to £45.

WHINLATTER PASS & THE VALE OF LORTON

Cyclewise Whinlatter
Whinlatter Forest Park, CA12 5TW (017687 78711 shop, 017687 898775 courses, www.cyclewise. co.uk/whinlatter). Open 10am-5pm daily. Hire from £17.50/3hrs.
Cyclwise can fix you up with a top-notch Cube hire bike and even a helmet camera with which to record the day's action. A limited number of children's bikes are available, but no child seats, buggies or tag-alongs, as they're not suitable for the demanding mountain bike trails in Whinlatter Forest. Pre-booking is advised, and ID and a credit card

Cyclewise Whinlatter

deposit are required. Skills and coaching courses are also offered, for adults, children and families.

Go Ape!
Whinlatter Forest Park, CA12 5TW (0845 6439086, www.goape.co.uk). Open Apr-Oct 9am-5pm Mon, Wed-Sun. Admission £30; £20 reductions.
Part of the national Go Ape! network of high-level rope and swing routes through the forest canopy, this place presents a vertiginous challenge. After careful instruction on how to clip yourself to the ropes and the all-important safety harness, follow a route of wobbly bridges, Tarzan swings, nets, ropes and zipwires, ascending ever higher into the treetops. It all adds up to an exhilarating (and exhausting) three hours. Participants need to be at least ten years old and 1.40m tall, and under-18s must be accompanied by an adult. Pre-booking essential.

COCKERMOUTH

Kirkgate Centre
Kirkgate, CA13 9PJ (01900 826448, www.the kirkgate.com). Open & tickets vary, check website for details.
Set amid a striking terrace of Georgian houses, just off the marketplace, this former school is now a volunteer-run arts centre, with an enticing programme of theatre, film and world music events.

Northern Lakes

North of the A66 between Penrith and Keswick lies a large section of the National Park that has no lakes, little fame and an extensive tract of rugged fells without roads or people. At its heart is Blencathra and the Caldbeck Fells, which together with surrounding fells account for one of the great high wildernesses of the Lake District – some 35 square miles with virtually no evidence of human activity except for cairns on the summits and long-abandoned mineral mines. Even the drystone walls dry up. The only way through is on foot via the Cumbria Way.

After such uncompromising terrain the comparative lowlands to the north and east are benign and inviting. The attractive villages of Uldale and Hesket Newmarket on the very northern borders of the Lakes are largely untroubled by tourist assault. Caldbeck's rich history brings more popularity. These were the hunting grounds of 19th-century folk song hero John Peel. To the east, castles and stately homes reappear and Penrith, a historic junction between north, south, east and west, is still a strategic stop for travellers entering or leaving the Lake District from the north.

BLENCATHRA & THE NORTH LAKES VILLAGES

Blencathra

It may be slightly overshadowed by its near neighbour Skiddaw, but there's no mistaking that Blencathra is big. At 2,848 feet high, it comes in at about number 17 on most lists of the Lake District's peaks, but as the first summit to confront the driver arriving on the A66 it more than punches it's weight and height. For years it was called Saddleback because of the dip in its centre, but Wainwright preferred, and used, the old Cumbrian name of Blencathra; such is his influence that that name gradually took over and Ordnance Survey now puts both names on its maps.

Wainwright devotes 35 pages to Blencathra and the various routes to its summit. Be warned that the arête of Sharp Edge is not named by accident – it is popularly regarded as a more nerve-racking knife edge than Helvellyn's Striding Edge. Indeed, forget about it in anything but guaranteed fine weather. The summit too can expose the unwary climber to frighteningly high winds, though there are wonderful views of the whole Lakeland range to the south and west.

Only the most hardcore Wainwright baggers continue onwards to the adjoining Mungrisdale Common with its indeterminate, squelchy summit. Wainwright confessed that it was the least loved of his nominated Lakeland 214 fells, with no more 'elegance than a pudding that has been sat on'.

Apart from Blencathra and Skiddaw, most people experience this slab of the Cumbrian Mountains on long-distance footpaths. From the car park at the Blencathra Field Centre, a trail follows Glenderaterra Beck to join the Cumbria Way halfway up the valley. Four miles in is the Skiddaw House Youth Hostel (*see p193*) – one of the most isolated properties in England – where the path splits. The longer and easier route goes out of the high fells and, 14 miles later, arrives at Caldbeck. The tougher route is two miles shorter, but cuts right through the mountains and over the highest pike in the Back o' Skiddaw range – the aptly named High Pike (2,159 feet). A welcome bench awaits on the summit.

Uldale

An engaging series of lanes and bridleways can be explored clockwise around the back of the fells. In particular, the strip of land that runs along the northern border of the National Park from Uldale to Caldbeck is as quiet a sector of the Lakes as can be found in summer, and is gently beautiful all year round.

The biggest stretch of water in this chapter, Overwater Tarn, is a tempting target – not least because it's occasionally fished by Bassenthwaite's ospreys. However, although it's owned by the National Trust, there is no public access through the fields, and the best view is from the road; the Uldale Fells, including the irresistibly named Little Cockup and Great Cockup, form the backdrop.

Uldale village, at the convergence of five minor roads, has commanding views all round, some of which can be enjoyed from the beer garden of the Snooty Fox (*see p208*). The scenery really takes off on the climb to Uldale Common, with its wide open spaces of moorland and pasture, and panoramic views from the Pennines to Skiddaw. It's not quite as empty as it looks. Designated a Site of Special Scientific Interest, it has significant areas of juniper, and merlin and red grouse flourish on the heather and bilberries.

The Uldale and Caldbeck Commons are also famous for minerals, and were once mined for barytes, lead and copper. Now the old spoil heaps are picked over by mineralogists seeking rare species: bechererite, chenite, claudetite and other

Blencathra. See p202.

esoteric '-ites'. There has been so much pressure on some areas that the National Park Authority has introduced a licensing system; permit applications can be downloaded from www.lake-district.gov.uk. Carry a permit or risk a £50 fine.

Under a traffic-light system, red plots of land feature rare and protected minerals; amber means some collection is permitted, while anything can be taken from green areas. All land between Uldale and Caldbeck is green; all amber and red territory is in the heart of the fells. The most determined mineralogists head for Fell Side, where the choicest finds are in Roughton Gill and the dead-end valley of Dale Beck. The little road that goes through the outlying farm settlements at Branthwaite and Fell Side initially looks as if it's headed into this mountain wilderness too, but then loops back close to Caldbeck.

Caldbeck

Caldbeck was alive with industry in the 17th century, when it had eight water-driven mills for corn, wool carding and bobbin making, and it remains quite an attraction by the backwater standards of these parts. Generously laid out around two rivers, Gill Beck and Cald Beck, it has a village green, a duck pond, pretty colour-washed houses with their corner stones picked out in black, and a choice of refreshment spots for anyone staggering in from a gruelling leg of the Cumbria Way. The church of St Kentigern has some lovely stained glass, including a contemporary piece featuring herbs and a chemist's bottle in memory of a local pharmacist.

Caldbeck's most famous son was the huntsman John Peel, who died at the age of 78 in 1854; his big white memorial stone is easy to spot in the graveyard. He seems to have been not much more than a roughneck farmer with a successful pack of hounds. This might have made his reputation locally, but when his friend William Woodcock Graves changed the words of nursery rhyme 'Bonnie Annie' to turn it into a folk song, 'D'ye ken John Peel', he was immortalised. A 1940s radio jingle for Pepsi-Cola sealed his international fame. The grave was attacked by hunt saboteurs in the 1970s, but has since been repaired. Legal hunting continues in the area, in the form of the Blencathra hounds, aka the John Peel Hunt. Like their namesake, they hunt on foot not on horseback.

Beyond the church is the restored Priest's Mill, an old watermill complex with a working wheel. It incorporates Neil Edgar's contemporary jewellery workshop, knitting yarn and textile co-operative the Woolclip (016974 78707, www.woolclip.com, closed Jan) and the deservedly popular Watermill Café (*see p208*).

Joseph Strong & Son's clog workshop occupies a former threshing barn in the centre of the village. Joe Strong made clogs for local millworkers; when the mills closed, he made them for Morris dancers instead, who would draw round their feet on a scrap of cardboard and post it to Joe. He died in 2010 aged 91, but his son Will continues the business.

The Woodwork Shop (016974 78252, closed Jan, Mon-Fri Feb) behind the pub specialises in hand-carved rocking horses, while the Old Smithy shop (016974 78246, www.caldbeckvillage.co.uk/old_smithy.htm) majors in organic and fairtrade produce and crafts, and has a tearoom. Art gallery and studio Hesta Scene (016974 78015, www.hestascene.co.uk, closed Jan, Feb), in the Tithe Barn, showcases paintings, textiles, jewellery and ceramics, and runs contemporary craft workshops. The Hayloft gift shop (016974 78237, closed Jan-Easter, mornings Easter-Dec) has an upstairs café. Meals are also available in the large dining room of the local pub, the Oddfellows Arms; it pays its dues to John Peel with period prints on the walls. There's also a village shop and post office.

A gently rising walk from the National Trust car park leads to the Howk, a limestone gorge with a wooded section and the substantial ruins of the 19th-century Howk Bobbin Mill. It once housed the largest waterwheel in the country, measuring 42 feet in diameter and three feet wide. The 1,110-foot-high mast visible from everywhere is one of the UK's earliest digital transmitters.

Hesket Newmarket to Mungrisdale

A mile and a half south of Caldbeck, Hesket Newmarket is a particularly appealing village of lime-washed cottages, stone houses, cobbled pavements and wide green verges. Once a market town for the nearby farms, it never developed further and settled for the peaceful life. There's a village shop and café, a chapel and an inn, the

Old Crown (see right): a proper local pub under co-operative village ownership and with its own brewery. A toy lorry in the window carries the livery of Eddie Stobart, who was born just outside the village and who turned a local farm contractors' business into one of the world's largest haulage firms with some 1,800 lorries and its own fan club. Hesket's other famous resident is the mountaineer Sir Chris Bonington, who led the first expedition to scale Annapurna.

As the road continues south round the Caldbeck Fells, the scenery becomes harsher. The flat lands to the east are peat bogs worked by Viking settlers 900 years ago; the first slopes of the fells are strewn with boulders. Hardy, semi-wild ponies make it feel like Dartmoor. Mosedale, little more than a handful of farm buildings, is the starting point for a walk to the remains of one of Britain's strangest mines. It's also the beginning of a climb once made by Charles Dickens and Wilkie Collins, and rated by Wainwright as the second best in the Northern Lakes – better than Skiddaw, in other words. It was a favourite with Coleridge too.

The mine comes first. By following the right-hand side of the River Caldew, heading into the fells through a juniper forest, a bridleway joins the Cumbria Way and after a couple of miles is the bulldozed remains of the Carrock tungsten mine. It closed in 1980 – presumably for good, although you can never be sure: it has closed several times in the past only to reopen whenever the price of tungsten rose enough to make it economic or, as happened in both World Wars, when foreign

Daffodil at Banks Farm. See p208.

supplies faltered. Lead, copper, arsenic and, if you believe the rumours, gold have been found here. A permit from the National Park Authority is required before you can help yourself to treasure or poison.

This is also the best place to start the climb up Carrock Fell, which has the foundations of a Celtic fort on its 2,168-foot summit. Bear in mind the chastening experience of Dickens and Collins, who got lost after their compass broke and the latter twisted his ankle. Most Victorians preferred the other side of Swineside Valley, where a track allowed them to reach Bowscale Tarn by pony and trap. Today's walkers can make a circular route by carrying on to Bowscale Fell (2,303 feet), and descending to the road at Mungrisdale via the Tongue – a smaller but no less arresting peak of 1,814 feet. Back at Mosedale, the Quaker Meeting House opens for teas in summer.

Mungrisdale brings the welcome sight of the first pub on this road since Hesket Newmarket, the Mill Inn (*see right*). The River Glenderamackin winds past the pub and through the village on its zig-zag route from under the Bannerdale Crags. The road splits in two here, and follows both sides of the river south until the A66 breaks the spell.

Where to eat & drink

Sophisticated restaurants are non-existent in these parts and, apart from Hesket Newmarket's Old Crown (*see right*), no truly distinctive pubs shout for attention. Beware, too, of restricted opening hours out of season.

Mill Inn
Mungrisdale, CA11 0XR (01768 779632, www.the-millinn.co.uk). Open 11am-11pm daily. Lunch served noon-2pm, dinner served 6-9pm daily.
Dramatically overshadowed by Souther Fell and Raven Crags, this 17th-century coaching inn is a trusty all-purpose retreat for footsore climbers and walkers. Cumbrian food and ales, a fire in winter and a riverside beer garden in summer are the main draws. Overnighters have six en suite rooms in pink and cream (£75 double incl breakfast) and can relax in the residents' lounge or take on the locals at darts and pool.

Old Crown ★
Hesket Newmarket, CA7 8JG (016974 78288, www.theoldcrownpub.co.uk). Open 5.30-11.30pm Mon-Thur; noon-2.30pm, 5.30-11.30pm Fri-Sun. Lunch served noon-2pm Fri, Sat, Sun. Dinner served 6.30-9pm daily.
When the village pub was threatened with closure, the enterprising locals of Hesket Newmarket pulled together and formed a co-operative to save the pub, Britain's first such scheme. It's now owned by 100 villagers, brews its own ale at the back and carries the whole thing off with a delightfully relaxed, non-conformist air. Mountaineer Chris Bonington is a local, and he launched the reborn pub by downing a pint of Doris's 90th. 'Same again please' for Prince Charles when he dropped in during his 'the pub is the hub' campaign (and reportedly left in a big black Mercedes, without paying). The rest of us will happily stump up for a pint of Great Cockup Porter, Blencathra Bitter or Skiddaw Special, and for a barnsley chop served with mint sauce.

FIVE AFTERNOON TEAS

Afternoon tea is a hallowed institution in the Lake District, and even the tiniest B&B will probably produce a complimentary tray of tea and cake on your arrival. For weary walkers, there's nothing more delightful than stumbling on a remote farmhouse serving summer teas on rickety outdoor tables; at the other end of the spectrum, it's a point of honour for every top-flight hotel to compete for the most elaborate and expensive tea ceremony, with beribboned doggy bags for taking home the leftovers. The following are five of our favourite teatime haunts.

Cote How Organic Guest House & Tea Room

Open at weekends and bank holidays, Cote How is a delight. Its Soil Association-certified menu is organic, Fairtrade and – most importantly – utterly delicious. The salmon in the salmon and cucumber sandwich is wild red; the chutney is home-made; and the Cumbrian tea bread, lemon drizzle cake and coffee and walnut cake are baked in-house. After a walk up Loughrigg Fell, relaxing in the bird-filled garden is bliss. See p93.

Flock-In Tea Rooms

A walker's tearoom par excellence, in the heart of Borrowdale. The barn and farmyard setting at Yew Tree Farm is picture-perfect – and none other than Prince Charles came to stay in the farmhouse B&B. Tea and coffee come in pint or half-pint mugs, but staff can also rustle up an espresso or a latte macchiato. Choose from Borrowdale tea bread, meringues filled with lemon curd or scones slathered with jam and clotted cream; savouries, meanwhile, include toasted cheese and chive scones and sturdy bacon baps. See p172.

Holbeck Ghyll Country House Hotel

Holbeck Ghyll offers the quintessential Windermere experience: fine china, silver sugar tongs and a three-tiered cake stand piled with finger sandwiches, miniature cakes and scones with jam and cream. Sit on the terrace with views across the lake or next to the fire in the lounge. It's not the most expensive show in town either, coming in at just under £15. See p33.

Snooty Fox

Uldale, CA7 1HA (016973 71479, www.snootyfox uldale.co.uk). Open 6.30-11pm daily. Dinner served 6.30-8.30pm Mon, Tue, Thur-Sun.

Good food is hard to track down in the further flung corners of northern Lakeland, but this typical black and white country inn – open evenings only – has some decent offerings in the form of roast peppers stuffed with risotto and feta cheese, steak with creamy wild mushrooms, and braised lamb shoulder with root vegetables and pearl barley. Yates and Ennerdale bitter is on tap at the bar; views to Binsey and Skiddaw are on offer from the garden. Three simple rooms are also available (£80 double incl breakfast). Dogs are welcome in the bedrooms and the snug.

Watermill Café

Priest's Mill, Caldbeck, CA7 8DR (016974 78267, www.watermillcafe.co.uk). Open 9am-5pm Mon-Fri.

A vegetarian café in the 1980s, the Watermill now serves meat and fish too, but still offers plenty of classic veggie options such as nut pâté, pasta bake and chickpea casserole, along with cakes and flapjacks. Own-made chutneys and preserves are sold here and at their stall at Kendal and Cockermouth farmers' markets. The café's lovely rustic setting features old pews, craggy whitewashed walls and a beamed ceiling. Even better, take a table under the trees by the river. Twice a month, the Watermill opens for BYO dinners; phone for details.

Where to stay

Modern bedroom and bathroom design has made few inroads into the prevailing patterns of accommodation. But then mercifully few modern inroads disturb the back-of-beyond pace of life around here. Daffodil at Banks Farm (*see below*) breaks the mould for farmhouse B&Bs, but otherwise rural seclusion is the focus. Pubs the Mill Inn (*see p207*) and the Snooty Fox (*see above*) also offer rooms.

Daffodil at Banks Farm ★

Hesket Newmarket, CA7 8HR (016974 78137, www.daffodilbanksfarm.co.uk). Rates £150 double incl breakfast.

The rutted lane up the hill might suggest *Cold Comfort Farm*, but in fact this is Cool Comfort Farm. Hens and geese peck around the farmyard and an Oxford Sandy and Black pig snuffles contentedly in its pen. Guests stay in Daffodil, a luxurious suite of rooms – bedroom, bathroom and dining room – that's all creamy colours and curvy plastered walls. The cooked English breakfast is almost wholly sourced from the farm. Teen Fisher will prepare an evening meal or you can have dinner at the Old Crown (*see p207*), drink your fill and take advantage of the complimentary pick-up. New for 2010 is Daisy, a second purpose-built apartment, and a wood-fired hot tub in the garden, from which there are lovely views.

High Greenrigg House

Greenrigg, CA7 8HD (016974 78430, www.high greenrigghouse.co.uk). Rates from £305-£450 per week for 2. No credit cards.

Farmers' quad bikes are more common than cars on this out-of-the-way backroad between Uldale and Caldbeck, where a restored stone hill farm provides three self-catering cottages (sleeping two, three and five). The well-equipped, sun-filled rooms are immaculately kept, and the floral theme is joyfully rampant through textiles, wallpaper, jugs of garden flowers and a cornucopia of silk flowers. Winding staircases enhance the cottage feel; sash windows open out to Knott and the Caldbeck Fells. Fans of Margaret Forster should recognise the secluded setting from *The Bride of Lowther Fell.*

Marlowe Cottage
Caldbeck, CA7 8HF (016974 76417, www.marlowe cottage.co.uk). Rates £515-£850 per week. No credit cards.
Cream walls with mushroom-coloured corner stones set the tone for this high-spec self-catering cottage on the western edge of Caldbeck village. A slate floor, leather sofa and twin fireplaces hold sway in the dining/sitting room; Shaker-style cupboards and fittings disguise a modern kitchen; brass beds, quilts and cottage furniture sit easily in the bedrooms (two double, one single). If the weather is good, the ample garden has a raised patio with barbecue.

Mosedale End Farm
Mosedale, CA11 0XQ (01768 779605, www.mosedale endfarm.co.uk). Rates £60 double incl breakfast. No credit cards.
A true hill farm, where JoAnne and Andrew Fell work with a full set of Swaledale sheep, cows, collie dogs and free-range hens (from whom you can collect your breakfast eggs, if you so desire). One of the two unfussy en suite rooms can be converted into a family room with the addition of bunk beds, and there's a guest kennel for a visiting dog. JoAnne bakes her own bread and cakes, while Andrew will drive guests to and from Penrith railway station – or the local pub.

Mosedale House
Mosedale, CA11 0XQ (01768 779192, www.mosedale house.co.uk). Rates from £190-£305 per week for 2 people. No credit cards.
The Granary cottage, Hayloft flat and Courtyard bedroom make a good combination for three couples or a family of six looking for superior self-catering accommodation. Local stone dominates inside and out in these farmyard conversions. The watchword is simplicity, and it couldn't sit better alongside the severely beautiful landscape of the Caldbeck Fells. Note that the convergence of kitchen, sitting area and bed in the Hayloft flat may be a little too cosy for some, and the Courtyard bedroom has no independent cooking facilities.

Overwater Hall Hotel
Ireby, CA7 1HH (017687 76566, www.overwaterhall. co.uk). Rates £170-£240 double incl breakfast & dinner.
It doesn't pretend to be cutting-edge – check out the heavy floral wallpaper on the hall staircase – and the castellation on the Georgian frontage is pretty superfluous too, but for a hideaway country house hotel, Overwater Hall could hardly be better hidden. It's down a drive, past a beck and a mill pond, and finally screened by trees in one of Lakeland's quietest corners. There can't be many drive-by customers. The best of the 11 bedrooms are large, with curved windows and high ceilings, some fabric restraint and views to the Uldale Fells. Sadly, Overwater Tarn is off-limits

Pheasant Inn

Howtown Hotel
Whether you've managed five miles on the Ullswater lakeside walk or taken a five-minute stroll from the Howtown landing stage, Mrs Baldry's timeless teas are the perfect reviver. Brew up leaf tea in a silver pot and sample the lightest of scones in the lovely garden under Hallin Fell, or commandeer an armchair in the antique-filled lounge. See p217.

Pheasant Inn
It may be more famous as a pub, but the Pheasant in Bassenthwaite can also turn out a textbook tea. Its sunny lounge is a vision of polished parquet, chintzy textiles, yielding sofas and starched napkins; a fire glows in the grate on chilly days, and trays of tea gleam with polished silverware. Cucumber sandwiches, scrumptious cakes and scones with jam and rum butter are very much the order of the day. See p191.

Places to visit

EAST TO PENRITH

Hutton in the Forest

Penrith, CA11 9TH (017684 84449, www.hutton-in-the-forest.co.uk). Open House Apr-Sept 12.30-4pm Wed, Thur, Sun. Garden Apr-Oct 11am-5pm Mon-Fri, Sun. Admission House & Gardens £8; free-£3 reductions; £19 family. Gardens only £5; free reductions.

This stately home based around a pele tower will stop an architectural historian in his or her tracks with its fearless amalgam of styles, from the austere castellated south front to the rococo east front. Built on and added to down the generations, the towers alone take a trip from the 14th to 19th centuries. Inside are paintings and ceramics collected by the Inglewood family over the years. The showstopping heart is the oldest part, a pele tower in which the wonderful barrel entrance hall with its swords, antlers and banners is pure Hollywood castle – but for real.

There's not an awful lot of forest left in Hutton in the Forest (and there hasn't been for centuries), but the country estate has enough grounds and gardens for a satisfying stroll. There's a leafy woodland walk, an old topiary terrace and a beautiful walled garden divided by yew hedges with herbaceous borders that are stunning in summer. Refreshments are available in the Cloisters tearoom. Various events are held throughout the year, but the highlight is the summer weekend Potfest (www.potfest.co.uk), when top international crafts people gather in the grounds to display their creations.

Little Salkeld Watermill

Little Salkeld, CA10 1NN (01768 881523, www.organicmill.co.uk). Open 10.30am-5pm daily. Admission £3.50; £1.50 reductions; £8 family.

Just north-east of Penrith at Little Salkeld, this is worth a little detour. For some 30 years Nick and Ana Jones have been running Cumbria's only operational watermill. You can tour the mill, buy the flour, eat in the vegetarian organic restaurant and even enrol on a bread-making course.

Little Salkeld Watermill

on private land, but a branch of the Cumbria Way passes nearby. Catering is Lake District hotel mainstream, with champagne bumping up the cost of afternoon tea to £23 and a strong showing of local meat and game at dinner.

EAST TO PENRITH

Heading eastwards to Penrith, take the foot off the A66 pedal for a while and follow the back roads. After the excitement of the Back o' Skiddaw and Blencathra, the countryside soon flattens out by the border of the National Park, but there are worthwhile diversions between here and Penrith.

Sitting on the course of an old Roman road, Greystoke has all the virtues of an English estate village. There's a green with an ancient cross, a stock of good-looking buildings (including a red sandstone church, St Andrew's, whose size and wealth tells of powerful benefactors), the Boot & Shoe Inn, the delectable Greystoke Cycle Café (for both, see p212) and, up a long drive, Greystoke Castle (017684 83722, www.greystoke.com).

The famous *Tarzan of the Apes*, a novel by Edgar Rice Burroughs first published in 1912, told of an orphan boy brought up in the jungle after his parents were marooned and died in West Africa. The boy's parents were Lord and Lady Greystoke. It is all fictitious, of course, with a tenuous connection in that the Howard family, who built the first castle here in the 15th century, believe that Burroughs may have borrowed the Greystoke name, having met members of the Howard family as a newspaperman covering the Boer War.

Today's Greystoke Castle is a fine Victorian pile, and still a private Howard home, but the estate opens up waymarked paths to the lakes and limestone pavements of its 3,000 acres. Less peacefully, 4WD drivers on castle-run courses rumble through the grounds just as tanks did in World War II when the army requisitioned the estate for training (and a German POW camp). Also on the estate are the gallops and stables of Nicky Richards, whose father Gordon W Richards, 'the Master of Greystoke', trained two Grand National winners here.

A mile along the Unthank road is another castle, 13th-century Blencowe Hall (see p212). A fleeting glance at its south tower might suggest it's ruined, but no – it has been superbly renovated into a desirable self-catering residence. Unthank itself has two attractions. The popular Upfront Gallery & Coffee Shop (see p212) pulls together in one complex art exhibitions, a craft shop, a sculpture garden, a vegetarian café and an innovative puppet theatre (see p213).

Around another corner is another castle and another legend. Hutton in the Forest (see left), an extraordinary visual journey through the centuries of stately home architecture, is the family seat of Conservative peer and former MEP Lord Inglewood, while Inglewood Forest, once the second biggest royal forest in England, is the legendary setting of *Sir Gawain and the Green Knight*, the medieval tale of Arthurian chivalry that is not beloved of all English literature students.

Penrith

Today, Penrith is a hard-working market town that feels disconnected from the lushness of the Lake District, and is fenced in by the M6 and West Coast mainline. Yet it's only five miles from Ullswater and equally handy for the Eden Valley or the Howgill Fells. Most Lakeland visitors hurry past on their way in or out of the National Park, but a judicious tour can be rewarding.

The town has a rich if violent history. Once the capital of Cumbria, it dates back to Roman times. Its ruined castle (run by English Heritage and free to enter), opposite the railway station, recalls Penrith's strategic position en route to Scotland. The town suffered countless border skirmishes and was torched three times by the Scots in the 14th century. In 1597 Penrith suffered an outbreak of plague, probably caused by anthrax, which killed 606 people. The plague stone is next to Greengarth Old People's Home in Bridge Lane.

St Andrew's Church, a Hawksmoor design in red sandstone, sits besides Penrith's oldest streets; Burrowgate and Sandgate. In the churchyard, the so-called Giant's Grave has two 11th-century crosses that supposedly mark the grave of the tenth King of Cumbria, with four more stones representing wild boar he hunted in Inglewood Forest. The old Tudor house beside the church was once the Dame School, which William and Dorothy Wordsworth attended after the death of their parents.

The Robinson School in Middlegate, dated 1670, now houses the small Penrith Museum. It details Penrith's geology, history and archaeology, and is also home to the Tourist Information Centre (01768 867466, closed Sun Oct-Mar). Out of hours, a list of available accommodation is helpfully pinned up just outside.

Penrith's main street is, regrettably, overstuffed with high-street chains, but the Bluebell Bookshop ★ (8 Angel Lane, 01768 866660, closed Sun) is a near perfect independent bookshop with a true booklover's sensibility behind the table layouts and labelling. Apart from a comprehensive Lake District section, there are second-hand books, CDs and maps, and a coffee shop upstairs. Arnison's, a timeless draper's shop in Devonshire Street, is where Wordsworth's grandparents lived.

Discriminating food shoppers will enjoy exploring Market Square. J&J Graham (6-7 Market Square, 01768 862281, closed Sun) is a splendidly old-fashioned grocer's full of Cumbrian produce, from sticky toffee pudding to Woodall's sausages, and including cheese, bread, cakes, quiches, cooked meats, pies and pastries. It's great for picnics or stocking up a self-catering cottage or even a last-minute gift on the way back home.

For fresh fruit and veg, Starfruits (17 Market Square, 01768 890255, www.starfruits.co.uk, closed Sun winter) is around the corner. The Fish Cellar (28 Devonshire Arcade, 01768 899408, closed Mon, Sun) has shrimps and sea trout from the Solway Firth and game from local estates. Buy a loaf of good rye bread or jars of pickle from the tiny Krakow (4A Corney Square, 01768 866554, www.cumbria.pl), which sells everything Polish.

A market is held on Great Dockray on Tuesdays, with a farmers' market every third Tuesday in Market Square.

On the south-west edge of town is Cranston's excellent Cumbrian Food Hall (Ullswater Road, 01768 868680, www.cranstons.net, closed Sun). Once a simple butcher's, Cranston's has morphed into a food hall specialising in the best of Cumbria. There's a town centre store in King Street (01768 865667, closed Sun), but this is the firm's flagship, an ultra-smart regional 'supermarket' that is notably strong on meat. The most recent addition, Café Oswald's (*see below*), is upstairs.

Finally, a gentle one-mile stroll up Beacon Edge, a road to the north of town, will bring you to Beacon Pike, a monument to the 1745 rebellion and the site of a Roman beacon that would have been lit to warn of invasion from the north. Now, as then, it provides a fine long-distance view of the fells.

Where to eat & drink

There's a fine selection of cafés and tea shops in the area; alternatively, given the admirable devotion to local Cumbrian produce (as strong here as anywhere in the Lake District), stock up with regional goodies at the excellent food shops in Penrith and head back into the fells for a picnic.

Bewick Coffee House & Bistro

Princes Court, Penrith, CA11 7BJ (01768 864764). Open 9am-4pm Mon-Sat.
Tucked behind the town centre shops, Bewick announces itself with a bright red-painted Georgian frontage. It's open from breakfast to lunch, with an emphasis on local specialities. Main meals might be slow-braised lamb shank, Bliekers smoked salmon or sea bass, rounded off with eton mess or glazed citrus tart.

Boot & Shoe

Greystoke, CA11 0TP (01768 483343, www.bootand shoegreystoke.co.uk). Open 8am-midnight Mon-Thur, Sun; 8am-1am Fri, Sat. Lunch served noon-3pm, dinner served 6-9pm daily.
Right on the village green, this is a 17th-century coaching inn with beams and a dark wood interior, plus benches and sun umbrellas outside. Food and beer is no-nonsense real ales and Cumberland sausage territory; we assume the mixed grill featuring bacon chop, black pudding and haggis is out of bounds for the jockeys riding out at the nearby John Graham Stables. There are four simple B&B rooms (£70 double incl breakfast).

Café Oswald's at Cranston's

Cumbrian Food Hall, Ullswater Road, Penrith, CA11 7EH (01768 868680, www.cranstons.net). Open Jan-May, Aug-Dec 8am-5.15pm Mon-Sat. June, July 8am-5.15pm daily.
This spacious new licensed café on the top floor of Cranston's Cumbrian Food Hall has a fresh airy feel from all the natural daylight. Food offerings roam around the best of Cumbrian produce, from hot porridge and a full breakfast to a local platter that includes Cranston's pastrami, roast ham, smoked pork loin, old applebian and black dub cheeses and Westmorland chutney.

Greystoke Cycle Café ★

Greystoke, CA11 0UT (017684 83984, www. greystokecyclecafe.co.uk). Open Easter-Sept Cyclists 10am-6pm daily. Non-cyclists noon-6pm Fri; 10am-6pm Sat; 10am-6pm second Sun in mth. No credit cards.
An old bicycle leans against an even older road sign. An idyllic little front garden, brimming with flowers, peeps over the wall to Greystoke Castle. An outdoor blackboard advertises 'quirky workshops' for bike maintenance and cupcake heaven. The year 1644 is carved into the studded front door. It's the first stop on the C2C Cycle Way (*see right*), and an official card-stamping station. Every day from Easter to September, Annie Swarbrick (a cyclist herself) opens her barn for bikers to oil chains, adjust saddles, shelter from the rain, make a brew and fill up with flapjacks and fruit juice. On certain other days non-cyclists can sit inside or out, front garden or back, to tuck into soup, bacon sarnies, pasta and chilli dishes, teatime scones and tray bakes, builder's tea or cappucino. A delightful halt on the Johny road junction just north of Greystoke.

Lowther Arms

3 Queen Street, Penrith, CA11 7XD (01768 862792, www.lowtherarms.co.uk). Open 11am-3pm, 6pm-midnight Mon-Fri; 11am-midnight Sat; noon-midnight Sun. Lunch served 11am-2pm Mon-Sat; noon-4pm Sun. Dinner served 6-8.30pm Mon-Thur; 6-9pm Fri, Sat; 6-9.30pm Sun. No credit cards.
The first stop in Penrith for CAMRA fans and much lauded for its changing selection of half a dozen real ales, this is an instantly recognisable version of the honest English pub. Daily specials freshen a menu that is as solidly familiar as the decor: hanging hops and horse brasses, bric-a-brac and brown wood, period pictures and old pottery.

Upfront Gallery & Coffee Shop

Unthank, CA11 9TG (017684 84538, www.up-front.com). Open 10.30am-4.30pm Tue-Sun.
Set back off the B5305, this attractive barn conversion trebles up with some of Cumbria's more interesting artistic talent, an innovative puppet theatre (*see p213*) and reliable vegetarian food. Two floors with uneven whitewashed walls and an open-raftered ceiling hold a craft shop and changing exhibitions. The spacious café is more than a coffee house; daily specials of vegetable curry and rice with pickle and naan bread, or quiche and salad may be accompanied by Jennings ale or a pot of speciality tea. Coffee cake, carrot cake and scones are also available.

Where to stay

The Boot & Shoe (*see left*) also offers B&B rooms.

Blencowe Hall ★

Blencowe, CA11 0DF (01386 701177, www.rural retreats.co.uk). Rates £4,819-£6,589 per week.
A mind-blowing, Grade I-listed, 16th-century castle. It looks like a proper castle should and sleeps 24 in 12 bedrooms. Built in the 1300s, it's said that Cromwell's army blasted it with cannon fire mistaking it for nearby Greystoke Castle. A spectacular restoration under the supervision of English Heritage in 2008 has won a string of awards. Most amazing is the modern glass bridge between the great top-to-toe crack in the south tower. Elsewhere, old and new complement each other with modern kitchens, four-poster beds, stylish

Things to do

Quirky Workshops

EAST TO PENRITH

C2C Cycle Way
www.c2c-guide.co.uk.
The Coast to Coast Walk (*see p143*) is well known; less famous is the C2C Cycle Way, which runs from sea to sea, from Workington or Whitehaven on the Irish Sea, through the Lakes and over the North Pennines to Sunderland or Tynemouth on the North Sea. Not that it's a secret, with 15,000 cyclists making the crossing every year, some in a single day. It's a 136- to 140-mile route, mostly on minor roads and cycle tracks, with the highest point topping 2,000 feet. The website is full of information on routes, guesthouses, guided support and a helpful note that the prevailing winds make it easier from west to east.

Greystoke and Penrith are stamping points en route and Penrith has been given 'cycle hub' status, which means it has access to circular cycle routes, proximity to the national cycle network, safe cycling initiatives and a clutch of bike shops. Five routes round the town can be downloaded at www.penrithtown.co.uk/visiting-cycling.htm. At Adventure Cycling (13 Meadowcroft, 077368 16700, www.adventurecycling.co.uk), qualified mountain bike instructors lead half-or full-day tours through the Lake District. Mountain bikes can be hired too, with prices starting at £60. Arragons (Brunswick Road, 01768 890344, www.arragons.com) is a family business run by real bike enthusiasts who sell and hire, do repairs, and are a stamping station for the C2C.

Greystoke Swimming Pool
Church Road, Greystoke, CA11 0TW (01768 483637, www.greystokepool.btik.com). Open May-Sept 3-6pm Mon-Fri; noon-5pm Sat, Sun.

An open-air heated 18m pool, with two children's play areas and a sports field. It's all not-for-profit, and run by volunteers.

Quirky Workshops ★
Greystoke Cycle Café, Greystoke, CA11 0UT (017684 83984, www.greystokecyclecafe.co.uk/workshops.htm).
The irrepressible Annie Swarbrick runs a full programme of courses and workshops from a restored barn at the congenial Greystoke Cycle Café (*see left*). Choose from willow weaving, botanical illustration, rag rug making or cycle maintenance. Or there's drystone walling, stone carving and blacksmithing. Or you can bake scones or make cupcakes. Lunch is taken in the farmhouse or, weather permitting, among the sculptures in the appropriately idiosyncratic garden. Prices range from £42 for one day to £155 for three days of stone carving, including lunch and afternoon tea.

Upfront Puppet Theatre ★
Unthank, CA11 9TG (017684 84538, www.up-front.com). Open varies, call or check website for details. Tickets £6.
Beside the Upfront Gallery & Coffee Shop (*see left*) is this much praised puppet theatre, the work of John Parkinson, who designed for English National Opera and Keswick's old Blue Box Theatre before settling in little Unthank village. Exquisitely crafted productions take place at Christmas, Easter and in the summer holidays, with opportunities to meet the puppeteers after some of the shows. Past productions have included the *Snow Queen*, *Sleeping Beauty* and *Stanelli's Super Circus*. The gift shop sells a wide range of puppets.

wetrooms, a spiral staircase and a snooker room. Prices are as high as you'd expect, and the minimum stay varies between three and seven nights depending on the season.

North Lakes Hotel & Spa
Ullswater Road, Penrith, CA11 8QT (01768 868111, www.shirehotels.com). Rates £140-£160 double incl breakfast.
No one's pretending that a roundabout off the M6 is Lakeland utopia, but this mid to upmarket hotel has appeal for families. Children under 16 stay free when sharing their parents' room, there's a 13m indoor pool and a games room, and there are discounts on Lake District attractions such as Honister Slate Mine and Rookin House Activity Centre. The hotel has 84 rooms and is an easy five-mile hop from the northern shore of Ullswater.

Stafford House
Greystoke, CA11 0TQ (017684 83558, http://stafford house.website.orange.co.uk). Rates £70-£90 double incl breakfast. Self-catering £20 per person per night.
This grey crenellated folly at the entrance to Greystoke Castle is slightly foreboding, but you'll find a warm welcome from owner Hazel Knight. Accommodation comes in the form of two traditionally furnished double rooms (one en suite), and one twin room with an attic sitting room and ground-floor dining room. Across the courtyard are three upmarket self-catering camping barns (one with disabled access), which sleep four, four and eight in dormitory-style bunk beds. Each is equipped with a drying room, smart wetrooms and kitchens. Sheets, towels and a self-service breakfast are included in the price; a cooked breakfast served in the main house costs extra.

Greystoke Cycle Café. See p212.

Ullswater

Nine miles long and three-quarters of a mile wide, Ullswater is the second largest of the Lake District's lakes after Windermere, and a lot more peaceful. Its devotees maintain that it's also the loveliest; its southern section, majestically framed by Place Fell to the east and Helvellyn to the west, is particularly gorgeous. Famously, this is where Wordsworth was inspired by 'a host of golden daffodils' dancing by the shore. Here too is the footpath described by Wainwright as the most beautiful and rewarding walk in Lakeland, and the Lake District's most celebrated waterfall, Aira Force. For the sure of foot, the narrow, precipitous ridge of Striding Edge offers an unforgettable route to the summit of Helvellyn.

As the first lake to be reached from the M6 at Penrith, Ullswater can become busy on its through road and at Pooley Bridge and Glenridding; by contrast, the quieter eastern shore ends at tranquil Martindale, home to the only pure-bred wild red deer herd in Britain. There are lovely little churches and picturesque tarns high up in the fells, but there's no better way to pass an idle half-hour than sitting on the wooden jetty at Howtown. Dangle your legs over the edge, attempt to spot an elusive pike and keep an eye out for the red funnel of a vintage Ullswater steamer, as it rounds the corner to take you out on the lake.

POOLEY BRIDGE & THE EASTERN SHORE

Best seen as a gateway to Ullswater rather than a destination in its own right, Pooley Bridge sits at the lake's north-eastern tip, on the River Eamont. A touristy place, it soon fills in summer with visitors staying at the two big campsites further down the shore at Park Foot and Waterside Farm, and with the many boaters that cruise these parts.

Of the village pubs, the Crown (017684 86955) on the main square has a garden running down to the river. On Main Street, the Sun Inn (017684 86205, www.suninnpooleybridge.co.uk) has hanging baskets and a beamed, bric-a-brac-filled interior, while the Pooley Bridge Inn (01768 486215, www.pooleybridgeinn.co.uk) offers an inviting, open-plan bar with sofas by the fireside. Outdoor shop Catstycam (Finkle Street, 017684 86401, www.catstycam.com) provides camping and walking essentials, and there's a smattering of gift shops, newsagents and general stores around the Market Square. Cross the bridge to reach the jetty, where you can take trips on the Ullswater Steamers (*see p233*) to Howtown and Glenridding.

A minor road runs from the village down the eastern shore of Ullswater, becoming increasingly narrow until it reaches a dead end in Martindale. As a result, this is by far the quieter side of the lake, particularly once the road has passed the two campsites and the discreet entrance that leads to the fabled Sharrow Bay hotel (*see p217*). Two miles from Pooley Bridge is Howtown, where there's a steamer jetty and, next to a wildflower meadow, the Howtown Hotel (*see p217*). Run by the Baldry family for more than a century, this fondly regarded refreshment halt has a beautifully

decorated walkers' bar and well-tended gardens; it's a lovely setting for afternoon tea.

From here, you can set off on a six-mile shoreline ramble to Patterdale at the lake's southern tip, celebrated by Wainwright as the most beautiful walk in Lakeland. After Sandwick Bay, a spot beloved by the Wordsworths, there are woods, fells and tumbling becks, and almost non-stop vistas across Ullswater to the towering Helvellyn range. A short diversion leads to the cascade of Scalehow Force. For an idyllic picnic location, leave the shoreline path for the grassy promontory of Silver Point, where two different reaches of Ullswater are revealed in panoramic splendour. Behind, the lower slopes of Birk Fell are clothed in ferns and foxgloves in summer, and a rocky outcrop erupts with purple heather, while tiny Norfolk Island lies straight ahead. On the opposite shore is lovely Glencoyne Bay, along with Great Dodd and Great Mell Fell. As Dorothy Wordsworth declared two centuries ago, it is a 'perfect summertime walk'.

If you're continuing south from Howtown by road, rather than on foot, you'll find a series of hairpin bends rising to the top of the pass and tiny, beguiling St Martin's Church. A church has stood here since the 13th century; this incarnation dates from the 16th. The spare interior has massive oak beams, ancient pews set against white-painted stone walls and a font said to have been a Roman altar; there's no electricity. The car park next to the church is the last place to leave vehicles before the road ends, and is the starting point for some wonderful walks in Martindale and Boredale. The immediate temptation is a steep but simple ascent of Hallin Fell (1,271 feet). Don't be discouraged by Wainwright's tart aside that it can be climbed in 'sandals and slippers and polished shoes'; he also

acknowledged its superlative views over Ullswater. You're unlikely to have it to yourself, though, unless you're visiting midweek in winter.

Two valleys point to the high fells. Just before the little tarn in Boredale, a clapper bridge is the start of a steadily angled climb to Place Fell (2,154 feet) and then down, more precipitously, to Patterdale. In Martindale is an ancient forest – home to what is thought to be the only remaining herd of pure-bred wild red deer in Britain. Up to 100 have been recorded on the western side of Place Fell in winter, and on Bannerdale Fell in summer. Ullswater's cruise boats run trips to see them in rut in October. Otherwise, the likeliest place from which to spot them is the Nab ridge. Look out too for semi-wild fell ponies, which roam the common land, and buzzards, peregrine falcons and England's only wild golden eagle, flying high over Riggindale Crags.

Where to eat & drink

Pooley Bridge offers thin pickings for discerning foodies. In fact, more than any other major lake destination, Ullswater may be the place for packed lunches and self-catered evening meals.

Howtown Hotel

Howtown, CA10 2ND (01768 486514, www.howtown-hotel.com). Open Easter-Nov 10am-11pm daily. Lunch served 1pm, dinner served 7pm & 8.30pm daily. No credit cards.

Quirky, time-warped and utterly unreconstructed (a gong announces the no-choice dinner), the Howtown Hotel remains hugely loveable. The red plush hotel bar and walkers' bar are two of the most charismatic drinking holes in Lakeland, while the cottage garden under Hallin Fell is perfect for a silver service afternoon tea while waiting for the Ullswater steamer. Dinner could be considered wittily retro, except that it probably hasn't changed significantly since the 1960s: soup, fruit juice, fish in creamy sauce, uncomplicated roasts and nursery puddings with custard. The bedrooms (£160 double incl breakfast and dinner) have an easy charm, with period furnishings and old-fashioned baths. Most rooms have uninterrupted views of Hallin Fell and the far shore of Ullswater. There are no TVs, telephones or tea-making equipment; instead, morning tea is delivered to your room. Five self-catering cottages (£440-£600 per week) adjoin the hotel. The location, close to the Howtown landing stage in the quietest corner of the lake, soothes the soul. Bring cash or a chequebook: it's no surprise to discover that credit cards are not accepted.

Sharrow Bay

Nr Howtown, CA10 2LZ (017684 86301, www. sharrowbay.co.uk). Lunch served 1pm, afternoon tea served 4pm, dinner served 8pm daily.

Set on Ullswater's eastern shore amid magnificent gardens, the Michelin-starred Sharrow doesn't do things by halves. Its unique styling is the legacy of founder Frances Coulson, who opened the hotel in 1948, and his partner Brian Sack; although it now belongs to the Von Essen group and has been pared down, it remains wonderfully idiosyncratic. The dining room is a study in glorious excess: a wine-dark boudoir of antiques, cherubs and gilded mirrors, where a six-course dinner is served. It's traditional fine dining fare

Weatherline

If you've ever toiled laboriously up Helvellyn, the third highest mountain in the Lake District, then spare a thought for Jon Bennett and Jason Taylor, the Lake District's two Fell Top Assessors. One of the doughty pair, who are employed by the Met Office and the National Park, must climb Helvellyn every day, seven days a week, throughout the winter.

Working alternate weeks between December and April, the duo supply mountain-top reports on the quantities of snow and ice, the temperature, the wind speed and the risk of avalanches for the Lake District's Weatherline (0844 846 2444, www.lake district.gov.uk/weatherline), a crucial service for walkers, climbers and locals. In 2009, for the first time in 34 years, they took Christmas Day off.

(roast quail with truffle fettuccine and wild mushroom sauce, veal medallion with foie gras and dauphinoise potatoes), with the odd lighter option and dedicated vegetarian menus. The five-course lunch is scarcely less indulgent, though there is a more modest three-course alternative midweek. Order with care to avoid a surfeit of richness and beware the odd ingredient oversight: risotto popped up in three courses on our last visit. Afternoon tea remains a legendary – and more affordable – way to sample the Sharrow Bay experience; book well ahead.

Liberally dotted with porcelain and antiques, the 24 bedrooms (£270 double incl breakfast) wouldn't shame a French château; they are divided between the main house and various buildings in its 12-acre grounds.

Where to stay

For those that favour more unusual accommodation, Ullswater is rich in spoils. Quirkier options range from the Duke of Portland's Boathouse to Martindale's remote shooting lodge, the Bungalow (for both, *see p218*). Then there's the inimitable Sharrow Bay (*see left*), the grandest dame of the Lake District's country house hotels, and the endearingly time-locked Howtown Hotel (*see above*), where infatuated guests return to the antiques-filled lounges and beautiful gardens year after year.

For a more conventional stay, all three of the pubs in Pooley Bridge (*see p215*) offer typical, pub-style accommodation. Camping is available at Waterside Farm (*see p232*) and Park Foot (*see p232*).

Sharrow Bay. See p217.

The Bungalow

*Martindale (01 7684 86450, www.dalemain.com/
accommodation/bungalow.htm). Rates £541-£1,109
per week.*

Built in 1910 by the Earl of Lonsdale (of Lowther Castle
fame) for Kaiser Wilhelm's visit to hunt red deer, this
former shooting lodge stands in glorious isolation in the
ancient forest at the furthest end of Martindale. Now part
of the Dalemain estate, it's let as a holiday cottage: up to 12
people can bump along the rough track for a minimum of
a week's stay. Superb walking routes lead to High Street,
Angle Tarn, the Knott and the high-level reservoir of
Hayeswater. You're also in prime position to witness the
annual rut of England's only wild red deer herd. It's an
indiosyncratic place and very popular; check online to see
if the odd week is free here and there.

Duke of Portland's Boathouse

*Pooley Bridge, CA10 2NN (017687 74060,
www.lakes cottageholiday.co.uk). Rates £650-
£2,080 per week.*

Beautiful, mossy-roofed old stone boathouses are one of the
iconic features of the lakes, and few are more eye-catching
than this little beauty, perched by the water just beyond the
Pooley Bridge pier. Much photographed, it has a colourful
history. Constructed in the 17th century, it was rebuilt in the
mid 18th for the third Duke of Portland, who was then forced
to sell after a decade-long legal battle with the Lowther

family almost bankrupted him. The duke might struggle to
recognise the boathouse's most recent incarnation as a
luxurious one-bedroom retreat, with oak doors opening on
to a balcony over the lake, Japanese teak bathroom fittings,
a sleek lounge and a teak, granite and Cumbrian slate
kitchen. Outside is a private jetty.

Hallin Bank

*Martindale, CA10 2NF (017684 86505, www.hallin
bank.co.uk). Rates £350-£490 per week. No credit cards.*

Set on the southern slopes of Hallin Fell, with Martindale
and Boredale at the front door and its own fields running
down to the beck, this 17th-century farmhouse has been
occupied by the same family for more than a century.
Attached to the whitewashed farmhouse, the Fold is a self-
contained stone barn conversion that sleeps up to five (one
on a folding bed). The master bedroom has aged beams,
while a steep staircase leads to the attic bedroom. Stone
steps descend into the lofty, galleried kitchen/living room,
with its exposed rafters, Aga and well-stocked library.
There's even a piano. The Chalet, a modern, one-room
wooden summerhouse, can be rented as an annexe for £80
per week; although less atmospheric than the Fold, it's a
handy hideaway for teenagers. Simply furnished, it has twin
beds, a table and chairs, a fridge and a little stove, but no
running water; the toilet and washbasin are in an outhouse.
Bed linen and towels are not provided in either property,
and electricity is extra.

THE WESTERN SHORE
TO PATTERDALE

The A592 runs the length of Ullswater's western edge, from Pooley Bridge to Glenridding and on to Patterdale. The shore is only intermittently accessible since much of it is privately owned, but there are some beautiful stretches, with views across to Hallin Fell and Place Fell; they're even more spectacular on a moonlit or starry night.

Heading south from Pooley Bridge, it's a couple of miles to Watermillock. On either side of the village are the luxury hotels of Rampsbeck (*see p225*) and Leeming House (*see p227*), both with enviable swathes of lakeside at the bottom of their gardens. Watermillock has a substantial marina, boat hire and a waterfront picnic area. It's also home to one of two Outward Bound Trust centres (01931 740000, www.outwardbound.org.uk) at Ullswater; the other is at Howtown on the opposite shore. The trust runs adventure courses for young people, which include canoeing, kayaking and raft building.

Head away from the lake, to the back roads around Matterdale, for superlative views. This is also where you'll find the eco-friendly Quiet Site (*see p227*) for campers, and, clinging to the skirts of Little Mell Fell, Lowthwaite Farm (*see p227*) – a near perfect farmhouse B&B with a Scandinavian

twist. Matterdale's church is a gem, with a craggy stone exterior and hefty interior beams; like most Lake District churches, it's nearly always open. If the pleasures of walking are waning, then Rookin House Equestrian & Activity Centre (*see p233*) offers all sorts of adrenaline thrills on wheels and saddles. The hamlets of Dockray and Troutbeck, meanwhile, have pubs as good as any on Ullswater.

Back on the shore road, three miles before the village of Glenridding, Aira Force and Gowbarrow Park (*see p221*) are two National Trust beauty spots attached to the same car park. It's a short walk along the shore to famous Glencoyne Bay (*see p221*); in March and April, you can follow in William and Dorothy Wordsworth's footsteps to admire the daffodils, 'fluttering and dancing in the breeze'.

Glenridding has no compelling attractions in its own right, and its primary function is as the great interchange point of Ullswater. Scores of visitors descend on its car park, then disperse to climb Helvellyn and Place Fell, catch a steamer to Howtown or Pooley Bridge, or simply hire a rowing boat. With the exception, perhaps, of the property on the beck, it's not the prettiest of villages. When the nearby Keppel Cove dam burst in 1929, it sent a quarter of a million gallons of water down the valley. No one was killed, but much of the village was destroyed.

WHEREVER CRIMES AGAINST HUMANITY ARE PERPETRATED.

Across borders and above politics.
Against the most heinous abuses
and the most dangerous oppressors.
From conduct in wartime
to economic, social, and cultural rights.
Everywhere we go,
we build an unimpeachable case
for change and advocate action
at the highest levels.

HUMAN RIGHTS WATCH TYRANNY HAS A WITNESS

WWW.HRW.ORG

HUMA
RIGH
WATC

Places to visit

THE WESTERN SHORE TO PATTERDALE

Aira Force & Gowbarrow Park
A592 between Watermillock and Glenridding;
CA11 0JS (017684 82067, www.nationaltrust.org.uk/
ullswaterandairaforce).
Of all the waterfalls in the Lake District, Aira Force is
the most famous and the most popular. It's located
half a mile in from the lake, surrounded by beautiful
woodland; the definitive viewing point is from an
arched stone bridge, just upstream from where Aira
Beck tumbles down a 65ft rocky ravine into the pool
below. It's the main – but not the only – attraction at
Gowbarrow Park, part of the hunting estate that once
belonged to the Howards of Greystoke Castle. In the
18th century, the Howards began landscaping the
park on an epic scale, planting half a million trees,
laying footpaths and building bridges. Intrepid plant
hunters returned from across the world bearing exotic
plants and trees – including some 200 conifers,
which have matured into enormous trees. Above Aira
Force, paths lead to High Force, another waterfall,
and the wilder Gowbarrow Fell, which offers stunning
views over Ullswater.

In 1906 the entire site was bought by the National
Trust, which has an information hut in the car park
and can provide an audio trail and details of wheelchair
and pushchair access. As Mrs Linton crisply observed
in her Victorian guide to the Lakes, the falls are 'within
the compass of any south country woman who can
walk beyond her own garden'. Two additional car
parks on the Matterdale road give higher-level access
points. Wordsworth referenced Aira Force in three of
his poems, but his most famous poem, 'Daffodils',
was inspired by nearby Glencoyne Bay.

Aira Force

Dalemain House
Dalemain, Penrith, CA11 0HB (017684 86450,
www.dalemain.com). Open House Apr-Sept 11.30am-
4pm Mon-Thur, Sun. Oct 11.30am-3pm Mon-Thur,
Sun. Gardens Apr-Sept 10.30am-5pm Mon-Thur,
Sun. Oct 10.30am-4pm Mon-Thur, Sun. Feb, Mar,
Nov-mid Dec 11am-4pm Mon-Thur, Sun. Admission
House & Gardens £9; free-£8.50 reductions.
Gardens only £6; free reductions.
This welcoming country house, two miles north of
Ullswater, has been home to the Hassell (pronounced
'Hazel') family for countless generations. It's a
distinguished-looking pile, with a 12th-century pele
tower and a pink sandstone Georgian façade. The
interior is something of a rabbit warren, with two
Elizabethan wings, winding Tudor passageways,
acres of oak panelling, military regalia in the Yeomanry
museum, family portraits running up imposing
staircases and an 18th-century Chinese room with
exquisite hand-painted wallpaper. It's the simplest
rooms that are easiest to relate to, though: the
nursery, with its classic toys, and the housekeeper's
quarters, with their rag rug, cast-iron fireplace and old
sewing machine (there's also a priest's hole, hidden
behind the store cupboard).

A fragrant rose walk, densely planted herbaceous
borders and an Elizabethan knot garden are among
the highlights of the garden; in May and June look out
for the display of Himalayan blue poppies. The tearoom
is set in the magnificent medieval hall, with a fire in
the grate, cakes made on the premises and a range
of preserves, cakes and treats to take home. Another
foodie attraction is the Marmalade Festival, held
here each February.

Wordsworth Point
Nr Glencoyne Bay (www.nationaltrust.org.uk/
ullswaterandairaforce).
On 15 April 1802 Dorothy Wordsworth came across
a bank of daffodils, close to where Aira Beck flows
into Ullswater at Glencoyne Bay. In her journal she
wrote of how they 'tossed and reeled and danced and
seemed as if they verily laughed with the wind that
blew upon them over the lake.' Two years later,
William began a poem, 'I Wandered Lonely as a Cloud'
(commonly known as 'Daffodils') and the rest is history.
Not all his contemporaries were impressed: poet
Anna Seward declared Wordsworth must be mad to
write so sentimentally of 'capering flowers', telling
Walter Scott 'Surely if his worst foe had chosen to
caricature this egotistic manufacturer of metaphysic
importance upon trivial themes, he could not have
done it more effectively!'.

There's a car park nearby, and the National Trust
guards the bay's host of fluttering flowers, while
camera-toting tourists mutter the immortal lines.

Ullswater. See p215.

One remnant of the area's industrial past can be seen at Greenside Lead Mine, a mile past the unprepossessing but friendly Traveller's Rest pub (017684 82298). The mine closed in 1962 after 250 years of operation. The YHA's Helvellyn hostel (see p227) now occupies one of the mine buildings: set 900 feet above sea level, it's a natural starting point for a northern ascent of Helvellyn.

Pick up more information on the area from the comprehensive Tourist Information Centre (017684 82414, closed Mon-Fri Nov-Easter) in the car park at Glenridding, and purchase essentials at the Mini Market in Eagle Road. It can be a relief to leave Glenridding on a hot summer weekend, though, and take to the water. Down by the lake is the steamer landing stage and café; a plaque marks the spot where, on 23 July 1955, Donald Campbell launched *Bluebird* to raise the world water speed record to 202mph. A short stroll away is St Patrick's Boat Landings (see p233), where you can buy ice-cream and hire a boat.

The road from Glenridding winds onwards to Patterdale, just beyond the southern end of Ullswater and the older and calmer of the two villages. There's a general store (017684 82220) and a post office, along with good-value accommodation at Patterdale Youth Hostel and Patterdale Hall (for both, see p227).

The village has a sturdy, slate-roofed Victorian church dedicated to St Patrick – who, it is said, came to the dale in the fifth century. It contains two notable embroideries by Ann Macbeth, an associate of Charles Rennie Macintosh at Glasgow School of Art. Between the church and the school is a signposted footpath to Side Farm Campsite and tearoom (see p230). It's also the start of the classic lakeshore walk to Howtown, or a more demanding climb up Place Fell (2,156 feet), which provides dizzying views across to the Helvellyn range, or to Angle Tarn (1,754 feet). Still more ambitious is the long circular tramp through Grisedale, to Grisedale Tarn (1,770 feet), higher still to the summit of Fairfield (2,863 feet) and back via the St Sunday Crags.

Considering the plethora of hiking and climbing routes nearby, it's no surprise that Patterdale Mountain Rescue (www.mountainrescue.org.uk) is one of the busiest rescue teams in the country. Staffed entirely by volunteers, it deals with scores of incidents each year, ranging from aiding stranded walkers on Striding Edge to rescuing snowbound drivers on Kirkstone Pass. Visit the team's website for weather reports, tips on keeping safe on the fells and a rundown of the service's latest incidents.

Where to eat & drink

Patterdale is short of decent eating options, although there's more choice in Glenridding. The Fellbites Café & Restaurant (Croft House, Greenside Road, 017684 82781, www.fellbites.co.uk, closed Mon-Fri Nov-Easter) serves light lunches and more sturdy evening meals: duck breast and red cabbage, say, or a hefty lamb shank and mash, washed down with a pint of Bluebird. Also licensed, Greystones Coffee House (017684 82392, www.greystones gallery.co.uk, closed Sat, Sun winter) doubles as a contemporary art gallery and café, with Wi-Fi access and a good selection of own-made cakes.

Inn on the Lake

Glenridding, CA11 0PU (017684 82444, www.lake districthotels.net/innonthelake). Open 11am-11pm daily. Lunch served 12.30-2pm, dinner served 7-8.45pm daily.

Patterdale

Steaming ahead

Ullswater Steamers (*see p233*), with their distinctive green livery and red funnels, have been sailing Ullswater for 150 years. The company's original remit was to carry the post, along with slate from local mines, lead from Glenridding and passengers. During World War II, the steamers did their bit for king and country, ferrying soldiers to their training base at the Ullswater Hotel (now the Inn on the Lake).

Wordsworth described Ullswater as 'the happiest combination of beauty and grandeur which any of the lakes affords', and its boats are equally stately. The grande dame of the four-strong fleet is the *Lady of the Lake*, who made her inaugural voyage on 26 June 1877, and is thought to be the oldest working passenger ship in the world. Her history is somewhat

chequered, mind: she sank in 1881 and again in 1958, and was so badly damaged by a fire in the '60s that she remained out of service for 14 years before a triumphant relaunch in 1979. *Raven*, launched in 1899, is the second oldest vessel, and was temporarily made into a royal yacht for Kaiser Wilhelm II's visit to Ullswater in 1912.

The latest recruits to wear the company's green and cream paintwork are *Lady Dorothy*, which joined in 2001, and *Lady Wakefield* (2007); all four of the 'steamers' are now diesel-powered, and run throughout the year (except Christmas Eve and Christmas Day). Taking a cruise remains a delightful, timeless experience: don a straw boater, assemble a picnic, and follow in the footsteps of Victorian day-trippers.

Its lawns gently sloping to meet the lake, Glenridding's most prominent hotel enjoys a spectacular setting. There's a restaurant with sweeping views and a rather elaborate three-course menu: for less formal eating, try the lounge bar for panini or club sandwiches, or the ramblers' bar for pizza, pasta dishes and pub grub stalwarts (hot pot, sausage and mash, scampi and chips) and big-screen sporting action on the plasma TVs. The 46 rooms (£150-£216 double incl breakfast) run from standard doubles to traditional four-posters, which are very popular with newlyweds: as you might expect, given its location, the hotel hosts any number of weddings.

Rampsbeck

Watermillock, CA11 0LP (017684 86442, www. rampsbeck.co.uk). Open 11am-11pm daily. Lunch served noon-1.45pm, dinner served 6.30-9pm daily.
In summer, Rampsbeck's grand front dining room lays Ullswater before you, along with an abundance of well-polished silverware and starched linen. In winter, a smaller room has the intimacy of a private dining club. The three-

or four-course menu offers elaborate dishes, waxing long and lyrical in its descriptions ('roasted fillet of beef with shallot confit, celeriac fondant, seared foie gras, pan-fried veal sweetbreads wrapped in Cumbrian air-dried ham and a Madeira wine sauce', for instance). The pomp and ceremony can be a bit of a strain, depending on your tastes, but the kitchen generally delivers, and staff carry out their duties with considerable charm. The 19 bedrooms (£140-£290 double incl breakfast) are sleekly appointed, with sumptuous fabrics, ornate wallpapers and antiques.

Royal Hotel

Dockray, CA11 0JY (017684 82356, www.the-royal-dockray.co.uk). Open 10am-midnight daily. Lunch served Summer noon-3pm daily. Winter noon-2pm daily. Dinner served Summer 6-9pm daily. Winter 6-8pm daily.
Views of the fells and an attractive garden make the Royal, located on the A5091 near Matterdale, a handy retreat. The real ales and food are honest, straight down the line and fairly priced: expect the likes of creamy garlic mushrooms to start, five-bean chilli or pie of the day to follow, and

Rampsbeck. See p225.

perhaps a homely rice pudding or apple crumble to finish. The ten comfortable, traditionally furnished en suite rooms cost £85-£95 for a double, including breakfast.

Troutbeck Inn

Troutbeck, CA11 0SJ (017684 83635, www.the troutbeckinn.co.uk). Open Summer 11am-11pm daily. Winter 11am-2pm, 5.30-11pm daily. Lunch served noon-2pm, dinner served 6-9pm daily.

Next to the junction of the A5091 and the A66, about five miles from Ullswater's shore, this was the former station hotel in the days of the Penrith–Keswick railway. Today it has a smart interior with muted tartan carpets, oak tables and high settles, and a menu with ambition (seafood crêpe with shellfish sauce; duck terrine with date and armagnac chutney; beef bourguignon with parmentier potatoes). If you're after accommodation, consider the seven bedrooms (£70 double incl breakfast) and three self-catering cottages (from £277-£425 per week for two people).

Where to stay

Patterdale has two inns with rooms, the White Lion (017684 82214) and the Patterdale Hotel (0845 305 2111, www.patterdalehotel.co.uk), both traditional rather than trendy. The Inn on the Lake (*see p224*) is a bigger, pricier affair. Away from the water, the Royal Hotel (*see p225*) and the Troutbeck Inn (*see above*) both offer inexpensive accommodation.

For country house hotel grandeur, choose between the Rampsbeck (*see p225*) and Leeming House (*see below*): half a mile apart, both boast imposing premises, stellar lakeside gardens, plush public rooms and more *grande bouffe* dining than anyone could (or should) stomach for more than a couple of nights in a row.

Helvellyn Youth Hostel

Greenside, Glenridding, CA11 0QR (0845 371 9742, www.yha.org.uk). Rates £13.95 adult.

Three-quarters of a mile beyond the Traveller's Rest pub and accessed via a rutted track, this 60-bed hostel is set in one of the old Greenside Lead Mine buildings. It's a good starting point for mountainous walks; staying here, you're already 900ft closer to Helvellyn. The hostel also organises weekend and week-long fell walking and rock climbing breaks; details on the YHA website.

Leeming House

Watermillock, CA11 0JJ (0844 879 9142, www.macdonaldhotels.co.uk). Rates £120-£200 double incl breakfast.

Owned by the Macdonald Hotels chain, this swish country house hotel stands in 22 acres of gardens and woodland next to Ullswater. Its 41 rooms are are swathed in yards of high-end textiles; the more expensive ones have lake views and half-tester beds, while the suites have private balconies. There's a helipad for guests in a hurry; on arrival, slow the pace right down with a leisurely game of croquet or an afternoon's fishing (the hotel has a private fishing licence). Tea is served on the terrace, haute cuisine in the Regency Restaurant; both overlook the lake. Come back down to earth by ordering a bacon butty for breakfast followed by a tramp through the woods.

Lowthwaite Farm ★

Lowthwaite, CA11 0LE (017684 82343, www.lowthwaiteullswater.com). Rates £60-£80 double incl breakfast.

In 2009 Jim and Tine Boving Foster opened this gorgeous B&B in their newly converted farmhouse, located in one of the most peaceful backwaters of the Matterdale valley. Tine is Danish, and the place exudes what the Danes call *hygge*: a sense of well-being, contentment and warmth. The four en suite bedrooms have a proper bath as well as a shower; they are named according to their respective views, which swing round from Blencathra to Helvellyn. The Garden Room has a sunny private patio, while the other rooms have access to a multi-level terrace. Breakfast is served on chunky wooden tables, with Tine's fruit salad, own-made granola and organic bread and muffins in pride of place, alongside traditional and vegetarian cooked breakfasts. Evening meals can also be prepared with advance notice. Children are welcome, and may find playmates in the two young Fosters.

Patterdale Hall

Patterdale, CA11 0PJ (017684 82308, www.phel.co.uk). Rates vary, check website for details.

Halfway between Glenridding and Patterdale, this 300-acre estate offers a wide range of self-catering accommodation. If the purpose-built chalets and lodges are too modern for your taste, consider the small hexagonal dairy, which sleeps two, the two-bedroom apartments in the coach house mews, or the snug, slate-built bothies, where the sleeping areas are tucked under the eaves. The surfeit of pine and flowery fabrics won't see the apartments featured in any interiors magazines, but they're good value and occupy a wonderful woodland setting. Alternatively, there are two larger cottages to the south of Patterdale Hall, which share a private garden and have splendid views.

Patterdale Youth Hostel

Patterdale, CA11 0NW (0845 371 9337, www.yha.org.uk). Rates £13.95 adult.

You'll find a mix of double-bedded rooms and dorms inside this slightly futuristic-looking 1970s building, just south of Ullswater on the banks of Goldrill Beck. Decor is cheery and retro. There's a laundry and drying room and a spacious common room with a stove; meals and packed lunches are available. It's a sociable place, often used by school groups and those attending YHA adventure weekends. In case of strains from coming down the fells too fast, or over-enthusiastic dancing at the Irish ceilidhs that are sometimes held here, the warden is a qualified sports masseur.

Quiet Site

Nr Watermillock, CA11 0LS (07768 727016, www.thequietsite.co.uk). Rates Camping from £17 per pitch. Pods £35. Cottages £600-£1,075 per week.

Set between Ullswater and Little Mell Fell, with terraced and sloping pitches for tents, hardstanding for caravans and motorhomes, and some funky timber pods for instant camping. Facilities include free showers (and, more unusually, baths), a shop, and an adventure playground and a games room for kids. The Quiet Bar in the old barn is decked out with beams, wooden wheels and old beer barrels, and serves a sterling selection of local real ales. Eco-friendly features include solar-heated water, a reedbed water treatment system and a recently planted wildflower

Side Farm Campsite. See p230.

meadow. Two holiday cottages (sleeping six and nine), can be rented together; with a trampoline and a wooden playhouse in the shared garden, children are in heaven.

k.
) is the stuff
se, then, that
ll but perfectly
ewing excellence.
quaff Mothbag – a
e, named in honour
ased moggie. Come
odied Red Bull Terrier
ely.

Foxfield
The Prince of Wales pub (*see p128*) near Broughton in Furness is home to the Foxfield Brewery. The beer range is constantly changing – hence the blank pump clips at the bar. If you fancy a light mild, opt for something from the 'Sands' range; the 'Encounter' beers are more bitter in taste. As the ingredients and strengths change, so do the names: Brief Encounter, Close Encounter and Third Encounter have all put in an appearance.

Hawkshead
www.hawksheadbrewery.co.uk.
The Hawkshead Brewery (*see p251*) is set on the River Kent in Staveley. Sample its range in the brewery's own Beer Hall, or look out for them at local pubs, both on pumps and in bottles. Award-winning Hawkshead Bitter is quaffed with great enthusiasm by weary fell walkers.

Hesket Newmarket
www.hesketbrewery.co.uk.
Owned by a village co-operative, the Old Crown (*see p207*) is a proper local boozer. A converted barn behind the pub houses the brewery. Blencathra Bitter, Pigs Might Fly and Sca Fell Blonde are among the idiosyncratic brews, dispensed in the pub and selected Lakeland hostelries. Tours include a meal at the Old Crown, and only cost a tenner.

Jennings
www.jenningsbrewery.co.uk.
One of Cumbria's best-known breweries, Jennings (*see p195*) was founded in 1828 and produces some characterful, and memorably named, beers. Tour the brewery's premises in Cockermouth, or conduct your own tasting session at any number of Lakeland pubs.

Keswick
www.keswickbrewery.co.uk.
A small, family-run enterprise, Keswick Brewery offers assorted seasonal and special beers in addition to its core range. The rich, malty Thirst Fall bitter is a classic, as is Thirst Run, a former winner at Keswick Beer Festival. Come Christmas, spread some festive cheer with the deliciously dark, spicy Thirst Noel.

Side Farm Campsite ★
Patterdale, CA11 0NL (017684 82337, www.lake districtcamping.co.uk/campsites/northeast/side_farm.htm). Open Easter-Oct. Rates £6 per person; £2 per vehicle.
There's no advance booking and no marked pitches at Side Farm, so arrive early to claim one of the the prime flat spots down by the lakeside. If you're successful, you'll find yourself in possession of one of the finest spots in the National Park: the steepest flank of Place Fell over your shoulder, Helvellyn dead ahead and the lower end of Ullswater in between. The other pitches (there are 70 in total) are sloping and somewhat stony; note that motorhomes are allowed, but caravans are not. Facilities are fairly basic: a stone-built toilet block, four free showers, a washing-up area with hot water and a laundry room with coin-operated washing machine and dryers. The tearoom in the old barn, serving flapjacks, slabs of fruit bread and ginger cake, ice-creams and mugs of tea, is strategically placed to tempt walkers descending from Place Fell or completing the shoreline walk from Howtown.

SOUTH OF ULLSWATER

Helvellyn
Ascending Helvellyn via the ridge of Striding Edge is probably the Lake District's most charismatic climb. Never mind that at 3,117 feet Helvellyn is England's third highest mountain; it's Striding Edge that is the real test of nerve for the average walker. Whether you set off from Glenridding or Patterdale, the paths converge at Hole-in-the-Wall. The rocky, mile-long ridge, falling away deeply and steeply on either side and very exposed, isn't quite a knife edge, but will probably feel like one. A lower and slightly less scary path follows the edge just beneath the apex; it also bypasses the rock tower of the Chimney, which intimidatingly blocks the route along the edge and involves a craggy climb. Finally, there's an unavoidable and steep – if less nervy – scramble to reach the Helvellyn summit and the relief of its plateau.

The textbook return to ground level involves negotiating a second arête – Swirral Edge, less intimidating and exposed than Striding Edge – before dropping down to Red Tarn. This is England's highest body of water to contain fish, with populations of wild brown trout and schelly. How the schelly got here is a mystery, as they're not known for climbing becks and waterfalls. Then it's downhill all the way back to Ullswater. The round trip is about nine miles, and takes some seven hours to complete. Don't undertake it unless you know what you're doing. It's not for the faint-hearted or the unfit, nor to be embarked upon in bad weather or poor visibility. The history of Striding Edge is littered with rescues and serious accidents, most poignantly in 1805 when a climber's skeleton was discovered two months after falling, his remains still guarded by his faithful dog. Warnings apart, it's a climb that will stay with you forever.

Lowthwaite Farm. See p227.

Things to do

Ullswater Steamers

Ullswater is great for taking to the water. There's a 10mph speed limit, but that's about the only restriction on the lake; it's technically a public highway. It has been a commercial waterway since ore and lead were transported from Glenridding, and mini submarines and flying boats were tested here during World War II. Boats and dinghies can be launched without the need to register your craft, and there are hire facilities at either end of the lake and halfway down at Watermillock.

You can also fish for perch (June to March) and brown trout (March to September). No permit is required for Ullswater and Brothers Water, though you do need a National Rivers Authority rod licence; daily, weekly or annual licences are sold at the Pooley Bridge and Glenridding tourist offices. Some say there are pike in Ullswater too, but the boat hire companies are so convinced that these are fishermen's tales they promise a free day's boat hire to anyone who lands one.

Sheltered bays and miniature pebble beaches are dotted along Ullswater's shore. Once you go beyond the shallows, though, the lake is extremely cold, even on the sunniest of days. Children should be supervised by a capable swimmer. In 2005 a man swimming from a dinghy died from the shock of the cold, while in 2006 three youths drowned after slipping off a shoreline ledge into 20ft of water; both tragedies occurred in summer.

POOLEY BRIDGE & THE EASTERN SHORE

Park Foot Trekking Centre
Park Foot Caravan & Camping Park, Howtown Road, Pooley Bridge, CA10 2NA (017684 86696, www.parkfootponytrekking.co.uk). Open Mar-Oct 10am-4pm daily. Rates 1hr £24; 90mins £35; 2hrs £40.
As well as running a large campsite, Park Foot offers escorted horse and pony trekking sessions for beginners and established riders. Hard hats and waterproofs are provided free of charge, and the scenery around Ullswater is glorious.

Lakeland Boat Hire
River Mouth, Eusemere, Pooley Bridge (017684 86800, www.lakelandboathire.co.uk). Open Easter-late Sept 10am-7pm daily (5pm low season). Rates vary, phone for details.
This friendly, family-owned operation has motorboats, rowing boats and Canadian canoes for hire.

Waterside Farm
How Town Road, Pooley Bridge, CA10 2NA (017684 86332, www.watersidefarm-campsite.co.uk). Open Mar-Oct 8.30am-5.30pm Mon-Thur, Sun; 8.30am-8.30pm Fri, Sat. Rates Camping £7-£11 per person. Boat hire £10 per hr; £25 half day; £40 full day. Mountain bikes £12 per day.
A mile or so from Pooley Bridge, Waterside Farm has a camping field on the lake's eastern shore, and also rents rowing boats, canoes and mountain bikes.

THE WESTERN SHORE TO PATTERDALE

Distant Horizons
Leeming Farm, Watermillock, CA11 0JJ (017684 86465, www.distant-horizons.co.uk). Open & rates vary, phone or check website for details.

There are outdoor activities galore to sample here, both on the water and in the mountains. Watery challenges include canoe and kayak skills sessions, sunset paddles and river descents, while land-based thrills run from canyoning, ghyll scrambling and rock climbing to navigation courses and winter skills training (think ice axes, crampons and finding out what to do in emergencies).

Glenridding Sailing Centre
The Spit, Glenridding, CA11 0PA (017684 82541, www.glenriddingsailingcentre.co.uk). Open Mar-Nov 10am-5pm daily. Rates Canoes & kayaks from £9 per hr. Sailing boats from £20 per hr. No credit cards.
You can hire all manner of craft here: sailing dinghies and single-handers; traditional little red-sailed boats; two- to three-person canoes and kayaks. Novice sailors can enrol on RYA-accredited courses, while the more experienced can hone their skills with expert tuition.

Rookin House Equestrian & Activity Centre
Troutbeck, CA11 0SS (017684 83561, www.rookinhouse.co.uk). Open 9am-4.30pm daily. Rates vary, check website for details.
The equestrian part of the centre provides hacks, treks and lessons, catering for riders of all ages, sizes and abilities. Adrenaline junkies can try quad biking, go-karting, clay pigeon shooting, JCB driving or the dizzying-looking 'human bowling'. More relaxed pursuits include archery tuition and fishing for rainbow trout.

St Patrick's Boat Landings
Glenridding, CA11 0QQ (017684 82393, www.stpatricksboatlandings.co.uk). Open Easter-Oct 9.30am-5pm daily. Rates £4.60-£11 per hr. No credit cards.
This shipshape enterprise hires out the jaunty little self-drive blue and white motorboats you'll see pootling about on the lake. Rowing boats, fishing boats and mountain bikes are also available, along with free customer car parking and a café.

Ullswater Steamers ★
The Pier House, Glenridding, CA11 0US (017684 82229, www.ullswater-steamers.co.uk). Open varies, check website for details. Tickets Round the Lake Pass £12.30; £6.15 reductions; £29.95 family. Single £5.60-£7.80; £2.80-£3.90 reductions.
The lake's historic steamers offer various fares and options. A Round the Lake Pass allows you to hop on and hop off all day, while a Walkers' Ticket gives you three stops. Alternatively, you can just pay as you go. In addition to the regular route around the lake from Pooley Bridge, with stops at Howtown and Glenridding, the company stages special events throughout the year: evening cruises with a talk about the lake from a National Park Ranger; a combined cruise and walk to watch the red deer rut in Martindale; photography trips with a professional photographer; or a Cumbrian fish supper cruise. *See also p225.*

Hartsop & Brothers Water

Two miles south of Ullswater, off the A592 to the east, is the tiny hamlet of Hartsop. It's one of the Lake District's architectural treasures and an official conservation area: no fewer than 12 of its 17th-century farm buildings and grey stone cottages, notable for their spinning galleries, outside staircases and circular chimneys, are Grade II listed. There are no public facilities except a car park outside the village, allowing for a peaceful, low-key exploration of what one suspects is more of a bijou weekend cottage community than a working one of spinners and shepherds. It's also the starting point for a stiff climb to Hayeswater, the Knott and High Street.

Just after the turn for Hartsop, on the other side of the road, sits serene, shallow Brothers Water, fringed by reeds and, in summer, dotted with lily pads. Called Broadwater until the 19th century, when two brothers drowned there and the name was changed, it's one of the Lake District's smallest lakes, less than two miles in circumference. Now owned by the National Trust, it's designated a 'quiet' lake, and no boating or leisure activities are allowed except trout fishing. Like Ullswater, the lake is believed to harbour the endangered (and protected) schelly fish – a legacy of the period when the two lakes were one. Sun-dappled woodland trails run close to the western shore to rejoin the A592 at Cow Bridge.

Half a mile south of Brothers Water are two secluded self-catering cottages (*see right*) that belong to 16th-century Hartsop Hall, a working hill farm also owned by the NT. From here, the road winds ever higher into a rock-strewn landscape of high fells and tumbling becks until it reaches the summit of Kirkstone Pass – the gateway to Windermere and Ambleside, and, at 1,489 feet, the highest pass in the Lake District.

Where to eat & drink

Part of the same site as Sykeside Camping Park (*see below*), the Brotherswater Inn (017684 82239, www.sykeside.co.uk) is a dependable option for a pint of real ale in the beer garden, a nip of whisky by the fire or some sturdy, unpretentious pub grub.

Where to stay

Hartsop Hall Cottages

Hartsop, CA11 0NZ (01229 860206, www.hartsop hallcottages.com). Rates £459-£856 per week. No credit cards.
On the southern side of Brothers Water, down a farm track at the mouth of Dovedale valley sits this traditional Lakeland farm. Its two self-catering properties, set among ancient barns and towering fells, are steeped in rural history. Dovedale Cottage occupies a wing of Grade I-listed Hartsop Hall; the interiors are traditional without being twee, and the garden is charming. Caudale Beck is a detached white-painted farmhouse, just off the Kirkstone Pass road. Inside, it's delightfully inviting, with an oil-fired Rayburn in the kitchen and oak beams and slouchy sofas in the lounge. The beck runs alongside the farmhouse, and there's a paved area for barbecues and alfresco suppers. Both cottages sleep six.

Sykeside Camping Park

Brothers Water, CA11 0NZ (017684 82239, www.sykeside.co.uk). Rates Camping varies, check website for details. Bunkhouse £14-£14.50 per person.
This is the last outpost of civilisation on the way up Kirkstone Pass – and as an all-year, all-weather retreat, its centrally heated bunkhouse and roadside pub are a blessing. The level camping field enjoys a superb location, surrounded on three sides by the high fells of Hartsop Dodd, Middle Dodd and Hart Crag, while a beck and footpath run down to Brothers Water. There are 19 hook-ups and hard standing for caravans and campervans. The bunkhouse is divided into two- to six-bed rooms, each with a toilet and washbasin, and there's a communal cooking area; showers are shared with the campsite. The shop has fruit, bread, milk, sausages, tinned goods and camping essentials, and a licensed bar, which also serves food, operates next to the shop in summer.

Willow Cottage

Hartsop, CA11 0NZ (017684 82647, www.hartsop.com). Rates £315-£470 per week. No credit cards.
Although it's called a cottage, Willow is actually a two-bedroom apartment on the ground floor of a barn conversion in the conservation village of Hartsop. The interior is simple and traditional without being old-fashioned, and uses local materials to charming effect: green-grey slate in the bathroom, and oak surfaces in the smart, modern kitchen. Views are good from the bedrooms, but note that the smaller one has a very narrow (4ft) double bed made specially for the space. The owners live in the apartment above.

Helvellyn. See p230.

Haweswater

Haweswater is one of the most fascinating destinations in the Lake District. It may be a reservoir, but it feels much more natural than some of the other man-made lakes, such as Thirlmere. Above, on Riggindale Crags, is the unique attraction of England's only wild golden eagle. Below is the enduring mystique of the drowned village of Mardale Green. It's also *Withnail & I* territory; Uncle Monty's cottage is just about standing and looks every bit as dismal as when the film was shot in 1986.

Most people bypass Haweswater because it's difficult to get to if you're ensconced in the heart of the Lakes. It entails leaving the National Park and re-entering it: from the northern lakes you have to approach via Askham; from the southern lakes the lengthy detour via Kendal, the A6 and Shap is an even greater deterrent. However, isolation brings its rewards. The simple, car-free valley of Swindale is one of the least known corners of the National Park. The summit of High Street is like no other in the Lakes, with its long plateau being both a former Roman road and an equally unlikely venue for horse racing.

Approaching from the north-east are several diverting sights: the biggest grass-covered building in Europe at the Rheged Centre; prehistoric earthworks at Mayburgh Henge and King Arthur's Round Table; and the stupendous ruins of Lowther Castle, alongside its feudal estate village.

Penrith to Haweswater

It's not strictly on the way to Haweswater, but just off the A66 west of Penrith is the Rheged Centre (*see below*). Despite all the Lake District's natural wonders, this has proved to be its second most popular attraction after Windermere cruises, with close on 450,000 visitors in 2009. It's certainly peculiar – a semi-subterranean, grass-covered mound with play areas and a 3-D cinema – but after that it's little more than a shopping centre.

Just south of Penrith at Eamont Bridge, amid the spaghetti of the M6, the A6 and the West Coast main rail line, are two large circular neolithic mounds and ditches going back some 3,000 years: Mayburgh Henge and King Arthur's Round Table. Both are tended by English Heritage, and are open all year, free of charge. Mayburgh is bigger, with a monolith at its heart, and its partner has a clearer layout and, despite its name, has nothing to do with King Arthur.

Following the A6 south, the village of Clifton is where the last battle on English soil was fought on 18 December 1745 – a skirmish between Prince Charles' Jacobite rebels and the Duke of Cumberland's Hanoverian forces. About 100 men were killed and each side has a memorial: the 'Rebel Tree' at the south of the village is the Jacobites burial spot, marked by a brass plaque, while St Cuthbert's graveyard has a memorial stone for the government men. Also in Clifton is the Lowther estate-owned George & Dragon (*see p241*), the most sophisticated pub for miles around.

East of Clifton, just over a mile away at Melkinthorpe in the Eden Valley, is Larch Cottage Nurseries. Landscape gardener Peter Stott has created an unusual enterprise here: combining garden centre, garden, art gallery and restaurant, it has 15,000 plant varieties, rare shrubs, old-fashioned roses, house plants and statuary. The Greenhouse restaurant (*see p241*) serves Italian-inspired lunches, and the Red Barn Gallery puts on changing exhibitions of contemporary British art.

Back on the A6 is Lowther, the estate village of the Earls of Lonsdale, a striking collection of tenant homes built to accompany the catastrophically

---

Places to visit

Rheged Centre
Redhills, CA11 0DQ (01768 868000, www.rheged.com). Open 10am-5.30pm daily.
Rheged is the name for the ancient Celtic kingdom of Cumbria, which has been curiously reborn two minutes from junction 40 of the M6. Designed to look like a hill, Rheged claims to be the biggest grass-covered building in Europe. Westmorland, the outfit behind the impressive Tebay Services (*see p236*) on the M6, call it 'an all-weather visitors' attraction' and can point to a 3-D cinema, an adventure playground, pottery painting, a soft play area, cafés and an exhibition space as elements of interest. But mainly it's shops. These are pleasantly arranged and cover local food, outdoor gear, books and lots of bags, scarves, jewellery and gifts. The self-billing as 'Cumbria's family day out' is stretching it. There's some potential wallet stretching too, with the adventure playground costing £1.50, soft play £1, pottery painting £3.50-£6.95 and a 3-D film £6.50 or £19.50 for a family ticket.

At your service

Motorway service stations are rarely praised, but Tebay Services (www.westmorland.com/tebay) – located between junctions 38 and 39 of the M6, with access northbound and southbound – is a noble exception. It opened in 1972 and belongs to a family firm, Westmorland. Good food and good service are the aims – and the surroundings are admirably different from the norm too, combining rugged stone and big beams with shiny white modern finishes.

Brand-name fast food is out; instead the takeaway stand offers proper soups and lamb hotpot, warm pies and hot and cold drinks. The dining area provides self-service hot meals and a central island laden with salads, decent sandwiches and tempting cakes. The tables have a view over a duck pond towards rolling hills and the Lake District fells. The shop sells fresh fruit and veg, local hams and smoked fish; there's also a deli and a cheese counter stocked with Cumbrian specialities, and a butcher's shop. The well-designed 'family area' features a kitchen with a sink, a place to warm up baby food and an indoor play area. If only all motorway services were like this.

ruined Lowther Castle, whose architect Robert Smirke went on to design the rather smaller British Museum in London. A public footpath runs from the village past the north front of the hulking shell of the castle and down to the River Lowther and St Peter's Church (another Smirke design, replacing a 13th-century church). Over the road is Askham Hall, a privately owned Elizabethan hall that became the family home of the Lowthers after they left the castle. The Queen and Prince Philip, friends of the 7th Earl, often stayed here when the Duke of Edinburgh came to compete at the now defunct Lowther Carriage Driving Trials.

Askham village, just west of Lowther, was absorbed by the Lowther estate in 1724. It's postcard-perfect, with two long, parallel village greens lined with rows of attractive cottages. It has two conventional country pubs in the Punchbowl and the Queen's Head, a toy shop, a post office with a coffee shop, and a heated outdoor swimming pool (01931 712168), open in the summer holidays.

Following the River Lowther further south along the valley, Bampton is the last settlement before Haweswater. Bampton's claim to fame is the red phone box in which Withnail rang his agent in

Haweswater. See p238.

High Street

the cult movie *Withnail & I.* Devotees of the film descend on the village from all over the world to track down locations such as Uncle Monty's cottage or the field where Withnail and Marwood take on the bull, or to re-enact the duo's drinking games in the excellent Mardale Inn (*see p242*) – it didn't appear in the film, but the landlord knows all the stories backwards. Bampton's store and post office has a sweet tearoom and B&B accommodation.

Haweswater ★

Haweswater was once a natural lake made up of High Water and Low Water. Alongside were the ancient farming communities of Measand and Mardale Green. Now it's one mighty reservoir, four miles long and half a mile wide, supplying tap water to Manchester and the north-west. Like Thirlmere, it is operated by United Utilities (which owns 26,000 acres of land and water in the Lakes), but it was built in 1935 by Manchester Corporation, which compulsorily purchased the valley, including the small settlement of Mardale Green that once stood here. The villagers were evacuated, the royal engineers blew up their houses, and the bodies were exhumed from the graveyard and reburied in Shap churchyard. The stones from the church went into the wall and tower of the dam (1,550 foot wide, 120 feet high) that was constructed at the reservoir's northern end. Local farms, long famed for their butter and cream, and the centuries-old Dun Bull Inn disappeared beneath the water. No one was paid any compensation.

Photographs bear witness to the last heart-breaking church service, relayed by loudhailer to the hundreds who stood in the hillside next to the packed little church. They sang Psalm 121: 'I will lift up mine eyes to the hills, from whence cometh my help.' In the crowd was the Reverend Barham, for 25 years vicar of Mardale, who the Bishop of Carlisle had not thought to invite to the final service.

In times of extreme drought the ruins of Mardale Green are exposed again. In 1984 the police had to close the road as sightseers, TV crews and a few former residents flocked into the valley to gaze at the drowned village. Each time there is less and less to see. The drystone walls, above and below the waterline, are the one prominent surviving feature.

Despite such torrid beginnings, Haweswater is a quiet and lovely place today. Even Wainwright conceded that Manchester Corporation did a reasonable job. Its lone road begins at Burnbanks at the north-east corner, where a few dwellings mark the encampment of the 1930s dam builders. The road runs for five miles along the eastern shore, with progressively fine views towards dales and fells. The only building on the road is the Haweswater Hotel (*see p242*), built in 1937 to replace the Dun Bull Inn at Mardale Green and sporting a vintage RAC sign outside. The road and reservoir curl to an end at Mardale Head, where a small car park fills up early with hikers setting off for walks up High Street, Harter Fell and Kidsty Pike.

Swindale

Make sure you bring powerful binoculars because Riggindale Crags, at the southern end of Haweswater, is the home of the only wild golden eagle in England. Follow a two-mile footpath from the Mardale Head car park around the western shore to the RSPB viewing platform in Riggindale. The first pair of eagles came here in 1969, but since the last female died in 2005, the last male, now about 13 years old, has had no mate and is increasingly unlikely to attract one. Some 16 chicks have been born down the years; the survivors are thought to have settled in Scotland.

Rumours spread during the winter of 2009-10 that England's last eagle was missing presumed dead, but at Easter 2010 the RSPB confirmed that his six-foot wingspan was still soaring above Haweswater and High Street. Close encounters can be scary. A golden eagle is a formidable bird of prey, capable of taking lambs and killing roe deer, and one walker reported having to protect his small dog from attack.

High Street

High Street, west of Haweswater, sounds as if it belongs more to Kensington than to the biggest mountain in the eastern Lakes, but it is well named, for, astonishingly enough, a Roman road ran right along the summit plateau and continued at high altitude for a good eight miles before dropping down near Askham. Not surprisingly, it's England's highest Roman road, peaking at 2,718 feet. It linked the forts at Ambleside and Penrith, 23 miles

apart; at Roman soldiers' mandated speed, it was a six-hour march. Today's track along High Street closely follows the course of the original road. An ancient ridgeway predated the Romans, and it remained a packhorse route into the 19th century.

The tradition of the annual Mardale Meet on High Street, where shepherds gathered for Cumberland wrestling and pony racing close to the summit on Racecourse Hill, ended in 1935 with the creation of the reservoir. To reach High Street from Mardale Head, cross Mardale Beck and take the relentless straight line over Riggindale Crags or follow Mardale Beck up to Small Water Tarn and then circle right over Mardale Ill Bell. To the west almost all the Lake District lies before you, and you can march on north on top of the world.

Beyond Haweswater

When Manchester Corporation built the Haweswater reservoir, road links were so sparse they had to create a concrete access road over the moors from Shap and the A6. Unmarked and little used, it makes a superb cycle track. Just before Swindale Beck, another minor road leads into Swindale. Few pass this way – it's impossible to park once you enter the dale at the cattle grid – and there's not so much as a bunkhouse or a farmhouse B&B, or any great sights to admire. As a peaceful backwater with timeless lakeland features of farm and fell, though, it's hard to beat.

It was just such peace and solitude that brought the Premonstratensian order to a quiet bend in the

The Lowthers

Nobody travels far in the Lake District without coming across the Lowther name. It features on castles and caravan parks, pubs and streets, plantations and free-range chickens, a river and a village. Their knights and earls and MPs have been Lakeland's dominant feudal family since the 12th century. It was famously said that in the 18th century you could walk from coast to coast across the north of England without leaving Lowther land, and despite financial crises and contraction the family retains some 72,000 acres of Cumbria and is the biggest private landowner in the National Park.

At the heart of this empire is the fantastic ruin of Lowther Castle, the seat of the Earls of Lonsdale. One of the biggest stately homes ever built, it stands high and hopeless on a hill overlooking the road from Penrith to Haweswater. It's been a windowless, roofless shell for 50 years, with 120 acres of overgrown gardens. Countless schemes to make something of the castle have come to nothing and now the plans go no further than making it safe and opening the grounds to the public.

The Lowther wealth came from coal and iron mines across Cumbria, from the development of Whitehaven as one of the most prosperous ports during the slave trade, and from a slave plantation in Barbados. The family fortunes survived the scandals of 'Wicked Jimmy' the 1st Earl, but took a drastic turn for the worse when the 5th Earl inherited in 1882. Known as the 'Yellow Earl' because he dressed his servants and fleet of motors in yellow livery, he was an all-round voluptuary, gambler and bon vivant and crippled the family financially.

The 7th Earl (who died in 2006) inherited the debts. Unable to find a buyer or a use for the castle, he sold the contents in the ultimate country house sale, stripped the roof and windows to avoid death duties, and effectively abandoned the place.

building called Sleddale Hall. Nobody has lived here for 25 years, and it's often been broken into, but its fame is international. Better known as Crow Crag, this is Uncle Monty's cottage from *Withnail & I*. When United Utilities sold the building at auction in 2009, the first successful bidder – at £295,000 – was the landlord of the Mardale Inn at Bampton. But the deal fell through and it was finally sold to a Kent architect, a fan of the movie, who has pledged to restore it in a way true to the spirit of the film. ('Warm up? We may as well sit round this cigarette. This is ridiculous. We'll be found dead in here next spring.')

River Lowther in 1199. They built the last abbey to be founded in England, Shap Abbey; it was also the last to be dissolved, in 1540. Lying about a mile west of Shap village, it's now cared for by English Heritage. All that remains apart from the foundation walls is the 16th-century west tower. Even so, it is not too hard to imagine the white-robed monks going quietly about their business. The best of the carved stonework was removed by the Earl of Lonsdale and used in Lowther Castle and for garden ornaments.

A footpath leads from the abbey south to Keld, where the National Trust's 15th-century Keld Chapel is another religious gem. With bare stone walls inside and out, a few rickety benches and a wooden table for an altar, it has humility and simplicity. A notice on the chapel door should tell you where to borrow the key.

The last diversion from the reservoir road is a right turn west to Wet Sleddale reservoir, a feeder for the Haweswater system. There's not much to see here and the setting can be positively dispiriting on a cold, wet winter day. A path circles the small reservoir and passes a semi-derelict

Where to eat & drink

George & Dragon ★

Clifton, CA10 2ER (01768 865381, www.georgeand dragonclifton.co.uk). Open 11am-midnight daily. Lunch served noon-2.30pm, dinner served 6-9.30pm daily.

Ancient and modern mix seamlessly in this stylishly revamped gastropub with rooms. It's on the A6, set back at the southern end of Clifton village. Exposed old stone sets off leather chairs; painted benches sit next to new oak tables; modern lamps spotlight the hanging hops. The lunch menu lists soup, sandwiches and hot dishes, such as Askham Hall rare-breed pork sausages and mash, and a pie, pasta, fish and risotto of the day. The more extensive dinner menu is in similar vein, with nothing over £13 and plenty of blackboard specials. Gloucester Old Spot pork, longhorn beef and roe deer are sourced from the landlord's Lowther estate. The ten bedrooms (£89-£135 double incl breakfast) continue the stylish, modern vibe. There's a family room with a double bed and two singles, plus a bike store and drying room that should please cyclists and walkers.

Greenhouse

Larch Cottage Nurseries, Melkinthorpe, CA1 2DR (01931 712446, www.larchcottage.co.uk). Open 10am-4.45pm daily.

George & Dragon

The best seats at this modern little café are those on the canopied terrace, overlooking the statues, fountains and plants of the nursery. The food has a definite Italian bias, with the accent on pasta dishes, paninis and pizzas (anchovy, black olive and mozzarella, say, baked in a dedicated pizza oven). Vegetables are organic and fresh from the garden. Desserts might be limoncello and blueberry cheesecake or pizza dolce: a ground almond and honey base, finished with Marsala custard. Cakes change every day, but the bestsellers are the Greenhouse (gluten-free) chocolate cake or sticky date cake – good with either morning coffee or afternoon tea.

Mardale Inn@St Patrick's Well ★
Bampton, CA10 2RQ (01931 713244, www.mardaleinn.co.uk). Open 11am-11pm daily. Lunch served noon-5pm, dinner served 6-9pm daily.
'A two-course farmers' meal £5' says the sign outside this nicely updated old inn. It has to be the best-value lunch in Lakeland. Delicious parsnip soup followed by venison pie, served among rustic benches and pine tables, is worth anybody's fiver. Walls are painted an on-trend chalky green with outbreaks of exposed stone. Lamps shine out of pretty wall sconces and, in winter, glowing logs burn in big grates. For dinner the menu scales up a little, with the likes of Allerdale goat's cheese salad, potted shrimps, lemon risotto with king prawns or Withnail venison burger. There are also four simply furnished double bedrooms with modern bathrooms (£80 double incl breakfast). Dogs are welcome, at no extra charge.
Scenes from *Withnail & I* were filmed around Bampton, although not at the pub. Don't bother demanding 'the finest wines known to humanity' and so on – they've heard it all before. In fact, the pub's website points pilgrims to a few nearby locations used in the film.

Yanwath Gate Inn
Yanwath, CA10 2LF (01768 862386, www.yanwath gate.com). Open noon-11pm daily. Lunch served noon-2.30pm, dinner served 6-9pm daily.
The oak beams, wood panelling, horse brasses and swirly red carpets might suggest just another time-warp pub with a microwave in the kitchen. In fact, the Gate's menu starts with half a dozen oysters and continues to moules marinière, black bream, wild venison steak and stuffed aubergine, with the likes of lemon cheesecake and champagne sorbet and good local cheeses to finish. Eat by the fire in the bar or trade up in the evening to the raftered dining room. There's a changing list of real ales on tap and a substantial wine list. A two-bedroom self-catering cottage is also available, costing £410-£715 per week. The pub is a couple of miles south of Penrith, just off the A6.

Where to stay
All the pubs mentioned above offer accommodation. Pick of the bunch is the George & Dragon (*see p241*), thanks to its attractive, boutique hotel-style rooms with glamorous bathrooms, crisp white linen and wool throws.

Haweswater Hotel
Bampton, CA10 2RP (01931 713235, www.haweswater hotel.com). Rates from £109 double incl breakfast.
The only hotel near Haweswater. It has its critics, but you can't fault the spectacular location above the north-eastern end of the reservoir, with uninterrupted views of the lake and surrounding fells. Built in 1937, it has 21 rooms, and retains something of a period feel in its fireplaces and windows. Refurbishment is taking place, so ask for one of the newer rooms.

Shap Abbey. See p240.

South Lakes & Kendal

Most people assume, naturally enough, that the Lakes proper start at Windermere. In fact, the National Park takes in substantial swathes of prime countryside to the east of Windermere, which are rarely explored as people hurry in on the A591 from Kendal, or rush home on the A590 further south. There are the long-fingered, dead-end valleys of Longsleddale and Kentmere, heading deep into little-walked fells. More popular, because it leads to the Kirkstone Pass and Ullswater, is the Troutbeck Valley. South of the A591 corridor, the Lyth and Winster Valleys combine to form a gorgeous section of undulating countryside, famous for its riotous spring blossoms and damsons. Instead of lakes and mountains, there's a web of rural lanes and some of the best eating pubs in Cumbria.

Just beyond the National Park boundary is Cartmel, a beautiful old town enhanced by the county's most decorated restaurant. Not far away are the grander destinations of three stately homes: Holker Hall, Sizergh Castle and Levens Hall, the latter famed for its outstanding topiary gardens. Arnside, in the southernmost corner of the region, is the start of one of the Lake District's most unusual guided walks. No peaks are involved; instead it's a three-hour trek across the treacherous shifting sands of Morecambe Bay. Finally, there's the town that sits less than a mile outside the Park, but is bypassed by millions of visitors every year. It has culture, museums, history and some excellent shopping treats. Don't forget Kendal.

SOUTH LAKES VALLEYS

Longsleddale

Most easily reached from the A6, but more enjoyably accessed via the back roads to Garnett Bridge off the A591, Longsleddale is the gentlest of dales. There are no lakes, no pubs, no B&Bs and no shops – not even a post office, in fact. And no mobile phone reception. Unless you're walking on to Kentmere Pike (2,397 feet) or Haweswater, it's six miles from dale end to dale head, and six miles back again – a journey followed by medieval drovers, and little changed in the intervening centuries. The River Sprint keeps you company, sometimes serene, sometimes darting ahead, while the single-track road undulates between age-old drystone walls covered in velvety moss.

Halfway along the valley stands the plain and simple St Mary's Church. To the left of the altar is a wooden spice cupboard, with '1662' carved on its door. A small piece of stained glass depicts the church's other treasure: a silver chalice, now held at Carlisle Cathedral for safekeeping. Facilities include a car park, a phone box, a picnic table and some public toilets. A little further on at Middale, footpaths branch out up and down the dale and over the fells to Kentmere.

As the dale narrows and steepens, amid the grey of stone and slate a whitewashed farmhouse stands out beneath Shipman Knotts. The tarmac road runs out at Sadgill, where once a day a red post office van crosses the humpback bridge at the end of its run. Seems familiar? Was that a black and white cat in the passenger seat? This was the inspiration for Postman Pat's bridge in fictional Greendale in John Cunliffe's children's stories. Happily, sleepy Longsleddale can't be bothered to exploit the connection. Its one concession to modernity is a community website, www.longsleddale.co.uk, which lists six self-catering establishments that will guarantee a week of peace in one of the quietest corners of the Lake District.

Staveley & Kentmere Valley

Midway between Kendal and Windermere the A591 bypasses Staveley, a little town that is not just the gateway to the Kentmere Valley, but an interesting example of business reinvention. The community once depended on the bobbin mill that supplied the Lancashire cotton mills, but now the Mill Yard is bustling with the new service industries of the 21st-century Lake District. There's award-winning artisan bakery More? (see p263); state-of-the-art cooking school Lucy Cooks; Wheelbase, a warehouse temple to cycling; and the Hawkshead Brewery (for all, see p251), a microbrewery that grew big enough to send its award-winning ales into 500 pubs and now runs brewery tours. Its on-site Beer Hall combines with neighbouring Wilf's Café (see p250) to keep any visitor to Mill Yard happily fed and watered.

After a few pints of Hawkshead Bitter, it might be wise to take the seasonal 519 Kentmere Rambler bus from Mill Yard to explore the Kentmere Valley. A dead-end road winds its way for three miles along the village, ending at Kentmere village. Watching the River Kent smash through the valley, it's easy to see how it once powered mills for bobbin-making,

spinning, dying and weaving. One former mill, at the confluence of the Kent and Park Beck, is an idyllic home for Kentmere Pottery (01539 821621, http://clients.thisisthelakedistrict.co.uk/kentmere pottery/contact.html). Pop in to admire (and buy) the handthrown pots.

On the left of the road, across a marshy expanse is Kentmere Tarn. Although popular with anglers, the straggly, one-mile-long pool appears unremarkable; nonetheless, it has its history. Archaeologists unearthed a 12-foot-long, 13th-century dugout boat there. And when it was drained for farmland in the 19th century, diatomite (a powdery rock valuable in insulation processes) was found on the lake bed. It created a thriving cottage industry until the lake was filled up again.

At the head of the valley the road ends for vehicles, with a small parking area next to the village hall. St Cuthbert's Church borders on the austere, but the villagers have brightened it with 100 or so wool tapestry kneelers depicting spring flowers, robins, crosses and rural scenes. Henry Marshall (Wainwright's first printer) is buried in the churchyard, but the grave of his son, Roger, who died climbing Everest in 1987, is empty because his body was never found.

Various demanding walks start from the village. It's a four-mile trek along an old rocky road via Garburn Pass to Troutbeck. The route is popular with mountain bikers, and is more peaceful than it used to be now that 4WDs and other off-road contraptions have been banned. En route you'll pass the standalone boulder known as Badger

Rock, which has acted as a training ground for generations of climbers. Alternatively, you could continue straight up the valley to Kentmere Reservoir and on to Haweswater.

The most compelling challenge is the Kentmere Round, a horseshoe walk of 12 miles, about ten peaks (depending on definition) and 7,500 feet of ascents. The summits include Kentmere Pike, Harter Fell, Mardale III Bell, Thornthwaite Crag and Yoke. There's a welcome cup of tea to be found at Mag's Howe in Kentmere in summer. Otherwise, it's back to Staveley for the nearest refreshment and other facilities.

Troutbeck Valley

After the seclusion of Longsleddale and Kentmere, the next valley west is altogether different. With a through road (A592) to the Kirkstone Pass and Ullswater, the footprint of civilisation is much deeper here, not least with summer traffic and the rash of holiday park timber lodges.

That said, Troutbeck's popularity is primarily down to its beauty. Nature sends Trout Beck gushing down from Thornthwaite Crag to divide Wansfell Pike and Applethwaite Common before feeding into Windermere. Humans have taken the local stone and slate to assemble one of the loveliest collections of old buildings in the National Park. Leave the A592 and take the back road through the Troutbeck hamlets, where nearly every house is listed and many are 300 years old. There are spinning galleries and mullioned windows galore. These are prized properties, with

Lyth Valley. See p247.

local pride most evident over the late May bank holiday when a dozen or so houses open for the biennial Troutbeck Garden Trail, followed by tea in the village hall. Details are available at www. troutbeck.org/village_association_garden_trail.html.

Many places belong to the National Trust, notably Troutbeck Park Farm (closed to the public), one of the farms bequeathed to the NT by Beatrix Potter and where she bred Herdwick sheep. On the branch road towards Ambleside, look out for the sign for the NT's wildflower hay meadow as the foreground to a tremendous view of Windermere. Just as the road splits is another Trust property, Townend (*see p254*). Not a stately home but a yeoman's house,

it was occupied by generations of the Browne family, farmers and businessmen, and has all the trappings of well-to-do 17th-century family life. The NT also owns the historic Town End barn opposite, built in 1666 and a perfect example of a 'bank barn'. It's still in daily use.

For refreshment, choose between the swish Queen's Head Hotel (*see p250*) or the less dolled-up Mortal Man (*see p249*). At Town Head, the back road rejoins the main road to resume its long climb north to Kirkstone Pass on the Lake District's highest road. Heading south, its only a couple of miles to Windermere, with Holehird Gardens (*see p34*) the last haven of peace before you hit town.

Troutbeck Valley

Lyth & Winster Valleys

The twin valleys of Lyth and Winster run parallel to one another between Kendal and Windermere, south from the A591. They may lack high-octane alpine scenery, but they do offer a lush slice of pure English countryside nestling between the Pennines and the Lakeland fells.

Their pastoral fame centres on the Westmorland damson orchards, which break out in spectacular white blossom every spring. Around Easter, Lyth Valley's Low Farm celebrates the revival of the damson orchards after their near demise following World War II with Damson Day. It's a proper country fair, with blossom walks and a thanksgiving service at St Mary's in Crosthwaite. Every sort of damson product is available, from gin, beer and wine to bread, jam and chocolate. Come September, when the fruit has ripened, roadside stalls pop up selling homemade damson jam and jars of bottled fruit.

Apart from untroubled country walks and dabbling in damson, the great attraction here is in eating at the area's four outstanding pubs: the suave and sophisticated Punch Bowl Inn, game specialist the Brown Horse, the quaint old Masons Arms (for all, *see p249*) and the polished Wheatsheaf (*see p250*). Call them what you will – gastropubs, dining inns or restaurants with rooms – but each has its own distinct flavour.

Bags packed, milk cancelled, house raised on stilts.

You've packed the suntan lotion, the snorkel set, the stay-pressed shirts. Just one more thing left to do – your bit for climate change. In some of the world's poorest countries, changing weather patterns are destroying lives.

You can help people to deal with the extreme effects of climate change. Raising houses in flood-prone regions is just one life-saving solution.

**Climate change costs lives.
Give £5 and let's sort it *Here & Now***

www.oxfam.org.uk/climate-change

Oxfam is a registered charity in
England and Wales (No.202918)
and Scotland (SCO039042). Oxfam GB
is a member of Oxfam International.

Be Humankind Oxfam

Where to eat & drink

South Lakes is definitely one of the best areas in the Lake District to find good food. As well as the Lyth and Winster Valleys' collection of trendy dining pubs, you'll find some smashing casual eateries, including Wilf's Café (*see p250*) in Staveley.

Brown Horse

Winster, LA23 3NR (015394 43443, www.thebrown horseinn.co.uk). Open 11am-11pm daily. Lunch served noon-2pm daily. Dinner served 6-9pm Mon-Fri, Sun; 6-9.30pm Sun.

When the bar is packed out with beaters from the local shoot, you can expect to find something gamey on the menu and game-cooking expertise in the kitchen. Sure enough, roast pheasant with all the trimmings, and tender loin of venison on creamed cabbage, both sourced from the local estate, were textbook-perfect. Food is served in an aged dining room that strangely but successfully mixes old oak with new leather, Swedish-style Gustavian furniture with a faux antique tapestry, assorted antlers and trendy candelabra. The bar has rougher edges, but whether you're drinking organic wine or local ale, the reliable mix of flagged floor, low beams and open fire does the trick. When the vegetable nursery and microbrewery are both on stream, the pub will be all but self-sufficient. There are nine smart bedrooms, with lovely views over the Winster Valley.

Masons Arms

Strawberry Bank, LA11 6NW (015395 68486, www. masonsarmsstrawberrybank.co.uk). Open 11am-midnight daily. Food served Summer noon-9pm daily. Winter Lunch served noon-2.30pm, dinner served 6-9pm daily.

Competition is strong, but for genuine olde worlde pub cosiness, it's tough to beat the Masons. Witness the warren of low-ceilinged rooms with their dark oak beams and rough wood tables and settles; the museum piece of a black-leaded range with hanging irons, spits and kettles; and the whitewashed exterior with parasols and hypnotic summer evening views across the Winster Valley. Food is rich and hearty: game pie with juniper berries, belly pork and black pudding fritter, and thick wedges of baked cheesecake made with clotted cream. The five bedroom suites and two self-catering cottages strike a more modern note.

Mortal Man

Troutbeck, LA23 1PL (015394 33193, www.the mortalman.co.uk). Open 11am-11pm daily. Lunch served noon-3pm Mon-Fri; noon-4pm Sat, Sun. Dinner served 6-9pm daily.

The name is explained by the inn sign and historic mission statement: 'O mortal man that lives by bread/What is it makes thy nose so red?/Thou silly fool that looks so pale/Tis drinking Sally Birkett's Ale.' The ale is still strong and, according to the specials board, the bread has upgraded to pheasant – great value at a tenner. On a sunny day the Troutbeck Valley looks perfect from the beer garden. Elsewhere, this sturdy old inn is in transition from dated naff decor to lilac throws and satin cushions in the 12 bedrooms (£80-£100 double incl breakfast).

Punch Bowl Inn ★

Crosthwaite, LA8 8HR (015395 68237, www.the punchbowl.co.uk). Open 11am-midnight daily. Food served noon-9.30pm daily.

Tasteful on the eye and tasty on the plate, the Punch Bowl sets the benchmark for sophistication among Lakeland's gastropubs. The bar is topped with local slate, the floor is polished oak and the lighting comes from fat candles and the glow of burning logs. The menu offers the likes of Italian fish soup, pot-roast pheasant breast, beef bourguignon and some inventive vegetarian dishes, such as macaroni cheese with black truffle cream. After tasting the local microbrewery ale, the globe-trotting selection of wine or champagne by the glass, it's delightfully easy to curl up on the giant leather sofa and drift away. There's more formality in the dining room for the evening à la carte, and nine glamorous bedrooms (*see p251*) for a full sleepover and a sterling breakfast.

Brown Horse

Wilf's Café

Queen's Head Hotel

*Troutbeck, LA23 1PW (015394 32174, www.queens
headhotel.com). Open 11am-midnight daily. Food served
noon-9pm daily.*

This upmarket dining pub with rooms looks as if it sees
more well-heeled wellies than muddy climbers' boots,
judging from the number of Range Rovers lined up in the
car park. The interior resembles an antiques warehouse
with its Elizabethan-style black oak and stuffed wildlife.
The log fires and candlelight couldn't be more comforting
on a raw day, and the menu is designed for feel-good
seasonal eating too – all sturdy ham hocks and lamb
shanks in autumn, for example. Fish specials might include
sea bream on lemon risotto with a crayfish sauce. With
bread and butter and side orders kicking in at £3.50, eating
à la carte can soon mount up – but it is top-quality fare.
There's also a £20 three-course menu du jour. The spirit of
the place is better embodied in the bars than the more
formal restaurant areas.

Wheatsheaf

*Brigsteer, LA8 8AN (015395 68254, www.the
wheatsheafbrigsteer.co.uk). Open noon-3pm, 6-11pm
daily. Lunch served noon-2pm, dinner served 6-9pm
daily.*

Don't drive past, thinking this is a typical roadside boozer.
Inside is a clean, uncluttered interior, where you can enjoy
terrific food in the bar or dining room. Start, perhaps, with
potted Morecambe Bay shrimps or Millom crab with lemon
and caper jelly and wholemeal bread; follow that with
Holker venison and confit potato or sea bass with buttered
samphire. To finish, there's baked white chocolate
cheesecake or rhubarb and custard crème brûlée with own-
made ginger biscuit. It all tastes as good as it reads. There
are also three guest rooms (£85 double incl breakfast).

Wilf's Café

*Mill Yard, Staveley, LA8 9LR (01539 822329,
www.wilfs-cafe.co.uk). Open Summer 9am-5pm Mon-
Fri; 8.30am-5pm Sat, Sun. Winter 9am-5pm daily.*

A cheerful daytime-only café adjacent to Hawkshead
Brewery (*see right*), Wilf's serves up hearty dishes such as
veggie chilli, welsh rarebit and baked potatoes. Eat inside,
sit on the terrace over the River Kent or slope next door to
the Beer Hall for a pint of Hawkshead Gold. In the summer,
free guided walks led by a National Park warden leave from
the café at 11am on Tuesdays and Fridays.

Where to stay

The excellent bevy of dining pubs in the South Lakes
also offer supremely comfortable accommodation.

In Troutbeck, the Queen's Head (*see p250*) has
15 rooms (£130-£150 double incl breakfast) above
the pub or across the way in the barn conversion.
They're all dressed to the nines with lavish throws,
cushions and curtains; expect to pay more if you
want a four-poster bed.

At the Brown Horse (*see p249*) in Winster,
take your pick from five charming cottage rooms
traditionally furnished with pine and flower-sprigged
curtains or the four new rooms, which have more
contemporary decor and full-length windows to
make the most of the valley views (£70-£100
double incl breakfast).

In Strawberry Bank, the Masons Arms (*see p249*)
offers five smartly equipped one-bed suites (£75-
£145), decorated mainly in a muted palette of
whites and creams, and two self-catering cottages
(£130-£175). Lyth Cottage sleeps two and Winster
Cottage four, though both also have a double sofa

bed. Enjoy a private sundowner on the terrace before repairing to the bar for some splendidly robust pub food.

The Punch Bowl Inn (see p249) in Crosthwaite has nine rooms beautifully kitted out with premium-quality everything, from the beds to the bathroom toiletries. The views are gorgeous, the service charming, the vibe appealingly relaxed and the breakfast delicious – though prices are hotel-high (£125-£245 double incl breakfast).

Cowmire Hall Bothy ★
Crosthwaite, LA8 8JJ (015395 68200, www.cowmire. co.uk). Rates £450 per week. No credit cards.
A converted bothy loft makes a seductive self-catering getaway for two (although you can fit two more in a gallery). It's simply and tastefully done out in white and old oak, with warmth from a Rayburn and a log fire. The ground floor is where Cowmire's damson gin is made (on sale here and at Fortnum & Mason). If you have a canoe or dinghy you can launch it at the farm's boathouse and slipway, tucked into the south-west corner of Windermere. Guests can also borrow a rowing boat and use the dayroom in the boathouse.

Howe Farm
Lyth Valley, LA8 8DF (07810 091008, www.howe farm.com). Rates £700-£1,150 per week. No credit cards.
Rustic 17th-century farmhouse meets colourful modern art in this three-bedroom self-catering property in the pastoral Lyth Valley. The characterful interior mixes half-timbered walls, invitingly plump sofas and a log-burning stove with contemporary white dining room furniture. The bedrooms (two double, one twin) have wrought-iron beds, while the rambling garden has its own sculpture, glorious views and a damson orchard.

Stockdale Cottage
Longsleddale, LA8 9BE (01539 823210, www. stockdalecottage.co.uk). Rates £390-£480 per week. No credit cards.

Things to do

SOUTH LAKES VALLEYS

Hawkshead Brewery & Beer Hall ★
Mill Yard, Staveley, LA8 9LR (01539 822644, www.hawksheadbrewery.co.uk). Open noon-5pm Mon, Tue; noon-6pm Wed-Sun. Admission free.
Hawkshead Brewery was launched in 2002 by former BBC foreign correspondent Alex Brodie, who, weary of reporting from the world's troublespots, started brewing beer in a 17th-century barn near Esthwaite Water. Four years later, demand outstripped capacity, and he moved lock, stock and beer barrel to Staveley to treble his production, now at 100 barrels a week. Hawskhead Bitter is the mainstay, alongside eight other brews. Overlooking the brewery is the daytime-only Beer Hall. Food comes in the shape of gourmet pork pies, sandwiches from More? bakery (see p263) next door and dishes from Wilf's Café (see left), the neighbour on the other side. Evening events include jazz and folk sessions, and a beer festival is held in July and November. Brewery tours are held on Saturdays.

Lucy Cooks
Mill Yard, Staveley, LA8 9LR (01539 32288, www.lucycooks.co.uk). Courses vary, check website for details.
Quite an enterprise: 24 fully equipped workstations for hands-on cookery classes, held every day. Whatever you want to learn, the effervescent Lucy empire probably runs a course for it. Options cover everything from Cumbrian food to Christmas cookery; sushi to budget meals for students. The £40 Demo & Dine evenings are a good introduction, with a demonstration of a three-course meal followed by a convivial supper in the dining room and terrace overlooking the river.

Wheelbase
Mill Yard, Staveley, LA8 9LR (01539 21443, www.wheelbase.co.uk). Open 9am-5.30pm Mon-Sat; 10am-4pm Sun. Hire adult bike £16 per day.
'The UK's largest cycle shop' is the claim, justified by a warehouse superstore big enough to cycle round. From a £3,000 Trek trail bike to child-trailers, from warm-up oils to blackcurrant energy drinks, bomber shorts to £150 'hydrophobic' sunglasses, Wheelbase has it all. The staff are all mad keen bikers, and the shop has its own cycle team, which competes all over the UK. You can hire entry-level mountain bikes for adults and kids, as well as tagalongs and trailers. If you're visiting in March, look out for the Big Demo Weekend, when 140 bikes are available to test-ride around the Lakes and a final party in the Hawkshead Brewery's Beer Hall.

CARTMEL PENINSULA

Walk the Sands ★
(015395 34026, www.grangeoversands.net/ morcambe_bay_guided_walks). Dates vary, check website for details.
Cedric Robinson, the Queen's Sand Pilot, has nearly 50 years' experience of guiding people across treacherous Morecambe Bay on an eight-mile trudge from Arnside to Grange-over-Sands. Armed with a stick and whistle, Cedric 'reads' the sands and understands the changing channels that could easily devour a double-decker bus. Held on weekends between May and September, the guided walks are organised by charities, but individuals are welcome to participate. Catch the train from Grange to Arnside where the trek begins at the shelter on the lower promenade. Expect it to take three and a half hours, and wear trainers not wellies, as the water can be thigh-high. A tractor and trailer is on hand for anyone in difficulty.

KENDAL & AROUND

Brewery Arts Centre
122A Highgate, Kendal, LA9 4HE (01539 725133, www.breweyarts.co.uk). Open 10am-11pm daily. Box office 10am-8pm Mon-Sat; noon-8pm Sun. Tickets vary, phone for details.
A vibrant base for cinema, theatre, dance, comedy, literature, visual art and music, as well as a useful resort for its cafés, bar and restaurant (see p260).

Cartmel

There's nowhere quite like Longsleddale for disengaging from the world, and the pure white walls and floors of this spacious self-catering cottage should soothe still further. There are two double bedrooms and an additional sofa bed, plus a kitchen/dining room and a huge sitting room upstairs. Exposed rafters and a log-burning stove supply the rural feel indoors, while outdoors you can climb Kentmere Pike and Shipman Knots. Alternatively, just sit on the terrace and watch the River Sprint run by.

CARTMEL PENINSULA

Cartmel

From Lakeside at the southern end of Windermere, it's eight miles via the B5278 to Cark in Cartmel and the vast neo-Elizabethan pile that is Holker Hall (*see p254*). The grandest stately home in Cumbria, according to architectural historian Nikolaus Pevsner, it's certainly a full-blooded affair, with all the expected trimmings of landscaped parkland, formal gardens, shops and cafés. Much power and wealth has been exercised within its thick red sandstone walls for more than 400 years.

A couple of miles north-east of here is the charming village of Cartmel. The centre is smart and picturesque enough to be in the Cotswolds, the prosperous feeling reinforced by chichi gift boutiques, expensive restaurants and exclusive-looking antiques shops. Among its many attractive buildings are the wonderful arched medieval gatehouse on the Square and the Priory Church of St Mary & St Michael (www.cartmelpriory.org.uk) – all that remains of the Augustinian priory built here at the end of the 12th century. The gatehouse belongs to the National Trust and is let to tenants, so is open only a few afternoons each year. Alongside is a venerable antiquarian bookseller, settling in after 75 years in the premises. The Priory Church has exceptional choir stalls and stained glass, and a bronze sculpture, *The Young Martyr*, by Anglo-Brazilian artist Josafina de Vasconcellos. A long-time Cumbrian resident, she died aged 100 in 2005. Guided tours of the church take place every Wednesday in summer.

For a week in summer, Cartmel makes the national sports pages with National Hunt meetings on its appealing little racecourse (www.cartmel-racecourse.co.uk), owned by the Cavendishes of Holker Hall. In 1974 it was the scene of one of racing's most infamous betting scams, which sent a trainer to prison for a horse-switching trick. At other times it's used for parking cars, walking dogs and hosting the village show in August. For gentler equine outings, Greenbank Farm (Aynsome Lane, 015395 33781, www.blackhorses.co.uk, closed Sat) can arrange a horse-and-carriage ride through the quiet lanes.

You will eat well in Cartmel. The argument over who invented Lake District sticky toffee pudding rumbles on, but Cartmel Village Shop (see p262), a specialist in Cumbrian produce, was one of the first and best. For organic goodies, Howbarrow Organic Farm Shop (015395 36330, www.howbarrow organic.co.uk, closed Mon, Sat, Sun), up the hill from the racecourse, supplies home-grown organic veg and masses of organic groceries, and can deliver a 'welcome pack' (vegetables plus breakfast basics) to self-catering cottages.

For eating out, the village hostelries – the Pig & Whistle, the Royal Oak and the Cavendish Arms (see right) – serve decent pub food. For more upmarket fare, Rogan & Company (see p257) is a first-rate modern bistro/bar. It's owned by Simon Rogan, who, as Michelin-starred chef-patron of fine dining restaurant L'Enclume (see p256), has put Cartmel on the culinary map. The most ambitious modern restaurant in the Lake District, L'Enclume is deemed one of the best places to eat in Britain. It's regularly dubbed 'the Fat Duck of the North' – not an epithet Rogan particularly relishes, but an undoubted compliment since the Fat Duck has been voted the best restaurant in the world.

Grange-over-Sands

From Cartmel, it's just a couple of miles to Grange-over-Sands, a genteel Edwardian seaside resort built for northern businessmen to enjoy the mild climate and fresh sea air. Today, nearly half the population is over retirement age and time seems to stand still. The biggest building in town is a nursing home, marked by a statue of a young World War I soldier. On summer afternoons musicians strike up in the bandstand, and gentle strolls are taken through the ornamental gardens. There's not much clubbing.

The jewel in Grange's crown is the mile-long promenade that stretches from the railway station to Blawith Point, alongside an expanse of green. Twenty years ago, these were the 'Sands', but the River Kent altered its course and sedimentation has turned them into more of a meadow. *Spartina anglica*, aka cord grass, grows and sheep graze; saltmarsh lamb has become a local speciality. A selling exhibition of Prom Art (01539 34026, www.grangeoversands.net/prom_art) is displayed along the walkway every last Sunday of the month from April to September.

There are still sands, forever shifting, out in Morecambe Bay, where the tidal 'bore' famously comes in faster than a horse, and where 18 Chinese cocklepickers died in 2004. Before the arrival of the railway, the quickest route to the east was across the bay, and the monks of Furness Abbey used to guide people over the sands. In 1536 the Duchy of Lancaster appointed the first Sand Pilot. The post still exists: Cedric Robinson, aged 72, is the 25th Queen's Sand Pilot and for nearly 50 years, for an annual stipend of £15, has guided walkers safely from Arnside to Grange-over-Sands (both stations on Northern Rail's Cumbrian Coast line). You can take advantage of his expertise too; see p251.

Where to eat & drink

Cavendish Arms
Cartmel, LA11 6QA (015395 36240, www.thecavendish arms.co.uk). Open 10am-11pm daily. Lunch served noon-2pm, dinner served 6-9pm Mon-Fri. Food served noon-9pm Sat, Sun.
A plastic box on the wall of this 400-year-old coaching inn contains a £5 note and a few coins, and is labelled 'Our first day's takings'. Things must have picked up since then, because both the tables and the ten en suite guest rooms (£65-£85 double incl breakfast) are very popular in summer. Sturdy decor matches a no-nonsense menu of comfort food: chunky hot beef and onion sandwiches, steak and ale pie, or sea bass with Morecambe Bay shrimps. And something called sticky toffee pudding, doused in butterscotch sauce and accompanied by a dollop of cream or ice-cream.

Cartmel Village Shop

Places to visit

Abbot Hall Art Gallery

SOUTH LAKES VALLEYS

Townend ★
*Troutbeck, LA23 1LB (015394 32628, www.national
trust.org.uk/townend). Open Mid Mar-Oct Tours 11am-
1pm, house & gardens 1-5pm Wed-Sun. Admission
£4.20; £2.10 reductions; £10.50 family.*
This wonderful 17th-century house, with its stout
chimneys and pretty cottage garden, is furnished with
intricately carved furniture, an enormous oak dining
table and a lovely old kitchen range, which is invariably
lit. Wander the rooms (afternoons only) or take the
guided tour to see what Cumbrian life was like for a
yeoman family in the 17th and 18th centuries. While
the carved four-poster beds and the simple servants'
quarters are diverting, deeper pleasures are in the
detail. In the Browne family's much-loved library (one of
the National Trust's most valuable collections), bawdy
stories sit next to books on law, cookery, religion and
agriculture – complete with mud splashes, seeds and
the odd horsehair. The large glass 'goldfish' bowl filled
with water was for magnifying the candlelight – important
in the dark interior of Townend – when attempting
close-up work such as sewing. The rush-light holders
illustrate how homemade rushes, dipped in animal fat,
could be held in the middle, thus allowing the Brownes
(unlike the rest of us) to burn the candle at both ends.

CARTMEL PENINSULA

Holker Hall ★
*Cark in Cartmel, LA11 7PL (01539 558328,
www.holker.co.uk). Open Mid Mar-Oct Hall 11am-4pm
Mon-Fri, Sun. Gardens 10.30am-5.30pm Mon-Fri, Sun.
Admission Hall & Gardens £10; free-£9 reductions;
£27.50 family. Gardens only £6.50; free-£5.50
reductions; £16.50 family.*
Holker Hall has never been sold. For 400 years the
Prestons, the Lowthers and the Cavendishes have
married and inherited in an impenetrable family
tree. The current owners (still residing in a wing of the
house) are descendants of Henry Cavendish, who, in
the 18th century, discovered hydrogen and the density
of the earth; his microscope is in the library. Henry was
so painfully shy he had a special staircase built in his
London home to avoid the servants; his lifestyle was
so frugal that he passed on a huge fortune to his heirs.

The red sandstone west wing, rebuilt in the 1870s
in Elizabethan Gothic style following a fire, is open to
the public. The exterior with its towers and cupolas is
magnificent enough; inside is just as opulent. There's
a great fireplace, an intricately carved oak staircase,
an Elizabethan-style long gallery, an enviable billiard
room and a mighty dining room laid out as if for a
period drama, with all the Wedgwood, Chippendale
and Hepplewhite buffed to the finest sheen.
The gardens are world-class, immaculately
maintained and voted among the best in the world
by the *Good Gardens Guide*. A mix of woodland and
formal garden, its features include clipped box hedges,
pleached laurel arches, herbaceous borders, a sculpture
trail and the national collection of styracaceae. Don't
miss the Great Holker Lime; planted in the 17th
century, it has a 26ft girth and is officially one of
Britain's 50 Great Trees. The Holker Hall Garden
Festival is held over three days in June. Further out
are the grouse moors, deer parks, farms, woods and
estuarine marshland of the 17,000 Cavendish acres.
For a price, you can shoot pheasant, duck and deer.
The peripherals of gift shop, food hall (*see p262*), café
and restaurant (*see p256*) are all of a high standard.

KENDAL & AROUND

**Abbot Hall Art Gallery &
Museum of Lakeland Life & Industry ★**
*Kirkland, Kendal, LA9 5AL (01539 722464, www.
abbothall.org.uk, www.lakelandmuseum.org.uk).
Open Apr-Oct 10.30am-5pm Mon-Sat. Nov-Mar
10.30am-4pm Mon-Sat. Admission Abbot Hall
£5.75; free reductions. Museum of Lakeland Life
£4.75; £3.40 reductions; £13.60 family.*
For a small gallery, Abbot Hall packs a big punch.
Housed in a Grade I-listed Georgian house on the
banks of the River Kent, it contains work by a stunning
roll-call of artists. Choose from Ruskin, Constable,
Turner, John Sell Cotman and Edward Lear or, if you're
keener on more modern art, Ben Nicholson, Roger
Hilton, Lucian Freud, Graham Sutherland, Frank
Auerbach and Kurt Schwitters. The gallery also owns
one of the foremost collections of work by 18th-century
portraitist George Romney, born at nearby Dalton-in-
Furness, including his 1776 masterpiece, *The Gower
Children*. But one painting, in particular, dominates.

The 'Great Picture' is a huge 17th-century triptych of Lady Anne Clifford; the two side panels are on display, but the central panel is so large that no one's worked out how to get it into the building.

Across a courtyard is the Museum of Lakeland Life, which beautifully explains the human history of the Lake District through a series of room sets, including a Victorian bedroom with a richly carved four-poster; a parlour with dark oak panelling; a typical Lakeland kitchen; and a street of Victorian shops. Also featured are artefacts to do with farming, mining, bobbin-making and the leather industry. The Arthur Ransome collection contains manuscripts and illustrations, as well as the author's desk, portable Remington typewriter, chess set and 20 of his huge array of pipes.

You'll find a discerning collection of art books in the gallery shop and a pleasant café (see p259) next door.

Kendal Museum
Station Road, Kendal, LA9 6BT (01539 721374, www.kendalmuseum.org.uk). Open noon-5pm Thur, Fri, Sat. Admission £2.80; free-£2.20 reductions.
Founded in 1796, this is one of the oldest museums in the country. Among its eclectic mix are 2,000 world-class mineral samples, many of them rare Lake District specimens. A veritable Noah's Ark of stuffed animals includes an aardvark and an armadillo, a three-toed sloth and an extinct Tasmanian wolf; most memorable is the enormous, fully grown polar bear. The Wainwright Gallery, tracing mankind's presence in Cumbria since prehistoric times, is named after the museum's honorary curator for 30 years, fell wanderer Alfred Wainwright. A reconstruction of his office contains original maps, drawings, handwritten reports of his walks and personal items such as his spectacles, rucksack and much-darned socks.

Quaker Tapestry
Friends Meeting House, Stramongate, Kendal, LA9 4BH (01539 722975, www.quaker-tapestry.co.uk). Open Apr-Oct 10am-5pm Mon-Fri. Admission £6.50; £2-£5 reductions; £14 family.
The Quaker Tapestry is a set of 77 embroidered panels stitched by 4,000 men, women and children from all over the world. It recounts events and movements in Quaker history, such as the abolition of the slave trade,

Quaker Tapestry

pacifism and the work of eminent Quakers including Elizabeth Fry, William Penn and the founder of Quakerism, George Fox. There's also a café (see p259), a shop selling embroidery items and regular embroidery workshops.

Levens Hall ★
Off A6, Levens, LA8 0PD (015395 60321, www.levenshall.co.uk). Open Easter-Oct House noon-4pm Mon-Thur, Sun. Gardens 10am-5pm Mon-Thur, Sun. Admission House & gardens £11; £4.50 reductions; £27 family. Gardens only £8; £3.50 reductions; £20 family.
Privately owned Levens Hall is a medieval house built around a pele tower, with much oak panelling and many tessellated ceilings. But the house's jewel is its world-famous, Grade I-listed topiary garden, widely acknowledged as the best in the UK. It was laid out in 1694 and has remained much as it was conceived. With nine miles of box hedge, enclosing swathes of violet verbena in spring, and yew trees shaped into wigs, birds, spirals, umbrellas, chessmen, cottage loaves, globes and pyramids, it is – in the words of Thomas West's 1790 *Guide to the Lakes* – 'the sweetest spot that fancy can imagine'. All that topiary takes an enormous amount of clipping and shaping. In autumn, three gardeners with electric cutters spend three months trimming the yews; the box hedging is done with hand shears.

Beyond the formal gardens is the park, where in 1969 Robin Bagot (father of the current owner, Hal), saved the avenue of oaks from being felled to make way for a dual-carriageway. Hal Bagot's steam engines take to the estate on Sundays and bank holidays. Tea and light meals are available in the Bellingham Buttery (the old servants' hall) or outside on the terrace. Levens' own traditional spiced Morocco Ale is a satisfying thirst-quencher on hot days.

Sizergh Castle
Off A591, Sizergh, LA8 8AE (015395 60951, www.nationaltrust.org.uk/sizergh). Open Mid Mar-Oct House noon-5pm Mon-Thur, Sun. Gardens 11am-5pm Mon-Thur, Sun. Admission House & gardens £7.15; £3.60 reductions; £10.75-£17.90 family. Gardens only £4.65; £2.40 reductions.
This striking fortified mansion, built around a 14th-century pele tower with walls ten feet thick, has all the portraits, four-posters, battlements and spiral staircases you'd hope for. It has been the seat of the Strickland family for 750 years. The prolific Elizabethan carved oak, reputedly the best in the north of England, includes 'linen fold' panelling – so called because it resembles folded cloth. The examples in the Inlaid Chamber are so fabulous that the Stricklands sold them off to the Victoria & Albert Museum in the 1890s to raise some cash, then took 100 years to buy it all back again. The beautiful grounds incorporate a notable walk-through limestone rock garden, ponds and a lake. The café and shop sit in a contemporary wood-and-glass building beside the car park, with outside seating and a menu of dependable NT favourites: sausages, quiche, soup, sandwiches and cakes. The shop and café remain open on Friday and Saturday, when the house and gardens are closed.

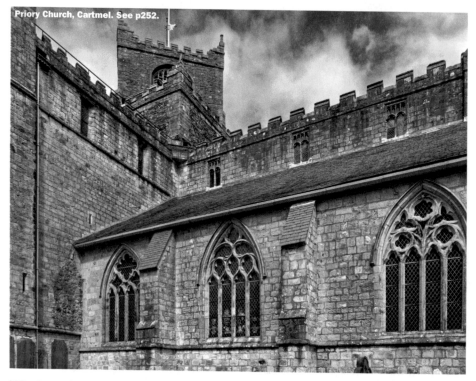

Priory Church, Cartmel. See p252.

L'Enclume ★

Cavendish Street, Cartmel, LA11 6PZ (01539 536362, www.lenclume.co.uk). Lunch served noon-1.30pm Wed-Sun. Dinner served 6.45-9pm daily.

Extraordinary, innovative and, according to *Restaurant* magazine, one of the best restaurants in the world. L'Enclume means 'the anvil' and Cartmel's old blacksmith's shop has been smeared with layers of whitewash to create a modern, minimalist setting for Simon Rogan's ultra-modern, Michelin-starred menus. In the bar, a smooth front-of-house team introduces spicy popcorn and a pine nut lollipop. The first dish to appear in the dining room is a martini glass of chlorophyll-green mallow topped up from a 'soda siphon' with foam of ginger beer, lemon juice, chilli oil and whisky. And so it continues through nine courses (for £55), and more still at £75 and £95. It might be easy to scoff at dishes such as 'skate belly with douglas fir bark foam', but far better to trust that Rogan's take on tastes, textures, ingredients and flavours are unique, and to ask whether you'd sooner pay for one amazing meal or two average ones. Ever restless, Rogan has started an experimental kitchen next door and taken the lease on Howbarrow Organic Farm, which is set to supply fruit and vegetables for the restaurant and all the herbs and flowers that are the hallmark of his remarkable cooking.

Hat Trick Café

Yew Tree Barn, Low Newton in Cartmel, LA11 6JP (015395 30577, www.hattrickcafe.co.uk). Open 8am-4pm Mon-Thur; 10am-4pm Fri-Sun.

An idiosyncratic set-up that is part architectural salvage yard, part arts and crafts centre, part cosy café. The hat tricks are the boaters and bonnets that decorate the eclectic interior, along with Oxo signs, old clocks and quirky lampshades. There are Lloyd Loom chairs and church pews to sit on, and rarebits, toasted sandwiches and jacket potatoes to eat. You can also visit for breakfast, or afternoon tea with tea bread and chocolate fudge cake. For drinks, try salep (a Middle Eastern milk concoction dusted with cinnamon and hazelnuts) or the own-made lemonade.

Hazelmere Café & Bakery

1-2 Yewbarrow Terrace, Grange-over-Sands, LA11 6ED (015395 32972, www.hazelmerecafe.co.uk). Open Bakery Summer 8.30am-5pm Mon-Sat; 9am-5pm Sun. Winter 8.30am-4pm daily. Café Summer 10am-5pm daily. Winter 10am-4.30pm daily.

Don't expect a skinny latte or flat white. Grange's best tearoom holds as firmly to its traditions as to its Victorian glass canopy and green and cream paintwork. Half shop, half tearoom, this is how grandma used to bake: iced buns, chocolate truffle cake, battenburg, coconut pyramids, vanilla slices and meringues, plus takeaway dishes of tatie pot and steak pie. In the primly turned out 'refreshment rooms', the tables have crisp white cloths, the tea has leaves, and it's fine bone china all the way.

Holker Hall

Cark in Cartmel, LA11 7PL (01539 558328, www.holker.co.uk). Open Cavendish Room Summer

10.30am-5.30pm daily. Winter 10.30am-4pm daily. Burlington Room Summer 10.30am-5.30pm Sun. Winter 10.30am-4pm Sun. Closed Jan.
The courtyard of Holker Hall (see p254) contains two eateries. The Cavendish Room is done out in blond wood and Farrow & Ball blue-green hues, and offers parasol-shaded outdoor tables in summer. Lunch on saltmarsh lamb hotpot or plaice with prawn and chive butter, or just sample the lemon drizzle cake or a cream tea. Emily Cavendish, daughter of the hall's owners, creates the soups and exotic ice-creams: elderflower and rosemary, honey and geranium, sweet chestnut and spiced chocolate. Next door, the Burlington Room offers Sunday lunch and more refined dining, but is often booked out by groups and coach parties.

Rogan & Company ★

The Square, Cartmel, LA11 6QD (015395 35917, www.roganandcompany.co.uk). Breakfast served 10am-noon, lunch served noon-2pm daily. Dinner served 6.30-9pm Mon-Fri, Sun; 6.30-9.30pm Sat.
Simon Rogan tones down L'Enclume's avant-garde leanings at his smart bistro by Cartmel bridge. Leather tub chairs and oak beams make for relaxed drinking (and eating) in the bar, while the restaurant has striped chairs, polished wood tables and a brighter feel. Begin with comforting dishes such as local crab cakes with watercress or a creamy butternut squash soup. Mains take homespun dishes for an extra spin, such as the Cumbrian beef burger with smoked bacon, emmenthal, spicy mayo, toasted muffin and chips.

L'Enclume

River Kent, Kendal

Where to stay

After splashing out on dinner at L'Enclume (see p256), go the whole hog and stay the night in one of its beautiful rooms. Six are located above the restaurant, four in nearby L'Enclume House (part of sister restaurant Rogan & Company) and two, both suites, in Cartmel Square. As you'd expect from this stylish operation, the rooms are expensively and individually decorated with gilded mirrors and Turkish rugs, smart leather and glass tables.

KENDAL & AROUND

Just a mile outside the National Park's borders, Kendal justifiably calls itself the 'Gateway to the Lakes', even though it's bypassed by most visitors to the region. Comfortably the biggest town in the Lakeland orbit, 'the grey auld town' has character and culture to spare.

The River Kent winds its way through the centre of town, crisscrossed by numerous bridges and with a waterside walkway. Highgate is the main thoroughfare; this is where you'll find the Tourist Information Centre (01539 797516, closed Sun), inside the Town Hall, where Alfred Wainwright worked for 20 years as borough treasurer. Look out for the 'old yards', the historic lanes that run off Highgate and once housed employees of the factories and workshops by the river. Market Square has its charms, with cobblestones and café tables.

Leading off it, Branthwaite Brow is an attractive street notable for the 1657 Chocolate House (no.54, 01539 740702, www.chocolatehouse 1657.co.uk, closed Sun) packed from floor to wonky ceiling with confectionary. Wainwright's Yard is a new development that includes upmarket gift shops and specialist food shop Artisan at Booth's (see p262).

Kendal has a rich assortment of historic calling cards. Wool was the major industry – hence the town motto, 'wool is my bread' – bringing wealth and jobs to the region since the 13th century. Of particular renown was 'Kendal Green', the coarse, water-resistant, greyish-green cloth worn by English bowmen and mentioned by Shakespeare in Henry IV. Footwear manufacturer K Shoes, once a household name, was based here until 2003, when the shoe factory turned into the K Village Factory Outlet Centre.

But the town's most famous export is Kendal Mint Cake, still made by three local firms, Romney's, Quiggin's and Wilson's. According to Romney's, the best-known manufacturer, the 'cake' was invented by accident in the 1860s when the mixture for glacier mints went wrong. Since then it has perked up walkers heading to Everest or the South Pole and clambering over every Lakeland fell. Also enduring is Samuel Gawith's, Kendal snuff makers since 1792.

Kendal Castle, a 12th-century ruin perched on Castle Hill Park, was the home of the Parrs and their famous daughter, Catherine Parr, the sixth wife of Henry VIII – the one who survived him. It's an attractive spot, free to visit and with lofty views across the town.

The Abbot Hall Art Gallery, the Museum of Lakeland Life & Industry (for both, *see p254*) and Kendal Museum (*see p255*) are fine cultural showcases, with particular appeal for fans of, respectively, portrait painter George Romney, writer Arthur Ransome and Lakeland hero Alfred Wainwright. While visiting Abbot Hall, have a pint in the tiny snug of the Ring O' Bells pub (39 Kirkland, 01539 720326); Charles Dickens is reputed to have squeezed in too. Embroidery fans should head to see the Quaker Tapestry (*see p255*), on display at the Friends Meeting House, whose 77 meticulously worked panels depict the story of Quakerism down the years.

The town centre is easily managed on foot, but it's a stiff five-minute climb to Beast Bank and Greenside, a residential street with a distinct villagey feel. *Postman Pat* author John Cunliffe used to live in Greenside and although Beast Bank post office, where Mrs Goggins sorted out Pat's letters, closed in 1993, a plaque marks the spot. The Rifleman's Arms pub, also on the street, doesn't serve food, but has guest real ales and folk musicians every week.

A few miles south of Kendal are two houses built around medieval pele towers: Sizergh Castle, owned by the National Trust, and the private Levens Hall (for both, *see p255*), internationally renowned for its historic, Grade I-listed topiary gardens. Don't miss it – the intricately sculpted box hedges and yew trees are dazzling.

Where to eat & drink

The Friends Meeting House, where the Quaker Tapestry (*see p255*) is showcased, has a friendly little café with courtyard seating. Queue at the counter to order the likes of pea and lettuce soup, quiche and salad, freshly made sandwiches, scones with jam, and Fairtrade coffees and teas. Vegan and wheat- and dairy-free dishes are available. Food shop Artisans at Booth's (*see p262*) also has a café.

Abbot Hall Art Gallery

Kirkland, Kendal, LA9 5AL (01539 722464, www.abbothall.org.uk). Open Apr-Oct 10.30am-5pm Mon-Sat. Nov-Mar 10.30am-4pm Mon-Sat.
Tranquil and minimal, the little café at Abbot Hall (*see p254*) serves a pleasant lunch – typically soup and a sandwich, smoked salmon and scrambled eggs, potted shrimps on toast, or cheese ploughman's. Alternatively, embellish tea or coffee with blueberry and lemon drizzle cake, caramel shortbread or buttercream and jam cake. There's seating outside on the lawn next to the River Kent.

Bridge Street Restaurant

1 Bridge Street, Kendal, LA9 7DD (01539 738855, www.one-bridgestreet.co.uk). Lunch served noon-1.30pm Wed-Sat. Dinner served 6-9pm Tue-Sat.
This lovely Georgian house on the corner of Bridge Street near the river houses Kendal's most accomplished restaurant. Chef/proprietor Julian Ankers presents a stylish modern menu that includes some sharing platters to start; seafood or duck (duck spring rolls, duck pancakes with hoi sin sauce, smoked duck noodle salad). It's grills and roasts for the mains: Kentmere lamb, slow-roast pork belly, fillet steak with duck-fat chips, sea bream or herb-crusted halibut. The setting is smart if somewhat austere, with

Quaker Tapestry Tearoom

Hazelmere Café & Bakery. See p256.

white walls and dark wood tables and brown seating. Look out for the good-value two-course lunch and 'tea-time special' set menu.

Grainstore Restaurant
Brewery Arts Centre, 122A Highgate, Kendal, LA9 4HE (01539 725133, www.breweryarts.co.uk). Lunch served 10am-2.30pm, dinner served 5-9pm daily.
Among its many virtues, the Brewery Arts Centre (*see p251*) packs in two cafés, a bar and restaurant. Downstairs are two casual cafés, the Warehouse and the child-friendly Intro Café with a soft play area. In the attic is Vats Bar, a name immediately explained by two enormous beer vats with a bite taken out of the side for seating. Next door, the Grainstore offers appetising bistro dishes: grilled mackerel with crushed potatoes, Waberthwaite pork and leek sausage with spring onion mash, tarragon crêpes with mushroom, and an assortment of pastas and pizzas.

New Moon
129 Highgate, Kendal, LA9 4EN (01539 729254, www.newmoonrestaurant.co.uk). Lunch served 11.30am-2.30pm Tue-Sat. Dinner served 5.30-9.30pm Tue-Fri; 6-9.30pm Sat.
This appealing restaurant stands out on the shopping street of Highgate, for both the clean, modern lines of its compact dining room and for serving some of the best food in town. Nicely balanced lunch dishes include linguine with ham and mushrooms or salad with houmous and quality bread. Pre-theatre casual suppers make it a handy, and good-value, choice before an event at the Brewery Arts Centre opposite.

Later in the evening, the à la carte moves up a notch to pan-fried calves' liver, perhaps, grilled sea bream or stuffed pork loin. Desserts (organic Windermere ice-creams, chocolate and orange torte and, of course, sticky toffee pudding) are particularly tempting.

Waterside Wholefood
Kent View, Kendal, LA9 4DZ (01539 729743, www.watersidewholefood.co.uk). Open 8.30am-4.30pm Mon-Sat.
A perfect spot by the river at Miller Bridge, with tables outside. Inside is a throwback to the days of beards and sandals, when furniture was pine and bread was wholemeal. Which is not to say this isn't a lovely, friendly wholefood café with an open kitchen, a community notice board, and the herbs and spices behind the counter giving off an enticing aroma. More goodness comes from cheesy leek and mushroom pie, tomato and mozzarella pizza, mushroom and butterbean strogonoff, flapjacks and carrot cake.

Where to stay

Beech House
40 Greenside, Kendal, LA9 4LD (01539 720385, www.beechhouse-kendal.co.uk). Rates £80-£100 double incl breakfast.
An overwhelmingly plush B&B in a Victorian terraced house, set high on leafy Greenside (close to Postman Pat's post office) with views over the town and a five-minute stroll to the shops. The six rooms – all en suite, graded classic or deluxe – are painstakingly schemed in a modish and modern style, with swags and tails, contrasting throws and plumped-up cushions. Beds have snow-white bedding, bathrooms sparkle and the complimentary toiletries come from local company Sedbergh Soap.

Lakeland Campers
Croft Foot Farm, Docker, LA8 0DF (01539 824357, www.lakelandcampers.co.uk). Rates £495-£550 per week
Wind through the Lake District lanes and wheeze over the high passes in a classic 1969 Volkswagen campervan. Dolly sleeps four (at a squeeze) via a double bed, a hammock and a child's bed across the front seat. There's a hook-up kit for electricity and you can hire an awning to create a bit more living and sleeping space.

Lapwings Barn & Curlew Quarters
Howestone Barn, Whinfell, LA8 9EQ (01539 824373, www.lapwingsbarn.co.uk). Rates £50-£90 double incl breakfast. No credit cards.
Bed and (brilliant) breakfast in a restored barn six miles north-east of Kendal, in the hamlet of Whinfell. There are two en suite double bedrooms: Curlew has a double (zip-link) bed and outdoor seating area, while the larger Lapwing has its own sitting room and terrace. The accommodation and accompanying smallholding, with its hens, sheep and pigs, is run by Mexican Rick Rodriguez, who married a Cumbrian girl 20 years ago. He cures his own bacon, stuffs his own sausages, makes half a dozen varieties of marmalade and bakes 100 loaves of sourdough a month for Kendal farmers' market. Breakfast is a feast. He doesn't grow the oranges, but he does squeeze them himself. For vegetarian guests, Rick will knock up huevos rancheros with corn tortillas and refried beans or a stack of pancakes with maple syrup.

Levens Hall. See p255.

BEST FOOD & DRINK SHOPS

If you're interested in Cumbria's culinary heritage, you're in the right place. Kendal and the South Lakes have excellent food shops specialising in all kinds of local produce and delicacies.

Artisan at Booth's

Wainwright's Yard, Stricklandgate, Kendal, LA9 4DP (01539 742370, www.booths-supermarkets.co.uk). Open 9.30am-4pm Mon; 8am-8pm Tue-Sun.
Booth's, the northern, family-run supermarket chain has long championed regional produce and runs a speciality food shop and café at its flagship Kendal store. Artisan has bread from local craft bakeries, top-quality chocolate, jams, chutneys, wine and beer, and one of the best cheese counters in Cumbria, set up in partnership with London's Neal's Yard. The café majors on regional produce too: rarebit made with local beer, Lancashire cheese on local Staff of Life rye bread, and Hawkshead beetroot relish. The fish and meat boards offer a selection of smoked and cured cuts. Even the duck eggs are name-sourced: Gladys May's Braddock Whites. ★

Cartmel Village Shop ★

Parkgate House, The Square, Cartmel, LA11 6QB (015395 36280, www.cartmel villageshop.co.uk). Open 9am-5pm Mon-Sat; 10am-4.30pm Sun.
There isn't a menu in the Lakes that doesn't contain sticky toffee pudding; even L'Enclume has 'stiffy tacky pudding'. For novices, STP is a light sponge, sweetened with dates and dark brown sugar and baked in a velvety caramel sauce that seeps deliciously into the sponge. And STP is to Cartmel what mint cake is to Kendal – because the Johns family, who run Cartmel Village Shop, claim to have made it first. Others dispute this, but the Johns certainly pioneered selling the pudding in a foil tray to warm up at home, and thus conquered the rest of the UK. Their version is undoubtedly one of the best, but there are plenty of other goodies to tempt here, including cooked meats, cheeses, Waberthwaite hams and local damson jellies.

More? The Artisan Bakery

Holker Food Hall

Holker Hall, Cark in Cartmel, LA11 7PL (015395 58328, www.holker-hall.co.uk). Open Summer 10.30am-5.30pm daily. Winter 10.30am-4pm daily.
Holker's beautifully presented food shop sells first-rate produce, featuring not only its own-label jams and chutneys, but even olive oil from the hall's Tuscan estate at Casa al Bosco. Local meat and dairy is the strongest suit: saltmarsh lamb reared on the Cartmel peninsula; beef from the estate's shorthorn cattle; venison and

game in season; Woodall's bacon; and Martin Gott's wonderful St James cheese, made at Holker Farm Dairy. A local producers' market is held one Sunday a month from March to September.

Low Sizergh Barn Farm Shop & Tearoom
Low Sizergh, LA8 8AE (015395 60426, www.lowsizerghbarn.co.uk). Open Farm shop 9am-5.30pm daily. Tearoom 9.30am-5pm daily.
Not just a vegetable shop, but a full-blown attraction with a tearoom, gift shop, art gallery and farm trail around Sizergh's 250 organic acres. The farm shop, housed in an old barn a few miles south of Kendal, is a glorious mini supermarket of Cumbrian produce, selling Lowther chickens, Cumbrian chorizo and salami, Withnail blue cheese, and Old Smokehouse and Mansergh Hall sausages, as well as the farm's own cheese, milk and eggs. The tearoom upstairs has a grandstand view of the milking parlour, while the craft gallery downstairs has taken over the old shippon (cow shed).

More? The Artisan Bakery
Mill Yard, Staveley, LA8 9LR (015398 22297, www.moreartisan.co.uk). Open 7.30am-4.30pm daily.
The best bread in the Lakes? Patrick Moore bakes proper, slow-fermented loaves with a chewy crust and soft interior. You can also buy cakes, fruit tarts, meringues, gateaux, cheesecake, Christmas pud and gluten-free muddees (chocolate brownies), which scooped the supreme champion prize at the Great Taste Awards in 2009. If you can't get to Staveley, the bakery's products are sold at the farmers' markets in Cockermouth and Holker Hall, and at Artisan at Booth's (*see left*) in Kendal.

Sillfield Farm Shop
Gatebeck, nr Endmoor, LA8 0HZ (015395 67609 www.sillfield.co.uk). Open 10am-5pm Thur-Sat; 10am-4pm Sun.
Peter Gott is a campaigner for real food, as well something of a media regular, turning up on TV and radio whenever they need someone to talk about happy animals. His farm shop is packed with produce from the rare-breed pigs, wild boar, Herdwick sheep and poultry on his 80-acre farm, located just off the M6 six miles south of Kendal. There's fresh meat, bacon, ham, black pudding, red wine sausages and assorted pies. Game lovers have wild boar pancetta, venison, pheasant and wild game pie. You can also buy a fine ewes' milk cheese made at Holker Farm by Gott's son Martin.

Low Sizergh Barn Farm Shop & Tearoom

Further Reference

TOURIST INFORMATION OFFICES

More details can be found at www.golakes.co.uk and at www.lake-district.org.uk. The main tourist offices are listed below.

Ambleside 015394 35282
Bowness 015394 42895
Cockermouth 019008 22634
Coniston 015394 41533
Keswick 017687 72645
Pooley Bridge 017684 86135
Ullswater 017484 82414
Windermere 015394 46499

USEFUL ADDRESSES

www.cumbrialife.co.uk
Cumbria Life magazine
www.english-heritage.org.uk
English Heritage
www.enjoyengland.com
EnjoyEngland
www.heritageopendays.org.uk
Heritage Open Days
www.metoffice.gov.uk Met Office
www.nationalrail.co.uk National Rail Enquiries
www.nationaltrust.org.uk
National Trust
www.ordnancesurvey.co.uk
Ordnance Survey
www.sustrans.org.uk Sustrans
www.thegoodpubguide.co.uk
The Good Pub Guide
www.thetrainline.com The Trainline
www.thewestmorlandgazette.co.uk
News, sport and weather for the Lake District, Kendal & Cumbria
www.visitbritain.com Visit Britain
www.visitcumbria.com Visit Cumbria
www.ukworldheritage.org.uk
UK World Heritage Sites

COAST & COUNTRYSIDE

www.babo.org.uk British Association of Balloon Operators
www.bbc.co.uk/coast BBC Coast
www.bcusurf.org.uk
Surf Kayaking
www.british-trees.com
The Woodland Trust
www.britsurf.co.uk British Surfing Association
http://camping.uk-directory.com
UK Camping and Caravanning Directory

---

www.classic-sailing.co.uk
Classic Sailing
www.countrysideaccess.gov.uk
Countryside Access
www.cpre.org.uk Campaign for the Protection of Rural England
www.golfincumbria.co.uk
Golf in Cumbria
www.goodbeachguide.co.uk
Good Beach Guide
www.lakedistrictfishing.net
Fishing in the Lake District
www.lakedistrict.gov.uk Lake District National Park
www.lakedistrictoutdoors.co.uk
Lake District Outdoors
www.lakedistricttouristguide.com
Lake District Tourist Guide
www.lidos.org.uk
Lidos in the UK
www.nationalparks.gov.uk
National Parks
www.nationaltrail.co.uk
National Trails
www.naturalengland.org.uk
Natural England
www.ngs.org.uk
National Gardens Scheme
www.ramblers.org.uk
Ramblers Association
www.river-swimming.co.uk
River & Lake Swimming Association
www.rya.org.uk Royal Yachting Association
www.ukcampsite.co.uk
Campsite reviews
www.ukclimbing.com
UK Climbing
www.uk-golfguide.com UK Golf
www.walkingbritain.co.uk
Walking Britain
www.walking-routes.co.uk
Walking Routes
www.wildaboutbritain.co.uk
Wild About Britain
www.wildswimming.com
Wild Swimming

FOOTPATHS/WALKS

Allerdale Ramble www.ldwa.org.uk Don't be misled by the name: this is a 54-mile 'ramble'. The route stretches from Seathwaite, in central Lakeland, all the way out to the sea at Maryport, where it turns into a coastal walk.

Coast to Coast Walk www.english-lakes.com/coast_to_coast_walk.htm An epic 190-mile walk devised by Alfred Wainwright, the Coast to

---

Coast sets off from St Bee's on the Cumbrian Coast, passing through the Lake District National Park before heading into the Yorkshire Dales and the North York Moors to finish at Robin Hood's Bay.

Cumbria Way www.thecumbriaway.info A 70-mile walk through the centre of the Lake District, taking in some spectacular scenery. It starts in Ulverston and heads north towards Coniston, Keswick and finally Carlisle.

Wainwright Society www.wainwright.org.uk Admirers of AW can sign up to help keep fell walking traditions alive, take part in organised walks, qualify for various members' discounts and receive a quarterly newsletter.

Windermere Way www.windermere-way.co.uk A circular, 45-mile walk around Windermere. It's divided into four sections, each of which can easily be completed in a day.

HOLIDAY HOME COMPANIES

The Big Domain 01326 240028, www.thebigdomain.com Big party houses for hire.

Cottages4you 0845 268 0763, www.cottages4you.co.uk Holiday cottages all over the UK.

Cumbrian Cottages 01228 599960, www.cumbrian-cottages.co.uk Self-catering cottages in Cumbria.

Go Lakes 01539 822222, www.golakes.co.uk Self-catering cottages (along with B&Bs, hostels and hotels), through Cumbria Tourism.

Lake Lovers 01539 488855, www.lakelovers.co.uk Holiday properties across the area, from quaint cottages and luxury apartments to sprawling traditional farmhouses.

Lakeland Cottage Company 015395 38180, www.lakeland-cottage-company.co.uk A cherry-picked selction of idyllic holiday homes across the region.

Landmark Trust 01628 825925, www.landmarktrust.org.uk Unusual, enchanting period properties, rescued from neglect by the Trust.

Little Domain 01326 240028, www.thelittledomain.com Romantic one-bedroom hideaways.
National Trust Cottages 0844 800 2070, www.national trustcottages.co.uk The NT has some exceptional Lakeland offerings, from simple bothies and cottages to imposing country mansions.

FICTION

Richard Adams *Plague Dogs* Adam's third novel tells the story of two dogs who escape a Cumbrian animal testing lab, and try to evade their pursuers on the fells.
Melvyn Bragg *A Time to Dance* Brought up in Cumbria, Bragg used the area in this story of an illicit affair. He set numerous other novels around Lakeland, including *The Maid of Buttermere* and *For Want of a Nail*.
Martin Edwards *Lake District Mysteries* Good, old fashioned 'whodunnit' murder mysteries, set against a Lakeland backdrop; try *The Serpent Pool*.
Sarah Hall *Haweswater* Set in 1930s Cumbria, Sarah Hall's powerful debut novel describes the construction of a reservoir, and the resultant loss of an ancient valley and farming community.
Beatrix Potter *The Tale of Peter Rabbit* The much-loved author and illustrator holidayed in the Lake District as a child, and later moved to Hill Top Farm in Near Sawrey. The scenery inspired many of her stories and drawings.
Arthur Ransome *Swallows and Amazons* A number of the books in Ransome's celebrated series of children's adventure stories are set around fictionalised Lake District locations.
Geoffrey Trease *Bannermere Series* The story of four children's adventures, set in a craggy, Lakeland-inspired landscape.
Sir Hugh Walpole *The Herries Chronicles* Details the history of a fictional Cumbrian family, over two centuries.

NON-FICTION

For more Wordsworth-related reading material, *see p89*.
Hugh Brogan *The Life of Arthur Ransome* An account of the writer's extraordinary life – which included being sued for libel by Oscar Wilde's great love, Lord Alfred Douglas, and marrying Leon Trotsky's personal secretary.

Celia Fiennes *Through England on a Side-saddle* In the late 17th century, the pioneering, intrepid Fiennes rode through every English country, gathering her observations in this work – published 150 years after her death. The Lake District, she wrote, was a place of 'inaccessible high rocky barren hills' which could 'appear very terrible'.
Richard Holmes *Early Visions, Darker Reflections* This accomplished two-part biography explores Coleridge's poetic brilliance, personal charisma, domestic tribulations and descent into opium addiction and ill-health.
Thomas de Quincy *Confessions of an English Opium-Eater* De Quincy resided at Dove Cottage for a number of years after Wordsworth moved out; his account of his laudanum addiction is his most famous work.
Jane Renouf *The Lake Artists Society, A Centenary Celebration* An illustrated history of the Lake Artists Society, set up in 1904 by WG Collingwood.
William Roberts (ed) *Thomas Gray's Journal of his Visit to the Lake District in October 1769* An evocative account of the poet's impressions of 18th-century Lakeland.
Alfred Wainwright *Pictoral Guide to the Lakeland Fells* First published in the 1950s and '60s, this series of seven books is regarded by many walkers as the definitive guide to the fells.

POETRY

Norman Nicholson *Collected Poems* Nicholson's native town of Millom and its inhabitants featured heavily in his poetry; admirers of his work include Seamus Heaney.
Robert Southey *Poems* A Romantic poet and biographer, Southey is considered one of the Lake Poets, and counted Coleridge and Wordsworth among his friends.
Samuel Taylor Coleridge *The Complete Poems* Coleridge moved to Keswick in 1801, going on to become one of the celebrated trio of Lake Poets.
William Wordsworth *The Collected Poems* The Cumbrian-born poet will forever be associated with daffodils, thanks to a spring walk around Ullswater in April 1802.

FILM

Miss Potter (Chris Noonan, 2006) A charming Beatrix Potter biopic, shot around the Lake District and starring Renée Zellweger.

Withnail and I (Bruce Robinson, 1987) 'We'll be found dead here next spring' is our dissolute hero's verdict on Uncle Monty's decrepit holiday cottage, Crow Crag; the scenes were filmed at Sleddale Hall, near Shap.

TV

The Lakes In this BBC series, penned by Jimmy McGovern, an unemployed man from Liverpool (a young John Simm) moves to Cumbria to work in a hotel, and becomes entangled in dark goings-on.
The Tenant Of Wildfell Hall Much of the BBC's acclaimed 1996 adaptation of Anne Brontë's novel was filmed in Cumbria – though the book itself is set in Yorkshire.
Wainwright Walks Television series paying homage to the work and walks of Alfred Wainwright.

MUSIC

Cecil Armstrong Gibbs *Lakeland Pictures* Eight piano preludes with Lakeland as their theme.
Arthur Butterworth *Lakeland Summer Nights* A piano solo inspired by the Lake District.
Alexander Clarke *Tales of Cumbria* Piano pieces inspired by the region's mountains and lakes.
John McCabe *Cloudcatcher Fells* An evocation of the mountainous Lakeland landscape, composed for brass band.
Jamie Sims *Beyond Reach* Sims composes music inspired by the Lake District, 'Where music, mountains and time collide'.

ART

John Constable In 1806, Constable embarked on a two-month tour of the Lakes, creating almost 100 drawings and watercolours
Thomas Girtin This 18th-century landscape painter's works include *Scene in the Lake District, near Buttermere*, now owned by the Tate. Tragically, Girtin died of consumption at the age of 27.
Sidney Richard Percy A popular Victorian artist, Percy captured the tranquillity of the Lake District's landscapes; Grizedale was among his subjects.
JMW Turner Turner's travels around the Lake District resulted in some wonderfully dramatic landscapes, including *Buttermere Lake, with part of Cromackwater, Cumberland, a Shower*.

Thematic Index

Ullswater. See p215.

A-Z Index

Derwentwater. See p173.

Loughrigg Tarn. See p76.

Where to eat & drink

Where to stay

Adverti...

Please refer to relevant secti...

Early

Books Cumbria
Waterstone's
The New Bookshop
The Waterhead Hotel
Temple Sowerby House
Augill Castle

Windermere

Gilpin Hotel & Lake House
Cedar Manor